UNDERSTANDING THE POWER OF ASTROLOGY

UNDERSTANDING THE POWER OF ASTROLOGY

Wally Krause

"An inside into the Motivation of the Mind"

GYAN

Understanding the Power of Astrology

Rs. 1415

ISBN: 978-81-212-1086-7

Published in 2013 in India by
Gyan Publishing House
23, Main Ansari Road, Darya Ganj
New Delhi-110002
Phones : 23282060, 23261060
Fax : 011-23285914
E-mail: books@gyanbooks.com
Website: www.gyanbooks.com

Lassertype Setting : Rudra Computer Graphics, Delhi
Printed at : Chawla Offset Printers, Delhi

Astrology is a science and not a fortune telling and as such it should be treated with respect.

Contents

The Author's Note to the Reader

This book is directed to the standard and basic astrological aspects. In guidance to help the reader become fully and comfortably aware of these aspects the author has used universal symbols throughout the book.

In order to understand Astrology on a universal level it is imperative for the reader to become very familiarized with the sequence and symbols of Astrology.

Briefly, the symbols are as follows:

☉	=	Sun
☽	=	Moon
☿	=	Mercury
♀	=	Venus
♂	=	Mars
♃	=	Jupiter
♄	=	Saturn
♅	=	Uranus
♆	=	Neptune
♇	=	Pluto
♈	=	Aries
♉	=	Taurus
♊	=	Gemini
♋	=	Cancer
♌	=	Leo
♍	=	Virgo
♎	=	Libra

♏	=	Scorpio
♐	=	Sagittarius
♑	=	Capricorn
♒	=	Aquarius
♓	=	Pisces

☊ ☋ = north and south node of the moon, also known as dragon's head and dragon's tail. The head symbolizes the positive, the tail symbolizes the negative influence.

M = Mid-heaven, also known as MC (medium coeli, latin for the "bottom of the sky")

A = Ascendant, also known as AC

Also of importance is the sequence of the planets, namely:

☉ ☽ ☿ ♀ ♂ ♃ ♄ ♅ ♆ ♇

Whenever the aspect refers to a planet that succeeds another in sequence the reading is taken from the preceding sign, i.e. ♃ ∗ ☉ is read from the aspect of ☉ ∗ ♃. This book will point to the earlier planet by stating the correct number of the aspect, which gives the interpretation (delineation).

Foreword

This book is written for anyone with, at least, some basic knowledge of astrology.

The sophisticated and ancient art of Astrology (the science of the stars) is a very wide and interesting field. It requires specialization of subjects that, in turn, require intense studies to understand and apply the principles involved, especially when Medical Astrology, Mundane Astrology (astrology of a country instead of a person) or Meteorological Astrology (forecasting weather patterns, especially earthquakes, rain or drought etc.) is involved.

The subject of Astrology is deep, intense and spreads from a basic interpretation to the most complicated medical advice when a doctor's diagnoses fails to deliver an answer to pain and suffering. Such an intense interpretation requires years of studying. It is beyond the understanding of basic Astrology and, thus, will not be considered much in this book with the exception that the author has considered the 6th house and the planets therein for an overall explanation of basic health issues.

Most books are far above the lay persons knowledge and understanding. They are works of exhaustive details, concentrating on the very minute and degree of a planet's transit, whereby considering nearly every possible angle, position and sub-position. To the contrary an overly generalized interpretation will not point directly to the obvious and may be so broad as to avoid any specific meaning. Don't you hate when your forecast sounds more like a newspaper horoscope? Forecasting needs to be accurate, not vague, embellished or derived from merely guess work.

It is not practical to grasp at all possible angles and meanings and overwhelm the reader, thus, this book is dealing primarily with interpretations and forecasts of a person's character, path in life and possible outcome of events, as shown in a chart by interpreting the aspects, transits and progressions.

This book is concerned only with major planets and aspects as all minor planets or sub-aspects (Chiron, Semi Sextile, Semi Square, Sesquiquadrate, Quintile and Quincunx etc.) will not have much effect unless there is a lack of major aspects at time of birth. As most people do not know their exact time of birth, predictions will be more general (sometimes within days or weeks of oncoming events) than hitting directly on the hour. (I am sure there are astrologers who disagree with me but everyone is entitled to an opinion based on their own long experience with these predictions).

A precise forecast is the intended result. Consideration of too many possibilities will muddle the issue and distract from the problem the client is inquiring. Also deserving consideration is the time a planet spends traveling around the Zodiac or Houses and, hence, will influence possible events for a longer duration.

There are 12 houses comprising of the 12 sun signs from January – December which form a circle of 360 degrees. The ecliptic is divided into 12 segments of 30 degrees each, beginning with the A (Ascendant) which occupies the cusp of the first house as determining the beginning of the 360 degrees. [1]

---

1. There are several systems to determine the size of the 12 houses. Not all of them divide into equal 30 degrees but provide for variation thereof. Today, the determination is varied by different Astrological Computer Programs. But for the purpose of this book an equal house size of 30 degrees works efficiently.

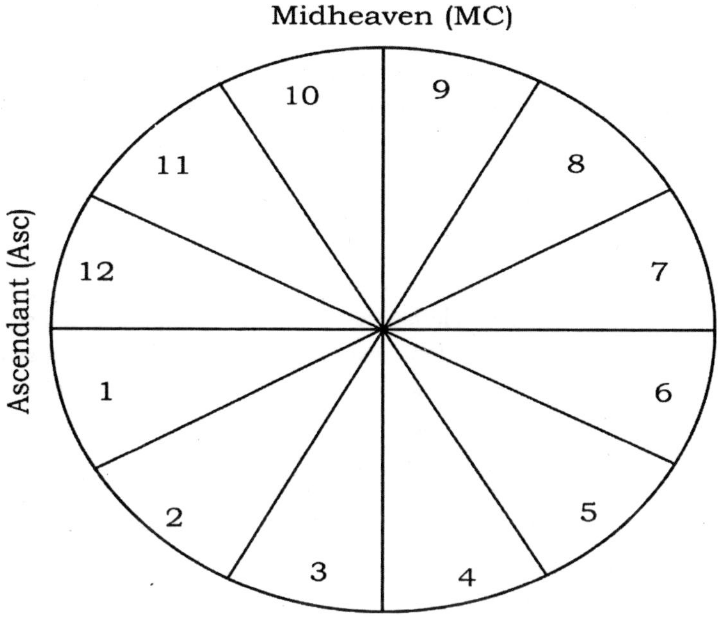

The planets travel through each house dependent on the sign they presently occupy. The duration a planet will take to travel through the zodiac (the 12 houses) is determined by the planet itself. [2]

	Planets travel through each sign:	*Planets travel through the entire Zodiac:*
☉	= 30 days	1 year
☽	= 3 ½ days	1 month
☿	= 3 weeks	1 year
♀	= 4 weeks	1 year
♂	= 5-6 weeks	2 years
♃	= 1 year	12 years
♄	= 2 ½ years	29 years
♅	= 7 years	84 years
♆	= 12 years	168 years
♇	= 12-20 years	248 years

2. The traditional division into 12 houses and 12 signs reflects the ancient division of the year into 12 lunar months circles.

Once the reader is very familiar with the function of forecasting major aspects intuition will develop and guide the reader through the sub-influences. The main reason for writing this book is the author's desire to make the process of interpretation easy and simple. A lot of people have a fanatic desire to consider each and every aspect, never mind how minor. They interpret small aspects into major events by imbedding emotional ties that a) never materialize and/or b) confuse the matter far beyond the understanding of the client. Let's not forget, the client wants to know the basics: love, money, job etc. and a psychological explanation of sub-planet's influences will not bring understanding why he/she has presently lost a job. There are also many Astrologers who desire to act as a psychiatrist as well and guide the client into a certain way to think and act. These subtle but forced influences can bring more emotional trouble and confusion to the client as these suggestions are based on the Astrologer's personal opinion of a situation and do not represent a clear reading of the why and how a situation has developed in the client's life based on the transit of the stars. The client needs to understand his/her own present situation. Future transit information should be considered as an avenue to utilize positive aspects or to avoid unfavorable aspects to any given situation. There are always two sides of the coin and the decision to be made is that of the client and not that of the Astrologer.

The author has also considered, in brief, the influences imposed by the stars on a child from birth to 3 years of age. These are the developing years in which the character and basic habit pattern are formed which the child will later apply to life. The author is considering writing more detailed about the subject of child development and medical issues in a later book, but for now, let's keep it easy and simple. Any * (sextile) in a baby chart shows available talent that needs developing.

As presented, this book gives plenty of information that is invaluable for basic and precise Astrological interpretation. Let's not forget, the reader is not comprising a newspaper horoscope that may or may not befit millions of people, but will concentrate on a single person's life path to determine the character given, the path laid out, the path chosen and the results achieved which allow a future forecast of where the road is going to lead and how it all will end. From the cradle to the grave the road is paved, and if well traveled, makes for a pleasurable life.

Experience has taught that people with rich and lucky lives are seldom seeking the wisdom of Astrology as they already have been given the ability to see past the obstacles and, saddled with good luck, have traveled far. The majority of people, unfortunately, have not been on the lucky path. Some have overcome extreme and sometimes hard breaking obstacles. Those are the clients that need understanding on how their own path is structured and must be traveled.

No one should feel discouraged because there are a number of adverse aspects in their chart. To a certain extent they appear in everyone's chart. The purpose is to remind us that there is work to be done, battles to be fought and won, difficulties to be overcome – and that, in victory over the self, lies sweet reward. In other words, weaknesses and faults denoted by adverse aspects should not be accepted as a handicap but rather as a challenge to develop talents, powers and faculties. By using adverse aspects, instead of being used by them, man may win his battle in life through the wisdom of the ages, astrology. The charts of many successful men and women show that they earned success, not because of good aspects, but because they overcame and utilized the so called "adverse" aspects. As the saying goes: "If life gives you lemons, make lemonade".

The aspects are but a guidance in life, however, man's responses are mostly poor or imperfect. Poor responses to the aspects spoil opportunity and the ability to grow. So, man brings himself into conflict, rather than into harmony with nature, and does so to his own detriment. Chinese people described it with clarity. "In life you have to wait until the time is ripe". Haste makes waste and other long established advises bring the issue down to the point. Plan, wait for the right time, and execute. If you sow at the right time the harvest will be plenty. History has revealed that nobility relied on their own private astrologer (under today's standard that would be an in-house position). Upon their calculation of the birth chart it was often attempted to delay the actual birth by a few hours in order to obtain a more favorable natal position via time of birth.

With that knowledge in mind, this book intends to be a guidance to understand the forces that turn the world.

Astrology is not a sort of fortune telling business. It is physical science. A chart is set out according to mathematical rules derived from astronomical observations.

1

The Function of Astrology is to Encourage, Warn and Exhort in Essence, Give Good and Unbiased Advice

Therefore, the knowledge of astrology should be applied to aspects that will develop based on the upcoming positions of the planets. A good astrologer will have the knowledge to help a person whose chart is being considered, as well as to avoid a good deal of trauma or even prevent a sad event altogether. Princess Diana's chart foreshadowed an accident via boat, car or plane which she may not survive. Her ♂ was heavily afflicted. Christoper Reeve may be still alive today had someone read his chart prior to the accident in which ♄ indicated a fall from a heightened position. (He fell off his horse) Delaying their activity would have helped avoiding the outcome. Sadly, we know that the indicated events took place and no forewarning was given.

This book will not get into the calculation of a horoscope. The author will skip that time consuming process and rely on a computer to do the work or if any reader has no access to one, lets just look to the ephemeris which is available in major bookstores and can be purchased in volumes of 100 years. (century to century). (See page 391 "Forecasting without making a chart")

Any astrologer's real task is to analyze events, as indicated by upcoming positions of the planets, and enable the client to put up the best defense or tactics against any upcoming danger or utilize, to the fullest extent, positive events. Advice should be given by letting the client know and understand what he/she could do from an individual position to any upcoming situation. It is not a good idea to induce the client to accept the astrologer's opinion on how to solve any upcoming problems, as the circumstances and desires of every person are quiet different. The client needs to develop and understand the power to alter circumstances to his/her own advantage. The function of astrology is to encourage, warn and exhort from what is contained in a person's chart.

What a client expects is some kind of assurance that the analysis makes a point, good or bad, that one can rely on. This book presents data upon which the reader can easily arrive at a precise interpretation.

Lots of material is available on the subject of Astrology through numerous books and other resources. To get the picture, that enables a precise forecast, one either has to have already substantial knowledge or must conduct a thorough search of many, many books to get the interpretations. Here, the author has combined available information with her personal and practical knowledge, gathered over 20 years, to bring out this book, which allows even a person with minimum knowledge of Astrology to be accurate in forecasting at a minimum investment of time.

Through many years of experience some astrologer have developed a sense of precognition which, together with material knowledge, will help to shed light on the events developing in peoples lives, or the world as a whole. [1]

Let's utilize any gained knowledge and apply it for the betterment of mankind. While we can't change the wind's direction, we can adjust the sails to reach our destination. Some people are lucky early in life but face a severe reversal. Others drudge, claw and overcome adversary to see a prosperous life later on. While some may never understand the light of day. There is a time and a place that is right for everyone. The 'when' and 'where' is to be discovered through astrology which opens the door through which man's opportunities and talents may flow.

Tradition has it that ♄ in ♎ and ♃ in ♋ (thus building a square) will bring great changes and alterations in the world. The next time such aspect will occur is closely to July of 2013. For the advanced, this is now an interesting subject to be forecast.

Los Angeles 2008 The Author

---

1. On page 453 the author has analyzed the events of September 11, 2001 by applying P (Pluto) transit to the chart of Manhattan/New York.

2

Any Interest in Astrology is a Good Investment of Knowledge that will Widen our Horizon

So, what is the lesson Astrology tries to teach us? Why did Christopher Reeve had his terrible accident and why did his seemingly nice and perfect wife had to die so young shortly after he did? Especially very religious people express a belief that a person brings any event "upon himself". But, by our standard of thinking, what could he and his wife had done that deserves such a horrific result? Well, first of all his accident was avoidable. It was visible in his chart, even without knowing his place and time of birth. But how could he have known that? So, what is the lesson given by life or God or the elements? Learn about astrology and be prepared for everthing or let it happen and deal with it. Of course, only humans who are prepared can guide their own life. That, however, requires knowledge of the elements in force. The intention of nature is evolutionary. Nothing stands still forever. Everything turns around. Birth, life and death are inevitable. Actions and reactions occur from which we learn to propel a matter forward.

The ideology, as applied in many Astrological and Religious books, that the "wise are those who bless every incident in their life", is not shared by the author. It would make more sense if "the wise would be the one being prepared and aware of what could happen to allow reacting in the most appropriate way to the incident. The answer hereto is left to the reader, as it is an individual's choice.

Just to mention but one example, a person may not be willing to struggle and fight but gives himself up to the flow of life, which eventually may bring him down. So, some would say he was too lazy, he should have done something. On the other hand there are lazy people who will not do anything. They may not even be blessed with any talent, but again, life endlessly provides for them. This is an indication that there is a higher control in place that may or may not require our action to be part of evolution. Therefore, the author believes that being aware of the future will in any case provide an advantage in life.

The first essential step is to become perfectly familiar with Astrological Symbols. Hence, this book will explain the symbols and thereafter faithfully use them in all text provided. The Astrological symbol is one universal language that has survived the ages. It can readily be understood by everyone on every continent, throughout the world.

The reader, who is already familiar with Astrology, will note that a lot of factors, such as applying or separating aspects, air, water, fire, earth, cardinal, fixed and mutable signs, angular, suceedent, sub-planets etc., are not considered in this book. The reason being that only many years of in depth study and experience will benefit a person's application of these aspects. Conducting a basic good and correct forecast is possible without consideration of these aspects. It is even possible, based solely on the birth date of a person and by using the Ephemeris, to give accurate forecasts to a person without even knowing any house position, as the human body is highly sensitive to atmospheric influences. These influences are caused by solar, lunar and planetary activity.

During adverse planetary aspects difficulties and obstacles are thrown into our path that inhibit progress. Feelings of anxiety, depression, nervousness and worry appear while we fight to safeguard our interests. The mind should be geared to see self-improvement in the acts necessary to overcome trouble and adversary. We are forced to think and act harder to retain our position and eventually gain positive changes. People who fought and clawed themselves out of poverty to become very wealthy are but one example that illustrates that the struggle must be accepted or gain will not follow.

A person born with no adverse aspects, or even no aspects at all, has no driving force for achievement and may meander through life like a boat bobbing the sea without ever reaching land. "Without a desire and a drive there can be no achievement".

To simplify astrology but still obtaining the best possible result, is the purpose of this book.

3

About Astrology

Man needs to understand the circle of life, its ups and downs. Don't plan at bad times, utilize good aspects, and most of all THE WISE MAN RULES HIS STARS, THE FOOL OBEYS THEM. Don't float in life, swim with a direction in mind.

Astrology provides knowledge by allowing more in-depth understanding of wisdom and meaning of life on earth. It is mostly the position of the O in aspect to other planets at birth that keeps us in bondage or let us be free. Of course, a strong person has, by will of mind, a means of influencing these natal conditions. That nothing is impossible should be foremost on a person's mind. For those advanced in Astrology it is enlightening and interesting to be able to foretell, prepare, and accordingly act to the situation that develops by identifying the aspects from the chart.

People very often talk about love and hate. The fact remains that a person who has not physically and mentally experienced these emotions and state of being will not be able to understand and define them. Quite often an Astrologer forecast an event that never comes to full fruition because the client is unable to absorb such an event through either lack of emotional experience, or simply by ignorance. However, through the circle of life, never ending changes force experiences upon us, in that the same transit, experienced again later in life, will then be in full force and effect when the person is ready and able to respond.

It is always interesting when taking the daily transit from the Ephemeris and staging the world's present transit. Obviously, we don't have a birth date for our earth. But by simply using, for example, today's transits of planets to each other we obtain an idea of the forces in place that bring evolution to this planet. The signs affected therein will point to the countries mostly involved in this challenge.

Among the most important and powerful transits is always the ☌ (conjunction). ☌ of planets are of major importance. Since ancient times the ☌ of ♃ and ♄ has attracted intense interests. Throughout history this ☌ is believed to bring new epochs, the rise and fall of nations, birth to new and great teachers, messiahs and it strongly influences civilization as a whole. This ☌, just short of perfection, occurred in June of 2000. We only have to look at the world's stage unfolding since that day to support the ancient belief. Look at China for instance, or India, both countries, once considered sub-developed, have floated to the top, giving the world powers a run for the money. This event may be compared with the end of the Roman Empire where ultimate powers ultimately destructed and destroyed. For those with lesser imagination it can be expressed in simple terms: when man has reached the top of the mountain there is nowhere to go but down.

While much has been written about the Universe and our consciousness thereto, man has not, and may never be able to, decipher the Universe as a whole. On earth everything has a beginning and an end. Nothing ever stays the same, we keep rotating. Look behind a curtain and there will be something else. In summary, for us the world is like a salami, it begins on one end, we savor it, and then it ends. But the omnipresent of the Universe with its vastness, does not have an end, or does it? If it had an end we would be wondering what lies beyond that curtain and beyond that, as that is our understanding as established by the rules on earth.

The main purpose of man is constantly enforced upon us, namely to understand nature (the wheel of life) and harmonize with its laws. Most religions preach harmony, piece and understanding. Once we're confronted with reality (which is not always to our liking) we tend to excuse it as God's will. But it is nature's never ending rotation that is forcing us to change. Thee who understands the forces of change and flows with it will avoid the struggle of swimming against the current. A chart, foretelling a possible accident, leaves man with a choice of trying to avoid it or blame it on God. The negative transits of ♂, ♄, ♅, and ♇[1] are manifestations of the full force of this change. Everything breaks up, annihilates, vaporizes, but out of the ashes a new circle begins. ♇'s hand may be felt about every 10-12 years. A new direction in life is enforced. As we are trying to hold on to what we have we will only extend the inevitable, a new direction, which is, even against our will, implemented and enforced. The greater the desire to resist change, the bigger and more prolonged the struggle will be. And, in the end, there will be change. Again, by the rules of nature, nothing last forever. The wheel keeps turning.

The natal chart is a good indicator of the person's ability to structure life or merely float in it. For example, if ♄ at birth is not aspected in any way (good or bad) the person lacks the drive and desire to succeed and will merely be carried by the flow of life without a personal desire and goal.

Forecasting can be tricky. Especially when forecasting an extremely good time ahead. Your client will mentally prepare for it, sit and wait in anticipation, but to everyone's surprise, nothing may happen or nothing has been realized to happen. So, the good time goes unnoticed without generating an impact on the person's life. Therefore forecasting, especially of good times, should not be glorified but observed with a grain of salt. The expectancy of the client may not be satisfied, thus, resulting in disappointment. While it is easier to prepare for bad times where the mind is alert to prevent the onslaught, good times let the mind drift and wander, rendering it unfocussed in anticipation that something great will just come along "quiet automatically". However, an unfocused mind may not be able to tune into the developing changes, which will ultimately turn into missed opportunity. In hindsight there were opportunities but not ready end results. As no action was taken to finalize the opportunities, no results could be achieved. It is therefore advisable to use good times to resort to well planned actions which, in turn, complete the opportunities with positive results. In other words, consciousness must be in place to utilize opportunities available at any given time.

The ☉ stands for heredity through the father and defines the vitality. The ☽ stands for heredity through the mother and her relationship to the child. If the child is born with ♃ in an unfavorable aspect to the ☽ the relationship with the mother will be inharmonious. The natal concept of ☉ to the ☽ determines a person's mental ability to act out and understand the masculine and feminine principle within the self.

The Ascendant (A) defines the personality per se. A baby chart will reveal the relationship of the parents to each other during the months of gestation. The first 3 years of life will form the character of the child based on the behavior of the parents toward the child and each other. As the child has no knowledge yet as to the concept of right or wrong the behavior pattern, as expressed by the parents, will be adopted as the norm in life. It is therefore of utmost importance that the parents be aware of their own behavior towards the child as well as to each other. The patterns instilled into the child, at this time, are hard to change in later life.

Many believe or want to believe that this life depends on past life experiences. As this argument is wholly fictional and as yet unproven, such assumption will not be applied here and unfortunately, remains an assumption, at best.

This author believes that rather then counting on the unproven theory of reincarnation, it seems more logical to assume that the position of the stars, in a person's natal chart, is based on the behavior pattern of the parents. If a generalization is permitted, then it will be that girls will have more similarity with the father and boys more similarity with the mother. Very often it applies to both, character and looks. This would permit the inference that the child is to play out and correct habits of the parents rather than habits of a former life. Throughout science it has been established that the unborn child is susceptible to its surroundings even prior to birth. It may be described as an antenna, via the umbilical cord, which connects it to the yet unseen world.

After age three the mind begins forming in that it notices surroundings, the environment per se which, in turn, forms impressions, and later on opinions and habits. The intellectual faculties begin to form and expand and will be colored by the way of life the child is subjected to. The maturing period begins and, actually, never ends except by death. In between the mind expands, learns and changes. Again, the rules of nature apply. The wheel is turning. Nothing stands still and nothing will remain the same. Not even man's opinion, which is subject to never ending adjustments in life. As the saying goes "a closed mind has no room to expand."

4

The Support An Astrologer May Provide

Awareness and preparedness help survive a challenging time much better. When does a person most probably consult with an astrologer? A much higher percentage of people will consult an astrologer when things are not working out and the person is lost in direction in life or just overwhelmed by circumstances. Whereas a happy and content person seldom needs to know when more good luck is flooding in. Therefore, the emphasis is placed on negative transits and progression. The awareness is centered on how to handle issues and get out from under pressing problems. These are the foremost issues an astrologer is faced with. Although, we know that people in general do not like to hear information that is rather unflattering and will not support positive expectations it is, however, a truthful, sometimes even painful way to make a person aware of what's going to go wrong. To keep full awareness of the fact of how the impact could be minimized and treated as a learning tool, especially when old habits have triggered an avalanche of unexpected reactions, is but one of the many tasks to be considered by an astrologer. Life, as such, is mostly a matter of acting in a certain way that will trigger expected or unexpected reactions thereto. There are situations that, if the outcome would have been considered beforehand, a different result could have been obtained. One thing is for certain, life as a whole is one big learning experience. The longer we repeat bad habits the less time we have to correct them. No one dies a person knowing all, having done it all, and thus becomes wiser therefrom. The compulsive non-learner can be found among people, who at the close of life, revert back to become children again. Their mental stage has reversed leaving them with temper tantrums and illogical behavior. Understanding the basis of life is the tool to astrology interpretations of a person's character, behavior pattern, and future events.

From years of personal experience an astrologer can attest that the prevailing transits and the awareness of either opportunities (good) or trouble (bad), may be kept under control. This places the person in a position to maximize or minimize transits. Bad transits have far less impact when the concept of awareness meets preparedness, is applied.

5

The Tools of the Trade

This book's purpose is to provide for every person, interested in astrology, a quick and easy overview of needed knowledge to read and interpret any chart. The instructions given herein include all applicable major aspects formed by the planets. The reader will be spared confusing or complicated calculations. Any chart may easily be calculated and printed out by a simple computer program (online even offers free chart printouts) and the reader may save enormous time. However, readers should be aware that computer interpretations of charts, although widely available, do not consider a person's individuality, hence its value is very generalized and mostly not much more than entertainment. So, from any chart printed, learning the correct interpretation is the substance given here that will be most helpful for any astrological work. As even computer programs are dealing with symbols the reader is urged to memorize the following symbols which are used throughout this book.

6

The Symbols

☉	=	Sun
☽	=	Moon
☿	=	Mercury
♀	=	Venus
♂	=	Mars
♃	=	Jupiter
♄	=	Saturn
♅	=	Uranus
♆	=	Neptune
♇	=	Pluto
♈	=	Aries
♉	=	Taurus
♊	=	Gemini
♋	=	Cancer
♌	=	Leo
♍	=	Virgo
♎	=	Libra
♏	=	Scorpio
♐	=	Sagittarius
♑	=	Capricorn
♒	=	Aquarius
♓	=	Pisces

☊ ☋	=	north and south node of the moon, also known as dragon's head and dragon's tail. The head symbolizes the positive, the tail symbolizes the negative influence.
M	=	Mid-heaven, also known as MC (medium coeli)
A	=	Ascendant, also known as AC

7

The Basic Representation by Each Planet

☉	The life, vitality, ego and power. It represents the masculine side.
☽	Emotions, domesticity, growth and life force for a women. It represents the feminine side.
☿	Intellect, the mind.
♀	Love and attraction.
♂	Passion and action.
♃	Religion, luck, legal involvement and optimism.
♄	Duty, work and authority.
♅	Sudden changes, independence, inventions and group involvement.
♆	The emotional side to life, its secrets and how we react to it.
♇	Life and death, annihilation, power struggle, break up and rebuilding.
☊ ☋	How we adjust and be seen by society.
M	Reputation and success.
A	Personality and wellbeing.

8

The Major Planet Formations are:

☌ = conjunction
∗ = sextile
□ = square
▲ = trine
☍ = opposition

Example:

☌ the planets occupy the same degree of longitude – i.e. ☉ 15 ♌ ☌ ♇ 15 ♌

∗ the planets are 60 degrees apart – i.e. ☉ 15 ♊ ∗ ♇ 15 ♌

□ the planets are 90 degrees apart – i.e. ☉ 15 ♉ □ ♇ 15 ♌

▲ the planets are 120 degrees apart – i.e. ☉ 15 ♈ ▲ ♇ 15 ♌

☍ the planets are 180 degrees apart – i.e. ☉ 15 ♒ ☍ ♇ 15 ♌

The influences of ☌ depend on the planets involved in a conjunction. Depending on a good or bad influence it may further a cause or hinder and delay, even obstructing the efforts made, leading to a negative result. The influences of ∗ bring opportunity through efforts and work. The influences of □ and ☍ bring disruption, obstruction, fate, and enhance bad conditions. The influences of ▲ bring expansion, luck, furtherance and benefits. It is the author's experience that the bad effect of □ acts more severely than the ☍ in its chief influences. The formations represent the following meanings:

☌ = This is the strongest formation and depending on the planets involved may produce a very good result or extreme friction that leads to break ups and, thus, change.
* = talents and opportunities need developing
□ = obstacles must be overcome
▲ = progress in life
☍ = stress and confusion. Bad habits need changing to give way to progress.

The reader is urged to keep in mind that any aspect in transit or progression must be considered first by the natal influences. If two planets are in good aspect with each other at birth, any bad aspect formed in progression will be much less negative. However, if the birth aspect was also bad, serious consequences may occur. If the progression is now positive, compared to a negative natal position, not much good will develop.

Here is a short explanation as to the main issues that arise through each particular house:

House 1 : Personality
House 2 : Personal income
House 3 : Short term travel, communications, siblings and neighbors (or the immediate environment)
House 4 : Home, family, end of life condition
House 5 : Children, love affairs, speculations
House 6 : Work, health
House 7 : Partnerships, lawsuits, public involvement
House 8 : Death and money belonging to others i.e. partner's money, taxes, insurance, inheritance, outcome of lawsuits, etc.
House 9 : Foreign land, religion, education, higher courts.
House 10 : Honor and professional standing
House 11 : Friends, hopes and wishes
House 12 : Karma, confinement, self-undoing, enemies.

(see page 56 for more information on houses and their meanings)

Man is subject not only to events applicable to his own private and individual nature, but also to influences arising from general and social causes.

The importance of the ☽ has been known to astrologers for a long time. Many old time farmers will insist that seeds sown when the ☽ is growing will germinate better. Battles have been won and lost due to the influence of the ☽. The same, of course, applies to individuals. Begin no quarrel, war, or controversy, neither invade the enemies country when the ☽ is in ♏ or ♑. Begin no quarrel nor invasion when the ☽ is combust, or within 12 hours after its conjunction with the ☉. If any quarrel, or war, or dispute is began in these hours, the beginner will be defeated, or much evil will befall this person. (with this in mind everyone is well advised not to begin any legal action when the ☉ and ☽ are combust) Even the ZULU tribe, native to South Africa, was well aware of it. The battle of Isandhlwana was fought during an eclipse of the ☽, visible in Zululand on January 22, 1879. The Zulus delayed their attack until the 23rd, thus demonstrated the knowledge of astrology and would not attack during the combust hours of the ☽, hence gained victory.

It is not a subject based on the assumption that a person believes in it or not. The concept of Astrology has proven, beyond doubt, that it is reliable and that, when well interpreted, will accurately and even timely forecast events that permit a person to either gain knowledge and take advantage of positive transits or avoid unfortunate events or, at a minimum, lessen its effect. Astrology will not change a person but any knowledge of the future always provides an advantage and may, to a certain degree, influence the outcome.

Astrology should not be confused with the horoscope in the daily news papers which purpose is solely to entertain and not to predict any event for any particular individual. A personalized chart relies on the data obtained from a person, namely, date of birth, time of birth and place of birth. If a major relocation has taken place in the person's life, said new location should be considered as the same indications of events, as shown in a natal chart, will fall into different houses, thus, having a slightly different effect and outcome.

It would be very enlightening if one could meet today the first person on earth who "discovered" the concept of astrology, thus laying the foundation for knowledge that is still applied today. What influenced that person and how was the concept developed? What was known at that time of our solar system that could have guided the person in his prediction? Well, it is a nice idea, but we will never know the real father of Astrology.

We all know, however, that no human being can avoid death. Most people are interested in discovering what lies on the path one travels throughout life. One thing, for sure, has proven true: 'we are all part of the universe and guided by the stars'.

A person with ample □ and ☍ in the natal chart may eventually be better off in life than a person with no aspects at all. While we all prefer the easy life, very few people are blessed to experience it. However, a person with no direct aspects, good or bad, has no direction in life. The will and desires are weak. Bad aspects at birth provide the energy, willpower and ambition to overcome obstacles and difficulties to obtain achievement.

Human behavior, as well as all other life forms, is mostly influenced by planetary action. Of course, there are but a few people on earth who happen to be unaffected by the planets. With that exception, the rest of us mere mortals, will be riding the waves of planetary influences from cradle to grave. By utilizing the ability to adjust and prepare for our future we can improve life and avoid major mistakes and even calamity, by being prepared as to when and how to act, in order to reap the best possible rewards or avoid disaster. While an individual's life is basically mapped out at birth the possibility of grabbing opportunity while the progressed planets provide a change of conditions over the natal chart, allows significant opportunities for change. The reader is well advised not to whitewash negative aspects or underestimate its influences. Beware of danger is a much better advice than to give a person the feeling that by ignoring bad influences they will go away. If the chart indicates an accident, a major illness, a looming divorce or loss of job, it is the duty of a good astrologer to make the client aware so that actions may be taken to avoid the approaching effects. Being aware of something helps minimize the impact. Warnings should not instill fear but suggest caution. There should be an awareness of action taken during the period the aspects operate. Astrology is intended to allow us to attain the consciousness to perceive the invisible.

A=ASCENDANT

The ascendant is the rising sign that appears on the cusp of the first house when the chart is calculated for the time of birth. Any aspect hereto influences the health and general well being. Each sign takes approximately 2 hours to rise above the horizon. (A new degree rises every 4 minutes. A new sign about every 2 hours and all signs rise in every place on earth in 24 hours). Any change in the time of birth will invariably alter the rising sign and subsequently the position of each house. The time of birth also determines the degree of the ☽ position in its sign at time of birth. While the planets, with the exception of a slight variation for the fast traveling ☽, will remain in about the same degree, even if a different birth time for the same date is calculated, they however, change position and may appear in a different house. While that does not change the aspects formed, it provides for a different meaning of those aspects formed at birth.

M=MIDHEAVEN

The Mid-heaven on the other hand is the highest point in a house chart and represents the cusp of the 10th house. It represents the spirit, the aspirations, the public image and social position in life. It also represents the parental influence over the person. The sign placed at M and its ruling planet will provide an insight into the person's professional ability. Transits hereto provide information about changes and social events during the life.

9

The Meaning of Retrograde

The planets move forward in one direction. At times, the motion of the planets relative to the earth's position in its orbit makes them seem to move backwards in the zodiac. This is called retrograde and is listed in the Ephemeris with an R. This retro-motion is only seeming, however, it has a very real effect in respects to the influence the planet exerts, as it is the angle of the ray which determines its influence on a person's life. The subsequent forward motion is listed as D (direct) in the Ephemeris. Please note that ☉ and ☽ are never retrograde.

When retrograde is noted in the natal chart, the affairs ruled by that planet seem on hold, unable to fully develop and benefit the person. The same applies to the progressed planets. On a daily transit, affairs of retrograde planets seem to develop their energy behind the scene. Action taken during this time will hardly propel forward but rather linger in a process of being developed rather than ripen into a completed action. The unveiling of actions or events will be catapulted into the open once the planet again proceeds in a direct, forward motion. For example, the time during which ☿ is retrograde, whether by transit or progress, any communication or entering into contracts should be done only with utmost cautions as unplanned problems will be experienced. It always pays to wait for any retrograde planet to proceed in direct motion before new plans should be entered into. During the retrograde phase plans should be carefully considered. Direct motion requires action to enforce those plans. Therefore, important decisions should wait until the planet's forward motion is activated again. Should the retrograde planet make important aspects to natal planets while in the retrograde state, the effect of which will only be felt on beginning of the forward motion. Retrograde motion renders the specific planet stronger in application. It does not, however, move the issue forward to completion. Retrograde is also known as the development phase prior to going into new experiences. A retrograde ♀ leads to emotional loneliness and frustration. ♂ delays, frustrates, brings inner uncertainties or lack of opportunity as well as lack of action. Nothing seems to move forward. ♃ applies to education, progress, optimism and litigation but will not fare well during this phase. ♄ symbolizes a lack of new opportunity but preparation and finishing old business may turn beneficial on forward motion. ♅ stands for unexpected old business. A friendship or partnership comes up for reconsideration before it may be concluded. ♆ creates deceptive situations. Strange feelings and circumstances may be experienced. ♇ brings secret and mysterious events and confrontations over power may develop. Confrontations with and withdrawal from society may be experienced.

10

Interpreting Progress

The Progressed horoscope shows the years after birth and the changes in conditions, temperament and characteristic of the person. Changes, new desires, interests and directions and a new line of thinking that occurs in people most of the time, will be intensified.

While the day on which a person is born establishes the natal (radix) chart, each day thereafter moves the planets ahead, thus, forming new aspects. For instance, if a chart is prepared for a 30 year old person, most planets have a different position than at time of birth. In the Ephemeris this position is shown by counting ahead 30 days, beginning from the day after birth. In summary, a chart is erected as if that person was born 30 days later. The progressed position of the planets to each other and their relations to the natal chart now determine the phase in life that prevails over the person. This may or may not be an improvement over the birth chart. The progressed planets now determine events together with transits to natal planets. It is always important to establish and analyze the original, natal position of the planets and the progressed position to determine the new prevailing influences over the person's life. Depending on the planets involved, these new influences may have a duration of several years.

While the natal chart represents the person's blue print, the progression represents the changes taking place based on structures or limits imposed at birth. Please note that a progressed aspect needs to be triggered by a transit in order to take effect.

If a transiting or progressing planet is forming an aspect with a Natal (radical) planet the interpretation should be taken from the house position of the Natal chart.

If a progressed planet is forming an aspect to another progressed planet, the interpretation should be taken from the house position in the Progressed chart.

11

What is a Transit?

A Transit is the daily passage of planets over or in aspect to the natal planets or cusp of houses. If an astrologer wants to consider the importance of a house cusp an accurate birth time is necessary. Any four minutes difference in the time of birth will move the cusp by 1 degree.

The passage of planets, via transit over or in aspect to progressed planets, will trigger the event identified by the position and meaning of the progressed planets. For example: a person is born with ♀ ▲ ♄. As soon as ♄ is in transit and ☌ ♀ the event (a business or enterprise established with a lover or marriage partner) will begin if no planet hinders or delays such formation. The same applies if the natal chart has no aspect between ♀ and ♄, but later moves via progress to ♀ ▲ ♄. The timing of the event will be established and becomes apparent through the transit.

12

Changes in Residence May Affect the House Position

Although the natal chart, when erected for the place of birth, will always be the strongest indicator of future events, a change of residence may affect the time of those events being set into motion. If the person moves to the east of the birthplace the difference in time should be added to the birth time. If a move is to the west of the birthplace the time difference should be subtracted from the birthplace.

A new calculation, based on the different time of birth, is necessary. The new location will result in the same planets being in the same signs and degree, however, they will be appearing in different houses, thus, changing their meaning and influences. This will affect the life in a different way. However, it is the author's experience that events will be so clearly noted in the natal chart that a new location chart may not result in a more accurate forecast. A more positive result, however, will be obtained if the new location results in a clearing of planets from the 12th and 6th house, hence improving karma and health.

13

Consideration of the Importance of Aspects is Necessary for Any Forecast

The primary marks of the chart to which attention should be paid:

A represents the Ascendant on the cusp of the first house. Its rising sign is the most sensitive cusp as it represents the character, the self-awareness and expression of vitality. It also indicates the physical appearance and behavior. While the ☉ sign will determine the individuality A denotes the personality.

M represents the cusp of the tenth house and denotes the position in life, honor, wealth, reputation or the lack of it and will indicate a rise or fall in life.

☽ represents the emotional side of the personality. The natal ☽ as well as the progressed ☽ has a strong influence on events when they render aspects to other planets at the same time as those planets form aspects between each other.

The cusp or beginning or edge of a house in the chart and the sign on the cusp thereon determines the ruling planet of that house.

♈ ruled by	♂
♉	♀
♊	☿
♋	☽

♌	☽
♍	☿
♎	♀
♏	♇
♐	♃
♑	♄
♒	♅
♓	♆

14

What is Required of An Astrologer?

The science of astrology is best suited for those people who possess an active 6th sense, a faculty of intuition. This is especially important when reading a chart as the senses tune in to the magnetic field of the person seeking advice. Merely learning the technical aspect and training associated with Astrology will not produce an equally good astrologer. Simply applying the standard interpretations to any given aspect will not incorporate the will and determination of the person seeking advice. The intuition of the astrologer is needed to bring an accurate forecast into the picture. Otherwise, forecasting may be faulty as not being applied to the personality expressed in the chart. Forecasting requires appliance of the truth and an earnest, unprejudiced interpretation of the chart.

The vibration of the planets in a chart endow the tendencies of its character. It will manifest and, by progression, determine the directions and events developing in the future. A precise forecast will support important events and minimize or avoid bad situations. Forewarned is fore-planned.

Not financial greed but a desire to genuinely appraise a person's ability in life should motivate an astrologer.

15

What is Required for the Exact Calculation of a Chart?

Every properly calculated chart is absolutely individual. In order to be precise the following information is absolutely necessary:

(1) Date of Birth

(2) Time of Birth

(3) Place of Birth

The Time and Place of birth are the basic factors in calculating the precise position of the **A** (Ascendant). Its position will determine the position of all other houses and their respective cusps. Latitude is the principle factor in locating the signs of the zodiac by means of the "houses". However, a determination of character and general forecasting events can be made solely based on the date of birth. (See page 391, Analyzing and forecasting without making a chart) It is, however, only a general definition and future forecasts may not occur at the exact time predicted. The events set out by the planets will occur. Just the exact time is left to speculation rather then calculation when the time and place of birth is unknown.

16

A Selection of Interesting Transit Interpretations

PREGNANCY AND SOCIAL DISEASES

When the ☉ transits and ☌ ☽ and is favorably aspected, women desiring to get pregnant will find this time favorable for any conception.

☉ ☌ ♆ and ☉ ☍ ♆ = unwanted pregnancies if the ☽ is also afflicted.
☿ □ ♇ = social diseases are often contracted under this transit.
☿ □ ♅ = social diseases are often contracted during this transit.
☽ ☌ ☉ = good for pregnancies.

♀ in good aspect through the 5th house can lead to a successful pregnancy.

BUSINESS AND JOB RELATED QUESTIONS

When the question is job or business related the planets refer to categories, as presented by examples:

☽ = Common employment
☉ = Government and position in public
☿ = Schools, intellectual affairs, all communications and publishing
♀ = Entertainment, Art, social functions
♂ = Mechanical work, manufacturing, building and munitions
♃ = Religion, legal and financial affairs
♄ = Mining, farming, bookkeeping and organizational professions.

♅ = Railroads, aerial and electrical industries, eccentric and innovative occupations

♆ = Oil and fishing industry, or other industries related to or near water.

♇ = Secret and underground involvement. Public power, politics and criminal involvement.

Here is a good reminder: No one knows it all! The subject of astrology is so engaging and a constant source of information that it requires a life time of learning. Ample good books are available for the curious and willing to delve into the depth of our Universe. This book is intended to simplify astrology, thus, allowing even the most busy-body to find the time to discover their talent and satisfy all their curiosity as to the events that structure our lives.

IMPORTANT INDICATIONS OF ☊ ☋
BY HOUSE POSITION AND SIGN

The ☾ nodes ☊ ☋ is not a planet but a point in the heavens where the ☾ crosses the ecliptic from north latitude to south latitude. It is also known as the "Dragon's head and Dragon's tail". ☊ is considered benefic and ☋ is considered malefic. It's influence on the person acts primarily on the individual's attitude and reactions toward social trends and behavior pattern. ☊ provides expansion in the social circles and indicates harmony with social trends and developments. ☋ restricts and hampers social relationships. The person has to fend without receiving social support, however, it allows the person to recognize negative trends, thus, it will not drag the person into the tide of cultural events and prevents from being swayed by others.

House 1: ☊ Provides the ability to blend in well with social and cultural patterns.

☋ The personality is reserved and cautious.
Conservative, slow in speech and not easily willing to follow social trends, the person is rather reserved and traditional in values. In the extreme it can also indicate some kind of physical deformity.

House 2: ☊ Following social trends and adopting social opinions will provide financial rewards. However, care is necessary not to overspend.

☋ Money is spent cautiously.

House 3: ☊ Current trends in usage of language are applied. Social activities are pursued and benefits are reaped from social involvement.

☋ Old fashioned conservative values and reserved attitudes prevent the person from jumping on the band wagon of popular ideas and beliefs.

House 4: ☊ The home and environment is trendy and used for social gatherings.

☋ The home is primarily used as a personal retreat for the person and family.

House 5: ☊ Current trends in entertainment, sexual attitudes and romance, bring social popularity.

☋ A conservative, formal and reserved attitudes is expressed towards social situations. Romance may be tainted by frustration and lack of fulfillment.

House 6: ☊ Creates popularity with co-workers and bosses.

☋ Rather a loner. The person avoids social working contacts and prefers to work hard on their own accomplishment.

House 7: ☊ Good skills for public relations are present. Agreements with current trends and attitudes attract positive cooperation.

☋ Caution is used when entering into personal relationships.

House 8: ☊ Beneficial business ventures, as trends, are successfully applied.

☋ A cautious attitude and care is needed when dealing with other peoples money. Litigation may end costly.

House 9:

☊ Education, religion, legal affairs and travel are undertaken to fit into social norms.

☋ Cautious and conservative, and not easily swayed by cultural ideas, the person avoids religious adherence and refuses to blindly follow trends even at the risk of becoming unpopular.

House 10:

☊ Current trends promote professional advancement. Popularity may lead to fame in early life. However, obscurity may follow.

☋ Struggle to gain acceptance and respect. The person's interest may not be in harmony with present social norms. Lasting values are more important than instant success.

House 11:

☊ Friendships are made easily. Current trends are adopted but the person may also be easily influenced by others.

☋ Responsibility is extended to friendships. Friendships are not entered into easily but may be enduring through strong loyalty. Meaningless social activities are rejected.

House 12:

☊ Moods and trends of the masses are tuned into. However, the individuality must be preserved or it will be absorbed by the social wave.

☋ Current trends and social favors are ignored or even rejected. Isolation and loneliness may be by choice. An inability to accept responsibilities may turn the person into a hermit.

17

A Moderate Inside into Medical Astrology

Parts of the body ruled by signs:

♈ Head and face
♉ Throat and ears
♊ Shoulders, arms, hands, lungs, collarbone and nervous system
♋ Breast, stomach and digestive organs
♌ Heart, upper half of the back
♍ Solar plexus and bowel
♎ Kidneys, ovaries, lower half of the back
♏ Muscular system, bladder, sex organs
♐ Liver, Thighs
♑ Knees
♒ Ankles
♓ Feet

18

Medical Astrology

Medical astrology is an extensive field that requires years of practice and in-depth knowledge. For the advanced, concentrating on medical astrology, when combined with knowledge of Palmistry, may be a very valuable experience. Such knowledge is supportive in a healing process. Excellent knowledge of these fields permit astrological diagnoses of diseases and hard to detect illnesses that have even eluded the abilities of medical doctors. Illness of children may be induced by surrounding unhappy adults. Mental pain may develop into serious diseases.

A natal chart reveals incipient diseases to which a person may be susceptible from cradle to grave. The reading of a child's chart may allow the use of treatments preventing an outbreak or may even permit actions that will ameliorate the seeds of diseases. Every person is, based on their star sign and planet(s) located in the 6th house, susceptible to specific illnesses. Prevention is a great part of the cure.

This book will not deal extensively with medical issues. It merely addresses the importance of considering the 6th house of a chart to familiarize the reader with some knowledge, permitting a forecast on basic health issues. Further studies, especially on this subject, are needed to perfect the subject of medical astrology.

The planets in the 6th house and the signs therein must be considered for any forecast. If there is no planet in this house then the sign on the cusp of the 6th house will show which part of the body is most susceptible to illness and suffering. When well aspected planets reside in the 6th house the ailments will be minor and may be overcome.

The following is a general indication of the signs and its influences over certain parts of the body. Depending on the aspects, good or bad, to the 6th house, the characteristic of induced illness is:

♈ Ailments to the brain resulting in neuralgia, headache, insomnia and affliction of the eyes and face.

♉ The throat, tonsils and neck area may suffer from disorder.

♊ The lungs, bronchial tubes, the respiratory system and nervous system are affected. The lungs are the weakest part.

♋ Conditions of the stomach, digestive tract, suffering from flatulency, fermentation and gastric trouble.

♌ The heart, excesses and inharmonious living and disorders of the blood are main complaints.

♍ The bowel and digestive system bring colic, constipation, dysentery and indigestion.

♎ The kidneys bring diabetes, bright's disease and suppression of urine that inflames the kidneys.

♏ The excretory system, generative organs and bladder produce ailments. It promotes inflammatory diseases, especially to the sexual organs and the excretory system.

♐ The purity of the blood is threatened by nervous upset and disorders of the liver.

♑ Colds and chills, imperfect circulation, mental depression and melancholia are present. It chiefly produces rheumatism, gout, constipation and skin trouble.

♒ The blood and mental faculties may be subject to disorder. Bad circulation, eye trouble, spasmodic cramps, especially in the lower legs, will be experienced.

♓ Impurities of the blood, imbalance in the body and its fluid system. Lack of cleanliness may produce disease. It fosters tumors and problems with the feet.

19

Planetary Rulership

☉ is the ruler of the system, the giver of life. It governs the heart, vitality, blood and brain. The right eye in a male, the left eye in a female.

☽ is the ruler of the natural functions in the body and the giver of life for a female. It governs the breast, stomach, fluidic and lymphatic system. The left eye in a male and the right eye in a female. When the ☽ is in progress the sign it travels through will identify the part of the body in distress.

☿ is the ruler of the brain and mind. It governs the nervous system, lungs, tongue, speech, hands, arms, mouth and hair.

♀ is the ruler of the throat, chin, complexion, cheeks, venous system, kidneys, and the internal parts of the generative organs.

♂ is the ruler of the nose, forehead, bile, gall, sinews, muscular system and external generative organs. It induces inflammatory ailments and suffering through accidents.

♃ is the ruler governing the purity of the blood, liver, arterial system, pleura, right ear and the absorbative system.

♄ governs the bones, joints, spleen, teeth, knees, phlegm and the secretive system. It is responsible for falls, strains and related injury.

♅ governs the nerve fluids, membranes of the brain, spinal cord and physical aura. It has a tendency to disturb digestion and creates gas in the stomach and fosters inflammation and contractions.

♆ governs telepathic functions, fluidic system and mental illness.

♇ governs social orders, and as such, creates weakness to outside influences. Especially excessive exposure to radiation will trigger a change of cells in the body.

A The position of the Ascendant at birth, by progression and afflicted by transit, affects the general health of the person.

An afflicted Ascendant may produce the following illnesses when experienced through the planets involved:

☉ causes physical disorders.

☽ causes functional disorders, irregularities of the system, problems with the body fluidic system.

☿ causes nervous and mental disorders

♀ causes excesses through pleasure, such as venereal diseases.

♂ causes inflammatory disorders and accidents, fever and wounds.

♃ causes blood disorders and diseases due to an excess in diet and liver problems.

♄ causes chronic complaints, cold and weaknesses and other lingering complaints. By its transit through the 1st house ♄ afflicts the health and may result in change of appearance, possibly leading to extreme loss of weight. During this transit the body throws of impurities and may fight ailments. A good ♄ to the ☉ promotes overcoming of illnesses.

♅ causes spasmodic disorders such as cramps, spasm and social diseases especially when bad with ☿

♆ causes disorders from drug and alcohol use, mental disorders, depression and insanity

♇ causes stress, depression and tension from breaking up of existing conditions. Illness may be induced by excessive radiation. Through serious illness a transformation may occur.

Some natal indications that deserve consideration on health issues.

If the ☉ and ☽ are afflicted by ♂ the person may suffer from blindness. The sign ♒ in particular rules over the eyesight. If ☉ ☌ ♄ in ♒ it is a strong indicator for blindness.

An affliction at birth between ♄, ♅, or ♂ may result in a person being born with distorted limbs. ♄ □ ♆ indicates malformations and produces an undersize of the physical body.

The ☋ in house 1, if badly afflicted at birth or by transit, may result in spinal injuries. A problem experienced either through accident or disease.

When the ☽ is afflicted by ♃ at birth the person may develop liver problems, especially when ♃ transits the 6th house. A person should avoid all operations at the time the ☽ travels through the signs signifying the part of the body that is considered for operation.

A negative ♂ transit may lead to cruel or abusive treatment in hospitals. Fever and infections may be misdiagnosed, especially when negatively aspecting ♆. Illness may be brought on by an emotional imbalance. Hospital treatment with improper medication may increase the illness.

☽ INFLUENCES ON THE HEALTH

In a female chart the ☽ is the giver of life and affects the general health and prospects of life. The health will be stronger when the ☽ appears in house 7-12. Should the ☽ be situated in ♏ or ♑ its influences produce impurities, irregularities of the feminine system and support habits that are adverse to the general health. If a negative ♃ is involved it may produce obesity. If the ☽ is afflicted in ♑ the health may be delicate overall and, especially in youth, produces ailing.

DEATH

Although, no one wants to talk about death, it is inevitable and, as part of life, ultimately unavoidable. However, until we are called upon to leave this earth situations may develop that permit us to avoid death and prolong life, especially when we can avoid accidents that are clearly shown in our chart. The 3rd house is a good indicator for accidents in and around our neighborhood. The 9th house warns us of foreign travel. ♇' hand may endanger our lives through chemicals or crime, while ♂ may indicate an accident or an unsuccessful operation. There is an endless list of possibilities that could end life untimely, either through others or even through our own hands. A good astrologer has the power to see such events when they appear in the developing stage. Dark clouds forecast the thunder. Certain transits are, in deed, dark clouds but we have the power to decide on changing our habits, at least, until the thunder has passed. If an accident is indicated it will be fairly easy not to drive for a number of days. A bad ♄ teaches us not to climb or be confronted with heights, so stay grounded until that transit has passed.

Every astrologer is well advised to consider transits that strongly suggest a negative influence. Together with the client, preventions can be set into place that minimize or even nullify any life threatening event. In the beginning of this book the author used the example of Princess Diana and Christopher Reese. A good astrologer could have saved their lives as their demise, via planetary influences, was clearly marked in their charts.

20

Natural Death

Observe the ruler of the 8th house and any planet therein. When there is any evil direction between the ruler of the 8th house and the planet therein, death may occur.

When ♇ ☍ or □ ☉ at birth and through progression again reaches a bad position or any transit is building a bad direction, death may occur.

Example: A women born on December 11, 1965 showing in her natal chart ☉ □ ⛢, ♇. The transit on March 20, 2003 is ♇ ☌ ☉ □ ⛢, ♇ death occurred on that day. Her desire for beauty brought on her demise. She died of complications from a liposuction operation that could have been avoided had someone, with knowledge of astrology, reviewed her chart. This is a tragic example of bad timing. While the ☉ represents life ♇ represents death.

♂ Is the chief influence for inflammation, infestation and all sorts of accidents relating to metal (boat, plane, car, operation by knife etc.) When appearing in or be aspected by a negative transit in the 6th and 8th house, it causes death through fever, loss of blood and all inflammatory diseases.

♄ In the 6th or 8th house denotes death through lingering illness affecting the part of the body ruled by the sign in which ♄ is placed. If ♇ is also negatively involved with ♄ by transit or progression, the chance of survival is slim.

People born with an afflicted ☉ in the 8th house may die young but may receive recognition after death.

It is important to notice when ♇' position affects any illness. All chemical treatments and medication should be avoided as they may turn out to be the source of death. The subject of death, although no one's favorite conversation, needs to be considered for the possibility of avoiding death and not to scare people.

21

Advice for Homoepathic Medication

(The Internal Clock of the Organs)

The energy required by the organs in the body is subject to a biological rhythm. The energy needed for the organs to function is regenerated during the course of a twenty-four-hour day. The treatment of illnesses, as well as the time of intake for medicine can be coordinated for the best possible effect. By taking homeopathic medicine during the time period of a specific organ, an illness can be treated by allowing the most energy to be utilized for the best possible results. The hours set forth below also show occurring times in which the body will remind us of its illness. As an example: repeatedly awaking at 1-3 am in the morning is an indication of liver malfunction or overproduction that disturbs the normal rhythm of the body.

LIVER	1-3 am
LUNGS	3-5 am
LARGE INTESTINES	5-7 am
STOMACH	7-9 am
SPLEEN/PANCREAS	9-11 am
HEART	11 am-1 pm
SMALL INTESTINE	1-3 pm
BLADDER	3-5 pm
KIDNEY	5-7 pm
GALL BLADDER	11 pm – 1 am

22

The Houses and Signs Therein

The 12 houses represent and accommodate the 12 signs of the zodiac through which the planets transit and progress. Each represents a department of life. A sign may be intercepted when it is placed between the cusp of two houses without affecting either cusp.

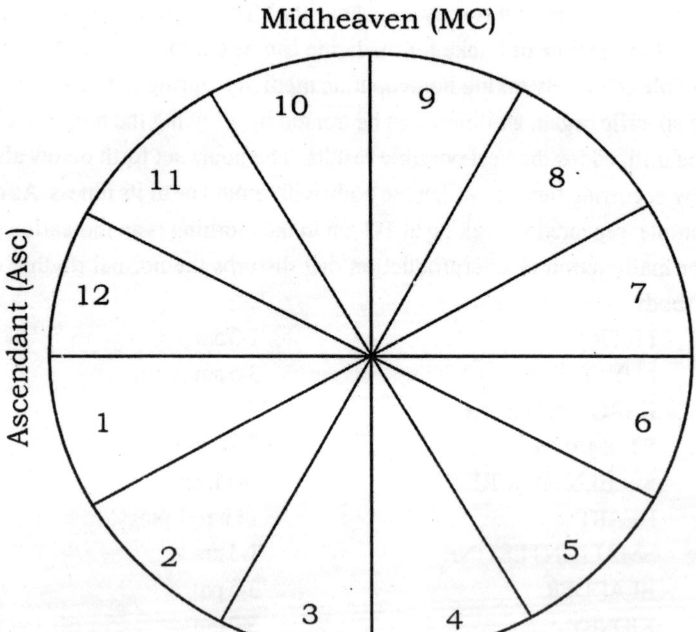

Example: *The cusp on the 3rd house is ♉. The cusp on the 4th house is ♋. Therefore the sign ♊ is placed in the middle position in the 3rd house without showing on either sign of the cusps. It denotes that this sign and its ruling planet are hindered in their expression and unable to perform to its fullest potential.*

23

1ST House

This house represents the beginning of life. It establishes the self as personality, physical appearance and attitude of the person. The sign at the cusp of the first house represents the rising sign or **A** (Ascendant). It defines the body, physical vitality and abnormalities. If afflicted, the parts of the body most susceptible to illness or injury, will be shown by the sign at the cusp.

♈ = The individual is driven by self-awareness and depending on any planets established in this house will either be strong willed, loving or ruthless in expressing directions in life. A self-starter and very direct in all approaches the person's character will absorb any qualities expressed by the characteristics of the nearest planets to **A**. In case there is no planet positioned herein the characteristics of the ruling planet will be expressed. (♂)

♉ = The individual is very practical, but also very often stubborn and strongly interested in financial resources as they provide for the good things in life.

♊ = The appearance is usually slender with sensitive nerves. The person gestures while communicating, is talkative and curious to investigate and has intellectual interests.

♋ = The mind observes everything. The mood is fragile, sensitive and tends to avoid unpleasant situations or delays solving of problems. The feelings run the mind. A close identification exists with the family and home.

♌ = The individual is proud and outgoing, loves to attract attention and dominate the crowd.

♍ = The person is very organized and practical but picky and critical. At times there are problems to believe and understand others as the mind will not fathom what isn't pre-programmed into their system. There is an ability to focus on small details but to the point of over-perfection, thus, annoying others.

♎ = The face may show dimples in the cheeks. The disposition is friendly and willing to cooperate but often is indecisive. There is an ability to express beauty and grace but always with a grain of self-interest. This person needs company to thrive.

♏ = The eyes are penetrating, coupled with a stern and blunt personality. The body oozes energy and willpower that needs an outlet for achievement.

♐ = The individual may be well built, is always on the move and loves to travel and flirt. The ultimate optimist if positively aspected who tries to accomplish enormous goals. The person will cooperate provided their self-interest is gaining.

♑ = The individual is serious and reserved with a strong money minded attitude. A disciplined and hard worker who's willing to pursue his goal.

♒ = A talkative person with a great humanitarian interest who loves adventure and functions well within groups. The independent and creative ability finds outlets through friends and groups.

♓ = This individual has very sensitive emotions. Dreamy by nature and subjected to various moods the person retreats into the self when things become unpleasant. Not an easy doer and, at times, stubborn but often practical, there is a desire to always stay close to the family. Often artistic and musical talents are present.

24

2nd House

This house refers to money earned through own efforts and the ability to handle the resources. It defines self-acquired wealth, losses through own actions and indicates the cause of death of the marital or business partner.

♈ = Money is flowing in and out as rashness and changes of emotions affect the spending. There is a strong desire to make money. However, with little persistence in staying the course to the end it is difficult to reap the full reward.

♉ = Money and goods of beauty are the prime motivators in life. A need for possessions is indicated and might be strongly pursued. However, placing too much emphasis on possession may deplete any mental contentment. In case there is no planet positioned herein the characteristics of the ruling planet will be expressed. (♀)

♊ = Money is often obtained through intellectual means, higher education and very often through dual sources. The person may work for a family business and invests in solid enterprises.

♋ = Frugality may be the right word. While willing to share with others to satisfy an emotional balance, at times, the stingy side prevails when the emotions are hurt. The person most likely would harbor a nest egg, which provides for emotional security.

♌ = The ambitions are strong but due to excessive pride and a display of arrogance this may require working alone to avoid confrontations. If employed, a position of authority is desired. A position in public may lead to success and afford the finer things of life.

♍ = The individual is capable of hard work, is well organized and can execute tasks down to the smallest detail, which makes this person a trusted and reliable employee. Willing to share, being practical and with no emotional ties to the income, this person saves for a rainy day but is not typically affected by money.

♎ = Money may come from partnerships, a legal profession or artistic endeavors. Seeking the good things in life, the person may, however, at times be frugal when acquired money is saved with a goal in mind.

♏ = There is a great amount of secrecy about money and possessions. An unwillingness to freely share with others fosters a constant desire to possess, which may be driven by a lack of self-confidence that is capable of turning jealousy into an art form. Money may be spent rapidly but with gain in mind.

♐ = The individual is not very generous with resources. There may be dual income from multiple sources. The person loves possessions, however, they should not curb any personal freedom. Money is spent on travel, education and religious institutions.

♑ = Money is a prime motivator in life. The desire for money and the accumulation of it may take over the emotions. At times the mind is so locked into the desire for more that miserly behavior may arouse conflict with others.

♒ = Income is gained from unusual sources, possibly from large organizations or inventions that are advanced in its field.

♓ = Money and possessions are strongly tied to the emotions. The income will fluctuate and is often derived from dual sources. Any business activity may be related to water or is located somewhere near water.

25

3rd House

The operation of the mind, the relationships with siblings and neighbors, as well as short-distance travel and mode of transportation are ruled by this house. The conscious mind is expressed in relation with others to either benefit or hinder the desires of the person. Thinking and communicating in the right, beneficial way and executing speech and written material are all governed here in ways expressed by the person. When the mind is underdeveloped or "closed" the person's acts are impractical, confused and even delusional and obstructive. It denotes the nervous system, the energy level, patience or impatience and degree of will power. It will indicate contracts and agreements, as well as loss of any property through contracts. It also applies to non-relatives who happen to live within the home.

♈ = The individual has an alert and restless mind that renders very impulsive decisions including sudden changes of directions.

♉ = The mind is slower and throughout, also very stubborn but willing to overcome obstacles.

♊ = There is an enjoyment of short travel. Rarely born as an only child the person has a changeable but highly intellectual mind where ideas need to be concentrated and pursued to final completion. In case there is no planet positioned herein the characteristics of the ruling planet will be expressed. (☿)

♋ = The mind is slow but retains a good memory. Mentally attached to the home, any communication may be confused or embellished at times. Travel by water is preferred. A critical streak may cause disagreement with others.

♌ = The person is a prepared traveler who always knows his way around and who loves to talk about travel. Craving the center of attraction, there is a love to dramatize appearances. Communications go well with siblings and neighbors.

♍ = The mind is organized and precise. A good problem solver who dips down to the root of the problem. Well spoken and presented the person is suitable for all practical and organizational work.

♎ = A well balanced mind that is willing to consider all angles. The person is cooperative, but often relies on and acts upon the opinion of others.

♏ = The individual is quiet, secretive and will suppress the feelings. Opinions are stated bluntly, with authority and often lack diplomacy.

♐ = A love to talk and communicate while ideas flow freely. Also a love for travel but with the desire to be the center of attraction. A craving for company, especially with family members, creates close relationships.

♑ = The individual is reserved and careful in communications. Words are selected to have the most impact and, at times, come across as harsh and calculated.

♒ = Unusual ideas for writing, adventure and travel, are strongly expressed. Communications can be erratic and way out for others to understand. An interest in humanity allows for interesting relationships with siblings, neighbors and friends.

♓ = Emotionally attached to family members, the person is very sentimental and sensitive in speech and expression. At times, there is a fear of travel or leaving the home. Very often the person is a dreamer encased in a different world.

26

4th House

This house represents the home environment, the parents of the same sex and conditions toward the end of life. It shows sorrow through family members and the finances of brothers and sisters, as well as delight or their demise. It denotes information about brother and sisters in law as well as the mother in law of male and father in law of female.

♈ = The individual is proud of the home and sometimes uses the home as a retreat to unwind and shelter from the world.

♉ = A very conservative individual, who doesn't want to move, therefore surrounds the home with a lot of comfort. The mind is stubborn and possessive.

♊ = More frequent changes of homes or dual homes are indicated. The person likes to cling to family records and traditions and loves to share the home with family members.

♋ = In early years, the person moves around with frequent changes of residence. Strong family ties bind, especially to the mother. A need for security controls the emotions. In case there is no planet positioned herein the characteristics of the ruling planet will be expressed. ☽

♌ = A comfortable and impressive home is used for frequent entertainment.

♍ = The person is a perfectionist at home to the point of annoyance to others. Pets are found in the home. A business may be operated in the home.

♎ = The home represents a refined environment. An artistic profession may be pursued from the home. Harmony is needed to derive mental security. There is a willingness to share with and entertain others. A strong interest in justice and a thrive for fairness exist.

♏ = There is secrecy regarding the home and family. Temper, jealousy and the desire to possess must be curbed to avoid disagreements with others. At times, the person may be gullible to the point of defeating his/her own guard.

♐ = There is pride and joy in the comfort of the home, which may be far away from the birthplace. The desire to entertain and maintain connections to the family is strong.

♑ = There is an inability to express the feelings, even to close family members, despite a strong bond with them. This creates mistrust. The person is frugal and conservative at home.

♒ = There are frequent changes of residence and a mental, rather than emotional, attachment to the home which is shared with friends.

♓ = The person is self-sacrificing for the family and loved ones. The home conditions may be restrictive. Sensitive emotions provide for ever- changing moods, which are affected by the environment.

27

5th House

It represents love affairs, intrigues, entertainment (all forms of performing arts), children, gambling and speculations. It indicates income from real estate, as well as causes of loss from business and reputation. It shows where in the world the securities are kept. The sign will identify the country or state.

♈ = There is restlessness and impulsive behavior. A possibility of love at first sight and a desire to dominate in all affairs is strong. Sex is important for a relationship. Ever changing conditions occur due to restlessness.

♉ = Possessive but passionate, there is a display of and desire to control others. The person is practical with children. Depending on other aspects, speculation may not be beneficial.

♊ = The individual may have multiple lovers, seeks intellectual partners, and may have several children.

♋ = The emotions are strongly tied to the lover, to children and the family. There is a desire to protect and mother others while seeking emotional security from the lover.

♌ = The person is dominant and demanding in love affairs. At times, the ego is greater than the love for children. If supported by other aspects, benefits from speculations may be received. In case there is no planet positioned herein the characteristics of the ruling planet will be expressed. (☉)

♍ = Being critical and nagging may create trouble in relationships. Emotional coldness may be expressed. The person may also be frugal and conservative in speculations.

♎ = The person demands attention but is a constant flirt with everyone. Musical talents should be developed. There is a preference to look after children of others instead of having their own children.

♏ = The individual engages in secret love affairs which may result in having children out of wedlock. Passionate but demanding, the person is a jealous lover. Dealings with children are rather forceful as there is a lack of understanding them. Unless supported by beneficial aspects, speculations are not fortunate. The emotions can reach great intensity.

♐ = There is a possibility of multiple love affairs. The person enjoys children if they don't curb the lifestyle. Good fortune with speculation may be experienced. All public forms of entertainment are enjoyed.

♑ = The individual is reserved, cool and conservative in a love relationship. As a parent, strict discipline and responsibility is taken towards children. A love to teach children may be experienced. The mind is constantly busy with accumulations that could be made, even at times of a vacation.

♒ = Unusual relationships are formed with lovers. A love to care for children is strong but having own children is mostly avoided. Care is required with speculations to avoid loss. An interest in dramatic art is expressed.

♓ = A very sensitive and extremely emotional side in love affairs is displayed. Anything will be done for love provided the emotional side is satisfied. The person has a desire for children and is strongly attached to the family. If unhappy, deep disillusionment may mentally separate and affect relationships.

28

6th House

This house rules the health, susceptibility to illness and diseases, work, servants and pets. It rules the service due to others. It identifies employee and employer, debts and limitations regarding a job. It denotes the residence of brothers and sisters and places where contract and agreements are kept.

♈ = The individual is restless at work, energetic and hard working but often makes job changes after disagreements with co-workers. Headache, sinus and fever affect the health.

♉ = A work providing for a superior position is desired. Disagreements with co-workers over dogmatic opinions may occur. The person hates job changes. The weight may fluctuate due to an inappropriate diet. Problems in the throat and neck area, thyroids and glands may affect the health.

♊ = Often multiple jobs are held to gain income. Sales jobs are very suitable. Flexibility is needed at work. Work may be performed for a family business. A need to learn to separate the private life from work is necessary. Jobs requiring intellectual capacities are preferred. Shoulder, arms, hands, and lungs are subject to injury or illness.

♋ = The individual has a talent to work with the public and cooperate with co-workers. Success is desired and work represents emotional and financial security. The person is easily influenced by others, due to a lack of self-confidence. The stomach, breasts and ulcer problems need extra care.

♌ = There is a need to be boss. Profits are gained from work for public organizations and government jobs. The person may be picky with co-workers. The heart needs protection from too much strain and the spine from too much overstraining.

♍ = Detailed work is performed methodically and behind the scene. There is a talent for research and investigative work. Disagreements may occur due to a stern opinion. The intestine and digestive system is susceptible to illness. Stress strongly affects the health. In case there is no planet positioned herein the characteristics of the ruling planet will be expressed. (☿)

♎ = The person works well with others and needs harmony to cooperate. There is an avoidance of blue color jobs. The individual may be associated with or married to a person with illness, however, benefits may be obtained from such arrangement. The kidneys need protection from disease.

♏ = There is a need to work alone as the person hates routine. Secret research and investigation work may be preferred. Work needs to be mentally stimulating to avoid boredom. Timely structured and restricted jobs are not suitable as they curb the person's desire for freedom. The sex organs and lower colon may be affected by illness.

♐ = Dual income may be received from numerous sources. The person is well suited for work in the travel industry. Lofty ideas sometimes render the person impractical. A talent for teaching could develop. The hip area is susceptible to disease.

♑ = A strong desire exists to obtain an executive position and to achieve honor, recognition and prominence therefrom. A work-a-holic attitude may rule in life. The person is very forceful to and demanding of others and likes to organize and rule. The spine and knees may suffer from arthritis.

♒ = The individual may work with or for large organizations with humanitarian interests and easily becomes friends with co-workers. At times the person displays dogmatic attitudes and unhappy working conditions attack the health. While very cooperative and generous with others there is always an expectation of others to perform their part of the task to completion. The nervous system, legs and ankles are vulnerable to injury.

♓ = Work may be very emotional and physically exhausting and creates a lot of worry. Work is suitable in hospitals and large institutions as there is a strong sense of responsibility toward others. The emotions and moods are strongly fluctuating. The nerves and a weak immune system may create health problems.

29

7th House

This house refers to marriage or business partnerships and its success or failure. There may be dealings with the public at large. It also applies to legal action by the lower court (the higher courts are indicated in the 9th house) and involvement with the public either due to scandal or by deed. It indicates any possible sexual perverseness (together with a reading of the 8th house) and any existing sexual problems. The outcome of illnesses, reputation as an employee, or being the employer, or how your employees are seeing you, are ruled by this house.

♈ = The person desires a more aggressive partner that is also physically and sexually attractive. Both may be very temperamental.

♉ = The individual is loyal, stubborn but money minded and seeks all the comforts money can buy.

♊ = The partner is chosen intellectually. Often dual relationships develop that require a lot of personal freedom.

♋ = The individual is possessive, sensitive, sentimental and may cling to a partner for emotional security. Very devoted if catered to but the feelings may fluctuate greatly. Due to the desire to constantly seek a 'mother image' in the partner, relationships may not hold together as the partner feels smothered by the overwhelming emotional needs of this person.

♌ = The individual is demanding, proud and seeks constant attention from others. Although, a loyal partner, constant ego boosts and praises are needed. A struggle for dominance may take place.

♍ = A steady but sometimes critical and nagging individual with fixed attitudes and opinions. A love to plan and execute is pursued by precisely going into all details. The partner may become a burden due to health issues.

♎ = The individual is tolerant, appreciates beauty and is concerned with the image of the relationship. Always a flirt and seeking the greener grass on the other side, this person may engage in several marriages before reaching satisfaction. In case there is no planet positioned herein the characteristics of the ruling planet will be expressed. (♀)

♏ = Passionate, blunt, jealous, possessive and direct in speech this person may thrive on secrecy and engage in secret liaisons. A strong sex drive is indicated.

♐ = There is a possibility of dual relationships or marriage of convenience to attain a material or social position in life. Marriage may be entered into in a foreign country or to a foreigner.

♑ = Due to a strong interest in making money, marriage may occur later in life. While expressing an emotional coolness, however, the person may be loyal and great responsibilities may be tied to the partner.

♒ = The individual seems unusual, independent and, at times, stubborn while demanding freedom for him/her self. A close friendship with the partner is required for a functioning relationship.

♓ = Possible dual relationships. Strong emotional ties exist to friends, lovers, partners and family. While seeking the ideal partner, disappointment will render the person nearly unable to solve problems and make any breaks. The partner may have health issues requiring a responsibility that may easily turn into a 'mothering job'.

30

8th House

This house relates to death and issues related thereto such as wills, trusts, inheritance etc. Endings, regeneration and the resources of others (partner, taxes, insurance, win-or loss of lawsuits etc.) or joint property, or money belonging to the spouse or business partner and sexuality, are ruled by this house. It indicates the cause of death, the sexual organs and muscular system as well as sexual diseases and the end of life condition of children. Any contracts related to partnerships are controlled by planets affecting this house.

♈ = Death may occur quickly by accident, fever or through head injuries. Resources may be spent impulsively and unnecessarily.

♉ = Death may occur due to choking, throat problems or diseases associated with the sex organs. Possessions mean a lot and at times hamper the way to happiness when they are not shared but used to bargain with others. Investments in real estate may be made with a partner. A conservative attitude prevails in sexual matters.

♊ = Death is possible through respiratory problems or may occur when in company of groups. There are often dual sources of income.

♋ = The stomach or the digestive track and surrounding areas may be the source of illness and death. A psychic sensitivity is present.

A positive attitude needs to be developed regarding life and death matters to avoid severe depression. Being very emotional and self-indulgent in sexual matters moods are variable and, at times, turn passive. The person may have possible premonitions of things to come.

♌ = The heart is the chief reason for death. Money is either inherited or obtained from a generous partner. A need to share with others is necessary to avoid overly proud and arrogant behavior.

♍ = Stress, the nervous system, the liver, diabetes and digestive disorders may lead to death. The person is not easily able to accept facts when presented by others. A critical attitude needs controlling. Friends should be made only after carefully scrutinizing their motives. Frigidity in sexual matters may be displayed.

♎ = The kidneys and any over-indulgence in food may lead to death. Harmony is required when dealing with others. A partner, who is generous with money, will be supportive. Legal difficulties could be experienced in obtaining an inheritance or loss through other legal matters. A strong self-indulgence in sex is noted.

♏ = Death may occur through the misuse of energy, illness of the sex organs or rectal problems. Time of rest and regeneration is necessary or the energy may be scattered. The person is secretive regarding resources and sexual matters. In case there is no planet positioned herein the characteristics of the ruling planet will be expressed. (♇)

♐ = Death may occur far away from the birthplace, in a different country or among foreigners. There is longevity and a partner who is generous with resources. Inner faith and religion may be practiced to balance the emotions. Money could be gained through inheritance or from legal action.

♑ = Old age, arthritis, degenerative disease or clocked arteries all may attribute to death. A strong responsibility to handle the joint resources with the goal to ever improve conditions.

Possessions are very important. Lack of diplomacy, when dealing with others, may be a source of confrontation. Sexual matters delve in the mind more often then in actual performance.

♒ = Death may come through circulatory problems and while involved with groups. Joint money and possessions may be grounds for eccentricity or strife. Sexual acts are ruled by the intellect. The person may have intuitive and psychic powers to heal and guide others.

♓ = Death may be triggered through poisoning of the system, or any abuse of alcohol and drugs, or by bacterial infections. The emotions are tuned in and are compassionate for the plight of others. Joint resources may be a matter of secrecy and will influence the emotions. Sexual fantasies may take over reality.

31

9th House

This house deals with foreign lands, travel, institutions of higher learning, religion, legal systems and laws. It also applies to publishing, especially when religious and philosophical subjects are brought to the greater public. It deals with the necessary teaching and governing of individuals and their development of social conscience. Profit and loss may be received from psychic experiences. Grand-children and parents of a partner are governed by this house. Losses that affect the reputation but also realization of wishes that have been properly planned and executed may come to fruition. Publication of writings may occur.

♈ = The person enjoys foreign travel and meeting foreigners but has trouble concentrating on pursuing higher education.

♉ = Travel will only be enjoyed if it comes with comfort and style. There is a possibility that religious views are expressed and practiced.

♊ = With a talent for languages travel in foreign countries is enjoyed. This may lead to publishing of writings on the subject of travel.

♋ = The person prefers to travel by water but is apprehensive about travel and rather stays close to home.

♌ = Of course, the king only travels in style. Suited as a preacher, the person may try to force beliefs upon others.

♍ = The mind is critical and cautious when it comes to religion and politics. A careful traveler who plans everything but has trouble accepting any sudden changes to his/her plans.

♎ = The person is often confused and impractical in travel and gets easily lost. The mind is swayed strongly by the opinion of others.

♏ = A very strong opinion is expressed that is hard to change. Travel is often pursued in secret or for a purpose other than vacation.

♐ = The person enjoys constant travel and the freedom it represents. At times, deep involvement in religious or political matters may lead to travel. In case there is no planet positioned herein the characteristics of the ruling planet will be expressed. (♃)

♑ = As money is always on the front burner of the mind, travel will, if possible, always be combined with business. The person is often drawn to a religious occupation.

♒ = Adventurous, independent and unconventional, this person likes to travel with friends to seek the most unusual experiences.

♓ = The person travels only when in the mood as the emotions are strongly tied to the home and family. Often, travel takes place more in dreams than in reality.

32

10th House

This house refers to the ambitions, reputation and standing in business, in the community and profession. Fame or notoriety may be shown in this house. For the employed it shows the kind of employer one has and how this affects any ambitions in life. If any ambitions are pursued rather ruthlessly a fall from high position may be the end result. A career in government may be attractive. It shows the degree of authority obtained, bosses and superiors attitude, and a general karmic reward based on past actions and plans. It denotes the security of the marriage or business partner, as well as losses and sorrows through actions of others. It identifies the cause of death of brothers and sisters. It deals with honor and recognition received. The parent of the opposite sex and money obtained from legal contracts are guided by this house.

♈ = Public recognition and an interest in a variety of social gatherings may be used to pursue a goal. However, a quick temper, rashness and lack of consideration for the rights of others may cause a loss of business, position and reputation.

♉ = A position will only be considered when it comes with power and authority as this person seeks material gain in any involvement. Tact, diplomacy and social consideration may benefit. Occasional any stubborn behavior may hamper the efforts to excel.

♊ = Numerous jobs or businesses are engaged in and the person communicates well with the public but, at times, tends to be too self-critical or suffers from lack of self-esteem. Spice in life, variety and constant changes are needed to avoid boredom. Intellectual communications may turn profitable.

♋ = The emotions may tune into the public's need. A business may be established from home and several career changes will be made in life. While hyper-sensitive the person uses tact and prudently attends to people and business but is also a worrier who suffers from suppressed feelings.

♌ = There is a hunger for power and fame. Unless the ego is curbed into moderation, reversal of position may occur. Despite a strong personality the self-confidence may be bruised when the desired success is not forth-coming.

♍ = A willingness to work hard is evinced. Persistence and determination will lead to success. Talent is indicated for teaching or analytical and organizational enterprises. At times the person is very reserved, even timid and self-critical, and prefers to work outside the limelight.

♎ = The person receives public favors and displays a love for the public and wants to be admired. Success is indicated in a business geared to the taste of the public.

♏ = The person possesses a strong desire and determination to reach a goal. At times there is a pushy and overbearing attitude with a strong self-interest. Hard work is needed to gain in life. Secretive in regards to work or business a profession is often chosen that involves secretive or dangerous elements.

♐ = There is always optimism and a desire for responsibility but also a demand to retain freedom. A good reputation is helpful in reaching success. There is an attraction to the public and a craving for social prominence.

♑ = Although very conservative, there is a display of executive skills. Responsibilities are desired as well as to climb the ladder of success in life. Placing business before any private life, this person seems to be working all the time. In case there is no planet positioned herein the characteristics of the ruling planet will be expressed. (♄)

♒ = Friends are helpful with success, which may come from large organizations. There is a strong loyalty toward friends and co-workers.

♓ = The mind is filled with imaginations, which may or may not fit in with reality. Changes in career are needed to accommodate the fluctuating emotions. The person may sense as to what the public wants. Talent in music and the arts may bestow prominence before the public.

33

11th House

This is the house of friendship and deals with hopes and wishes, social acquaintance, friends and group activity, which may be supportive in life. The natal planets will determine the social position in life. Whether friendships last and be helpful will be determined by the planets found in this house. It deals with the standing in society, fines, penalties, taxes imposed and penalties per se. It denotes stepchildren. It shows the ability to overcome obstacles.

♈ = Aggressive in making friends, a display of push and shove may be used toward achieving the goal.

♉ = Steadfast in friendships, the person always hopes that everything materializes.

♊ = To keep company with intellectual friends is all important. Due to being impatient in waiting for gain, friendships may be changed in hope of more favors.

♋ = The person may become possessive of friends. Although sociable and caring, there may be such an emotional craving for hopes and wishes to come about that said clinging to others becomes an embarrassment, hurting more than helping.

♌ = The desire to dominate any friendship and social gathering is strong. Although loyal to friends, the ego always craves center of attention for the self.

♍ = The individual is critical of friends and may avoid social gatherings.

♎ = A strong craving for attention and compliments from friends and at social events is prevalent. Being seen in the right company seems very important as friends are selected by their status and ability to benefit. Social climbers come under this aspect.

♏ = The person does not seek active participation in social gathering but does so more as a way of pursuing business. Friendships are used for gain or mental support.

♐ = A love of the crowd and participating at social events to satisfy the constant desire for attention is pursued in aspiration of hopes and wishes.

♑ = There is a certain seriousness associated with friendships. Social gatherings are not everyone's favorite but are attended as they may expand business. In general, the person is conservative and pushy to achieve hopes and wishes.

♒ = Friends come from all walks of life. Hopes and wishes may be expressed in unusual ways and possibly be pursued through groups rather than as an individual. If planets in this house are negatively aspected friendships will be made, however, the friends are not in a position to help. In case there is no planet positioned herein the characteristics of the ruling planet will be expressed. (♅)

♓ = Friends are made especially with the underprivileged, handicapped or those suffering from other serious problems. The mind vacillates about hopes and wishes. Dreams may be a substitute for actual achievement.

34

12th House

This house is ruling primarily over karma. The ability for self-undoing is heightened when mistakes are repeated despite nature's warning to change course. It also stands for secrecy, hospitals and other institutions as well as incarcerations or other places of solitude and confinement. Old habit pattern may need revision to comply with progress made by the person. Mental problems may lead to an illusionary existence and could result in self-deceit. Karma may be unfolding based upon past actions. It is difficult to overcome the restrictions placed on the personality by this house. Karma is the great teacher that gives and takes depending on the person's action and behavior. Seclusion, exile, or diseases confining the person are indicated by this house. It shows secret affairs and the cause of death of one's own children. It denotes any involvement with crime.

♈ = Strong optimism may feed the imagination and help overcome problems. At times the energy is directed against the self, leading to loss and dissolution. The person may hold strong grudges and has trouble being forgiving to others.

♉ = Unwilling to change or part with possessions, a need exists to relax and learn to express real feelings. Music will soothe the nerves. An excessive social life may lead to insecurity and self-undoing as keeping up with others may not befit the goal and purpose of life.

♊ = The mood will fluctuate and create trouble especially with relatives. The mind absorbs the tension of others creating anger and insecurity. The person may be close to the mother or be dependent on the mother.

♋ = Constant changes in moods and feelings may exhaust others. There is a strong feeling of being unloved. Unable to be decisive may strain the mind.

♌ = While being demanding a display of egocentric behavior may be expressed while any sensitivity toward others is ignored. Inner faith needs confirming and the true feelings need to be expressed instead of being suppressed.

♍ = The mind revolves around the health. Certain imaginations may cause illness. Too much criticism will affect the health and reputation. Dreams may disclose real events. Work in hospitals or mental institutions may be pursued.

♎ = Marriage, partnership or business of a secret nature may lead to self-undoing. The person may see life through rose-colored-glasses always hoping for the best. Overly selfishness may lead to undoing.

♏ = The person is involved in secret work or investigation or spends time being incarcerated. Any misuse of power may lead to undoing. Strong emotions must be controlled. Sexual problems may lead to withdrawal from society.

♐ = While the person is definitely optimistic, hard work will not always equal rewards. However, strength is there to overcome adversary.

♑ = Deep concentration, a powerful drive for achievement and a strong desire to seek gain and recognition, are instilled into the character. This person may get involved with institutions as means of doing business. Self-undoing may occur through lack of concern for the rights and feelings of others.

♒ = There is a strong need for freedom and lots of it. While the desire for adventure and the unusual is strong so is the desire to help humanitarian causes. The person may possess psychic abilities.

♓ = Volatile emotions need solace and require working out which, in turn, requires a lot of self-sacrificing. Overly strong emotions will lead to mental illness if not addressed properly. In case there is no planet positioned herein the characteristics of the ruling planet will be expressed. (♆)

35

Signs, Rulers and Meanings

Each of the twelve signs has a ruler and certain characteristics assigned to it that define the person born under that sign. If the degree of the sign falls towards the beginning or end of a sign, the previous sign or the following sign may need to be taken into consideration as they will also extend an influence over the person.

♈ = RULER ♂

" I AM" stands for new beginnings. There is creative energy and enthusiasm. There is a drive to prove oneself through action. However, thinking before action is taken needs to be learned. Impulsive action could bring an inability to listen and consider matters before action is taken. Projects are not always finished. Good leadership is given and a desire to seek fame exists. Wealth and comfort, as well as authority, is desired. However, excessive aggressiveness may result in loss. More diplomacy is needed. Defeat will not be accepted, however, more love should be spread to create harmony.

♉ = RULER ♀

"I HAVE" is the principle. Determination, power and efficiency will pursue the good things in life. The mind is focussed on material rewards. There is a love of money, beauty, comfort, pleasure and luxury. No interference is permitted when the goal is in sight. Security is foremost on the mind. Others will be selected as to the benefits that could be derived from them. Friends may be made with people who have problems in order to gain superiority over them. Jealousy may reach the point of being absurd and applies to material goods as well as to sexual matters. A great possessiveness is used to cover up insecurity. The nature is very emotional and ruled by motives. A strong will may be overpowering to the point of severing relationships. More self-analysis is needed. A tendency to change others to one's own point of view is strong but the self is unwilling to change.

♊ = RULER ☿

"I THINK" relates to communications. Speech and writing is very important but could turn the person also into a chatterbox. The mind is thirsty for knowledge and is eager to study. When the education is poor inner satisfaction will not be obtained and may render the person unbearable to others. When well educated there is charm, refinement and intelligence. Interested in a variety of subjects life becomes busy but nervousness may not allow for tranquillity. While the mind is always in control calmness needs to be learned to allow the body to rest. Travel and constant changes are welcome. While material things are not considered the number one in life, money is needed to support a style of personal freedom. Higher education should be pursued to accommodate the talent of the mind. There is a strong individuality.

♋ = RULER ☽

"I FEEL" is strongly ruled by the emotions. Material, mental and domestic security is needed to calm the emotions. Hypersensitivity may result in withdrawals from society to protect the emotions from being hurt. A steady home and family life will provide security and attract a sense of responsibility towards the family. The person can be strong, sweet and charming but in the next moment weak, melancholic and distant but always will try to be a diplomat to avoid confrontations. The easily hurt emotions may behave illogical and will refuse to collaborate with others. The nature vacillates between grown up, childish and stubborn behavior. Inner thoughts are difficult to fathom and at times, are hidden altogether, to avoid arguments. There is a willingness to be helpful. Love can be smothering and possessive. However resentment and despair will easily follow. There must be physical and mental comfort. The mind will indulge in powerful imaginations and, at times, be unable to understand the fine line between real and imagined. The person must learn to answer Yes or No and any control of the temper and moods is very important. Egotistical to a fault, there is often passive resistance to the point of becoming unapproachable. If forced against their will, the mind becomes immovable, unwilling to see any point presented. Ideas of others may be confusing as their own thinking will always take precedent over suggestions of others. Responsibilities will be shunned if the agenda does not befit the mind and emotions.

♌ =RULER ☉

"I WILL" is embedded in the self-expression. Generosity, nobility and a desire for center stage, together with a desire for a spacious and extravagant home, will be pursued provided there remains personal independence. Children are liked. A strong attraction to the opposite sex, a desire for money, and the pursuit of a goal is foremost on the mind. There may be over-confidence to the point of annoyance to others. Repetition and routine are creating boredom and dislike. The mind gets easily obstinate and impatient and disagreements may turn into a battlefield. The ego needs to be liked and placed on center stage. A sense for the dramatic is instilled, if nothing else, but for self-approval. There is a hate to compromise for an 'everything or nothing' attitude. The ego needs authority and loves to dominate others. If the authority is not forthcoming laziness and boredom may prevail.

♍=RULER ☿

"I ANALYZE" by seeking knowledge. The mind likes to work and control but also needs to harvest wisdom. Work will be performed meticulously by concentrating on the smallest detai!. Work is performed in service for others rather then for themselves. This person makes a good employee who is very reliable. At times trivialities may take over the mind by turning to nagging over unimportant things. The mind may be critical to a fault. The health needs protection from overwork. This may be the work-a-holic who frets and worries over work, thus neglecting his personal life. If ill there is great power of recuperation. Holistic medicine is more potent than conventional medicine. No food should be eaten when angry as it is harmful and negatively affects the intestine. A love for good clothes, food and comfort is given. Attention is paid to fashion labels. A love of gossip and chattering and to show off, as well as a desire to obtain constant attention, results in spending in a big way. Problems finding the right mate may be the result of setting the standard for a partner too high. Any desire is tainted by financial consideration. If married, the person wants to be boss.

♎ = RULER ♀

"I BALANCE" with charm and grace. There is a desire for popularity but the help and cooperation of others is always needed. Companionship is pursued. A talent for public relations and a love to mingle with the famous is expressed. A strong sense of justice and a good intellectual ability bring important friends. Help is needed to solve personal problems. If angry, the mind unleashes like a tornado and may close of any logical application. After the outburst the body may shake and become ill. The memory is very good, especially with names of people considered important.

♏ = RULER ♇

"I DESIRE" power. The will drives intense emotional desires which are subject to a constant struggle within. The sex drive is very strong, the mind is very possessive and filled with jealousy. At times a violent streak appears. There is potential for good and evil with serious consequences to follow. A problem to delegate responsibilities exists as the desire to be in control and to be a perfectionist stands in the way of communicating ideas. Despite any weakness, the staying power is tremendous. Although, not known as a diplomat, help may be given to others. The mind is secretive, investigative and likes to fight. The eyes are penetrating trying to pray into the mind of others. Once a goal is set there is no turning back but to reach accomplishment.

♐ = RULER ♃

"I SEE" brings love for freedom and adventure. A fondness of travel, being straight forward and energetic, the mind engages in positive thinking. A good luck factor will accomplish many tasks. Social interaction are desired. A serious thinker who is concerned with the wellbeing of society. Harmony is needed or the mind will be narrow minded and bigot. Religious interests may turn fanatic. There is an all or nothing attitude to life. Jumping to conclusion may hinder consideration of the entire issue. The person can be a merciful enemy and, when pressured or under anxiety, may become severely depressed. The mind may dwell on a possible insight into the future. A strong creativity to accomplish is present, however, there is no fondness of housework. Independence is always stressed. When rolling out the charm many social accomplishments can be achieved.

♑ = RULER ♄

"I USE" to develop and accomplish. There is always property that needs looking after and business to be done. Independence is very important and money will be used to obtain more possessions. A steady climb will be achieved. There is a love for law and order. The mind will be demanding, be very dogmatic and always tries to utilize everything. The desire to have and obtain may become overwhelming to the point of neglecting a personal life. This sign is good for finding solutions for the most difficult problems and the person is driving a hard bargain, which may lead to more material wealth. Either methodical and neat, or the opposite, a desire to drive others hard may lead to conflict. Jumping to conclusions may distract from considering all angles. The mind may become so fixed on something that it will be unable to see the entire picture. The desire for money is very strong and the main motivator in life. Being frugal or outright stingy, and at times greedy, may hinder happiness. Early in life the health may suffer but otherwise a long life is indicated. This is a one man show that, at times while even lonely, wants to do for the self. The need to be appreciated is very strong.

♒ = RULER ♅

"I KNOW" freedom, adventure and friendship. Very loyal to friends but eccentric in temperament. Determined, even stubborn at times, the person wants to accomplish what others see as impossible. The mind gets irritated when others do not comprehend the ideas presented. While willing to argue they will part with friends that are not advanced enough. Snobbery is not in the system. There is a love to be equal and independent.

As the mind is constantly searching for the new and undiscovered loneliness may not be part of the system. Exchange of ideas with others furthers the intellect. Everything is addressed on the mental level, which rules over the emotional part. An appreciation of nature, beauty and comfort is there but not greed to get money above all else. Not too much into sport, the mind is more exercised than the body. Although often appearing calm, the mind may be filled with anxiety, which may render the body ill. A hard and excellent worker with great sense of responsibility who works well with others and large organizations. The mind is very creative, likes to obtain knowledge and loves mental freedom. An interest in humanitarian issues always find an outlet as sympathy for human problems and solving of human problems are foremost on the mind. An aura of confidence emanates from the person who is a tireless worker and who will pursue any worthwhile goal.

♓ = RULES ♆

"I BELIEF" in sensitivity and feelings. Desperately wanting to do the right thing but the mind has very little will power and is easily influenced by others. A fear for the unknown my cause anxiety. The emotions sway between happiness and despair, agreeing and disagreeing to the point of becoming immobile. Unable to decide, there may be a withdrawal from contact with others to avoid involvement. The mind is not combative. Struggle will cause procrastination and lack of decision making. Rather suffer than fight is the motto. If provoked, the mind may be impossible to calm down, this will result in health problems. The mind is stubborn and unwilling to compromise when provoked. A sense of personal significance needs appreciation. Charm and humor may shine through the fragile emotions. The person may be very impractical and unable to control the temperament. Life is lived in highs and lows without a precise plan in mind. While materialistic, the business of providing may become irritating. Doing nothing may be preferred over hard work. The mind is aloof at times and care must be exercised when controlling money. Unhappiness is often self inflicted as the real world is substituted for a dream world. Musical and artistic talents are present and need developing. The imaginations may be overblown and removed from reality. A talent for healing is indicated. Devotion, unselfish sacrifices and accepted suffering may be exercised to find the self. A craving to reach out in blind devotion is extended to loved ones, even when undeserved. There is a strong need to face reality. An independent action is needed to escape the personal creation of reality. Direct orientation is needed to succeed.

36

Planet ○ SUN

The position of the ○ in the chart represents the place in the sky, at the time of day, when the person is born. If born around sunrise the ○ must be near the Ascendant, if born between sunrise and noon the ○ would be somewhere in the 11th house. At noon, the ○ will be at M (mid heaven) and towards the 8th house by the middle of the afternoon. At sunset, the ○ would be around the 6th or 7th house and later in the evening, it would have traveled furthermore, towards the 5th house. If born at midnight, the ○ is near the nadir (opposite M) and if born in the early hours of the morning, the ○ will be around the 2nd house. When positioned at birth in the second house, and not badly afflicted, it provides for wealth through the person's own efforts.

The ○ is the giver of life without its rays no life, as we know it, could exist. However, if the ○ happens to be in the 6th house or 8th house, its power may be somewhat lessened. The 6th house, being the house of illness, may weaken the person's vitality and powers of recuperation. The 8th house deals with death. If the ○ is found herein at birth, it may signify a weak constitution and a short life. For talented artists it may deny any recognition until well after death. If the ○ was placed in the 12th house and not well aspected, the early years of the person may be spent in poverty or be subjected to abusive parents.

The ○ represents dignity, strength of will, courage, pride, honor and responsibility, which makes the person reliable in love and friendships and bestows generosity. If well aspected, it brings friendships with and favors from people in high social positions, which help financially and with advancement in life.

An afflicted ☉, however, reveals a lot of opposition and negative traits such as over-ego, self interests, love of adulation and abuse of power, which may bring ruin. A strong desire for leadership exists but the person is willing to abuse it once said position is obtained. Any over-extended energy may lead to loss of health. A very negative ☉ may produce a person whom one should neither trust nor depend upon.

The ☉ signifies employers, superiors, judges, government officers and any other person having power to command or hold any authority. The ☉ is masculine and stands for the father and the man in a woman's chart. (in a man's chart the ☽ serves the same purpose) It is an indicator of health and energy in a man's chart (the ☽ in a woman's chart) but both sexes receive their energy and well being from the rays of the ☉. A very weak and afflicted ☉ indicates a short life.

☉ IN THE HOUSES

While the natal position determines the influences over the person which progresses in life any transit through each house has a duration of only 30 days. Transits by and through itself do not trigger sizable events unless a major aspect is activated during transit. The characteristics of each house will then apply.

1 ☉ (1) A very strong will, abundant vitality, intense self-awareness, feelings of importance, desire for power and leadership are indicated. A strong determination is present to pursue life by his/her own rules. The power of recuperation is strong to overcome afflictions of every nature. The person works long and hard to achieve success.

If afflicted, there is excessive pride, egotism, compulsive behavior, false ambition and the desire to rule others.

2 ☉ (2) There is a need to learn the correct use of material resources. This aspect will provide a clue as to the way the person will acquire and utilize wealth.

If afflicted, there is a belief that wealth justifies the means. The will may be imposed on others for purposes of material self-

aggrandizement and money may be squandered on display for purely ego gratification.

3 ☉ (3) An intense strong drive to achieve distinction through mental accomplishments is present. There is a strong urge for knowledge. The person is eager to investigate and attempt new things that include mental leadership. A strong desire is instilled to travel and explore. Brothers, sisters and neighbors are part of an exchange of ideas.

If afflicted, there is arrogance, snobbery and a tendency to force ideas onto others. Disagreements with siblings and neighbors, as well as difficulties through communications, may cause trouble.

4 ☉ (4) There is a strong interest in the home and family, and a desire to improve and make the home the center of interest. The first part of life may be a struggle with more ease experienced later in life.

If afflicted, there may be too much pride, an inability to get along with the family and a tendency to dominate in the domestic scene.

5 ☉ (5) Bestowed in the person is a love of life, a powerful will and desire to seek pleasure and appreciation. Artistic pursuits are undertaken, especially in drama, pleasure and romance, and become a big part of life. A sunny and happy disposition my turn childish and egocentric attitudes may develop. There is a possibility of prima donna behavior. Beware of blind confidence. A love of children is indicated but if the ☉ is in ♈, ♌ or ♐, the person may never have his/her own children. There could be an involvement in an all consuming love affair, and if the ☉ is in ♉ or ♏ possessiveness and jealousy could be prevalent.

If afflicted, there is trouble with children, loss in speculations or loss in investments and possibly a confrontation with authorities.

6 ☉ (6) The health is delicate and a lengthy recuperation time is needed. There is a strong desire to seek distinction through work. If appreciation is not forthcoming ill feelings may develop which are likely to cause a change of job. Employers, with the sun in this house, can be demanding and be authoritarian towards employees. A health related career in the medical field might be pursued. Difficulties in obtaining a well paid position may hinder advancements.

If afflicted, long periods of unemployment may be experienced. The self-esteem and dignity is linked to work and service. The sign in the 6th house gives indications as to the body part most susceptible to illness.

7 ☉ (7) Close personal relationships and loyal friendships are made when the sun is well aspected. Under favorable conditions marriage becomes all important and attracts a loyal partner with great affection. Success may increase after marriage. The self-confidence allows for great dealings with superiors and improves public relations. This person favors occupations dealing with the public on a larger scale.

When afflicted, there is a desire to dominance by the person or it is received from either a partner or others. Arguments over partnerships may lead to break ups or legal actions.

8 ☉ (8) A great interest is expressed in the matter of death and after life. Fame may be achieved only after death. The will is strongly applied for furtherance of interests. Dealings will be made with superiors or authorities regarding taxes, insurance, goods of the dead, corporate and business partner's finances, and if the ☉ is well aspected, a good inheritance could materialize.

When afflicted, litigation may result over these matters. In case of divorce an unfavorable outcome may result. The marriage or business partner may squander resources. Almighty attitudes of superior being must be avoided or it will trigger adverse conditions.

9 ☉ (9) Religion, foreign interest, higher law, education and philosophy fall under this house wherein the ☉ indicates foreign travel and residence. Good aspects are in force when ♄ or ♃ also reside in or travel through this house. It indicates either interest in law or a job related to foreign travel.

When afflicted, a narrow-minded attitude prevails that can lead to fanatic and bigot believes and may be wrongly expressed by overly desiring to be an authority. The social order and its laws are areas of conflict. Imposing one's view on others should be avoided as well as eccentric religious beliefs, which will lead to difficulties, especially with foreigners or institutions of higher education. A strong ☉ may be expressed by overbearing and condescending attitudes or hypocrisy.

10 ☉ (10) Ambition to attain power, authority and responsibility is combined with a strong will to succeed. There is a good ability to lead. A birth into a higher social standard is possible. The birth time is around Noon.

If afflicted, there can be an overbearing dictatorial demeanor, excessive love of power and a tendency to use unscrupulous means to achieve power, fame and position. Reversal and disgrace may be indicated by afflictions to ♄.

11 ☉ (11) There is a strong interest in friendships and group activities and it is possible that help is received from powerful and influential friends. The drive for achievement is strong, so is the desire for recognition and the ability to lead groups.

If afflicted, there will be domination of or by friends for selfish gain. With a strong negative ♄ involved said selfishness will eventually backfire and cause reversals.

12 ☉ (12) The person wants to stay out of the public eye and has a behind the scene approach to life. Loneliness and estrangement from normal human contact may be experienced. An interest in healing, psychology, hospitals and institutions may be turned into a way to make a living.

If afflicted, neurotic tendencies, shyness, secrecy, actions taken behind the scene and self-undoing are possible. There could be a constant fight against powerful enemies, which prevents progress.

☉ IN THE SIGNS

13 ☉ (♈) A vital strength is present which provides ample energy to defend against diseases. The personality is rather aggressive, direct, full of energy and enthusiasm and eager to dive into action. The compulsive drive to act needs support from the brain. Learning to think before barreling ahead is necessary. The short attention span of ♈ makes the person headstrong and, at times, unwilling to accept the advice of others or is unable to finish what was set out to be done. The desire to be first, seek fame, recognition and wealth, may turn into a strong drive overlooking what else lies on the road. The search for positions of authority and superiority is

accompanied by aggressiveness and a willingness to use force, if necessary, thus, ignoring all rules of diplomacy. The foolish desire to make it at all cost brings trouble and defeat. But the person is always ready to go the full distance again if the reward is promising. The ability to reach out to others, cooperate with them and consider their point of view, must be cultivated or there will be dire consequences.

14 ☽ (♉) Physical strength is evidenced and financial fortune are pursued but sometimes depleted by sheer extravagance and the desire to show off. The desire for wealth, pleasure and comfort is strong and beauty is not only eagerly desired but also used as means to get ahead. The person seeks emotional and material security, hence, is willing to attract people who are of use to them. The emotions can be intensely loyal but resent interference and be plagued with jealousy and possessiveness, which may become a burden to others. Plotting and applying willpower will let the person endure for a long time if that means reaching the desired goal.

15 ☽ (♊) The ☽ brightens the mind and intellect and gives a pleasant disposition. The mind is geared for intellectual pursuits, writings and all kinds of communications. At times, the person becomes a compulsive talker and is also very expressive with the hands. The learning capacity is large and always hungers for more. A well educated ♊ may be a very charming, refined and diplomatic person. As the symbol of ♊ is made up of two lines, a person represents mostly one or the other, in short, positive or negative. While the emotions are most of the time under control, occasional bouts with depression occurs when things don't turn out right. If the mind is not happy the body is not happy, either. Times of tension need to be addressed with calmness and logic. The person is fond of travel and changes and is not particularly bound to specific persons or places. Financially frugal at times, however, he/she is generous with resources belonging to others. Occasionally being belligerent and rebellious, the person likes to break rules and work against established authority. Cooperation is needed for the unruly ♊ to fit in.

16 ☽ (♋) A certain amount of laziness and retreat from responsibilities may be noted under this sign. The feelings are tied to emotional,

material and domestic security. The mind is sensitive and fearful to the point of immobility and the person protects its vulnerability by seeking solitude or avoids any confrontation. A desire to have a family is very strong, but at times, the person will neglect rather than support his own family. The desire for security is so pressing that it becomes the focal point of the mind. Investments are placed into secure institutions rather than into gambling or involvement with other major risk factors. The mind vacillates between being a strong adult or resorting to the vulnerability of a child. When pursuing a goal this person will be sweet and charming, however, once that act has played out he/she will turn melancholic, distant and disinterested. The person prefers diplomacy if that is what is needed to clinch the deal. However, if the object is unobtainable the person resorts to childish, stubborn and immature behavior refusing any cooperation with others, thus, damaging their own cause. While being possessive to a fault this person demands all freedom for him/her self. If aroused or hurt this person becomes a bitter enemy out to destroy and get even. Female ♋ can be obsessed with motherly, smothering love to the point of annoying others. Neatness and cleanliness are not the usual habits of this person and moodiness, intolerance, timidity and excessive desires to hurt others when things are not working out, can make for vehement enemies. Being told what to do does not work well and at times may lead to a refusal to perform.

17 ☉ (♌) The ☉ acts as the spotlight bringing out the desire to shine and perform. The personal independence, the desire for a home, family and children, are highlighted. ♌ being the ruler of the heart, may be generous and strongly attached to the opposite sex. The mind is set on money as it can buy all the luxury a ♌ desires. Being somewhat outspoken and opinionated, the person may run into difficulties when not willing to consider others pace and point of view. The personality carries a sense of the dramatic and superior that may result in self-approval when others are not willing to support the cause. A position of authority and responsibility is desired and pursued endlessly. Especially women can be very dominant and will fiercely defend their family. However, some ♌

are not willing to play the game. They are lazy, disinterested in any business, inconsistent in any action and the weak ○ leaves them with little desire to pursue anything.

18 ○ (♍) An extensive interest in acquiring knowledge to further the intellect, is intensified. Meticulous attention is paid to details, efficiency and organization. A willingness to help others, practicality and intelligence, all make for an excellent and reliable employee. The mind is so much focused on work and related subjects that the person is unable to establish a private life. Sometimes the mind is focused entirely on trivialities at the expense of the bigger picture. When not appreciated, the person may criticize to a fault. The health needs attention as overwork and worry affect the digestive system. The body does not react well to artificial food or medicine. When angry or worried the person should abstain from eating as the system has trouble digesting anything. When engaged in the food business the person makes a good chef or worker in the health food business. A certain sternness and desire for perfection may prevent close friendships or even marriage.

19 ○ (♎) Charm, grace and beauty are instilled by this sign. There is desire to marry, or at the very least, to have great relationships and many friends. Any kind of work related to public relations, the arts and any social interaction and cooperation, is gladly accepted. If intellectually interested, becoming involved in the legal profession, becoming a judge or mediator or counselor, will be suitable. When aroused, this person is able to burst out in anger which may affect the health. A good memory is part of a well balanced mind. However, at times the person may be so overly confident that ventures are undertaken where angels fear to treat. Surely, trouble and disappointment will follow.

20 ○(♏) The person possesses a very strong will power and intense emotional desires, which are primarily expressed in a strong sexual drive. This desire is filled with passion, possessiveness and immense jealousy. In extreme cases the uncontrolled emotions may resort to violence and criminal involvement. Very thick headed, there is a liking to fight to the bitter end regardless of costs and sacrifices involved. Although, willing to help others, the person may demand favors in return. Any desire or opinion is expressed

rather forcefully. The person loves to act secretively and may hold grudges forever.

21 ☉ (♐) The person loves personal freedom, is outgoing and loves to travel, seeks involvement with foreigners and prefers to deal with all in a straightforward and open manner. Generally generous and well supported by luck, the person craves center of attention and involvement in the upper society. If the harmony desired is in imbalance, the person may suffer from anxiety, becomes narrow-minded, jumps to conclusion and engages in bickering incurring nervous ailments that are hard to treat. Religious fanatics may develop under this sign when the person loses his/her own identity and is swept up by the masses. The urge for creativity is strong. Many outlets are pursued to please the ego and gather rewards. Women tend not to be very domesticated due to the strong independent nature and desire to mingle in society rather than stay at home. When putting on the charm side this person will collect many friends.

22 ☉ (♑) The person likes to be around and get involved in a lot of different things and pursues the desire for independence and financial security. Interested in law and order the person will get involved, however, always keeping in mind the reward of security. Attachments to others, who mentally and financially will be helpful, are tainted to improve the status in life. Their own interest is a priority in all actions and will not be deterred even when different problems arise. At times suffering from perfectionism the ♑ demands a lot from self and others and strives for executive positions. The intense desire for security makes money the prime motivator and despite riches, the person may turn stingy and greedy. The emotions may turn to depression, melancholia and feelings of loneliness when goals are not reached.

23 ☉ (♒) Born under this sign bestows an interest in great humanity, spiritual energy, astrology, as well as forming loyal friendships and companionships to balance the emotional side. The mind may be stubborn and temperamental and difficult to understand. Full of inventive ideas the person may be "well ahead" of the time, grasping ideas that will only be accepted by the masses at a much later time. Straightforward and honest the person dislikes strife,

egomaniacs, hypocrisy and a pushing ahead for gain regardless of the costs, attitude. ♒ is concerned about the well being of all rather than just their own personal advancement. Logic rules the emotions and the intelligence. Openness, charm, and calmness will bring them ahead. If overworked or subjected to anxiety and mental pressure health problems will develop.

24 ☉ (♓) The emotions are very sensitive and react to the feelings of others. The personality is very changeable, moody and, at times, unsure of the self. Not being a fighter, the mind may suffer from anxiety, exhaustion and depression when problems need solving. Procrastination may be the middle name which is covered up with humor, charm and persuasion. At times the optimist, then again the pessimist, ♓ may irritate others by a constant change of moods. The pursuit of goals, money and possession in any ambitious fashion lacks the staying power and drive to see things through. Often encased in a dream world the artistic and musical ability may be strong and could produce astonishing results. As the mind is mostly overactive and spread out it is hard to focus and make precise decisions. Unhappiness will lead to illness. When close with their family and friends the unselfish and devoted side may turn up when help and service is needed.

☉ IN ASPECT WITH OTHER PLANETS

25 ☉ ☌ ☽ The combustion of both of these planets brings emotional impulsiveness and health problems due to overuse of energy. Indecisiveness and a conflict of masculine and feminine behavior may add to the level of anxiety and mental burnout.

26 ☉ ☌ ☿ A good memory and a receptive mind will support all matters to do with writing and communications. Depending on other aspects, however, the mind can be placed on overdrive resulting in a blocked mind or over-extension of one's self-image and ability. The intelligence should be used wisely. Together with the rays of the ☉, a stimulation of energy, productivity and talent should be utilized to benefit the person.

27 ☉ ☌ ♀ The person is charming, cheerful, optimistic and full of energy and life. Involvement in the arts, music and social events is

indicated. There is a love of children, a romantic expression and a strong drive to seek emotional fulfillment through the affections. When blessed with great beauty the person may be preoccupied by extreme narcissism. A well aspected ♃ supports speculations.

28 ☉ ☌ ♂ A strong desire for action, fueled by will power, endurance, strength and courage, is evinced. The person displays restlessness, aggressiveness and, at times, a rather pushy behavior when things don't move along well enough. Dealings with authority may be subject to disagreement.

29 ☉ ☌ ♃ The ego is well supported by luck and expansions. Social circles will be beneficial and their own generosity is repaid by well serving connections. Popularity will support many undertakings and projects will gain tremendously from the taste and favor of the public.

30 ☉ ☌ ♄ The ego is hampered and limited in the self-expression and achievement of goals. Extreme hard work is needed to achieve any gain. Due to frustration and delays in setting goals the person tends to retreat into depression, melancholia and possible self-depreciating. Maintaining a strong discipline and pushing ahead, despite obstacles, may produce achievement in the end.

31 ☉ ☌ ♅ Through being unpredictable, eccentric and ego driven the person may achieve some unusual task or be misunderstood by others. The mind may be so advanced as to invent or assume things that are still well into the future for others, which makes it difficult to communicate with everyday folks.

32 ☉ ☌ ♆ The desires and emotions are subject to flights of fancy, confusion, self-deception, or if well aspected, may lead to musical and poetic talents. An ability to be psychic, involvement into mystic, astrology, clairvoyance or religious inspirations, may come to the forefront. Dependent on the overall aspect to the sun the ego and desire for greatness and publicity may lead to confusion or even fraud. When the mind has left reality in search for self-glorification the imaginations may be so inflamed by a desire to create what just isn't there that self-delusion or even mental illness is the result.

33 ☉ ☌ ♇ The will, the ego and the desire for power are very strong. If not kept under control the ego may turn to use the mind in a

destructive, dictatorial way in search for the ultimate power and glory. If carried too far a downfall will ultimately occur.

34 ☉ * ☽ The emotions harmonize allowing for good relationships with others. The principle of masculine and feminine is balanced providing for close emotional ties to the opposite sex. Love and marriage fare well and the health is strengthened by this aspect.

35 ☉ * ☿ The mind is eager to engage in correspondence. Travel may be considered also for educational purposes. Cooperation from authority is received and a broad and optimistic outlook brings benefits.

36 ☉ * ♀ Financial, social and love matters will be engaged in and utilized for the person's benefit. Happy relationships may produce marriage and settlements may be entered into bringing an advantage.

37 ☉ * ♂ Bursting energy provides the person with a well focussed and active mind. The will is strong and ready for action and will take on any task worthwhile accomplishing.

38 ☉ * ♃ From ♃ generosity expansion and luck emanates, thus, empowering the expansion of the mind. Actions are initiated which support dealings with authorities. An expanded optimism will benefit the accomplishment of goals set out and followed through. Helpful to others, eager to travel and involved in religion, this person acquires wealth and generosity by way of association, friendship and marriage.

39 ☉ * ♄ There is patience, endurance and self-discipline to follow any project to completion. A great amount of loyalty toward friends, combined with hard work, will help achieve set goals. Due to a strong sense of responsibility, prudence and planning the person is sought after as a reliable employee who is trustworthy and hard working.

40 ☉ * ♅ An unusual mind, coupled with a strong will power, provides the basis for an enduring drive to accomplish and succeed. Interested in humanitarian causes, open-minded and talented in occult, astrology and psychology issues, the person will be a pioneer on these subjects.

41 ☉ * ♆ The rays of planet ♆ promote creativity, art, music, poetry, writing, religion and all aspects involving the immense feelings

and imaginations needed to be excellent. The vision and imagination, however, has to be kept in check to avoid drifting away from reality into a dream world.

42 ☉ ∗ ♇ Strength and willpower are the main characteristics of this aspect. The person tries to use the energy to reform, renew or starve off existing conditions.

43 ☉ □ ☽ Due to a lack of self-confidence and insecurity the emotions are in disharmony, especially when dealing with the opposite sex.

44 ☉ □ ☿ The mind is filled with worry and anxiety, is unsettled, unable to come to a satisfactory conclusion, and is prone to make mistakes. Stubbornness, argumentative behavior and a critical attitude may prevent conclusions to undertakings and if any agent, lawyer or employee is involved, this aspect spells trouble. No contract should be signed without full realization of its meaning. The health may suffer due to tension of the nervous system.

45 ☉ □ ♀ Loss of money, relationships and disagreements create sorrow and disappointment. Arguments and bickering may hurt close relationships. The mind is bitter, the feelings are hurt and society in general will not be well disposed toward the person.

46 ☉ □ ♂ The person acts very impulsively, rash and without consideration of the results. The mind is plagued by anger, arguments, frustration, and displays a bully and egotistical behavior. In time this will bring resentment and disagreements. Applying patience and foresight under this aspect will be beneficial to the outcome of affairs.

47 ☉ □ ♃ An attempt at applying overconfidence, together with an unrealistic, exaggerated and egotistical display, leads to disagreements and disappointments. Self-development and application of the will should be held in check to avoid ill-considered acts that may turn detrimental.

48 ☉ □ ♄ The road is littered with obstacles and hardship. The fulfillment of desires, plans and goals may be threatened. Only strict adherence to discipline, organization and hard work may overcome this aspect. Nothing is gained the easy way and illness, suffering and ongoing problems may lead to a pessimistic mind and depression.

49 ☉ □ ♅ The will, the ego and eccentric and erratic behavior leads to unwise action. The energy is depleted before it can be applied

to reach any results. Irrational behavior, self-dramatization and a constant nervous strain may push the person ahead despite a warning or knowledge that this road should not be followed. Uncontrolled acts may lead to defeat or will even destroy what had previously been accomplished.

50 ☉ □ ♆ The feelings are used for self-deception which arise from the overblown desire of importance and fame. Utterly impractical, strange emotional desires and attachments are engaged in, or even secret affairs, which bring scandal and downfalls, that will further hurt the already sensitive emotional state. The mind may resort to living in a dream world unwilling or unable to see reality for fear of being disappointed. Involvement in cults and quick money making schemes should be avoided or they will end in loss and degradation.

51 ☉ □ ♇ Headstrong and dictatorial, there is a desire to rule others according to one's own standard in life. The display of aggression and "I am always right", attitude should be carefully monitored or it will create opposition and dislike of the person.

52 ☉ ▲ ☽ Good health, stamina and harmonious, balanced emotions, make the person attractive and liked by others. The person is very self-confident, charming, optimistic and loves company. There is a good rapport with family and friends and a fondness of children and animals.

53 ☉ ▲ ☿ The sharpness of the mind increases so does the health of the mental faculties. Study and involvement in correspondence, signing of agreements and travel for educational purposes, will be beneficial.

54 ☉ ▲ ♀ Financial gain, domestic bliss and happy emotions will be experienced. Help from social sources is received and new love relationships may be entered into that will be harmonious and happy.

55 ☉ ▲ ♂ A display of leadership ability, of willpower and courage is ready to push ahead. The body is physically very fit, engages in sport, but always has a decisive interest in the own advancement.

56 ☉ ▲ ♃ Optimism and honesty bring honor, success, lots of social engagements and confidence. Cooperation is received from others

which brings benefits. A sensing of future trends will bring popularity.

57 ☉ ▲ ♄ There are characteristics of good organizational abilities coupled with a strong concentration, frugality, conservative behavior and practicality. A willingness to work hard brings co-operation with authorities, which will fare well and be beneficial.

58 ☉ ▲ ♅ The ego is channeled to constructive creativity. A strong will, together with leadership abilities and humanitarian engagements, will involve the person in unusual business and relationships. Authority figures will be supportive of new ideas and endeavors.

59 ☉ ▲ ♆ The person has a talent for the arts, music and writing. Religious involvement are furthered by this aspect. The emotions are balanced and well applied to face reality and intuitively sense new trends, which will bring benefits and advancements.

60 ☉ ▲ ♇ The ego is strong. The willpower and concentration, when applied correctly and not abused, will transform the life of the person and bring favors from society.

61 ☉ ☍ ☽ The mind and the feelings are at cross-purpose causing stress and misunderstandings, especially in relationships with the opposite sex. The health may, at times, be weak and further be eroded by restlessness, nervousness and a desire to engage in arguments. Relationships with children may not be satisfactory and parenting may be a strain rather then an enjoyment. The aspect to other planets will determine how the person reacts and where the confusion to the self-expression is manifested.

62 ☉ ☍ ☿ Arguments should be avoided as disputes will arise over one's point of view. Not a good time to start anything new or engage in travel. The nervous tension is high, thus creating health problems.

63 ☉ ☍ ♀ Bitterness, conflict and arguments, especially in the domestic sphere, should be avoided. Advice should be taken at this time and foolish spending, for ego gratification, should be avoided or loss will be incurred. Investments will not bring gain and speculations should be avoided.

64 ☉ ☍ ♂ The ego desires to act hastily and impulsively creating an aspect of disagreement, anger and attack. A good deal of aggressiveness is projected onto others or received from them. Coercion is used to win at all costs, however, enmity is willfully created that leads to estrangements. Aggressiveness is strongly displayed with the opposite sex, and together with jealousy, makes for explosive behavior that leads to loss and disappointment. The health, especially the heart, is due to suffer.

65 ☉ ☍ ♃ By being too optimistic more promises are made than can be delivered. This may incur mistrust and damage to the reputation. If the ego is not held in check a degree of arrogance, pomposity and unrealistic expectations may bring an involvement in schemes and enterprises that are not at all beneficial and will lead to loss.

66 ☉ ☍ ♄ The personal manners seem aloof and cold. The person suffers from general depression. Lack of cooperation and a negative attitude may result in being disliked and shunned by others. Hard work needs to be performed and many obstacles hamper the ambitions. As ♄ hinders and delays in all aspects of life the person may marry late, or never and if there are children, either problems or estrangements, may occur. The vitality is very low. Teeth and bone problems may be experienced.

67 ☉ ☍ ♅ The desire for independence and a bully attitude, together with super sensitivity of the emotions, bring unexpected dislikes and disagreements. The nerves hover on the edge, the mind is tense, irritable and ready to explode at the slightest occasion. The displayed eccentricity and ego-gratification causes confrontation with others.

68 ☉ ☍ ♆ The mind is distorted and confused. Fantasy thinking, wishful thinking, unreliability and, at times being deceived by others, or resorting to be deceitful for personal gain, may occur. Romantic feelings may be subjected to illusion and unrequited love by the desired object. Religious fanaticism or occultism should be strictly avoided to prevent mental and financial disappointment.

69 ☉ ☍ ♇ A strong will, as well as a big ego and desire for power may be exercised in the quest to dictate to others the world according to them. Disagreements will follow. A need to establish diplomacy

and harmony in relationships and business is required to obtain cooperation and results. Aggressiveness in all matters of life, especially in romance, but also with authorities, should be avoided.

☉ TRANSITS

The duration of the ☉ *transit is short, lasting only a few days. Its influence depends on its position and aspect at birth, thus, rendering positive or unfavorable conditions.*

70 ☉ ☌ ☽ There is an increased activity in domestic affairs, in social gatherings and activities with children. This is a favorable time for women to get pregnant if no negative aspect is received hereto. The ego and emotions are activated resulting in impulsive behavior. If done to an extreme, it will trigger health problems. Otherwise, harmonious and controlled emotions will bring independence and stability. The impact of this transit will, to a large extent, depend on the natal position of these two planets. Lawsuits should not be filed during the brief hours of combustion between these two planets.

71 ☉ ☌ ☿ An increased mental awareness will lead to involvement in communications, or even short trips related to education. Writers and teachers may get inspired during this time. Dealings with agents and lawyers may be beneficial. If negatively aspected otherwise, communications may not fare well and the combustion of these planets may render the mind overloaded and unable to focus. Deceit may be practiced on others.

72 ☉ ☌ ♀ Romantic and artistic involvement bring pleasure and advances. An optimistic attitude, a will to cooperate and attending social engagements will do well at this time. If afflicted, the person may be a social butterfly, attaching to losers in society. Extravagance and narcissism could develop. Under good aspects, marriage may be offered, leading to financial gain.

73 ☉ ☌ ♂ Involvement in physical activities will increase so does the sex drive. Aggressive furtherance of ambitions, more self-confidence, a desire for power and authority, may all manifest during this time. Rash acts, as well as aggressive behavior and lack of consideration for others, should be avoided as it will cause

problems and loss. Aggressive sexual encounters may lead to trouble. Depending on the natal position of these planets, this may be an exiting, energetic and daring period or a critical and troublesome time. Stay calm, focus and be in control of the emotions to avoid confrontations and accidents.

74 ☉ ☌ ♃ Optimism, kindness and generosity apply to this transit. A good time to approach those having authority and power and to begin any kind of higher education. Legal, travel or religious activities will do well if no natal affliction exist. Cooperation with children will work well. Pregnancies may result during the influences of these two planets. During this time the person may be more inclined to social gatherings and will eat more food then usually, resulting in increased weight. Business may bring success and greater popularity. If negatively aspected, foolish optimism and an inflated sense of self-worth may result in loss.

75 ☉ ☌ ♄ Any ambition will be stimulated and activated to improve business conditions. If well aspected, honor and recognition may be due at this time. An increased workload, as well as problem solving may also occur. To avoid frustration, work should be executed detail by detail. Any stress could result in disagreements, especially with older individuals or the boss, if employed. Children may become a burden or make demands testing the patience and responsibility. The body needs to be kept warm or rheumatism and colds will develop. It seems to take more effort than usually to get anything done, as the body's energy level is low.

76 ☉ ☌ ♅ Impulsive action, as well as a strong drive for more freedom and independence are activated. Unexpected events may occur such as friendships, romantic attractions or avenues for leadership could open up in a specialized field. If the aspect is negative, lack of considerations and responsibilities may nullify any advance offered. This is a favorable time for the study of astrology and occult subjects. An impulsive inner drive, activated at this time, may lead to erratic heart beats. The unpredictability of ♅ may result in peculiar happenings, all with the desire of more personal freedom in mind.

77 ☉ ☌ ♆ The imaginations are strongly activated and, depending on the natal aspect, may further artistic undertakings or lead to secret affairs, self-deception and psychological aberrations. Dreams may become more vivid and influential. Speculations and gambling may not be profitable. Under negative aspects, this transit may bring unwanted pregnancies or alcohol and drug abuse as the ego is now influenced by its inability to render constructive decisions.

78 ☉ ☌ ♇ The ego combined with will power is seeking leadership, authority and changes that permit self-improvement by discarding the old and worn out. Issues regarding taxes, insurance, inheritance and money belonging to the partner or associate, may surface now. The tendency to dictate, coerce and control others should be avoided. Moodiness and sexual aggressiveness need controlling. Contacts with criminal elements must be avoided to prevent unfortunate events from developing. If badly aspected otherwise the physical strength will be diminished and heart problems may develop or even lead to death.

79 ☉ * ☽ Increased vitality and interest in domestic affairs will develop. A good time to consider real estate transactions and travel. Improvement of health and relationships will take place. There is harmony between the ego and the emotions.

80 ☉ * ☿ Creative ideas and communications, as well as artistic expressions, emerge during this transit. Authorities will be favorable to new ideas. Short trips may be related to education or correspondence. A good time to improve knowledge through study.

81 ☉ * ♀ Enjoyment of social life, art, romance and music takes place. A love of beauty and a desire to participate in entertainment is increased. Charm and happiness will help gain rewards and bring support from others. Financial improvements may be received.

82 ☉ * ♂ A growth in self-confidence and energy is used and applied to constructive plans and activities, thus, obtaining furtherance of business and beneficial connections. The body builds extra strength and stamina resulting in increased physical activities and an increased sex drive. The mind is alert and willing to forge ahead. New friendships and love affairs may result from this transit.

83 ☉ * ♃ The enthusiasm is high. Greater interest in educational or other studies will develop. Any form of education, such as teaching, will benefit under this transit. Authorities will be favorable. A good time to advance in legal matters and financial speculations. Benefits may be received from foreigners. This is a prosperous time if prudently applied.

84 ☉ * ♄ Ambitions, coupled with prudent planning and executing of business, will be profitable. Authorities will be supportive of business enterprises. Friendships can be formed through business ventures. This is a time of opportunities that, if attended to in a steady and progressive manner, will be greatly beneficial. Responsibilities are handled well and especially older, more reliable and powerful individuals, will provide gain. Career changes, due to new opportunities, may be presented.

85 ☉ * ♅ Original, eccentric and creative ideas may flow and will be supported to materialize on new inventions. This is an excellent time to study astrology, science or engineering subjects and make supportive new friends or join interesting groups. Sudden and positive changes may occur.

86 ☉ * ♆ The mind is tuned into positive imaginations. A good time for all kinds of visual arts. This is also a favorable time to seek hospital treatments as it promises positive healing results. Intuitive and clairvoyant talent may be activated via meditation, which will bring understanding and solutions of prior problems. The ego is calm and content, thus able to decide on positive changes.

87 ☉ * ♇ The willpower is strong and used to improve and activate positive changes. A willingness to leave the old behind for a new beginning. The mind is resourceful in planning new business ventures. Gain, through the resources of others, may materialize.

88 ☉ □ ☽ Difficulties and conflicts within the domestic circle arise due to volatile emotions. Emotional outbursts by women will be experienced. The self-expression is disturbed by laziness and self-indulgence a the cost of others. Expenditures may outstrip income to satisfy the disturbed emotions. Any domestic or real estate dealings need to proceed with caution. Frustration and lack in confidence may linger until this transit has passed. The health needs attention as emotional upset may trigger illness.

89 ☉ □ ☿ Ego conflicts may create communication difficulties, thus resulting in social rejection and problems with authorities and contracts. Worry and anxiety, by an unsettled mind, will lead to mistakes. This transit may affect the mental health.

90 ☉ □ ♀ Excessive expenditure are made due to self-indulgence. A need for excessive attention and admiration is expressed to satisfy a self-centered attitude. Misunderstandings and poor taste could prevent social acceptance.

91 ☉ □ ♂ Aggressive and impulsive behavior leads to confrontations. Accidents may happen. Extra care is needed and authorities must be approached with caution to avoid conflicts. Unbridled passion and aggressive sexual behavior cause trouble and will strain relationships. Stay clear of disputes. Estrangements and disappointments may follow. Beware of scandal and injury to honor and reputation. Be discreet, avoid rash acts and quarrels with others.

92 ☉ □ ♃ Undue optimism, extravagance and an inflated sense of self-worth create conflict with others. To promise more than one can deliver may result in loss of friends or position. The body may retain excessive weight. There may be laziness and legal trouble or problems with authorities.

93 ☉ □ ♄ Business and authority will not cooperate. Frustration of ambitions and social rejections will lead to loneliness. The ego may be bruised and mannerism may turn harsh and autocratic. Tiredness, depression and strenuous working conditions may deplete the vitality. Any selfish behavior will back fire. This is not a good time to ask for favors. Disappointments with children may cause strife. The emotions are rigid and will be uncooperative.

94 ☉ □ ♅ Any desire for freedom at all costs could result in breakups and estrangements. Do or die is the motto as erratic attitudes render the person unreliable and egotistical. Sudden attractions occur but they soon resolve as there is no stability of the mind. Financial hardships could arise. Joint finances, speculations or gambling might create dramatic losses. The heart beat may be irregular and affects the health. Erratic and foolish acts may destroy hard earned gains. No changes should be made during this transit. Protect the status quo. Machinery may suddenly break down. The mind is stressed, thus travel and controversies should be avoided.

95 ☽ □ ♆ The mind is encased in dreams creating self-deception. A desire to escape responsibility, abuse of alcohol and drugs, as well as secret sexual involvement, all distort reality leading to uncontrolled imaginations and confusion of the mind. Deception and unwanted pregnancy may occur. Delusion of grandeur can cause involvement in disastrous financial schemes. If ♆ is afflicted at birth this transit might have serious consequences. Deep depression will affect the health. Morals may be abandoned and delusions will replace reality.

96 ☽ □ ♇ A power struggle or intrigue and secrets regarding other people's money could lead to confrontations. Sexual aggression, jealousy and harsh behavior take over personal control. Breaking and disintegration of current conditions will occur demanding radical changes in life. Relations with authority will be difficult and may result in financial loss. Breakdowns of machinery demand costly repairs.

97 ☽ ▲ ☽ Good relations with the other sex are kept as the mind and emotions are balanced. Domestic arrangements work out well. Romantic relationships may blossom during this transit. Generally, this is a favorable transit.

98 ☽ ▲ ☿ Intellectual activities, to further the goal and self-expression, are undertaken. Improvement of self-confidence brings greater social rewards. The forming and execution of contracts and agreements will be beneficial. This is a good transit to begin studying as the mind is very receptive and sharp.

99 ☽ ▲ ♀ A happy and content period. The personal charm is greatly increased, thus attracting suitable partners. Kindness and a willingness to help others will not go unnoticed. Financial gain may be made if other aspects are positive to this transit. Help is received to further any goal. Society will be supportive and help improve the position in life.

100 ☽ ▲ ♂ The ego is strong, so is the energy level. Actions will be taken to improve on business, health and personal relationships. Dealings with authority will be more positive.

101 ☽ ▲ ♃ Lady luck provides for a positive attitude and brings favors from those in power and authority. An excellent transit for

self-improvement and entering into schools of higher education. Romance may appear while studying. Foreign travel or dealings with foreigners promises rewards. During this time legal affairs may resolve favorably. This is a transit where opportunity will present itself and finances will improve. Don't allow laziness to prevent from reaping new opportunities.

102 ☉ ▲ ♄ Old relationships may be renewed and responsibilities are accepted in a constructive way. Older individuals may prove reliable and helpful. Plan well at this time to reach a steady progress in business. During this transit legal affairs may be handled favorably. Utilizing this transit to the fullest will bring rewards and opportunity, however, patience and perseverance is always required when ♄ provides a hand in life.

103 ☉ ▲ ♅ Unexpected and very sudden benefits may come through authorities. Social circles will widen and the popularity will increase. Greater personal freedom will be experienced. Business established with partners or associates may expand. Unusual opportunities may present itself during this time. This is a good time to study astrology. Gain may be reaped from investments and friends. Some positive changes could be made.

104 ☉ ▲ ♆ The imaginations will expand and become very creative. Depending on other aspects in the chart this may be the time when ideal love knocks on the door. This transit is very positive and supportive if a hospital stay is necessary. A good time to meditate and structure the mind. Artists find outlets for their talent.

105 ☉ ▲ ♇ Increased willpower and a desire for improvement could lead to gain in business and professional affairs. A good time to start a new business or benefit from the resources of others. Any project involving investigation and research will profit from this transit.

106 ☉ ☍ ☽ Difficulties arise in expressing emotions, in dealing with the family, authority, the public and partner. The ego stands in the way of emotional expressions. Health problems affect the vitality. Spending should be scrutinized to avoid depletion of resources. In general, this is a tense period that might lead to separations.

107 ☉ ☍ ☿ Arguments and disagreements ensue over ego issues, restlessness and trouble through communications. Contracts and

agreements entered into may include unfavorable terms that were previously overlooked. Disputes should be avoided as well as travel and new endeavors. The nerves may be strained, needing rest under this transit.

108 ☉ ☍ ♀ The internal harmony is disturbed creating friction in relationships. Financial problems, over-sensitivity and temper tantrum, all create trouble that exhaust relationships. Bickering and hate may surface creating conflicts and estrangements.

109 ☉ ☍ ♂ Ego-confrontations interfere with business and other relationships. Rash, impulsive and aggressive acts cause resentment and estrangements. Difficulties with the law and authorities could lead to physical confrontations, even arrest, if the aspects in the 12th house support such a conclusion. Beware of accidents. A period of disappointments where the emotions should be kept under tied control. Any tension will induce health problems. Avoid dealing with finances or new undertakings and curb any self-centered tendencies or loss will follow.

110 ☉ ☍ ♃ Over-confidence, inflated self-importance, unwise action and financial depletion might occur. Expecting too much of others while neglecting their own duties and attempts to control others through display of emotions and temper may create resentment. Narrow-minded attitudes, especially on religious matters, could lead to fanaticism or abuse by others. The main issue here is going overboard with everything, getting caught up in schemes or other events that turn unfavorable. Legal difficulties may result therefrom. Disappointment will be experienced unless some mental restrain is exercised.

111 ☉ ☍ ♄ A hard, unsympathetic and unreasonable attitude, as well as selfishness and confrontations with authorities, may occur under this transit. Insecurity is masked by rigid attitudes creating strong oppositions. Loss through authorities, older people and financial matters must be guarded against. No progress for hard work will be achieved. Set backs in business or forced changes of occupations could come up. The health is suffering. Disappointments, obstacles and losses will affect the mind. Cold and distant emotions hurt the self and others. A very trying time if caution is not practiced.

112 ☉ ☍ ♅ Rebellion against the established norm and a demand for extensive freedom regardless of responsibilities, is displayed. The behavior is unpredictable, eccentric, unreliable and unstable leading to estrangements from friends and relationships. An urge to change the current conditions may be executed in a rebellious way. Speculations will lead to loss. Joint finances become the subject of strife. This transit provides for sudden, undesired changes. Not a good time to travel as sudden accidents or break downs could occur. Avoid disputes and legal involvement. Anxiety will affect the emotions.

113 ☉ ☍ ♆ Delusion of grandeur occurs. The ego is confused about reality leading to self-deception and loss. Unwanted pregnancy may create agony. Alcohol, drugs, sex and gambling should be avoided especially during this transit. Neurotic behavior will affect relationships. Uncertainty about life creates worry, confusion and collapse of plans. Laziness may derail from pursuing goals.

114 ☉ ☍ ♇ A strong ego attempts to coerce and dominate others. Conflicts result therefrom that break up business or private relationships. Problems over joint finances, insurance, inheritance, taxes or partner's resources could develop at this time. Sexual aggressiveness may end affairs. Dealings with authorities may result in power confrontations. Machinery could break down during this time. Old systems, as well as sexual and financial engagements, may end and cannot be resumed.

☉ PROGRESSED

115 ☉ ☌ ☽ Depending on the position of both planets at birth this aspect will produce change. Whether any change represents advancements, or indicates a critical period, is dependent on the natal aspect. If the natal aspect was favorable positive domestic and honorable change will occur. If negative, loss will be experienced. As this combustion of vital life forces will strongly influence the health and vitality, fever may result as the extra heat generated by this aspect permeates the body.

116 ☉ * ▲ ☽ Fortunate for the wellbeing and progress this aspect makes the mind cheerful and positive. Beneficial attachments may

be made and the person is able to take full advantage of all opportunities that will present itself. Positive changes may now be made for an overall improvement of the mental and physical conditions.

117 ☉ □ - ☍ ☽ The intense power of both planets may affect the general health. It brings unfortunate conditions and sorrow into the life. A death in the family may occur. Many disappointments will be experienced, leading to separation and estrangements.

118 ☉ ☌ - ✱ - ▲ ☿ The ☉ brings increased vitality and opens the mind. Travel, literary work and all kinds of correspondence are undertaken with a new zest for achievement. Dealings with attorneys, agents and all who could be beneficial, will now bring gain. The groundwork for future benefits can now be positively executed.

119 ☉ □ - ☍ ☿ Mental trouble, leading to worry and anxiety, will be experienced. The mind is unsure, changeable and prone to make hasty decisions, leading to mistakes. Great care and prudence is required when dealing with agents, servants, lawyers, business partners and literary persons, especially when signing of contracts are involved. Said contracts either never come to fruition or turn out to be in the disinterest of the person.

120 ☉ ☌ ♀ Love and life experiences are intensified. Beneficial connections will be made that promise support, sympathy and affection. The pursuit of pleasure and happiness brings great fortunes. New friendships help improve the status of the person and marriage may result therefrom.

121 ☉ ✱ - ▲ ♀ Financial and social gain is indicated. Opportunities will present itself resulting in advancement, recognition and attachments which will all be beneficial to the person. Investments will profit. The feelings and emotions will be uplifting.

122 ☉ □ - ☍ ♀ Overspending leads to loss. The feelings are subject to disappointment and sorrow. Loss of friends and relationships occur and disagreements will result within the family circles. Matters to do with pleasure, entertainment and society at large, will be unfavorable.

123 ☉ ☌ ♂ This is a critical time where anger and excitement rash to the forefront. Aggressive and restless behavior override the sense

of logic, which leads to quarrels, disappointments and possible dire consequences. The health needs special attention, especially the purity of the blood, which may cause severe fever.

124 ☉ ✶ - ▲ ♂ Independent actions lead to new enterprises and ventures. It increases the vitality and brings new and exiting acquaintances. The mind is alert, ready for adventure and risk taking, and is interested in making positive changes.

125 ☉ □ - ☍ ♂ This is a very unfortunate aspect. The health needs attention (especially feverish complaints and inflammatory diseases). Accidents must be avoided and dispute with others must not be entered into. Serious domestic trouble, estrangements and disappointments will end in sorrow and despair. All changes should be avoided until this aspect has passed. Nothing should be done that produces scandal or injure the reputation. Act as discreetly as possible as the urges to act rashly and impulsively will end in misfortune.

126 ☉ ☌ ♃ Gain, success and good fortune is indicated by this position. Social connections are increased and financial rewards result therefrom. Travel and association with foreigners, or outcome of lawsuits, will be favorable. The health will be good with a strong vitality. New unions, attachments and friendships will be made, and if the ☽ aspect is good at the same time, the person will meet with success on every level. In case of an afflicted ♃ at birth, over-confidence, ego expansion, foolish extravagance and excess should be avoided.

127 ☉ ✶ - ▲ ♃ A prosperous and successful time with general improvement of all affairs. Lasting attachments may be formed that bring gain and happiness. This is a time when ambitions may be fulfilled. Travel, or involvement with foreigners, bring beneficial changes. Solid investments will lead to prosperity. Actions taken now become more thought out and wisely, thus, bringing furtherance and improvement.

128 ☉ □ - ☍ ♃ Trouble and difficulties will prevail affecting money, the domestic affairs, social and legal matters. Loss will be incurred and death, separation or estrangement will bring sorrow. It is necessary to guard against deception, treachery and hypocrisy. Disappointment and disagreement will result with partners and

friends and trouble through them may develop. The person should neither be too expectant nor indulge in any excesses as those bring health trouble creating long and serious suffering.

129 ☉ ☌ ♄ All affairs tend to go wrong at this time. The mind will be warped, full of worry and suspicion, as loads of responsibilities wear the person's health and energy down. While it stabilizes the character and increases ambitions it also imposes more perseverance as it becomes now harder to succeed. The health may be affected by poor circulation, bringing on rheumatism, blood disorders, cold and chills. The antidote hereto is optimism and physical exercise to maintain a healthy mind and body.

130 ☉ ✱ - ▲ ♄ The person becomes more reliable, adheres to a moral character and will meet with elders or authorities who are helpful, sincere and able to benefit and may even become friends. The mind is steady, concentrated and persevering as to increase honor and reputation. A position of trust should be obtained that will serve well in the future. This influence will bring gain rather than fulfill any material desires. Sound and solid investments will improve the financial conditions in the long run.

131 ☉ □ - ☍ ♄ A period of worry, anxiety, sorrow and grief. A death in the family or domestic trouble could be on the horizon. The person should not make any changes and be especially careful of older people and authorities. Depression and despair should be avoided. A need to guard against health problems arises. The mind should be kept steady and calm as disappointments and oppositions will be suffered. Financial difficulties will occur and any selfishness could backfire at this time.

132 ☉ ☌ ♅ Great changes in life will enhance the mind. If positive, new attachments with people of higher social standing, may be made. If afflicted by other planets, estrangement will be experienced. Unusual friendships could be formed but should be entered into only with great caution as they may be of a peculiar nature that may ultimately not be in the person's best interest.

133 ☉ ✱ - ▲ ♅ Unexpected and sudden benefits may be obtained that could include some travel which was not originally intended. The mind will sharpen, become expansive and inventive, thus creating

impressive original ideas. The study of occultism, astrology or mystical matters may be encouraged by others. As ♅ brings new friendships, acquaintances and involvement with groups and issues of society, this aspect might bring advantages. Sudden gain in investments or by speculation is possible.

134 ☉ □ - ☍ ♅ Sudden and severe disappointments will come into the life. Unexpected trouble will turn all plans unfavorable, creating disagreement, opposition, conflict and cause separation. The mind will turn irritable, the health will suffer, and nervous disorders will affect the mind. Any planned changes and matters of importance should be on hold until after this aspect has passed. Disagreements and disappointments with close relationships cause annoyance or even disgrace. Travel should be avoided and if the ☾ aspect is unfortunate at the same time, caution is the big word and should be adhered to otherwise trouble may occur during those critical times. Careful consideration of consequences preceding any action may prevent major mistakes and disappointments. Any dispute, legal affairs or actions, which may lead to disgrace and ill repute, should be avoided.

135 ☉ ☌ ♆ Some psychic awakening could become apparent and may strangely affect the feelings. This experience may entail some incarceration or restriction or hospitalization.

136 ☉ * - ▲ ♆ Musical and poetic talent may be awakened and improved. The position ☽ ▲ ♆ may bring unexpected luck (even a possible lottery winning) with a good ☉ aspect to ♆. It also brings some benefits of an unusual nature. Some kind of improvement to material affairs will come into being.

137 ☉ □ - ☍ ♆ A deep depression may grab hold of the emotions. Neurotic tendencies may surface, and if ♆ is much afflicted at birth, the moral fiber is weakened and may bring ruin to the person. This time is layered with tremendous obstacles. Great stamina is needed to overcome this depressing aspect as most plans will suffer from confusion and, thus, will not materialize.

138 ☉ ☌ ♇ Moody and egotistical behavior, with a strong desire for leadership and power, may change the personal position. Dealing with people in authority may lead to opposition or a stand off in a power game. Criminal elements should be avoided at all costs as

such involvement may backfire leaving the person at the mercy of authorities and loss is certain. The person may feel devoid of energy, have disappointments, suffer from confusion and gets involved in purposeless action that lead to breakups. Remember that the sun creates life, ♇ symbolizes death and rebirth. With that in mind, something in the life of the person will end.

139 ☉ * - ▲ ♇ A strong sensitivity may engage the person in helping the underdog. Transformations to improve the power and standing may develop. Any changes considered should be carefully scrutinized before being put into action. The will and ability to concentrate is strengthened and brings endurance to work toward improvement.

140 ☉ □ - ☍ ♇ Relations with superiors and authorities become difficult and create opposition, which leads to radical changes. Ego problems and bossiness will bring struggle and money problems. Outright power struggle will result. No changes should be initiated and no contract or new agreement should be entered into until this aspect has passed. Machinery may break down. If changes are enforced they should be followed to avoid further disappointment. Avoid any situation that could lead to violence. Dominance, self-centeredness, aggressiveness, belligerence, power struggle, financial problems and sexual encounters will become a source of trouble. The nerves are on edge and the physical vitality is weakened. Keep good control of your energy, don't overdue anything, be moderate and mostly keep calm and practice diplomacy.

BABY CHART

The conditions at time of birth, whether mentally or physically, as well as the social conditions of the parents, reflect on the child. From the moment of birth, until about 3 years of age, the child directly and subconsciously adopts the actions of the parents as normal and based thereon forms its own character, habits and beliefs that continue throughout life. Charts erected especially for children will help prevent later complications resulting from any latent weakness instilled at birth.

141 ☉ ☌ ☽ One parent is very strong, domineering and acts as father and mother. This could be because one parent is missing or one parent takes over the responsibility while the other parent acts like another child.

142 ☉ ☌ ☿ As ☿ travels close to the ☉ there are no aspects between them at time of birth.

143 ☉ ☌ ♀ is similar to ☿ and never far from the ☉.

144 ☉ ☌ ♂ The father is acting quickly and impulsively which the child imitates. A quick healing power goes with this position if no other negative influences prevail. If afflicted in ♋ or ♓ the emotions are easily boiling over.

145 ☉ ☌ ♃ Born into wealth and good standing, however, if other negative influences are present, happiness is lacking. Good relations with and support from authority figures will be beneficial in life.

146 ☉ ☌ ♄ The father may be domineering and stifling the child's development. The child adopts mannerism of the father or elderly person and becomes slow to act out of its own energy. Resentments develop towards the father or authority figures and more reliance is built on the mother who may has to run everything. An inferior complex may develop in the child. The lack of humor and joy of living is shadowed by seriousness and guilt of duty. This may create depressions. The health is weak. Inhibited self-assuredness often creates lack of self-worth, which in turn creates fault findings with everyone. Overly serious mannerism and a constant searching for approval may hinder the forming of great relationships. There is a need to learn peace of mind, self-confidence and to step out of daddy's shadow.

147 ☉ ☌ ♅ There is an unusual upbringing and an erratic and rather eccentric lifestyle and behavior. The father's influence is strong leading to an unusual approach to life, which may not be understood by others and judged merely as being eccentric. The child is very independent making it hard for the parents to exercise control.

148 ☉ ☌ ♆ A strong spiritual father influence's the child and may not allow the child to develop a positive image of a father figure. The

child submerges in a world of fantasy and may discover secrets of the parents, thus creating mistrust in the family. If guided correctly, the child may develop into a creative and very artistic person. If not properly guided it will spend a lifetime trying to find a way of creative expression. Due to extreme sensitivity drugs and alcohol may be used to avoid the harsh reality of life. A lack of stability may lead to delusion or uncreative outlets, or suicide, to end the mind's confusion.

149 ☉ ☌ ♇ The father is important for the development of the child. He may be overwhelming, controlling or manipulative. He will instill traits on the child who will adopt such behavior as normal. Relationships will fail due to constant manipulations. If there is a power struggle going on between the mother and father, the child absorbs such behaviour as normal, creating intense relationship problems later on in life. The mind vacillates between being completely in control or being completely neurotic, whichever tactic will gain the most. Feeling out of control creates disaster, therefore, the game never ends. Obsession, righteousness and display of all kinds of emotions, in order to gain and control, zap the energy out of everyone else.

150 ☉ ∗ ☽ The parents enjoy a good relationship, however, the child may not quite comprehend the parents behavior. The father's positive authority serves the child well in the future when having to deal with authorities. The child, when reaching adulthood, is so convinced of its own positive point of view and idealistical beliefs, that the feelings may suffer in a relationship when the other person does not befit the ideal as visualized by the child.

151 ☉ ∗ ☿ As ☿ travels close to the ☉ there are no aspects between them at time of birth.

152 ☉ ∗ ♀ is similar to ☿ and never far from the ☉.

153 ☉ ∗ ♂ The parents provide a good and constructive influence on the child. The talents of the child need to be channeled in order to develop.

154 ☉ ∗ ♃ Confidence is instilled in the child providing benefits in career choice and drawing benefits through co-operation from others. Understanding the needs of the self and others is important.

155 ☉ ✱ ♄ The child develops well to work with authority and learns through positive actions of the father. The learning process will help prepare for the business world and cooperation in society.

156 ☉ ✱ ♅ Creative, innovative and talented, the child understands ethics, moral and the need of society. If the talent and energy is structured and expressed positively a mentally advanced person will emerge.

157 ☉ ✱ ♆ The father encourages the child. If the child's talent is understood by the parents and developed a creative mind will emerge. If the talent is not nurtured, blind adherence to religious sects will stifle the self-worth.

158 ☉ ✱ ♇ A constructive balance between the will, the ego and usage of power, is in place. Helpful parents instilled cooperative attitudes into the child.

159 ☉ □ ☽ This affliction indicates that mom and dad did not go along when the child was born. This will later affect the child's development of self-worth and may affect responsibilities as the feelings remain unstable.

160 ☉ □ ☿ As ☿ travels close to the ☉ there are no aspects between them at time of birth.

161 ☉ □ ♀ is similar to ☿ and never far from the ☉.

162 ☉ □ ♂ Rash actions against the self-interest, to the point of self destruction, create havoc. The father is unhappy with his life and work and is not functioning on a constructive level at the time the child is born. The social environment born into is difficult for the development of the child. The child may never understand a sense of danger. Diving into difficult and dangerous situations is done without considering any possible consequences. If the parents display anger, possessiveness and emotional control, the child will not express its own feelings but react likewise. This spoils over into relationships, especially when it involves a sexual relationship. The child will later react to life emotionally and not intellectually, always in a hurry, restless and out to satisfy the physical desires but neglecting the intellect. The concept of self-worth is confused. 'Think before you act' should be the first concept this person

needs to learn. Internal unhappiness, emotional pressure and stress may lead to serious diseases.

163 ☉ □ ♃ The father does not like himself, nor what he does or his situation in society. Problems are over dad's head. There is a lack of or indifference to communications between father and child. The father may disappear during the early years of the child creating a dislike for men. The knowledge of 'who I am' is distorted and poorly developed and creates relationship problems. Selfishness, always blaming others for every wrong without considering his own involvement, may destroy all efforts to belong, thus creating unhappiness and tightness of physical being, which, in turn, may lead to serious illness. A need to learn to love the self, accept responsibility and sharing emotions with others, is needed.

164 ☉ □ ♄ The father does not like who he is, a trait taken over from his father. He is unhappy with his lot in life, thus passing feelings of dissatisfaction onto his child and often, he leaves his children. The signs of ☉ and ♄ give indication of the unhealthy patterns that the child will unwillingly adopt. Resentment towards the father, authority figures and all kind of restraint, will turn to 'anti' tradition for organizations and anything of dislike related to rules and order. If the mother is the domineering part of the parents she is anti men, anti social rules and authority, creating dislike in men by children of both sexes. In later life, without respect and value of their partner, homosexuality in women and a desire to use older persons for personal gain, or a desire to destroy and get even with their mate, will destroy any attempt at harmony and happiness. A tendency to load on and lay blame of all their problems onto others by refusing a self-examination, distracts from the ability to learn the roots of the problem. Feeling good is something that needs to be learned here.

165 ☉ □ ♅ The family is eccentric and may live outside established social norms. The father's desire to change the world instills radical and revolutionary desires in the child. A difficult and sometimes estranged relationship between the parents and the child develops. When the mother is the dominating force in the family opposition against the father is expressed.

166 ☉ □ ♆ The family needs spiritual development and either practices strict and blind adherence to religion or is atheist displaying disdain for any religion. The parents impair their children's concept of reality, this in turn, affects the child's future concept and understanding of reality. Inability to decide and acknowledge reality may subject the child to follow gurus and cult movements.

167 ☉ □ ♇ The father dislikes groups, society and its rules. The child may alienate itself from society in order to avoid dealing with it. A feeling of not belonging develops creating uncomfortable involvement in crowds. There may be feelings of paranoia when confronted with masses of people. The child needs to learn to be in control of the self without trying to control others.

168 ☉ ▲ ☽ The parents enjoy a good relationship, however, the child may not quite comprehend the parent's behavior. The father's positive authority serves the child well in the future when having to deal with authorities. When reaching adulthood, the child is so convinced of its own positive point of view and idealistically beliefs, that the feelings may suffer in a relationship when the other person does not befit the ideal visualized by the child.

169 ☉ ▲ ☿ As ☿ travels close to the ☉ there are no aspects between them at time of birth.

170 ☉ ▲ ♀ is similar to ☿ and never far from the ☉.

171 ☉ ▲ ♂ This aspect is excellent for any cooperation with authority. The father imputes positive images in the child and teaches the child how to set out and accomplish goals. The child receives help and encouragement from family and friends and has ample opportunities to succeed.

172 ☉ ▲ ♃ Raised in a positive and comfortable atmosphere instills a reliance of always being taken care off. Reliance on others to provide help may later lead to using partners to provide the comfort without making an effort to provide for themselves.

173 ☉ ▲ ♄ The father calmly influences the child and encouraged free thinking, thus creating a serious personality with positive self-expression. Good relations with authorities will be developed.

174 ☉ ▲ ♅ Good family relationships encourage growth. The parents will be unusual, unconventional, encouraging and foster the child to new ideas and ways of thinking.

175 ☉ ▲ ♆ The family, especially the father, displays a spiritual goal and expression. The danger is that he will expect the child to follow his path, which may not be in the child's best interest. The child's talents must be expressed and developed even if different from the father's interests. Each individual must find its own self-expression.

176 ☉ ▲ ♇ There is constructive expression, which is very good for any contact with the public, mass-media or communication. The parents make great efforts to teach the child and prepare it for a role in society and dealings with authorities. The father is positive which creates a mental security for the child.

177 ☉ ☍ ☽ This affliction indicates that mom and dad did not go along when the child was born. This will later affect the child's development of self-worth and may undermine the responsibility due to unstable feelings.

178 ☉ ☍ ☿ As ☿ travels close to the ☉ there are no aspects between them at time of birth.

179 ☉ ☍ ♀ is similar to ☿ and never far from the ☉.

180 ☉ ☍ ♂ The family is not liked or accepted by the community and there is strife within the family. The child lacks the ability to sense danger which may manifest by sexual aggression or pursued of dangerous situation or dangerous occupations while ignoring any consequences. Both, male and female may have disagreements in life or attract likewise partners, thus increasing trouble and discontent. A conflict between the wants and the execution to achieve it may be at cross-purpose. The energy is unproductive and wasted by the inability to act according to plan. This creates a lack of accomplishment, which may lead to indifference and laziness. The will to succeed may not be established. As adults, there are difficulties in establishing a warm and loving relationship.

181 ☉ ☍ ♃ The father does not relate to himself. The mother may be dominating, using the child against the father, to gain the upper hand. The child lacks attending to its needs. Internal tension and mental turmoil may, later on, develop into physical illness.

182 ☉ ☍ ♄ Mental restrictions, imposed on by the father or loss of the father, either by leaving or emotional unavailability, hamper the self-expression. The child needs to learn to detach, especially from

the father's grip and oppression. A feeling of disdain towards authority and the law, disillusion and a sense of failure, may develop. A female may attract partners just like daddy was, continuing the destructive circle into her own life. The constant tension will attract illness. Self-righteousness may prevent cooperation with others.

183 ☉ ☍ ♅ Being unsure and non-productive is a trait that is adopted by the child from the father. Life may be hard and subject to obstacles and disappointments. Behavior pattern may be erratic, eccentric and maturity will be slow to develop, possibly leaving a dislike for the father. The family resentment must be overcome to enjoy an unusual lifestyle and advanced mind.

184 ☉ ☍ ♆ The child may be neglected on a spiritual level. The father may be emotionally unavailable to the child creating confusion and insecurity. The child may fill the void with fantasy, illusion, or create a dream world to make up for what is not available. Relationships will be very difficult as the mind is not always on "this planet". Difficulties to share emotions will develop. Unrealistic expectations turn into disappointments.

185 ☉ ☍ ♇ A strong psychic energy is present. Dominance, as well as manipulation and control may be executed, as adopted from the father in the home atmosphere, which seem to drain others physically and emotionally. Once the control level is reduced or removed, positive energy can flow and develop. This will involve freeing one self of the parental control.

☉ TRANSIT OR PROGRESSION TO A (Ascendant)

186 ☉ ☌ A The person has a strong character with as definite view of the future. A strong constitution helps the body recuperate and provides for good health. If negatively aspected, the ego will be inflated. Unanticipated results may bring down the ego. The health may also suffer. During transit outburst of energy, eagerness and confidence will help with gain.

187 ☉ * A A balanced ego and self expression is displayed. The mind is well developed providing for abundance of energy and creativity. If not negatively aspected, good fortunes may be received.

188 ☉ □ A The ego, as perceived by the person, is differently expressed when in public and dealing with society. The behavior is inharmonious, thus creating difficulties in getting along. During transit health problems develop as well as conflicts with superior and person in authority. Relationships suffer causing worry and anxiety.

189 ☉ ▲ A. Optimism, self-confidence, a well as a balanced ego and cooperation with others, especially with authority and superiors, provide for advancement.

190 ☉ ☍ A refer to # 188.

☉ TRANSIT OR PROGRESSION TO M (Mid heaven)

191 ☉ ☌ M A position of prominence and influence may be achieved. The sign involved may provide an indication as to the direction this aspect will take. During transit leadership maybe adopted which brings popularity. If afflicted extreme shyness and worry will stifle the emotions.

192 ☉ * M A good rapport with authorities and the public will bring increased honor and recognition. Intense feelings and properly controlled emotions provide for good public relations.

193 ☉ □ M Trouble with authority is indicated. Difficulties may arise in dealing with society or achieving any desired goals. The honor and reputation could suffer. Changes in mood will affect all affairs creating tension and unhappiness.

194 ☉ ▲ M Increase in honor, reputation and career is promoted. Public life, politics or public fame may follow. During transit the body is able to positively release tension. Relationships and co-operations will be beneficial. A good time to deal with public issues.

195 ☉ ☍ M refers to # 193.

37

☽ Lunar Aspects

The position of the ☽ at birth and its aspects to other planets form the most important meanings, which must be considered first when reading a chart. The ☽ regulates the ebb and flow of the tide and is responsible for regulating the juices in our body. Without its influence the body could not function, thus, life could not be sustained. Any dysfunction of the body can be traced to the ☽ influences and may lead to permanent disease or even death.

It takes the ☽ about 28 days to transit all 12 houses. While passing through the various houses forming aspects to natal or progressed planets, it produces emotional reactions, situations and afflictions of the health. The exact influences, while in transit through any house, is identified by the sign it is in. How and when an event is triggered by the ☽ closely affects other planets. Therefore, all aspects formed to the ☽ will either substantially improve conditions or will affect the person through loss, which is primarily related to the emotions and actions taken thereon.

*The ☽, **A** and **M** are the most important aspects at birth. When progressing they influence the well being, reputation and honor of the person.*

The ☽ transit is not particularly of importance to major forecasts as it travels so fast (13 degree per day) that its influence may only have an effect when combined with other major aspects, especially a conjunction, or progression of the ☽ to major aspects.

Most people do not know their exact time of birth and therefore any reliance on the ☽ position may be deceptive due to guesswork rather than actual knowledge of the time of birth. A few minutes difference in birth time can delay an event up to a year and therefore, the reader is urged, when making important forecasts, to take the accepted time of birth and based on past events, thereafter calculate the possible time of birth that would trigger major future events to other planets.

The ☽ aspects are only of vital significance when coinciding with other solar and mutual aspects. It applies to the female side. Any major event, good or bad, involves women as well as the characteristics of the other planets and signs involved. Hence, the ☽ needs to be judged by its aspects to other planets, at the time of progress, in that it bestows influences to the aspects due at the time. However, if those aspects are minor or no aspect is formed by progression, it will then not produce important events. People who are more susceptible to the ☽ rays, i.e. ♋ are affected by full moon on a regular basis through their volatile emotions. For a man the ☽ represents his marriage partner and will affect actions taken thereon. The ☽ progression after birth indicates the woman to whom he will be attracted. The ☉ applies to the man in a woman's life. For a woman the ☽ is responsible for her health. The ☽ is seen as the potent fertili,er through which the other planets act, thus, inducing growth. Planetary aspects alone do not operate into action. An aspect of the progressed ☽ and transits of the affected planets combined will trigger the event.

NATAL ☽ IN THE HOUSES

196 ☽ (1) The emotions rule self-awareness, expression and actions. Early childhood experiences color most of the life. There is a restlessness and strong desire for constant changes of environment and occupation. Unless the mind is steady and strong the person may be easily influenced by others or used by them. The mind is changeable, moody and may suffer from lack of direction and purpose. An insatiable wanderlust may be present. If

the ☽ is positive, psychic and mediumistic abilities are present. A very vivid imagination is evident and the person is quite intuitive. There is a strong emotional need for personal recognition and approval by others. There is fondness for food and related occupations. Some involvement, good or bad, with the mother or mother figures, is indicated. It determines the strength of the constitution and may also bring the person in touch with the public.

197 ☽ (2) Changes, fluctuation in income, and sometimes impulsive urges to spend money, is apparent. Women may assist with finances. Material possessions represent security, however, the ability to hold on to money depends on the aspects to the ☽. There can be a strong and overwhelming desire to acquire money and possessions. The wish to surround oneself with luxury and all aspects of the good life, even if the income available would not support such a lifestyle, may lead to trouble. Spending, just to satisfy the emotions, should be avoided.

198 ☽ (3) Short and medium distant travel may be connected with the job. The job may involve any kind of communications, possible Television, Film or other mass media, which requires the mind to focus on constant new changes. Some study to gain knowledge in these fields may be undertaken. Friendships, especially with women, may be made among siblings and neighbors. The mind may be highly imaginative and curious but lacks sustained concentration. The emotions dictate speech, correspondence and the intellect. The person may be prone to day dreaming and fantasies and the mind is strongly influenced by the imagination. Trivial matters may pre-occupy the mind, thus preventing real matters to emerge and be considered. In conjunction with a well aspected ☿ the person could gain a position of prominence.

199 ☽ (4) There is a desire for frequent changes of residence or for re-decorating the home. Work may be performed from home and may involve real estate or food related activities. A strong sensitivity and emotional attachment exists to the mother who may reside within the home and with the family. Unless there is a meaningful home or a place to reside, unhappiness will prevail. A fondness of cooking and housekeeping is strong. A lack of harmony and many

changes in residence could result if afflictions are noted to the ☽. Finances may be improved later in life.

200 ☽ (5) Being a strong personality who craves the center of attention, romantic attractions, pleasure and gambling, will influence the imagination and emotional needs. The affections are very changeable because of emotional instability. Emotional dependency on others or interference by the family with a romantic partner, is possible. For females, this may be an indication of fertility and the bearing of many children, especially if the ☽ is in a water sign. Emotional impulsiveness can lead to speculations, unhealthy affairs or estrangements from children. Fluctuations in love affairs and an unwillingness to be faithful may lead to trouble in marriage. If well aspected, it indicates fondness of and gives children.

201 ☽ (6) The emotions are a source of health problems. There could be functional health disorders, trouble with allergies, or maintaining the water balance in the body. Hypochondria or psychosomatic illness may result. Emotions are tied to work and any efficiency is dependent on happiness and harmony. If afflicted, there will be difficulties in retaining stable employment and if the person is the boss, trouble with employees could result. Frequent job changes or temporary jobs are indicated. Jobs may be taken in the service industry and emotional relationships or friendships are formed with co-workers. A proper diet is necessary to balance the health and emotions. This position is good for cooks, and all other jobs related in some way to food and its preparation. Usually the person likes pets and will take good care of them.

202 ☽ (7) Men seek a mother image in their partner. Women love to mother their partner. A strong desire exists to marry for emotional and domestic security. If fortunate, it supplies success in marriage, partnerships and brings popularity. If afflicted, it will make the marriage unstable, bring loss in litigation and public disfavor. The opinions of others will strongly influence any decision. Obtaining an emotional fulfillment through relationships is a constant desire. Jobs and affairs related to dealing with the public may be sought out.

203 ☽ (8) The emotions vacillate between extreme high and low. The partner's financial affairs may fluctuate and spending is strongly

tied to the emotions. Sexual frustration could lead to shopping excursions resulting in needless purchases of goods which are later discarded when the desires turn to new objects. With a good ☽ there could be gain through inheritance, taxes, insurance or partner's finances. The ☽ may be a source of ill health that leads to the person's demise. The emotional reactions are strong. There is an interest in spiritualism because of the desire to stay somehow in contact with family members who have passed on. Over sensuality and over-involvement in a strong desire for sexual outlets may lead to physical depletion and emotional unhappiness. If afflicted it could worsen the financial position after marriage and legacies bring lawsuits leading to loss.

204 ☽ (9) The emotions are easily influenced by attachments to religion, social values, affairs and interests in foreign countries. There is either a strong religious interest or disinterest. A dogmatic attitude and bias, related to religion, may be obvious. The parents may influence any religious thinking or dictate said thinking. Guru worship should be avoided as the person is easily influenced by such concepts. A strong interest in higher education may be pursued that leads to a decree in law or business. Setting up residence in a foreign country may be considered, or at the very least, traveling to foreign countries will be enjoyed. If badly afflicted it denotes trouble and loss, especially where travel is concerned.

205 ☽ (10) The ☽ in this house brings success in business which caters to the public. The emotions influence professional changes, and a strong desire for security, fame, honor, reputation and recognition is evident. Contact with the public, public officials, politician and known celebrity are desired to improve one's own position held in life. When the ☽ receives bad aspects the possibility of scandal and public disgrace is intensified. The person may be born into a prominent family who demands a high standard and displays ambitions. A strong mother influence, as well as women in general, will influence the career. A chance to gain prominence before the public, and ambitions favorably to enter into politics, may be pursued. At an extreme any logic will be replaced and the mind will be ruled by emotions.

206 ☽ (11) The mind will focus on activities and desires of hopes and wishes. Benefits derived from friendships will be fruitful if the ☽ is well positioned. Female friends will be easily made but expectations of gain and possessiveness may determine the duration thereof. Friendships are influenced by the emotions and may undergo drastic changes. Friendships, initiated through the family, will considerably influence opinions and actions. The desire not to be alone is strong and the person always wants to be emotionally connected to someone.

207 ☽ (12) Men will suffer through women. Uncontrolled emotions may be the source of self-undoing in this house of karma. The unconscious mind is ruler of the emotions. If the mind is in control it can be used for psychic and intuitive learning. Shyness and easily hurt feelings make the person retreat from the public and seek seclusion. If the ☽ is afflicted, neurotic tendencies and loneliness, sometimes to the point of needing medical help, or even hospitali,ation for physical and mental illness, may occur. Secret acts, secret love affairs and secretive behavior, to disguise emotional instability, can cause trouble. It favors work performed in seclusion, such as in prison, hospitals or charitable institutions. Afflictions tend to bring out secret enemies, trouble and persecution.

☽ IN THE SIGNS

208 ☽ (♈) There is an intolerance when the sense of idealism is upset or when others will not have the drive and intensity to proceed. A conflict between the idealism and the thrive for worldly success will create emotional tension, which in turn will disturb associations. The spirit of enterprise, if properly asserted, will bring success and happiness. Love and friendships need constancy, sympathy, and mutual harmony to prosper. The character is impulsive, emotional, restless, independent, ambitious, aggressive and headstrong. The person has courage and is not easily defeated. Quick actions are taken on an emotional level and sudden flare ups of temper occur. When the character is attacked the person either emotionally dominates others or is dominated by others. There is

persistence and defeat will not be accepted. Unless the ☽ is very badly aspected, ultimate success will be obtained.

209 ☽ (♉) A conflict between the desire to achieve wealth and a tendency to avoid responsibility may create setbacks and loss. If artistic talent is present it should be expressed and trained. Behavior in regard to affection should be checked so that obstinacy is not allowed to persist. An unwillingness to change, as well as emotionally unstable behavior and la,iness, could create backlash. A strong need for financial security is present. Steady emotions and common sense should be used. Old actions should be completed before handling any new ones. Proper planning will attract wealth and beauty. Material comfort and a stable domestic situation is desired. Perseverance, forethought, kindness and self-reliance will attract the good things of life.

210 ☽ (♊) The creative energy is strong and interested in intellect, literature and science. Independence, strong sympathy for others, and personal dignity are displayed and provide strength to overcome adversity. The emotions are sometimes divided in that one side wants freedom and adventure while the other side wants to help and educate. When well aspected, it provides kindness, friendliness and generosity, which attracts helpful associations. Emotional tension may cause the person to say or do things that will be hurtful, causing antagonism which leads to separation. Under adverse aspects there should be an awareness of the words used that may be upsetting to others. A sharp intellect, a quick emotional nature and resourcefulness is used, but at times, vacillating instead of acting, creates unwanted results. Talking incessantly may distract from expressing the real emotions. Restlessness, with frequent changes of residence, nervousness and a constant desire for new adventures, could create unstable conditions. The self is spread too thin. The mind has great ideas but is unable to follow through. The distortion of the emotions leads the person astray, thus creating confusion and superficiality. Traveling salesmen and other occupations that meet with people, are favored.

211 ☽ (♋) The exercise of mental discipline is necessary in order to avoid la,iness and day dreaming. If la,iness is permitted to take control a personal inability to perform may manifest. There is a love to drift with the tide and only sheer necessity will force them into action. Keeping the feet on the ground will go a long way to cooperate with others. The attitude of better now then never should be adopted to promote progress. An intensity of emotions is displayed, especially at times of full moon. Strong ties exist to the mother, the family and home. There is an unwillingness to motivate change. The status quo is preferred. Domestic security is the prime motivator and influences the emotional wellbeing. Sensitivity exists to the opinion of others, which can lead to imagination of slights. If negative it instills insecurity, thus, the person easily retreats, withdraws and broods. An emotional instability and a tendency to smother others with emotions or goods in order to emotionally dominate them, will bring disappointment.

212 ☽ (♌) Quick mental reactions, great instincts and an ability to grasp opportunities, is present. A desire for happiness and contentment, at home and at work, as well as in social circles, is expressed. A position that is great for friendships, especially with women. Ill considered emotional rash acts may bring setbacks. Logic should always control the feelings, which may be stacked with ego pride. A proud person, with a flair for dramatics, desiring the center of attraction and the spotlight for themselves. A desire to be admired and appreciated is displayed. Romance and affection are sought. Normally, there is a strong liking of children, parties, arts and entertainment. A tendency to be self-centered, with prima donna behavior, creates estrangements. The need for dramati,ation should be curbed. The desire to dominate and a childish desire for self importance can be overbearing and disturb relationships. An ability for organi,ation and self-reliance helps attain leadership positions. If positive it bestows popularity.

213 ☽ (♍) The mind is analytical by nature with a very good memory. Reliable work performance gains respect and increases material and financial well being. The person may be frugal or at the very least, very economical in any spending habits. When taken unfair

advantage of by others the mind becomes critical, nagging and irritable. The speech may become caustic causing disturbing circumstances. Being hard working and very practical with a desire for neatness, cleanliness and organi,ation, the mannerism is rather reserved and of quiet demeanor. This makes for a good housekeeper and cook who is concerned with health issues. A desire to be behind the scene, because of shyness and a wish to serve others, comes into the open. Not being very curious, the person likes to keep things private. An affliction brings an overly strong desire with details and the attitude can, at times, be very critical. Perfectionism can stand in the way of achievement.

214 ☽ (♎) Strength of will and a desire for balance in life, together with a marked sensitivity to the speech and actions of others, requires a sense of humor. Tension and difficult circumstances should be faced with courage and determination to solve it promptly and restore harmony. Rest and recreation are important to restore energy. While artistic and intellectual work is preferred, domestic duties are considered exhausting and are carried out with certain disdain. A strong sensitivity to attitudes and reactions of others, as well as upset by inharmonious conditions, especially in relationships, adversely affect the health. A display of charm and elegance in mannerism and appearance furthers social activities. Being mostly courteous, gracious and kind their well being depends on feeling good. A balanced attitude is good for public relations. On the negative side, there is often agreement with others for the sake of harmony and to influence others while in fact, they would not agree with the opinions stated. There may be emotional dependency on others that can become degrading. A talent for art and music is indicated and needs developing.

215 ☽ (♏) A strong driving force with courageousness and sustained energy may emerge when circumstances compel swift actions. Shyness or an inability to express oneself may create misunderstandings with others. Feelings and opinions are sometimes expressed in a rather forceful way. Jealousy, resentment and bitter feelings may alienate associations and friends. Fantasy thinking should be strictly controlled and acts, in hope to gain

sympathy from others, may not have the desired effect. A wish to induce guild feelings in others may end such relationships rather than resolve any conflict. Strong bias emotions and acts, expressed in a willful and uncontrolled manner, such as blunt speech, a quick temper and threats to gain the upper hand, should be curbed. The desires rule the emotions. Personal affairs are taken very seriously and possessiveness and extreme jealousy may emerge. The person loves to hold grudges and plans revenge when angered. Brooding and revenge are serious defects in the character as well as the strong desire to restructure family and friends to their own point of view. The person seeks dominance of others and is very stubborn when their own desires are at stake. The motivations behind their actions are not always apparent, not even to themselves.

216 ☽ (♐) The person is alert and active, loves to talk and enjoys all forms of physical exercise, as well as travel, study of law, religion or occultism. The character is optimistic, good-humored, friendly and outgoing. The mental and physical energy is high but creates a conflict between impulsive acts and carefully considered actions. Sudden impulses may override logical reasoning. When annoyed, the reactions may not always be practical and of sound judgment. Patience and proper consideration of an issue must be applied prior to any action. Tension is created when the impulses move the person to go ahead at any cost versus logical application of reasoning. This tension brings trouble with associations and relationships. A balance of emotions and reasons must be achieved. The character is unsteady, emotionally idealistic and at times very optimistic and cheerful. The person is fond of travel and likes to take up residence in a foreign country. A distorted sense of reality and a refusal to see facts as they are may lead to a lack of considering other's point of view. This could involve unfairly playing on others. A narrow-minded view, extreme arrogance and egotistical, holier-than-thou attitude can lead to conflict. Unconsciously motivated emotional reasons may play a part when personal advantages in society are sought.

217 ☽ (♑) When well aspected it brings abundance of help from others even if the person is to weak to push himself forward. Hard work

will be required throughout life. The constant desire to critici,e, being impatient and a show of temper, will cause set backs or end relationships. Cooperation is required for any lasting success. The concept of give and take must be learned together with the ability to laugh at life, this will go a long way towards constructive relationships. The nature is reserved and cautious. Considerable coldness and austerity may be displayed toward others. Things are taken very seriously and the emotions identify with money rather than spiritual values. There are high ambitions, a willingness to work hard but the person is driven by bias, slanted towards status and financial security. Money and power, as well as status for themselves, are prime motivators. A display of shyness and insecurity about their own worth and a display of over-sensitivity to real and fancied slights, will get them into trouble. Under afflictions there are calculating tendencies to achieve power at any cost without respect for the feelings of others. Liability to slander is indicated. An insane fear of losing possessions and money may turn them miserly, even denying themselves all the comfort they could have. They have little feelings for themselves and none for others.

218 ☽ (♒) When well aspected, it gives a very vivid imagination and well developed intuition. Great self control, a sense of duty and responsibility make this person a loyal and efficient employee. Abundance of energy, charm and idealism, together with dignity and poise will always bring practical solutions to any problem. Friends are made easily. Personal relationships must also be based on being great friends to gain happiness. There is an interest in humanity and in human nature. Flashes of knowledge of deeper meaning and future events may emerge. There is a desire to be friendly to all. A personal desire for freedom and unusual friendships is pursuit while an interest in group activities is used for the betterment of man kind. However, the person has to be careful with drinks and drugs, as the self-control is weak. An unfavorable ☽ brings stubbornness, a strong opinion and a strong need for freedom, which may cause friction. The person is very sensitive to personal involvement and displays fear of being curbed of personal freedom, which may result in isolation.

219 (♓) A blind trust in others, based on insecurity, may lead to frustration and loss. There is a desire to perform under one's own terms without the push and demand of others. A willingness to be of service, when coupled with pleasant working conditions, may lead to a job in the social welfare system, or a nursing position. The health depends on a happy and content emotional wellbeing that, once disturbed, will lead to chronic ill-health. The person has a supersensitive nature that absorbs emotions of others. There is emotional vulnerability and a display of frequent withdrawals into seclusion. A vivid imagination, which if used constructively, supports the arts, music and any other artistic endeavor. The emotions may easily be tied to others, thus, having trouble letting go of others due to a feeling of dependency. Guilt may result from undesired complications. Afflictions may bring super sensitivity, easily hurt feelings or could develop into a persecution complex. Neurotic tendencies can interfere with daily tasks. Irrational dominance, as well as excessive shyness, may bring a desire to act in a hidden and secret manner. A disposition to indolence, self-pity, vacillation and faint heartedness may lead to sorrow. Great sensitivity may result in enjoying pompous behavior.

☽ IN ASPECT WITH OTHER PLANETS

220 ☽ ☌ ☉ This position may deplete the vitality and render the health fragile throughout life. If of weak character the person may become dispirited and suffer from melancholia every time there is a full moon.

221 ☽ ☌ ☿ Communications are guided not by logic but by the emotions and at times, the emotions win the upper hand. Hypersensitivity to personal remarks, criticism and attacks, may leave the person emotionally drained. An interest in domestic affairs, especially in food and health products, may lead to an occupation in that field. A good memory and well articulated speech may influence people and support success. If this conjunction is afflicted, the mind becomes very changeable and abrupt.

222 ☽ ☌ ♀ The emotions are attracted by artistic fields and beauty. Talent in the arts may manifest and be used for involvement in the

clothing or food industry, decorating business and all kind of domestic interests. The personality is charming, sensitive, tactful, affectionate, kind and sympathetic. A good ☽ promises success and love in relationships. Negatively, it tends to promote self-indulgence and could subject the feelings to be abused by others. In a man's horoscope a well aspected ☽ indicates the forming of a happy marriage. However, in a woman's chart the emphasis is upon the health. For both sexes it indicates love of pleasure, music and art. Depending on the ☽ position, the finances may be fluctuating.

223 ☽ ☌ ♂ The feelings are subject to outburst of anger and prone to temper tantrums. Jealousy, anger, emotional frustration and great intensity may make any cooperation difficult. If ♂ is strong and negatively afflicted, this person can make dangerous and vindictive enemies, as the emotions are bound to boil over and get out of control. If common sense does not get the upper hand the person may suffer from runaway emotions that will create havoc in life. This conjunction may strengthen the health and could attract a domineering partner. If ♏ is involved toward this aspect, the sexual desires may turn abnormal. The person is mostly restless and unsettled and may resort to physical battle.

224 ☽ ☌ ♃ Good luck, sympathy and generosity, as well as good karma may be attracted by exceptional deeds. Optimistic, trustworthy and generous, there is a desire to help others. A major affliction to this aspect brings waste, self-indulgence and pompous behavior. A good aspect provides good health and a strong emotional attachment to family and friends. It provides for popularity.

225 ☽ ☌ ♄ The emotions are tied to the material world. The more the better is the motto. The personality is rather somber and at times suffers from emotional depression and melancholia and is unwilling to use any energy. Common sense, great concentration, practicality and self-discipline, together with hard work, may get the person to reach the goal. This conjunction may create health problems in a woman's chart, especially where the digestion is concerned. In a man's chart, if afflicted by transit or progress, it may result in the death of the marriage partner.

226 ☽ ☌ ♅ The emotions create original imaginations and erratic impulses as well as mood swings that lead to erratic actions. An affliction hereto will foster erratic, cranky, irritable and unreliable behavior, bringing havoc and loss in its wake. A craving for the uncommon, the unusual, for adventure and excitement, may lead to extremes. Emotional attachments will undergo sudden and inexplicit changes. Secret affairs could have disastrous results. Health problems occur when transits trigger this aspect.

227 ☽ ☌ ♆ The emotions are very sensitive and will easily absorb the emotional state of others. Fantasies should be kept separate from facts or the mind will drift into a dreamland. A vivid imagination may be used for musical and artistic abilities. Upon affliction, the mind builds castles in the air to escape reality. A positive aspect supports religious and spiritual inclinations.

228 ☽ ☌ ♇ The emotions are ruled by the desire to dominate others. An interest in death, and life after death, may become a subject of study. Fearless behavior is displayed. An attempt is made to make drastic changes in their lives. Abrupt behavior towards family and friends may force sudden changes or will alienate others through brusque and overbearing behavior.

229 ☽ * ☉ Good harmony and established friendships with the opposite sex, for harmonious family relations and marriage, is indicated. The basic constitution is strengthened and harmonious emotions promote success in life.

230 ☽ * ☿ A receptive mind and a good memory support success in life, especially in literary circles and all occupations requiring communications. On the negative side, there could be a tendency to change the mind unexpectedly, hence rendering the person somewhat unreliable.

231 ☽ * ♀ The home life, family, marriage and relationships will be happy and successful. Displaying a certain grace and sweetness as well as an excellent housekeeping ability, renders the person affectionate. Close ties are kept with loved ones. Abundance of charm brings general popularity. For a man, it is a signification of a happy marriage. In a woman's chart, it primarily operates upon the health, but also provides love of art and pleasure. This position

makes the person very kind, affectionate and attractive to the opposite sex.

232 ☽ * ♂ An abundance of energy and self-determination is used to carry action to completion and succeed. Able to fight if necessary, there is a strong persistence. This aspect strengthens the health and helps overcome illness. The power of endurance is increased, allowing the person to survive hardships and setbacks much easier than a person without this aspect would manage. The combination of emotions and actions give a tendency to engage in rash acts, but under favorable conditions, this will render the person resourceful and able to overcome adversary.

233 ☽ * ♃ There is generosity and a display of sympathy for others, especially for the family. Money is spent on comfort and pleasure. The person is devout and idealistic in religious matters. Being optimistic, cheerful and friendly will support success and financial rewards. Business may involve the home, real estate or anything related to food and may be carried out from the home. Honesty, fairness and friendliness guarantee popularity. A strong mind and the ability to heal the sick are derived from this aspect.

234 ☽ * ♄ Endurance, patience, resourcefulness and practicality in professional matters, together with good organi,ation, integrity and frugality, support a well run enterprise. Keeping financial and other matters well organi,ed will assure a steady climb. However, often the mind tends to be too stern and too disciplined. The general outlook of life may seem rather depressing. Self-reliance, tactful and diplomatic dealings with others support a trustworthy, responsible and honorable position in life. A slow but steady persistence will, eventually, achieve the goal set out.

235 ☽ * ♅ The emotional responses are vivid and quick, the instinct knows how to take charge of new opportunities. The imagination may be well developed. Great opportunities may be presented with the help of women. A good rapport with friends, groups and organi,ations, can be achieved. The mind tends to be independent and is attracted to the study of astrology, There is an interest in clandestine love affairs or an unconventional union.

236 ☽ * ♆ If very well aspected, the person may develop psychic abilities. An interest in the occult and a highly charged imagination could lead to work in television and film. The mind works especially on an unconscious level and, at times, displays severe emotional sensitivity which will have an affect upon the family ties. Depending on the development of the soul, religious or occult interest may be pursued.

237 ☽ * ♇ The emotions and imaginations are guided by a strong will that is applied to improve life. Old habits or things are parted with and a move onto a clearer future is attempted by removing obstacles lying in the path.

238 ☽ □ ☉ A conflict between the conscious and the unconscious will restrict the self-expression, causing emotional insecurity. The mood is changeable, the person is procrastinating and, at times, very unreliable. Difficulties with women and persons in authority, is indicated. The hyper-sensitivity displayed, especially towards women, is affecting the cooperation and brings misunderstandings.

239 ☽ □ ☿ The mind is preoccupied with the past, hence is interfering with the logic and reasoning process. Narrow-mindedness and a constant nervousness affect the emotions. Focusing on trivialities leads to incessant talking. Communications are muddled and create misunderstandings. The memory and mental stability may lack direction. A liability to hysteria, excessive worry and lack of attention, results in errors of judgment.

240 ☽ □ ♀ Financial and social problems are created by being too trusting of others and by unwise financial and sexual involvement. Marriage may be troubled or delayed. Unhappiness and emotional stress may be manipulated for gain by others. For a man it indicates the destruction of domestic happiness by the wife. For a woman it indicates health problems, public scandals, slander and problems related to inconsistent emotions.

241 ☽ □ ♂ The emotions are ready to burst. The temper is domineering and uncontrolled. Jumping to conclusions and a display of emotional outbursts create grief. A desire for total independence resents any interference. Disagreements with others, especially with the family, cause emotional turmoil and unhappiness.

Uncontrolled emotions and a display of aggressiveness interfere with relationships and work. Men will be very forceful towards women. Alcoholism, rash and uncontrolled speech, and physical acts may lead to personal undoing. If the anger is suppressed physical disorders could result. Foolishness and the use of physical force may disturb relationships. The person may resort to lies to cover emotional hurts. Impulsively formed relationships are not of long duration and will be upsetting. Patience and endurance will be severely tested and could result in unwise action.

242 ☽ □ ♃ Too much generosity and desire to help others may deplete finances. This could lead to emotional disappointments when the reali,ation sets in that one has just been used. To avoid any emotional excess there is a need to learn discrimination. Otherwise constant disappointments will follow. The attitude can sway between over-optimism to fanaticism and emotional extremism, which needs to be balanced. Wanderlust and boredom may need constant satisfaction. Either la,iness or excessive activity will confuse any goal. Misfortunes in foreign lands or with foreigners is possible. Trouble through litigation, indecision or lack of forethought, may be encountered. Disagreements with the mother are common. For a woman this aspect produces ill health, especially to the digestive track and the liver.

243 ☽ □ ♄ Unhappiness, worry, melancholia and the lack of vitality can block a positive outlook in life. Depression may render the person unable to respond to life in a positive way. Seeking isolation could eventually turn into loneliness. Somehow the past stands in the way of attending to the future. Optimism and faith need encouraging. Men feel uneasy in the company of women. Money obtained may disappear again. At an extreme, this person may resort to battery, selfishness, be unscrupulous and ignorant to the feelings of others. ♄, the gatekeeper of karma, may hold the person down until the lesson of relating to others is learned. In a man's chart it may indicate the death or disappearance of the marriage partner. A woman will experience health problems. Many delays will be experienced before progress can be made.

244 ☽ □ ♅ The imagination is strong but the emotions are subject to sudden changes in mood. A relentless search for adventure may lead a person to suddenly abandon a job or relationship in hope for more excitement. Life is ruled by unstable situations. A change of residence, of work or surroundings and touchy feelings will be upsetting, creating hurt and confusion. This results from erratic changes and over-sensitivity. When intolerant of others, personal relationships will suffer and co-operation becomes very difficult. Possible secret affairs could result in break ups.

245 ☽ □ ♆ The mind is immersed in fantasy to the point of ignoring any reality. Life may be disorgani,ed, muddled and dirty. Addiction to drugs, alcohol or sex are possible. In extreme cases delusion may set in which could lead to institutionali,ation. Relying heavily on others to always help them through problems and difficulties, the person desires to obtain personal advantages out of the situation. Deception may be practiced or experienced.

246 ☽ □ ♇ A desire for affection and dominance is intensified and makes others feel uneasy. The mind is abrupt, detests interference and sometimes rejects material things. Trivialities, petty details and delving on unimportant things may stand in the way of achievement. Relationships may be forced rather then entered into by agreement of all involved. Associations, especially with females, may come into the life and after a while pass out of it, and in many instances, will never be resumed. The feelings are hurt but need to understand that a condition of permanency cannot be obtained by a one sided desire.

247 ☽ ▲ ☉ Favors from society, general success and health, as well as financial rewards, are supplied if this aspect is not diminished by other negative aspects. Harmony in emotional responses and good recuperative powers are indicated. Good optimism, self-confidence and grace help attract the opposite sex and provide for a content family life.

248 ☽ ▲ ☿ The memory is strong and sharp. Well delivered communications and good business sense will help with success. A talent for languages is given as well as a fondness of travel.

249 ☽ ▲ ♀ Increased feminine virtues, such as beauty, charm and affection, together with artistic and musical abilities, bestow harmony and luck onto the person. All work related to home and food is favored and may result in a prosperous business. This aspect makes for a happy marriage, great attraction to the opposite sex and any engagement in pleasure. Finances will be obtained from business or relationships or marriage partner but if there is any affliction to this aspect, the finances may fluctuate throughout life.

250 ☽ ▲ ♂ The physical energy level is high. Engagement in business is prosperous and pursued to completion. If the strong feelings are kept under control, the person is able to go far. If needed, the person will fight for what is right and is able to apply the will to overcome any obstacle.

251 ☽▲ ♃ There is an emotional interest in religion, in the development of the spirit and a helpful attitude is kept towards others. Devoted to their families, partner and children, the person has the ability to create harmony and wealth.

252 ☽ ▲ ♄ Conservative and honest with a lot of common sense, combined with good organi,ational abilities, bestow a great business sense or make for a well sought after employee. Real estate matters are especially favored. The desire to perform with great responsibilities and integrity may, at times, make the person seem cold and aloof, however, the interest to perform well and the ability to be self-disciplined serve the person well.

253 ☽ ▲ ♅ New original inventions, coupled with a desire for enterprises and supported by sheer energy and determination, bring achievements of an unusual kind. The conditions are rather unusual and favor studies in astrology.

254 ☽▲ ♆ A good positioned ♆, free of any bad influences, renders the person extremely mediumistic and gives psychic abilities. Intuitions that guide the mind may be able to deal with psychic phenomena's and the unseen, or make connection with the deceased. Otherwise, hypersensitivity, exceptional artistic talents, dreaming and engaging in fantasies, may come under this influence.

255 ☽ ▲ ♇ The emotions are intense and powerful. Guided by the power of ♇ great courage, determination and endurance may be possible to overcome any obstacle.

256 ☽ ☍ ☉ The conflict between the will and the feelings creates stress, especially in relationships, domestic and financial affairs. A strong restlessness, nervousness and even hysteria, will drain the energy and create disharmony. A bad childhood experience may prevent the person from being a good parent. These old stress factors, hate and feelings of unhappiness, interfere with the role as parent. A problem to engage in prolonged detailed and hard work could interfere with efficiency. The constant emotional tension disturbs the concentration and will power.

257 ☽ ☍ ☿ The mind is confused creating irritations when dealing with others. In order to conceal insecurity the person may talk incessantly without a specific subject in mind. Criticism may be taken too personally creating hateful reactions that will be expressed in unwise choice of words. Confused communications lead to misunderstandings.

258 ☽ ☍ ♀ The feeling of being unloved may be overwhelming. The over-sensitivity creates domestic and material problems as tendencies of self-indulgence could drain the finances. Over-indulgence in sexual matters may lead to more empty feelings. Excessive display of emotions should be curbed by learning to love and accept the self.

259 ☽ ☍ ♂ A fears temper, coupled with rash and overemotional reaction to life, will create unpopularity. Alcohol and drugs are dangerous as well as involvement in heated arguments that are triggered by alcohol consumption. Self-control is the word. Impulsiveness must be curbed as well as carelessness with money and possessions of others. Disagreements with the parents, especially with the mother, will color later relationships. Having a short attention span creates serious trouble, even to the point of getting involved in violence. Under very serious afflictions the person may have criminal inclinations.

260 ☽ ☍ ♃ Optimism and kindness are often bestowed onto the wrong person. Promising more than what can be delivered, applies. La,iness, self-indulgence and unwillingness to cooperate or

participate may create problems. A negative ♃ can put on extra weight. An emotional dependency on others, in hope for support, may become an annoyance. A denial of reality may create private or religious controversies. A need to let go of old habit pattern and to adopt a more realistic attitude, is desirable.

261 ☽ ☍ ♄ Depression, worry and stagnation force change to occur. Relationships, jobs, family affairs, are all unsatisfactory and the inability or unwillingness to see things more optimistically will create frustrations. ♄ forces the emotions to undergo changes, or even through circumstances, will enforce said changes. Cooperation, by willingly responding in a more appropriate manner, will ease this process considerably and makes it less upsetting. Social interactions should be made in a more pleasing manner and the coldness, instilled by a negative ♄, should be overcome. A dislike for authorities creates difficulties in getting along.

262 ☽ ☍ ♅ The emotions are out of control. A sudden instability, as well as constant changes of mind, create confusion and havoc with relationships and family. This unpredictability will exhaust all involved and irritability will prevent long term relationships. The mind jumps from one interest and idea to another. Constant and unplanned changes bring undesired results. Irresponsibility towards loved ones causes separation.

263 ☽ ☍ ♆ The mind and emotions are confused and unfocused. Wrong attachments cause disappointment and loss. Associations may lead into drug and alcohol dependency. Investments should be carefully scrutini,ed before entering into any deal. Being sloppy and unkempt, the domestic affairs are in disorder. The lack of initiating anything leads to procrastination and outright la,iness. Personal weakness may attract others who leach on them. This aspect may give parasitical inclinations.

264 ☽ ☍ ♇ A strong desire to control prevails that forces the will onto others. Relationships are forced onto others which creates difficulties and break ups. Disputes over money leads to quarrel, especially when females are involved. Aggressive emotions and a powerful, even bully desire to control, will bring unpopularity and loss.

TRANSITS

265 ☽ ☌ ☉ see # 70

266 ☽ ☌ ☿ Communication in the domestic sphere is increased. More visits to the home take place. Meetings, especially with women, friends, neighbors and co-workers are initiated. An increased interest in food and home products could lead to more efficiency. The health may improve if no negative aspect to this transit is in place.

267 ☽ ☌ ♀ Social activities are increased. The emotional side is happy, kind and attentive to romance. Charm is displayed, providing a serene cooperation with others. Business activities prosper and bring financial gain. New friendships will be initiated. Any affliction hereto will induce la,iness, sentimental feelings and a desire to overindulge in food and drinks, which will negatively affect the health.

268 ☽ ☌ ♂ Any rash acts, anger, temper tantrums and quarrels will interfere with relationships. The energy may be misdirected to become aggressive, thus annoying others, especially women. The emotions need to be kept under tight control or health problems will surface. Any afflictions to this transit could bring accidents or inflammatory complaints.

269 ☽ ☌ ♃ Any action in and around the residence will be beneficial. The mind is optimistic and kind. Business and financial affairs are bound to prosper under positive transits. A great time to commence pleasure and entertainment. If afflicted, however, over- indulgence and over confidence could bring undesired results.

270 ☽ ☌ ♄ Emotional and financial difficulties may surface leading to depression and all kinds of problems. The vitality is low. Personal coldness, negative expressions and lack of consideration for others create confrontations. Burdensome responsibilities will be imposed that further deplete the energy. No changes should be contemplated. Business affairs may not run to satisfaction and need extra hard work, at this time, to function. Old friendships may be renewed with women. Health problems will affect the digestion. Dealings with elders may result in arguments, loneliness and estrangements. Beware of emotional spending as it could deplete the finances.

271 ☽ ☌ ♅ Unexpected changes of moods disrupt the domestic life. Due to a craving for excitement, daily routine at home and in business maybe neglected resulting in disagreement and loss. Involvement with money belonging to others can bring sudden turns in fortune. If afflicted, accidents may occur. Sudden and unforeseen events could challenge the person. Any personal attachment may be of an illicit order. Losses by or through women is indicated.

272 ☽ ☌ ♆ The imaginations get inflamed by the emotions drawing unconscious memories and experiences. These may be disturbing and depressing hindering the mind to apply logic. An unwillingness to cope and attend to social duties, as well as day dreaming and absentmindedness, may interfere with daily affairs. This transit is only positive for hospital stays if not afflicted. Education may be delayed due to a confused mind. Contacts with peculiar persons may cause loss. Do not indulge in alcohol or drugs. Beware of self-delusion.

273 ☽ ☌ ♇ The ego is aroused. Involvement with money belonging to others may benefit or hurt the person. A strong desire for change, especially in domestic conditions or a change of residence or the death of a family member, could occur. Beware of being belligerent, coercive and bully as the emotions are subject to overwhelming, intense experiences. Jealousy and possessiveness should be curbed.

274 ☽ * ☉ see # 79

275 ☽ * ☿ Positive emotions rule the mind. Communications will increase. The mind is practical, curious and seeks mental exchange with women. This is a good time to solve problems.

276 ☽ * ♀ The mind and emotions are cheerful and balanced. Business dealings may increase the finances, especially through domestic products and real estate. For artists this is a very creative time. Increased pleasure and romance will occur. A positive time for home entertainment.

277 ☽ * ♂ An open expression of emotions and feelings, particularly with women, is displayed. Business will be promoted. The energy and emotions are used to further ambitions. Work can be performed

efficiently and with great energy, self-reliance and courage. The body shows more energy and the health is improving. Avoid any rash acts. Planning and executing with precision will bring the best results.

278 ☽ ✱ ♃ Emotional dealings with foreigners or travel with the family to foreign countries may take place. Women will show more optimism and kindness. General prosperity will increase. Financial gain may be received from the family. Inner harmony and support from others makes this period a good time for public relations.

279 ☽ ✱ ♄ Increased responsibilities in domestic affairs promote stability. Serious work or education is pursued that will steadily increase the finances and provides progress toward a goal. Help is received from women, especially from more mature authority figures. Advancement is gained through persistence, stability and serious concentration. New friends can be made who have helpful connections. Old friendships are renewed with family members.

280 ☽ ✱ ♅ Unexpected emotional joy may be experienced. New ideas or new friendships with women turn into great opportunities. While feeling restless and exited, the mind is elevated to a new level of consciousness permitting beneficial changes to occur. This is a time for advancement.

281 ☽ ✱ ♆ The feelings, the mood and all approaches to life are super sensitive. Emotional dealings with women bring deeper understanding of life. Whenever the ☽ is positive with ♆ and not afflicted, lottery winnings are possible. Artists enhance their creativity. Meetings with strangers and unusual individuals will take place. Dreams depicting future events will be experienced. A positive time to meditate.

282 ☽ ✱ ♇ A good time to improve social relationships and deeper interaction with family members. Business could be improved for higher gains. Income could be derived from the resources of others. Reliable solutions to old problems are found.

283 ☽ □ ☉ see # 88

284 ☽ □ ☿ The emotions interfere with the mental process. Lack of focus and concentration, as well as excessive talking, interfere with job efficiency. Financial resources are depleted due to lack of

concern over expenditures. Important details may be overlooked while the mind will focus on trivial matters. Contracts and agreements should not be entered into at this time. Emotional problems surface. The speech may turn sarcastic creating in harmonious situations. Traveling and new endeavors should not be started. Any correspondence should be executed with utmost care in mind. Affairs with relatives are strained.

285 ☽ □ ♀ The emotions are hypersensitive to the slightest misunderstandings. Social events will not work out to any advantage as the feelings retreat easily. Discord is created in relationships. Dealings with women will not work out well at this time. Smothering others with emotions to gain more approval and love may backfire. Business and financial problems occur due to over-sensitivity and financial extravagance. Problems are not solved but avoided, hence, creating bigger obligations in the future. Caution is needed in all dealings as the emotions are unstable and not well adjusted to handle disappointments. Over indulgence may be used to satisfy the fragile mind.

286 ☽ □ ♂ Rash acts, anger, frustration, irritability and impulsive action will create problems, especially with women. Family relations do not operate smoothly at this time. In extreme cases, severe health afflictions will be created by the emotions. Accidents could happen. Business problems surface and cause irritability and loss. Inflammatory or feverish complaints are common. This is not a good time to approach the opposite sex. Do not travel. Do not make important decisions as conflicts will arise.

287 ☽ □ ♃ Over-optimism will lead the emotions astray, which hunger for excessive approval. Emotional dependency on others, especially on women, may occur. Inertia could bring life to a halt. Unrealistic expectations may lead to disappointments. Expenditures may outstrip any income. Gain of weight or through overindulgence, will strain the health. Extreme dependency on religious beliefs may remove the mind from reality. Beware of arrogance.

288 ☽ □ ♄ Depression, extra responsibilities that require hard work, digestive problems and the ability to succeed are all afflicted during this transit. Any dealings with older, established authority figures,

especially women, create difficulties. Life seems on hold or, at the very least, on a slow down. Anticipated earnings may not materiali,e. Worry, anxiety, negative attitudes and the general state of affairs have an adverse effect on the daily life. Feelings of rejection could lead to discontent and depression. Avoid making changes. Take care of the health. Extra domestic duties may trigger resentment. Disagreements in the domestic circles or problems in the living arrangements may come up during this transit.

289 ☽ □ ♅ Erratic emotional outbursts and inter actions, especially with women or family members, affect relationships. Separation and estrangement may occur. Financial loss or even the unexpected death of a friend or family member could occur. Unanticipated changes or problems will disrupt the flow of life. The mind is too erratic to focus on necessary issues. Avoid harsh and sarcastic speech or trouble will follow.

290 ☽ □ ♆ The mind and emotions are in a state of utter confusion. Neurotic tendencies surface during this transit. Waste of money, impractical actions, uncontrolled imaginations and day dreaming, all interfere with daily responsibilities. Weird attractions to religious organi,ations and cults, or guru worship, will take hold of the mind in its search for peace and belonging. The logic may be so distorted that the mind withdraws into a private world. Deceit might be practiced or received as the mental confusion creates disorderly understandings of reality. Inferior complexes may stifle the self-expression. Food allergies may develop. Intense dreams may influence daily tasks.

291 ☽ □ ♇ A deep desire to control others surfaces thereby creating conflicts with family members, especially women. Trying to remake everyone, or the dividing of resources or expenditure on the home, will be subject to disagreements. If the ☽ is badly aspected at birth, this transit could trigger a death in the family. Sudden urges should be subjected to careful scrutiny and control as deep seated, and long standing problems, rise to the surface.

292 ☽ ▲ ○ see # 97

293 ☽ ▲ ☿ Communications and interactions with others are harmonious. There is a desire to improve domestic conditions and

personal appearance. The mind is more active, more concentrated and focused. A good time to travel and to make changes. Family affairs will do well and contacts with women will be favorable.

294 ☽ ▲ ♀ Happy and content emotions bring enjoyment of life. Social and romantic interactions, friendly relations with women and family will serve the mind well. Finances will improve. Entertainment, attachments and romance will flourish. A good time to reap success and gain.

295 ☽ ▲ ♂ A high energy level brings harmonious action and improves relationships. Ambitions are activated leading to improvement of business. Courage, confidence and emotional interactions will be beneficial. Sexual relationships will improve under this transit. Travel will be adventurous but caution against impulsive risks must be taken.

296 ☽ ▲ ♃ Harmonious emotions and co-operations in all relationships will bring progress. Financial and domestic conditions improve. A splendid time to plan a vacation. A favorable time for pregnancy, child rearing, or family interactions. Religious, social and educational institutions, as well as visits or treatment in hospitals, will be favorable. This transit may trigger the desire to engage in higher education. Spiritual uplifting may be experienced. Gains are reaped from investments, speculations or unions, if the position of the ☽ is favorable.

297 ☽ ▲ ♄ Somber and serious but stable emotions will be applied in a positive manner to responsibilities in family and business. Loyalty to others, co-operation and seeking and accepting advice from older people will all be beneficial. Any rapport with women is developing well. A good organi,ation will steadily increase the finances. The emotions are under control while the mind is realistic. Difficulties will be accepted and overcome. Opportunities through women will develop. Stability in family circles and romance will add to establish permanency.

298 ☽ ▲ ♅ The mind provides inspirations and unusual ideas. The emotions are balanced through interaction with family and friends. Interactions with women will be beneficial. A good time for pleasure and excitement. A perfect time to engage in public relations.

Unexpected income from the resources of others, such as a possible inheritance from women, may all be gainful. The residence may be changed at this time and will bring new opportunities. The mind is inventive and geared for improvement. Sudden remarkable new friendships could be entered into. Gain from investments is indicated if the ☽ has a positive natal position.

299 ☽ ▲ ♆ The emotions and imaginations work harmoniously together. Compassion and understanding is strongly emphasi,ed by this transit. Relating to women and their emotional needs furthers good relationships. Artistic talents are enhanced and expressed. If a need for hospitali,ation arises, this transit will support any treatment necessary. Dreams may point to further events.

300 ☽ ▲ ♇ The emotions and the will power are strong. Improvement of present conditions is considered and implemented. Benefits may come through the resources of others, such as insurance, taxes, winning in lawsuit or inheritance or from the spouses resources. Any business related to domestic matters and real estate will prosper. The emotions are intense, the mood is serious. Obsessive behavior should be avoided. This is a time for self-improvement.

301 ☽ ☍ ☉ see # 106.

302 ☽ ☍ ☿ Incessant talking without any substance, disagreements with family over domestic matters, and difficulties in any kind of communication occurs during this transit. Confusion, disagreements and arguments will cause strife. Gossip and confused conversations should be avoided. The mind is nervous and irritable and displays problems of concentration. There is a conflict of feelings versus reasons. The stress experienced may affect the health. Signing of any contracts or agreements should be postponed. This is not a good time to engage in travel.

303 ☽ ☍ ♀ The feelings are very sensitive. Family, romantic attachments, business and social issues cause emotional upset. Women may easily break out in tears. Hurt feelings surface and may turn into drama as the emotions do not want to see reasons. Expenditure based on emotional hurt may turn costly. Avoid disharmony. Overindulgence in food, drinks and social activities could drain

the energy and result in illness and other problems. Cooperation should not be denied.

304 ☽ ☍ ♂ Rash, ill considered acts, quarrel, anger and conflict will create confrontations with the family and relationships. Estrangements are possible due to the over-forceful nature. Sexual aggressiveness causes resentment and creates battles. Spending should be curbed before it goes out of hand. Internal tension will affect the health. Accidents could occur. Fever and inflammatory conditions surface and affect the well being.

305 ☽ ☍ ♃ Overdoing about everything should be avoided. Optimism versus pessimistic outlooks as well as financial extravagance will all lead to problems. Disagreements with women occur. Critical attitudes bring resentment. Inertia, procrastination and an attitude of let others do it, not me, bring arguments and problems. Weight will be gained due to emotional overeating. Changes of any kind should not be made during this transit. Travel should be avoided. A bad time for separation or legal affairs.

306 ☽ ☍ ♄ Indigestion, lowered energy, depression, loneliness and general ill health could develop during this transit. Family relations are strained. Responsibilities are avoided and nothing is gained except by hard work. Dealings with elders, authority and women are strained and not supportive. Domestic responsibilities seem overwhelming. Lack of self-confidence causes a strain on the emotional system. Business and financial affairs will neither be productive nor produce any gain. Governmental agencies may impose heavy restrictions that become burdensome. Disappointments bring depression and melancholia and restrict any willingness to cooperate. A death may occur in the family circles further producing a timid, fearful and depressive attitude. This transit slows the body functions and may lead to illness.

307 ☽ ☍ ♅ Unstable, erratic and disruptive family affairs develop. Unexplained changes of mood, a strong desire for personal freedom and an unwillingness to cooperate, all create severe difficulties. Fluctuations in finances, loss in investments and sudden break downs of machinery occur. Trouble over taxes or money belonging to others could lead to separation and estrangements. Strange and peculiar attractions maybe formed that will dissolve as soon as

they have outlived its purpose. Beware of accidents. This is not a good time to travel or contemplate any changes. Problems with friends, especially with women, may come up.

308 ☽ ☍ ♆ Mental confusion interferes in daily activities. The mind may be preoccupied with dreams and fantasies, thus, evading necessary responsibilities. Excessive use of alcohol and drugs will affect the mind. An untidy appearance, distortion of facts, idleness and a lack of cooperation, bring strife. Ideas may be far out, unrealistic and merely an excuse for not attending to any daily task. Money can be spent indiscriminately depleting the resources. Mental illusions may follow. Attractions to undesirable characters may lead to fraud and weird experiences.

309 ☽ ☍ ♇ The mind refuses to consider the emotions and well being of others. Confrontations, estrangements and a desire to dominate, especially in the family circle and with women, will leave an unpleasant aftermath. Enforced changes in business, residence or even the death of a family member or friend could create havoc on the emotions. Difficulties with taxes or inheritance may take a long time to resolve. A previous circle of life is coming to an end. Guilt, jealousy and possessiveness will torture the mind. Legal affairs may be prolonged and end unfavorable.

☽ PROGRESSED THROUGH THE HOUSES

In the progressed chart the ☽ aspects are only of importance and impact when they coincide with the ☉ and other mutual aspects. When the ☽ is on its own very little will manifest. The progressed ☽ passing through the various houses in the natal chart, without forming aspects to other planets, has very little value to forecast events. The progressed ☽ should be considered, not only for any aspect it forms to the ☉ and all other planets, but also be applied to Mid heaven (M) and the Ascendant. (A)

The following indications for houses and signs may be applied to the progressed ☽ to natal planets and also to the progressed planets aspecting the natal ☽.

310 HOUSE 1: Matters to do with the personality, attitude and actions thereon come to pass. It always indicates breaking up of existing

conditions, changes and possible health afflictions. Attention should be paid to the changes desired as mistakes made will affect the person negatively.

311 HOUSE 2: Matters to do with the personal finances come up. If the ☽ is in a good position with other planets, the finances will improve otherwise loss will result.

312 HOUSE 3: Matters to do with mental conditions, communications, short travel, siblings and neighbors will be activated by this position. The mode of thinking and absorbing of information will bring changes. The mind will be stimulated but may tend to be depressed or resorts to thinking very deeply. A desire to alter existing conditions or even make changes to the surrounding conditions may be desired. This position will activate, through the emotions, the relationships with family, friends and neighbors. A very bad ☽ may trigger an accident to the person, to siblings or children of close friends.

313 HOUSE 4: Matters to do with the home, domestic affairs and family are of prime concern. The restlessness experienced during progress of the ☽, especially when in ♈, may induce the person to move the residence or make changes to the home.

314 HOUSE 5: Matters to do with increased emotions, the pursuit of love affairs, pleasure, gambling, investments or children will be highlighted. The feelings should be reigned in and guarded by logic to avoid emotional and financial losses. Prudence is always required. If the ☽ is in evil aspect to other planets, the emotions will run wild and speculative matter will lead to loss.

315 HOUSE 6: Matters to do with health and work are activated by this position. Depending on the ☽ aspect, illness may result or the health may improve. Working conditions are also affected.

316 HOUSE 7: Matters to do with marriage, partnerships, association and exposure to the public are influenced when the ☽ passes through this house. Depending on the ☽ aspect these may be favorable or not. Should the ☽ be afflicted while progressing through this house no union or attachment should be formed and no lawsuit should be entered into until this effect has passed.

317 HOUSE 8: Matters to do with death, inheritance and money will come up, which have a deep and lasting effect. It could be influential in the outcome of matters related to inheritance, money from the spouse or any other money received. Good aspects bring gain and adverse aspects tend to present sorry, trouble and losses.

318 HOUSE 9: Matters to do with religion, occult, publishing, higher education, law and foreign travel or interactions with foreigners tend to occupy the mind. Sometimes higher education is pursued. With a favorable ☽ all matters will develop positively whereas a negative ☽ tends to separate and prevent any gain.

319 HOUSE 10: Matters to do with business success, honor and reputation will emerge and bring some kind of responsibility. Depending on the aspect made it will either lead to advancement or downfall and some kind of publicity, or of issues before the public that include honor and reputation, may be involved.

320 HOUSE 11: Matters to do with friendships and help or hindrance from friends to achieve hope and wishes, are foremost of importance. Under positive conditions the ☽ influence will bring new and helpful friends that greatly assist in life. Adverse aspects deny any help even if the friends want to help they are unable to do so. Care should be taken in the selection of new acquaintances.

321 HOUSE 12: Matters to do with karma, isolation, sorrow and trouble are guided by this house. The ☽ herein is, even under positive aspects, considered unfortunate. It confuses the emotions and leads to situations that negatively affect the mind and the emotions. As a house of karma, the person is forced to deal with unresolved issues of life, excessive habits that need changing and will receive results of former acts toward self and others. In other words, this house my have a boomerang effect on prior actions. Men may suffer through the acts of women.

☽ PROGRESSED TO ITS NATAL POSITION AND OTHER PLANETS

322 ☽ ☌ ☽ Any result from the natal ☽ to the progressed ☽ depends on its position at birth. If favorable it brings prosperity, a negative aspect brings misfortune. Changes in residence, occupation, relationships, traveling or habits will tend to give effect.

323 ☽ ✱ ▲ ☽ Pleasant and beneficial changes are indicated. New friends may be made and the person could come before the public and reap rewards.

324 ☽ □ ☍ ☽ Projects could end in uncertainty, indecision, unpopularity and disfavor or create other kind of loss. The health, based on emotional turmoil, will be affected.

325 ☽ ☌ ☉ An increased confidence may support changes that are presented by the ☉. Either planet may affect the residence, or environmental changes, business and personal unions. All depends on the natal aspect and current transits. Therefrom positive or negative effects will result. If an opportunity presents itself this is the perfect time to take full advantage of the situation and bring it to a fruitful conclusion. It also affects the health. The conjunction of both stars, when the ☉ is combusting the ☽, could bring liability to fever, circulatory problems and other emotional and physical illnesses. In case of a very badly affected conjunction nothing new, especially with regards to lawsuits, business ventures and new relationships, should be undertaken. It should be postponed until this progress has passed or nothing but loss will result.

326 ☽ ✱ ▲ ☉ Confidence, an increased energy level, gain from others, especially from authorities, will help any undertaking. New attachments and ventures will develop positively and favors from superiors are forthcoming. Ambitions should be pursued during this time as opportunities to improve the life are placed before the person. The emotions are happy. Joy and pleasure is given and received and friendships may be formed which increase honor and wealth. The health will be steady or even improving at this time. It is up to the person to utilize all opportunities that will be presented.

327 ☽ □ ☍ ☉ Life will be disorganized. Either the own health or that of close friends and family members, will be in decline. Great care should be placed on the health, which, if affected by worry and anxiety, will cause physical afflictions. Changes should not be made at this time. At an extreme, it may bring death into the family and social circles. Depending on other aspects, a bad direction will reach its high point and bring sorrow. Separation, by death or otherwise, may be experienced. The honor and social standing

may be affected. It is best not to get involved in any dispute, particularly with superiors, or to let the emotions get out of hand.

328 ☽ ☌ ☿ The mind is alert, receptive, methodical, logical and is supported by a good memory. All kinds of studies and mental activities will further the interests. The power of concentration is enhanced and should be applied to avoid dissipation of valuable energy.

329 ☽ * ▲ ☿ This is the best time to enhance the intellectual faculties, broaden the hori,on and engage in studies to expand the mind. All kind of communications, travel and planned changes will fare well under this influence. The stimulation of the brain will further latent talents and be fortunate. Literary undertakings will prosper if planned and executed properly. It is the will power to mentally grow that determines the outcome of this aspect.

330 ☽ □ ☍ ☿ The domestic affairs will be in disarray. Disputes will arise with family and friends that are very upsetting. Great care with words, spoken and written, should be exercised to avoid confrontations and misunderstandings. Travel should be avoided at this time. No dealings regarding contracts or agreements should be entered into. There is a possibility of libel or slanderous attacks on the reputation of the person. The mind may be on overdrive, hence, overstepping social bounds and turning indiscreet. This will reflect upon the reputation and cause opposition. The mind may distort things, apply the wrong judgment or misunderstands what others are trying to express. The mind delves in anxiety and worry and the emotions may overflow in an uncontrolled and unintended manner. Great care should be exercised before any action is taken.

331 ☽ ☌ ♀ Good fortune will come to the person. It will brighten the mind, inclined to pleasure and adventurous social connections. It may bring new attachments that produce affections by both parties. If both planets have been positive to each other at birth these attractions may turn happy and lasting. Artistic talent will bloom and the person should further any interests at this time.

332 ☽ * ▲ ♀ A clear mind, happy emotions and a desire for affection will help form successful and beneficial unions and relationships. The pleasantness of this aspect should be utili,ed to the fullest

advantage. Finances may increase dramatically and the person will prosper. The entire period, during which this progress applies, will be very satisfactory and profitable. If the natal aspect of the ☽ and ♀ are very good, this time indeed, will become memorable and full of opportunities.

333 ☽ □ ☍ ♀ Trouble in respect to the feelings and emotions is indicated. Disagreements, disappointments, separation and upsetting events will cause sorrow and anxiety. Monetary difficulties or outright losses could be experienced. If the emotions are sensitive this aspect will easily hurt and upset the feelings. Avoid any attachments and financial involvement. There may be death in the family or of a female in the social circles.

334 ☽ ☌ ♂ The desires surface to explode in rashness and uncontrolled impulses. Passions may turn to anger, jealousy, hate and extreme behaviors that may lead to accidents and ill health, especially inflammatory diseases. All relationships should be carefully scrutini,ed and travel should, if possible, be avoided all together, as accidents could occur. The emotions should be tightly controlled until this effect has passed.

335 ☽ * ▲ ♂ The person becomes courageous and adventuresome. A good time for positive change, for travel and entering into enterprises that require free-thinking and action. Affairs can be pushed to completion. If the emotions are controlled and guided and not permitted to undue over-enthusiasm and excitement, this time means positive progress.

336 ☽ □ ☍ ♂ The emotions will act very impulsively, hasty, rash and without consideration as to the outcome. Fever, inflammatory ailments, accidents or involvement in violence and crime may occur. If possible all travel should be avoided, no contracts or agreements should be entered into, and all dealings should be restricted to really trustworthy people as there is a liability for things to go wrong which will bring sorrow. Dealings with women should be avoided as the own hasty and bully attitude and subsequent behavior will be inimical, hence causing trouble. The temper must be curbed as any hasty impulses to forge ahead at all costs, without due consideration of the situation, will bring dispute and quarrels. It is necessary to be very discreet and curb all acts made by impulses

to avoid trouble and sorrow while this aspect lasts. The old saying that "haste makes waste" applies here.

337 ☽ ☌ ♃ Fortunate while it lasts, this aspect brings benefits from friends and general social circles. Improvements in opportunities, finances, and pleasurable travel are indicated. The health will improve, the mind will expand, becoming more optimistic and eager for new undertakings. This aspect should be utili,ed to its fullest to reap all available benefits.

338 ☽ * ▲ ♃ Social gain, opportunities and many benefits will bring good fortune. New undertakings will be successful and bring financial gain. The health will improve and travel will be beneficial. Investments fare well at this time as the mind is geared to throughout secure the transaction from which gain will be received. The extent of this fortunate aspect depends on the natal aspect of both planets. The better the position at birth the greater the benefits will be during progress.

339 ☽ □ ☍ ♃ Financial and social affairs will not turn out well. Expenditures should be carefully watched as they could financially deplete the resources. New acquaintances should be carefully scrutini,ed, as they may not turn out as expected. The health will suffer, especially the purity of the blood. A wrong diet and an extreme mode of living may create internal problems. Family and friends are not cooperative and no new undertakings or changes should be considered during this time. Any kind of extravagance and all legal affairs should be avoided.

340 ☽ ☌ ♄ The actions are hindered and bring depression and sorrowful experiences. Dealings with authority and elders, will not bring support but rather lack of sympathy for the person's cause. This leads to further depression. The health must be watched carefully, especially cold and chills must be avcided. It signals the beginning of changes that will affect both the health and the general conditions in life. It demands that all affairs are carefully planned prior to execution.

341 ☽ * ▲ ♄ Merits and persistence, prudent actions, trustworthiness and thriftiness will produce gains. The acceptance of responsibility and the proper execution of affairs will bring stability and improve

security. The person is very serious, persevering and frugal. Attracting faithful friendships and benefits as well as receiving help from people in authority, will increase honor and bring recognition. This aspect will produce gains when the person is already older and is fully prepared to work hard to utili,e these benefits to the fullest extent.

342 ☽ □ ☍ ♄ Domestic and financial trouble creates worries and loss. Depression and discontent with the surroundings and job will affect the daily life. Changes should not be made at this time, as the outcome would not be favorable. The general vitality is very low making it even harder to move ahead. Only after this aspect is over (about 4 months) will the power of recuperation support a gaining of vitality again. It may bring not only sorrow and grief, but also possible death into the domestic sphere. It will certainly hinder and delay any projects planned at this time. Depression and melancholia should be avoided. The finances will suffer, important affairs will not progress and anxiety will prevail. The person should not trust others and stay away from older persons or authority as much as possible, as this aspect triggers quarrel and misunderstandings with them. Carefully assess any kind of response, verbally or in writing, while this aspect last. Positive thinking and maintaining of a courageous attitude will go a long way in overcoming this unfavorable time.

343 ☽ ☌ ♅ Sudden and unforeseen changes may occur. There is a possibility that sudden attachments be formed, however, they may involve either a married person or some kind of illicit connection. As it always brings out the unpredictable behavior, great care must be taken not to make irritable, hasty or uncalled for decisions. Refrain from sarcastic speech that will be offensive to others. On a positive note original ideas and inventions may be developed. It is a time for the emotions to readjust to new conditions in life.

344 ☽ * ▲ ♅ Sudden, unexpected changes of a positive and fortunate nature will be triggered by this aspect. New, intense and remarkable friendships may be formed which bring gain. An interest in astrology may develop. The mind is full of inspirations and desires to invent and create. Changes undertaken at this time, when no

other destructive transits are in force, will bring beneficial results and will guide the future.

345 ☽ □ ☍ ♅ Sudden, unexpected changes, adverse to the interest, will occur. Removals and changes, made at this time, will give reason to regret afterwards. The mind will act in an erratic and eccentric manner causing disagreements. Attractions pursued and relationships entered into at this time are not of a long duration and may bring remorse. The speech should be well guarded as any tendency to be sarcastic or insulting will have adverse reactions. A time of caution in which obstacles must be overcome and separation occurs. Existing habits undergo changes and the mind should focus on personal improvement. If possible, no travel should be considered until this aspect has passed.

346 ☽ ☌ ♆ A peculiar state of mind may attract strange and weird people. If not careful, loss may occur when such associations are formed. Weird dreams may disturb the person. This is a time to get a grip on reality to avoid disappointments.

347 ☽ * ▲ ♆ Dreams may occur that signify some warning if the person is able to correctly analy,e such dreams. Strange individuals will come into the life and if all transits to this aspect are good, gain will be obtained through such associations. If the natal chart shows a good position between these planets musical and poetic talents will be awakened that should be nurtured and improved. This aspect also supports psychic readings as the mind is so sensitive and fine tuned that it is able to sense the feelings and emotions of others. Women appear to be helpful. Enemies are subdued. Any existing latent action that was made with the intention to discredit the person will surface, giving opportunity to defend against it. A connection with water, may be via travel or relocation near the water, may be considered.

348 ☽ □ ☍ ♆ Deception and loss will prevail if warning signs given are not considered. Dealings with others may be deceptive, fraud may be committed on the person or in the extreme, by the person. Dreams will be rather disturbing and give way to strange experiences. Most of all, common sense should prevail as the mind has trouble to distinguish between right and wrong. Undesirable people may try to get the person's confidence just to abuse it for their own gain.

Fraud and shams may occur as well as separations, estrangements and break ups that are not entirely desired by the person.

349 ☽ ☌ ♇ The emotions are more susceptible to the reaction of society. Intense feelings may be placed on relationships that, if uncontrolled, may be overbearing, leading to breakups. Do not permit the emotions to be ruled by obsession. This aspect intensifies the emotional needs, which may turn into possessiveness and jealousy. Dealings with taxes, wills and inheritance, through a female person, may emerge.

350 ☽ * ▲ ♇ The emotions will reach more depth and feelings than previously. Creative changes on the domestic front and personal side will be desired. Important new relationships will be formed which are far more emotional for both parties and may be part of a public display.

351 ☽ □ ☍ ♇ Tension, opposition, obstacles, aggressiveness and anger will boil over emotions. Hidden resentment and anger, swallowed long ago, will come up and create havoc. Some kind of emotional power struggle will take place and will be destructive for the well being. Jealousy or guilt will control the mind. Relationships with the opposite sex should be guarded or, if possible, avoided at this time. Best, avoid all emotional confrontations during the pendency of this aspect.

BABY CHART

Prepare your child for a happy childhood and content adulthood by paying attention to the vibes shared with your child, which are most important from gestation to 3 years of age.

Until the child is 3 years old it absorbs the emotions and behavior pattern of its parents. Astrology points to the behavior of the parents based on the position of planets in the child's chart. These aspects need attention in order to free the child from bad behavior learned from their parents. The choice is simple: "understand the problem and solve it", or carry on a circle of unhappiness and restrictions by passing it on to the next generation. To understand the problems that a person carries over from childhood, the baby chart should first be set up to determine the problems or advantages associated with the childhood development out of which the adult emerged.

352 ☽ ☌ ☿ The open expression of emotional feelings, which depend mostly on the emotional state of the family, is either based on a content environment or reflects nagging and complaining. The emotions mostly depend on the issues expressed by the sign in which this conjunction takes place. The mother's behavior played a big role on how the child will react later in life.

353 ☽ ☌ ♀ A strong, sometimes unbreakable bond exists with the mother. Mother will always be part of the child's life even if the mother-child relationship is not satisfactory. A female child may develop homosexual relationships in which the partner resembles mom. As the child sees mother as infallible the father is viewed more as an assessory rather than an authority figure. A male child may develop love-hate relationships with mom or cite with the father against the mother. Confusion about mom may turn a male into a homosexual as he can't deal with a woman's sexuality because of his close emotional ties to his mother. Changes can only occur if the strong bond to the mother is loosened to permit the personality and own feelings to be developed and understood. As nature teaches us, once a child is grown it needs to develop its own life.

354 ☽ ☌ ♂ The mother's hurt feelings are reflected by allowing anger and emotional upset to be expressed in a self-destructive way, which the child absorbs as normal. The child explodes or implodes their hurt feelings creating disapproval and disassociation in life. The super-sensitivity, instilled by the mother, must be understood to be channeled into physical energy.

355 ☽ ☌ ♃ Overindulgence, over confidence and reliance on feelings rather than logic may create a lack of foresight. In order to feel and experience everything, as mother tends to do, the child may not learn what consequences of action could mean. An extensive closeness to the mother may be chosen instead of developing its own life and responsibility.

356 ☽ ☌ ♄ The childhood is symboli,ed by illness or suppression and restrictions that emerge from the parents relationship. The father may suppress the mother's emotions by restricting her own

development, making her depressed, unfulfilled and unhappy. This emotional state is absorbed and adopted by the child as the norm of being. The relationship of the parents may center around providing the daily necessities without considering personal feelings. One parent is the provider the other submits to it. The emotional deprivation, as exercised by the parents, creates depression, melancholia, temper tantrum and an inability to form close relationships. Wife bashers may develop for their inability to share feelings and relate to others. Physical illness may develop due to restrictions on the flow of the body's juices, triggered by an emotional imbalance.

357 ☽ ☌ ♅ Erratic emotional responses are copied from the mother. Feelings are not expressed in a pleasing manner but rather in emotional outbursts without much differentiation between happy, angry or sad. These emotional outbursts are sudden and unpredictable and disturbing to any relationship. They may prevent happy relationships all together as the partner is worn out by the behavior. In extreme cases, these emotional outbursts create a situation of violence, as a battle of will develops. To avoid drama and destruction the feelings need to be considered, discussed and channeled into a reasonable manner before being hurled onto another person thereby creating insults and breakups. The inability to share emotions may lead to many break-ups as soon as pressure is placed on the emotions. Sharing feelings with others must be learned to overcome this aspect.

358 ☽ ☌ ♆ The relationship to the mother is clouded by confusion, illusion and her inability to relate. In the child it instills confusion about the role a woman should play in life. Strange expectations of women, and an inability to see a person in reality, creates disappointment. A child reacts more by intuitive actions than to actual reality of a situation. The perception of right and wrong is distorted. "What is the role of a woman and what is her position in society", is severely unanswered by the mother, thus leaving the child bewildered and unable to fully relate to women. The concept of love may be so distorted that the person is riddled with guilt rather than love when involved in a close relationship. The overall concept of love, sex and relationship is not functioning on a level of reality.

359 ☽ ☌ ♇ The mother's energy is manipulative and controlling by attempting to be in charge at all times. This way she will not be shocked or surprised because she makes the rules. The child absorbs this behavior and progresses into a control freak. Only by letting go will the child be able to relax and let positive energy flow to dissolve all emotional difficulties.

360 ☽ * ☿ Talent in communications is present. The mother teaches the child to express emotions, which allows for balanced relationships and provides for an ability to communicate well in business.

361 ☽ * ♀ The child finds it easy to relate to others as the mother prepared the child to love and appreciate love, art and creative expressions. However, endurance must be present for productive achievements.

362 ☽ * ♂ Emotions and actions are in harmony. The mother will teach the child to cope with emotional and sexual needs in an open and constructive manner. Relationships will be constructive and well balanced.

363 ☽ * ♃ The mother feels good about herself and provides a healthy and warm atmosphere for the child. The child will be caring in relationships and openly express its feelings.

364 ☽ * ♄ A seriousness, slowness and emotional control is instilled by the parents. Feelings and commitments are taken seriously. The person is very responsible.

365 ☽ * ♅ The mother teaches the child to be original and to deal with problems and to relate well with others.

366 ☽ * ♆ The family provides a constructive emotional environment. The mother teaches the child to respond positively to spiritual influences and growth.

367 ☽ * ♇ Emotions are shared with friends and the public. The energy absorbed from the mother flows constructively. The child has talents that need developing, which will benefit from contact with the public.

368 ☽ □ ☿ The mother does not discuss her feelings and needs. Emotions are bottled up until the pressure explodes in anger and frustration. The child will imitate such outbursts and consider them a way to express opinions or feelings. An inability to share feelings

will cause difficulties in any relationship. Communications with the mother are restraint. Peace and harmony will not be easily achieved. Sensitivity and expression of feelings must be understood to achieve any emotional security.

369 ☽ □ ♀ Bottled up feelings of resentment exist to playing the role of motherhood. Inferior feelings of being a woman are instilled. The mother expresses an inability to create a loving bond with the child, as she may not want any children. A male child may develop a dislike for women as his ability to love and care is smothered by his mother's dislike of herself.

370 ☽ □ ♂ The energy is not expressed constructively but ruled by emotions. Sexual relationships may not be emotional fulfilling as they may be tainted with roughness or violence. The mother expressed an emotional lack of fulfillment, of unhappiness, or is subjected to violence. She is easily angered and has suppressed stress and tension until it rises to the surface and explodes. Health problems will manifest from the tension retained in the system. The child absorbs this pattern and gets involved in physical relationships, which could be subject to violence. These relationships do not offer any emotional gratification.

371 ☽ □ ♃ The mother's inability to relate to herself and her own needs reflect on the child in that the child will not express emotions, but angers easily and neglects the self. Not considering desires and needs will lead to frustration, lack of affection or overindulgence to the point of mental and physical exhaustion. A lack of emotional needs and display of affection will result in rejections, which may be acted out through excessive sexual desires. Responsibility for the self must be developed. Overindulgence on food and drinks will lead to excess weight and health problems. Over or under relating must be controlled to permit healthy relationships.

372 ☽ □ ♄ The father has thwarted the mother's personal expression by restriction, limitation and by controlling her desires and feelings. The mother's resentment towards the father instills in the child a lack of trust to show emotions. As an adult emotions are shared hesitantly just to take them back when the feelings are hurt. This withdrawal complex will hinder the forming of a happy relationship,

as neither party is sure of the other's emotional involvement. A female child will accept that all men are restrictive and controlling, thus seeking a partner who plays out daddy's control. The result will be resentment, depression, bitterness and internal loneliness. The pattern of the parents must be discarded to allow joy to enter life and nurture the soul. Especially a female child should nurture her feminine side in order to blossom.

373 ☽ □ ♅ The eccentric mother reacts abruptly, brusque and ends relationships or jobs or friendships suddenly, at times without apparent reason. Not being sure in any involvement will prevent stable and consuming relationships. Everything may end abruptly leaving others in a state of shock. Facing situations that are unpleasant and that hurt must be learned so that the situation can be resolved rather than deserted. A crisis needs a resolution not a flight of abandonment in order to develop compassion, understanding and growth.

374 ☽ □ ♆ Mother's actions towards the child foster delusion. The child may perceive the mother as other than what she is. Secret and hidden acts by the mother, later surfacing, will change the child's perception as to who mother really is. The concept of the role of the father may be clouded by the mother's behavior. The child perceives misunderstandings as normal and later carries on this belief into its own family life.

375 ☽ □ ♇ The mother is manipulating the Universe. She is in control of everything and everyone. The child adopts such a behavior and becomes obsessed with people. Especially love relationships may experience rejection instead of understanding. Helping people may be tainted by expectations of return so that friends have to be eternally grateful. The child needs to overcome its insecurity and establish a sense of self-worth to break this pattern.

376 ☽ ▲ ☿ The mother enjoys relating to the child and will communicate her feelings in a constructive manner. Social grace, sharing of feelings and creativity will be instilled in the child. There may or may not be a close relationship to the father as the main influence of this aspect comes from the mother.

377 ☽ ▲ ♀ The mother bestows affection and emotional awareness and warmth on the child.

378 ☽ ▲ ♂ The mother's influence on the child creates a happy and emotionally balanced individual. The emotional and sexual needs are positively expressed creating supportive and helpful relationships.

379 ☽ ▲ ♃ Warmth, affection, energy and generosity are showered onto the child, by the mother.

380 ☽ ▲ ♄ Slowness, seriousness, steadiness and responsibility are instilled in the child.

381 ☽ ▲ ♅ The mother teaches solutions to problems, dealing with responsibility and fosters the child's emotional development. Original ideas are promoted to create positive energy.

382 ☽ ▲ ♆ A need to be creative, to learn meditation and spiritual growth emanates from the mother to the child. However, spiritual growth should not replace a healthy life and development and should not be adopted to the point of relying on God rather than on oneself.

383 ☽ ▲ ♇ A warm, open and cooperative emotional outlook exists during early childhood. Cooperation with society and social issues, that service the masses, will be beneficial.

384 ☽ ☍ ☿ Difficulties to express and communicate emotions, as well as difficulties to share emotions, exist as the mother has never expressed her own emotions. Bottled up feelings will explode in anger and cause resentment as communicating and listening are not experienced in childhood.

385 ☽ ☍ ♀ The absence of the mother, in the early years after birth, may have left a void in emotional love expressions to the child. A sense of abandonment will instill in the child creating fear of commitment and lack of emotional satisfaction. In later life the person will either suppress emotions or become the underdog in relationships or at an extreme, revert to homosexuality to avoid the male/female confrontation.

386 ☽ ☍ ♂ The mother has difficulties to express her sexual and emotional needs and is torn between a profession and being a mother. This smoldering dissatisfaction may be expressed by emotional outbursts. Her emotions so overrule logic that she attempts ill-planned events that lead to failure and further

dissatisfaction. The child, however, perceives this behavior as normal. When growing up it creates conflict between a relationship and a job, sex or love, all leading to dissatisfaction and separation. Anger and emotional satisfaction need to be understood and positively channeled into energy, or the emotional over-sensitivity will ,ap all energy, leading to a wasteful existence.

387 ☽ ☍ ♃ Tension in relationships, due to suppressed emotional responses, are adopted from the mother's behavior leading to strife, overindulgence in food, alcohol and neglect of body and soul. Relationships may be formed without any idea or consideration how to sustain it, without any plans for the future and without sharing emotions. The child will grow up suppressing the emotional side creating internal pressure and unhappiness.

388 ☽ ☍ ♄ There may be a loss of one or both parents in early life or communication of emotions are cold and receive no response from the parents. The father is extremely restrictive, suppressing any open display of emotions. Thus creating a sense of loneliness and despair. Feeling happy and at ease may be perceived by guilt, leading to suppression of open display of love and affection. A need to establish a self-worth is necessary. A relationship needs mutual sharing to be positive and functional.

389 ☽ ☍ ♅ The mother's eccentric behavior of willfulness and erratic display of emotions is adopted by the child. The mother may not stay long in any place, job, or relationship and abruptly walks out when her feelings are hurt as she is unable to discuss her reasons. Emotional hysteria may override a logical conclusion creating an unwillingness to compromise.

390 ☽ ☍ ♆ A veil of delusion or illusion clouds the understanding of who "mother" really is. Being mentally dependent on mother may lead to a constant comparison of women to mother with none good enough to match her. A woman may be disappointed of her man when he turns out different to her expectations. A determination of personality must be made to avoid becoming a blind follower of some guru worship and be taken in for lack of believing in the self.

391 ☽☍ ♇ Mother keeps a controlling grip on everyone. Spontaneity and happiness are disturbed by extreme willpower and

manipulations that smother everyone. Loss of control will create emotional chaos. The child adopts this obsessive need and either alienates himself from others, or draws relationships repeating this pattern until a change is made.

☽ TRANSIT OR PROGRESSION TO A (Ascendant)

392 ☽ ☌ A The emotions are closely tied to the general health. An involvement in public affairs is possible. This may indicate the birth of a daughter.

393 ☽ ∗ A The emotions are balanced. For a man it indicates harmonious relationships. For a women it provides good health. Relationships will be harmonious and helpful. Gain through friends is indicated.

394 ☽ □ A Difficulties in self-expression will be experienced as the emotions are unbalanced, thus creating problems in work and private relationships. The mind vacillates and delays or hinders any decisive decisions. This will affect the health creating illness, especially through tumors that may develop into cancer. As conflicts arise, it pays to wait for any important decision until this transit has passed.

395 ☽ ▲ A refer to # 393

396 ☽ ☍ A refer to # 394

☽ TRANSIT OR PROGRESSION TO M (Mid heaven)

397 ☽ ☌ M Popularity may be received and leads to fame in the public eye. Progress and success through women may influence the life. The social standing could be elevated. The career chosen may be connected with a family business. Domestic success could be achieved. Real estate and business connected to food and home issues will develop well. If not negatively affected by other aspects, this will lead to public popularity. If afflicted shyness, worries and fears stifle the emotions.

398 ☽ ∗ M Harmonious relationships may be formed which help increase the honor and popularity. Cooperation will be received.

399 ☽ □ M Emotional problems hinder any fulfillment, especially when related to honor, reputation and business. Scandal is possible. The public does not receive the person well. Domestic affairs may be disorderly. Problems with women, or the death of a woman, may

occur under this aspect. During transit attend to any domestic affairs and stay close to your family.

400 ☽ ▲ M Professional success and favors by the public and authority may further any goal.

401 ☽ ☍ M refer to # 399.

38

☿ Mercury

This planet rules the mind, the thinking process, the education and mental development. Its focus is directed to all kinds of communications, whether by writing, phone or otherwise. Short trips may involve business and/or family members, neighbors and friends. This planet, when retrograde, puts on hold activities which began in the retro phase. Such undertakings may terminate prior to completion or do not develop as originally planned. Important events should not be started before ☿ returns to its forward motion, at which time, the planet will support any undertakings. Any transit through a house is completed within less than 30 days with the exception, whenever the planet is retrograde and intensified, before continuing forward again. The transit will affect any logical thinking and communications as well as written agreements.

☿ IN THE HOUSES

402 ☿ (1) There is an intellectual outlook in life that absorbs everything. Logic and reasoning are foremost applied. A strong intelligence is provided and the person is very talkative. An intense desire to express themselves in speech and written communications is prevalent. The mental will power is strong and may be utilized in occupations such as writer, doctor, researcher, teacher, librarian, secretary or any job involving communications.

403 ☿ (2) Business and money affairs predominate and money is obtained via communications, publishing, broadcasting, teaching etc. Money making endeavors are carefully planned and executed. Any occupation related to organizing, planning and careful execution is suitable. If negatively aspected, financial deals turn sour as the mind maybe mislead by others.

404 ☿ (3) Intellectual ability and an interest in all kinds of communications is indicated. Writers and speakers fair well under this position. Short distant travel for purpose of teaching, speaking, as well as an involvement in telephone and other communications, are predominant. If the planet receives negative aspects, an indiscrete speech, false, erroneous or distorted information is expressed and difficulties through contracts, promises and agreements will be experienced.

405 ☿ (4) Education, communication or work from home in these fields is possible. The person likes to collect things and hangs on to family history. An interest or work in real estate or earth related occupation is indicated. If afflicted, changeable conditions in the home may lead to disputes and disagreements.

406 ☿ (5) Artistic and creative work related to writing and all kinds of communication, as well as an ability to be forceful and dramatic in communications, is instilled by this aspect. If well aspected, gambling, investments, or jobs in that field, will perform well and the education of children is important. Mental excitement and stimulation is expected from any romantic partner. If afflicted do not gamble, speculate or blindly trust others. Being critical towards others should be avoided.

407 ☿ (6) A love for detailed work exists, especially if related to any kind of communications. As this is the house of health, jobs in the medical and hospital field may fair well. A thriving for perfectionism which, if carried too far, can cause a mental break down. If afflicted, mental ill health, preoccupation with trivial details, and an overly critical nature may result.

408 ☿ (7) The person engages in mental activities and communications with the partner or the public. There is a talent for sales, public

relations, arbitration, law and all work involving written and verbal communication. Concern is expressed about how others perceive and think about them. A preference exists for well educated and intelligent partners. If afflicted, problems with communications, misunderstandings, clashing of opinions and with contracts and agreements, will occur. If there is a connection to the 6th house marriage may take place with a co-worker.

409 ☿ (8) The interest centers on money belonging to others, such as insurance, inheritance, partners money, or corporate finances. Work may be related to these subjects. Secret actions for personal gain may be initiated. A love of mystery and intrigue is apparent. Possible travel, associated with death or secrecy, may be connected with an inheritance. The nervous system is subject to diseases, grudges, vindictive behavior and revenge, all may prevail if negative influences are present.

410 ☿ (9) There is an interest in higher education, foreign travel, philosophy and law. The person is concerned with attitudes, facts and desires a constant upgrading of their own education. Great interest is expressed in foreign cultures and religion but if negative, guru worship, pride, snobbery, and dogmatic beliefs, may alienate them from others.

411 ☿ (10) The pursuit of professional ambitions, success in business and increase of intelligence and knowledge, is a prime motivator. There is a desire to seek prestige, a lucrative career in any field of communications with people of power and leadership. A governmental job in a higher position, with executive power and the ability to communicate well, is also indicated. If afflicted, however, scheming, plotting, selfishness and dishonesty, where ambitions override moral principles, is possible. If negative to ♄ a rise in power will be followed by a severe downfall.

412 ☿ (11) Engagement in communications with friends and groups for mental challenges is provided. The mind is original, objective and constantly produces new ideas, especially with investigation, astrology, philosophy and interest in humanitarian improvement. If afflicted, the person may be eccentric, unreliable, impractical and may use friends for any personal advantage.

413 ☿ (12) Habits, as well as unconscious memories rule the mind. Feelings rule decisions rather than logical thinking. The person is secretive and provides little expression about feelings and thoughts. The person is rather shy or unresponsive to intellectual challenges of others. The mind works fast and the imagination is constantly active, at times depriving the mind of needed rest. If afflicted, neurotic tendencies, mental illness or indulging in the past may preoccupy the mind. Learning difficulties and problems remembering learned knowledge may interfere with the ability to be precise.

☿ IN THE SIGNS

414 ☿ (♈) The person possesses decisive and impulsive thinking and enjoys debates and arguments. The mind works fast and produces quick and sometimes original ideas. The personal view can be somewhat narrow-minded. Tendencies to impatience, egotistical and headstrong attitudes may exist. This leads the mind to act before thinking the matter through which results in frustration and backlash for hasty and inaccurate decisions. Sometimes an idea is abandoned before it is acted out. Irritability and quick temper are trades that follow an afflicted ☿.

415 ☿ (♉) Practical, material and financial considerations are foremost on the mind. Originality and common sense allows for making shrewd decisions that provide for good management ability. The mind works slow but persistent. Once the mind is made up it takes great efforts to change the decision reached. Arguments and disharmony are disliked but will be imposed to protect financial interest and security. By restricting the attitude, that only the big things are of interest, small matters will be ignored and important things may be overlooked. Great stubbornness is ruling the mind. On the negative side, there may be intellectual obstinacy, overblown opinions, avarice and extreme materialism.

416 ☿ (♊) The desire to rule on a mental level with logic and an application of the intellect is extremely high and well applied. The person is interested in facts, unbiased opinions and has an ability to seek the truth, which is apparent with a well situated ☿. Good

education is a must. The ability to write and communicate well is supported by this position. The mind is constantly on overdrive by absorbing external stimuli, which can put pressure on the highly sensitive nervous system. Any over stimulation of the mind could lead to fatigue, confusion, irritability and a stressed emotional system. Periods of solitude are required. The practice of meditation is a good source of relaxation. The mind is very curious but is involved in so many projects that focusing on a particular matter becomes difficult. It negates the intellectual ability away from a positive decision. Confusion is created when the mind undergoes constant changes in opinion and points of view, resulting in being fickle rather than precise. Mental originality is present as indicated by a positive ☿. Jobs involving speech and writing or generally any kind of communication is favored by this aspect. Any negative influence could lead to incessant talking which becomes an annoyance to others.

417 ☿ (♋) The emotions rule the mind. Unconscious desires will interfere with logical thinking leading to decisions that are devoid of facts. The memory may be clouded by emotions overlooking the actual facts. Attitudes and opinions of others will, at times, be blindly adopted for sake of being accepted by others. The personality is very sensitive and easily hurt. Harmony in family and home is essential to the well being while jobs related to the ☽ (food, real estate, consumer goods, home products) are avenues of satisfaction.

418 ☿ (♌) The will is strong and, at times, overbearing. Good concentration is given as well as a good problem solving ability. A position of authority is desired. Speech and behavior tend to be dramatized for attention, but if carried too far, arrogance will alienate others. The desire for the big and mighty may distract from the small details that may catch the worm, if applied properly. The mind may overlook and refuse to consider the immediate focus on interesting matters that would change the overall outcome, had it been considered properly. Opinions are formed slowly and not easily changed. The ability of teaching others, as well as good planning, is indicated. Work may be connected to travel while artistic and money making endeavors are favored.

419 ☿ (♍) The mind is analytical with great practicality, able to make decisions that are thought through. Sometimes, however, considerations of trivial matters, when blown out of proportion, delay urgent decisions. Organized and efficient, orderly surroundings at work are a must. This aspect is great for research work and specialized job skills related to communications. If work is done behind the scene the person may be shy and retiring from the public to a certain extent. Detailed work is very suitable.

420 ☿ (♎) The mind will concentrate on human relations, psychology, the law and rules of society. An interest in the thinking and motivation of others makes for a good psychologist, astrologer, public relations officer, lawyer or judge. Mental partnerships with others will be profitable. There is a great ability to consider all aspects first before making a decision. However, if negative, these desires may lead to indecisiveness, loss of opportunity and impatience. Mental stimulation is received from others, which are being judged by their personal appearance and mannerism. Coarse speech and inappropriate dress appearance are off putting. A demand is made for a high degree of mental discipline from others. In extreme cases the person will agree with others for the sake of popularity and acceptance.

421 ☿ (♏) There is an interest to delve into the intuitive mind of others. Critical attitudes and using sharp language, will at times, be insulting to others rather than bring the desired result. They say it as they feel it. The person loves to act in secret and communicates only the necessary information. Strong emotions may lead to plotting, scheming and ulterior motive in order to gain an advantage over others. However, strong determination is also a trait of this sign. Detectives, researchers, or investigators are ideal occupations. If negative, the mind is preoccupied with sex, is mistrustful of others, and the person has either secret affairs or acts in secret.

422 ☿ (♐) All contact with foreigners, foreign lands, society, religion, philosophy, law and higher education, as well as social motivations, are considered. However, if the mind is overloaded it can lose track of facts and adopt strange attitudes. Illogical thoughts can undermine any undertaking. The person may get involved in prophecy and be influential in mass karma and destiny. The speech

is direct and a strong demand is made for personal freedom. Hypocrisy may develop when the moral standard is below their preaching and is ruled solely by attitude. Because there is a desire to adjust to the opinion of the popular social norm, there may not be realization that the general attitude may not be the prevailing truth. Places of social control attract such as Churches, Universities and Government to achieve intellectual authority. When negative, the person may conform to corruption or other means of winning the game while expecting from others to adhere to the truth without considering the truth of their own opinion. Lofty goals and ideals can take precedent over real facts and situations.

423 ☿ (♑) The mind is ruled by ambition, shrewdness, practicality and is organized and interested in the gain of material resources. A good concentration is indicated. The person will follow up but may not be very original in the thoughts applied but rather follows a trend of good education and joins business or science to reach financial and social status. Conservative and realistic, there may be a lack of humor. At times, the mind is too stern and serious. If carried too far this will be used to attain a goal without regards to any values. Money may become the one and only goal overriding values and all other considerations.

424 ☿ (♒) The mind is open to the new and unusual, is truthful, unbiased, objective, and always seeks originality. Bestowed with the ability to see beyond the present state of society and eager to explore the beyond of today's knowledge, any new adventure and unexplored issues, are of interest. A great ability to be telepathic is present. An interest in humanitarian issues is pursued rather than blindly running after the money. This is an excellent ability for the study of astrology and involvement in occult. The person seeks mental stimulation through groups and friendships.

425 ☿ (♓) Vivid imaginations and photographic abilities to recall memories, is given. The mind is able to be active on the unconscious level of thinking, thus, bestowing intuitive acts, as well as the ability to absorb the thinking of others. Like a sponge, the mind absorbs the vibes of others. However, it also reacts internally to problems absorbed from others by acting less on logic, but rather on intuitions of the unconscious mind. When in a

negative state, the mind distorts reality, indulges in day dreaming, in woolgathering, and suffers from neurosis. It may vacillate to the point of turning the person into a mental basket case. There is a strong desire to seclusion and secrecy. Great artistic abilities are instilled and should be developed. Increased sensitivity may result in personal criticism.

☿ IN ASPECT WITH OTHER PLANETS

426 ☿ ☌ ☽ This position bestows a receptive and keen mind. It inclines to and favors studies requiring the exercise of the mind with ideas and gives strong concentration. Any kind of communication, especially with women, will be positive. When afflicted, quarrels and arguments will result.

427 ☿ ☌ ♀ Grace, harmony and a pleasant and diplomatic communication is bestowed under this aspect. There is literary talent and all forms of entertainment will be beneficial. Any cooperation with others, and a balanced mind, will help with gaining achievements. Any afflictions to this conjunction may render the person unreliable, fickle and a social butterfly in search of the self.

428 ☿ ☌ ♂ The mind and energy are highly charged. Occupations requiring the gathering and assimilation of information are suitable. The speech may be harsh and aggressive and, at times, hasty to the point of becoming insulting. Being very fond of debates, the person may enter politics or get involved in controversial issues. If this conjunction is negatively afflicted the person may engage in heated arguments, hence letting the emotions override all logical reasoning.

429 ☿ ☌ ♃ A well developed mental ability, together with an eloquence in speech supports any public position. Occupations such as teacher, writer, advisor or head of institutions, or catering to society at large, are very suitable and bring success, respect and recognition. Work may be connected with travel, bringing advancement and financial rewards. The person will be highly respected, be an authority or has standing in any high public position, such as head of a university.

430 ☿ ☌ ♄ The mind is driven by logic, visualizes well and will plan carefully prior to executing any idea. Hard working with an interest

in education and a precise following through every step necessary to completion of a project, will bring success. However, gaining of recognition and success requires overcoming a lot of obstacles on the way. If this aspect is negatively influenced by other planets the person may be a constant worrier, and suffers from depression and melancholia. A degree of self-doubt may also be experienced.

431 ☿ ☌ ♅ The mind is brilliant, quick and produces original and inventive ideas. The ability to sense the feelings of others may be utilized in professions such as astrologer where the person may tune in and have telepathic abilities. The mind acts independently and may be advanced over present society. Any affliction to this conjunction, however, produces very eccentric, unreliable, thick headed and conceited individuals.

432 ☿ ☌ ♆ The mind produces vivid imaginations which produce good writers, especially on the subject of occultism and astrology. The person may possess clairvoyance ability and is able to channel into higher consciousness. At times submerged in dreams, the mind seeks seclusion to indulge in fantasy thinking. Photographic talents are indicated. Any affliction hereto will produce a reclusive and deceptive person acting secretly and underhandedly to avoid detection. In extremes, the mind completely loses touch with reality.

433 ☿ ☌ ♇ The mind senses the thought of others, discovers secrets, is strong willed and resourceful in an attempt to get to the bottom of things. An interest in changing society and improving conditions is applied during the life. Detectives, policemen, private investigator and all professions dealing with secret information are suitable. If afflicted, this aspect produces ruthless individuals, ready to deceive for personal gain. The desire to remake others will bring unpopularity and opposition.

434 ☿ * ☽ The intellect is promoted and supported by strong feelings. This is a good time to begin studies, to travel, deal with friends and solve difficult problems.

435 ☿ * ♀ Eloquent speech, skillful communications, a graceful appearance and talent in the arts or entertainment are bestowed by this aspect. There is musical talent especially by the use of the voice.

436 ☿ * ♂ The mind is sharp, well trained and ready for action. The person can be relied upon and any undertakings are planned well and thoroughly. The person is practical, has intellectual and engineering abilities and enjoys engaging in conversation and games that challenge the mind.

437 ☿ * ♃ The mind seeks expansion, especially in education, the law and religion and may deal with foreigners or the person chooses to reside in a foreign country. This aspect favors writers and provides mental and financial fulfillment.

438 ☿ * ♄ The mind is disciplined, responsible and well organized. Prudence and frugality will serve well and support detailed planning and execution of endeavors.

439 ☿ * ♅ A solid memory, a quick, sharp and intuitive mind produces occult, astrology and scientific abilities. The person displays independence and is able to find solutions to even the most difficult problems. The ability to be in a leadership position is well developed.

440 ☿ * ♆ The person expresses mental harmony, a fertile imagination and an ability for telepathy by sensing other people's feelings and thoughts. This aspect favors writers and photographers. The person prefers to work in secret to avoid interference with the mental process.

441 ☿ * ♇ Interests in science and physics are indicated. The person, by sheer willpower and creativity, is able to accomplish any task.

442 ☿ □ ☽ The mind could be sarcastic, thus, interfering with relationships. Any travel, new undertakings or execution of documents or communications of any kind, should be avoided. Relationships with relatives or loved ones will be strained.

443 ☿ □ ♀ The concept of love and communication is at cross-purpose resulting in arguments and tension. Communications, especially through speech and writing, should be carefully guarded as the mind should not engage in mindless chattering and gossip.

444 ☿ □ ♂ This aspect produces individuals who are fond of heated arguments, who have a nervous and irritable disposition, and who do not mince words. Lack of diplomacy, an overblown ego, jumping to conclusions before knowing all facts, fondness of debates and

strives are characteristics under this aspect. Any tension created by this square will often affect the health and produce nervous breakdowns.

445 ☿ □ ♃ The ideas are exaggerated, unrealistic, often impractical or unobtainable. The mind conjures up projects that are either not fully developed or beyond the ability to deliver. Over-optimism may sweep away logic and reality as the saying goes "Fools rush in where angels fear to tread." Commonsense is lacking. The person may be indiscreet or be talked into commitments that prove later on not to be in the best interest of the individual. Excessive talking may create unpopularity or disagreements. The ego and pride must be kept on a realistic level and be subject to strict control.

446 ☿ □ ♄ Consumed by excessive worry, pessimism, lack of imagination, narrow-mindedness, and rigid thinking or mental limitations, may prevent happiness and success. It is hard for this individual to think outside the box and be inventive. There is a fear of change and failure and a holding on to old beliefs due to a lack of self-confidence. To cover up such inadequacy the person my resort to belittling others in order to look superior. Written contracts and agreements may be a source of trouble.

447 ☿ □ ♅ The mind is nervous, erratic and changeable. Ideas come suddenly but the mind is too erratic to consider the fullest extent of executing them, thus, the ideas may be impractical, too grandees, way-out and beyond the person's experience. Rejecting advice from others while at the same time changing their own mind constantly allows the mind to jump to conclusions instead of applying a logical process to consider it. Tactless behavior, bitter and cutting remarks and obstinacy are used to please the ego.

448 ☿ □ ♆ The mind has trouble concentrating on details, thus, making it forgetful or confused. Keeping a secret seems impossible as the feelings boil over just to divulge what was promised to be kept hidden. Communications will be confused as the speed of the mind exceeds the ability to form those words.

449 ☿ □ ♇ The speech is harsh, bitter and direct. The ego gratification is so great that words are used to bully others. Secret actions or involvement with underworld figures may lead to disgrace and disruption of freedom.

450 ☿ ▲ ☽ The brain is very active and full of energy. Undertakings will be successful. All contacts with family and loved ones, especially women, will be favorable. This is a good time for new endeavors, traveling, contracts and general changes.

451 ☿ ▲ ♀ The mind is at ease creating a friendly and agreeable atmosphere. A good time for amusement or business related to the arts and beauty.

452 ☿ ▲ ♂ The mind is alert, full of energy and eager to learn. The speech is forceful and to the point, thus benefiting writers, engineers and all occupations which require a mechanical or communicative skill. The person desires to be a mental authority and seeks out public display.

453 ☿ ▲ ♃ A great interest is expressed in higher education, publishing, writing, religion, travel and dealings with foreigners. The mind is alert, well educated and communicates with ease and self-confidence. The vocal faculty is pleasant and well developed. It appeals to the public. If well aspected by other planets the person is honest, ethical and fair in all dealings with others. A display of generosity, harmony and an enjoyment of intellectual debates is used to broaden the horizon. Optimism and positive thinking will bring recognition and achievement.

454 ☿ ▲ ♄ The mind is well organized, practical, concentrated and able to consider even the smallest detail. Bestowed with good memory the person is eager to educate, teach others and work hard. There is a strong perseverance until the task is completed. A bit serious and sometimes a loner, the person makes loyal friends.

455 ☿ ▲ ♅ A talent for research, investigation, mystery, unusual ideas and inventions comes with this aspect. The mind is especially suited for the study of astrology and is able to think ahead of the times.

456 ☿ ▲ ♆ The feelings and thoughts of others can be sensed and visualized so well as if it were for real. Photography, movies and all forms of visual art are a suitable choice for the person. Artistic, musical and poetic ability is present as well as excellent writing skills due to the ability to utilize the vivid imagination so well. The voice is soft and the feelings are delicate. In extreme cases the

senses may tune in on the public's mind and are able to manipulate through subtle suggestions and influences.

457 ☿ ▲ ♇ A strong will, an excellent concentration, secret actions and a flair for the mysterious bring benefits through mystery writing, research, investigation or secret service involvement.

458 ☿ ☍ ☽ A time of conflict between the feelings and reasoning. Quarrel, tension and opposition may arise. Due to an overall disharmony in the domestic and business sphere, no travel should take place and communications should be kept at a minimum to avoid confrontations.

459 ☿ ☍ ♀ Worry, conflict and tension result from a clash of passion and intellect. Lack of tact, hypersensitivity and being too critical may all create disagreements.

460 ☿ ☍ ♂ The person is argumentative, engages in heated verbal exchanges and is rushing into communications that may later give reason to repent. Such bickering and narrow-mindedness bring unpopularity. The ego and feelings are quick to boil. The mind is unwilling to consider other's point of view. Logic, reasoning and good judgment is often abandoned for harsh and cutting words used as defense mechanism when others disagree with the individual. Relationships with family and friends are not harmonious and subject to constant strife that leads to estrangements.

461 ☿ ☍ ♃ The mind is over-optimistic and inclined to promise much more then the person is able to deliver. Projects are abandoned prior to completion and boredom is experienced when new projects are not quickly forthcoming. The beliefs may be dogmatic, fanatic or outright illogical and difficult to implement in reality. When higher education is pursued it may not result in a degree suitable to earn a living. The mind is kept under stress, displays a poor memory and has difficulties to adhere to confidentiality. The strain on the mind will create health problems.

462 ☿ ☍ ♄ Suffering from anxiety, suspicion, depression, defensive behavior, unreliability and a tendency to be constantly looking at the dark side of life, result in missing valuable opportunities. In extreme cases the person is outright dishonest and ready to get involved in schemes for personal gain. Bickering, nagging and sadness makes the individual unpopular. Others may deny their

cooperation. Difficulties in communications are experienced as overly conservative thinking will not permit the mind to see another point of view.

463 ☿ ☍ ⛢ The mind is eccentric, way out and conjures up new ideas continuously that, because of the fast changes of the mind, never come to fruition. The speech is caustic, tactless, arrogant and conceited and makes it difficult to obtain lasting friends. Being extremely opinionated may make any cooperation difficult. The mind jumps to conclusions prior to having considered all the facts. The nervous tension will affect the health. Unreliability and an inability to see projects through to completion will create trouble.

464 ☿ ☍ ♆ The mind tunes in to the senses of others and may use deceitful tactics to exploit the emotions of others. Straightforwardness and honesty is required or mistrust will result. The mind is confused and rather occupied with dreams and fantasy thinking and is unable to acknowledge reality and facts. Confidential information will be unknowingly divulged as the mind is unable to accept the real from the imagined.

465 ☿ ☍ ♇ Connections to secrets or a possible involvement in the underworld strain the mind. Will power creates tension that may lead to health problems. The manners are harsh, abrupt and insulting or others will subject the person to such experiences. A tendency to interrogate others or use a manner of speech that is imposing on them, should be avoided.

TRANSITS

When ☿ during transit turns retrograde affairs will be on hold and either dissolve before its next forward motion or develop only thereafter.

466 ☿ ☌ ☉ refer to # 71.

467 ☿ ☌ ☽ refer to # 266.

468 ☿ ☌ ♀ Any personal communication or any business related to beauty and art will advance. Entertainment will be enjoyed and financial gains will be attracted. In the extreme, however, the mind will be bewildered, letting the person chatter along without reaching a point. Public relations go well at this time. Applying charm will

help advance issues along. The intellect will be heightened bringing increased optimism and romantic attractions.

469 ☿ ☌ ♂ A strong point of view is aggressively presented and defended. The energy should be used to further business affairs. All arguments and friction should be avoided as they lead to impulsive decisions that may not be in the person's best interest. Accidents, inflammations and other injuries may occur. Investigations may involve the person. Do not act in haste. Restraint actions are the best remedy at this time.

470 ☿ ☌ ♃ The mind will concentrate on an optimistic outlook, increased mental activity and a desire for achievement. Higher education is entered into. A prosperous time for writings, publishing and entering into contracts and agreements. Trips taken for educational purposes will enhance knowledge. Gain from investments can be made but prudence is still required to avoid loss. An increased zest for life is experienced. Positive thinking will improve present conditions.

471 ☿ ☌ ♄ Proper planning, cooperation and discipline is applied to improve business conditions. Improvements in health and diet will be beneficial. While heavy responsibilities and hard work are still required, more ease is applied in performing them. Any worrying or depressing thoughts should be let go off. Slowly but surely, the necessary tasks should be performed. Involvement with older and more established persons may reap good, practical advice or other gain. Business contracts may be entered into. If negatively aspected, separations or loss of employment may occur due to narrow-mindedness. The speech must be controlled. Any tendency to gloom and doom must be curbed. Do not get involved in cheating or addicted sexual acts. Not only will it deplete the fragile vitality but bring other troubles too.

472 ☿ ☌ ♅ Sudden exiting ideas or meetings with unusual people will take place. A heightened interest in astrology could develop. Concerns over taxes and money belonging to others may surface at this time. New friendships or group activities will be entered into that include communications and public relations. If afflicted, conflicts and disagreements over attitudes will be encountered.

As the mind is in a heightened state, control should be exercised to not let it jump to conclusions prior to knowing all the facts. Beware of accidents. Lots of originality could develop during this transit.

473 ☿ ☌ ♆ Depending on the natal position, the mind is either inventive and full of imagination or will be distorted, rendering it unreal. Day dreaming should be avoided. A strong transit will expose any latent talent for telepathy and clairvoyant ability. Visual artists will benefit under this transit. Drugs and alcohol should only be used in moderation as it inflicts the mental and physical health. This is not a good time to enter into contracts as the mind is not particularly alert to hidden factors. Confusion may create misunderstandings.

474 ☿ ☌ ♇ Secret action may be taken to avoid detection of decisions made, which revolve mostly around other people's money. Critical information about family and friends may be received that forces plans to be changed. Domineering attitudes should be avoided. The mental activity is heightened but old ideas may need revisions to survive.

475 ☿ * ☉ refer to # 80.

476 ☿ * ☽ refer to # 275.

477 ☿ * ♀ Communicating with others is harmonious. A transit that is great for public relations. The appearance is refined, the manner is kind and diplomatic. A good time to enjoy pleasure and entertainment. Social and legal events should conclude well.

478 ☿ * ♂ The mind is alert and self-asserting. Work efficiency will be improved. A good time to plan, execute and enter into contracts and agreements. More energy is drawn from the mind giving a stronger drive for achievement. Beware of rushing into commitments. Plan wisely. Personal relationships may be balanced and sound at this time.

479 ☿ * ♃ Optimistic and positive thinking, as well as engagements in higher education, serve the mind well for writers, teachers and professions involved in communications and publishing. Contracts and agreements may be favorably executed reaping benefits therefrom. A good time to pursue hopes and wishes. Legal matters could improve.

480 ☿ ✶ ♄ Planning, organizing and executing of goals are all based on realistic thinking and will develop well. Enhanced education, especially to further any talent in communications, is well received. Business or partnership agreements, executed at this time, will enhance prosperity. Contact to long forgotten friends may be reestablished. Advice from older, more established and experienced people will be gainful. Pay attention to your health.

481 ☿ ✶ ♅ The mind is interested in unusual and new ideas that can greatly improve present conditions. Great advances can be made in the study of astrology. The mind is geared toward advancement. Friends and groups will be supportive in developing new ideas.

482 ☿ ✶ ♆ The mind is sharp and willing to visualize new ideas. A good time to deal with hospitals and institutions. Creative work, such as filming, photography, writing and other artistic expressions will do very well during this transit. A very good time to study and write.

483 ☿ ✶ ♇ Information, even secret information, will be made available and be beneficial. Good correspondence with society will happen. Issues with joint finances may come up or provide gain. The mind is willing to consider mysterious or complicated matters, trying to analyze everything in detail.

484 ☿ □ ☉ refer to # 89.

485 ☿ □ ☽ refer to # 284.

486 ☿ □ ♀ Difficulties appear in social and romantic relationships through misunderstood communications. The emotions may be hypersensitive, reacting to every word said in a disturbing manner. Gossip may interfere with work and can change the reputation. Expenditures should be checked, as the emotions want to overindulge to compensate for being under mental tension.

487 ☿ □ ♂ Mental irritation, rash and sarcastic conversation, as well as expression of anger, will all create personal and business disagreements. Beware of accidents. Slow down and take care before making any decisions. Inflammatory diseases may create high fever and affect the overall health. The temperament needs controlling. All correspondence is subject to irritation and conflicts. Calm the nerves. Don't argue and avoid any sudden impulses.

488 ☿ □ ♃ Over-optimism, outright laziness and unrealistic thinking bring confusion to the mind. This is not a good time to travel or have dealings with foreigners. In fact, this is not a good time to make any changes. Ideas may be impractical and grandiose, wasting money and energy. Details to contracts must be carefully scrutinized to avoid loss.

489 ☿ □ ♄ The mind is negative, depressed, pessimistic and ruled by worry and anxiety. Communication, especially with older people, superiors or other authority figures, is difficult and could lead to estrangements. Friendships may end or cool off. Lowered vitality requires extra hard work to achieve anything. Legal difficulties or difficulties with authorities consume the mind. The health will suffer under the strain and tension. Beware of misunderstandings. Negotiating and entering into contracts should be avoided during this transit.

490 ☿ □ ♅ Sudden and unstable changes, impractical decisions or erratic communications present problems and interfere at work and with relationships. Irritation, nervousness and a confused mind may give way to associations with eccentric or unreliable individuals who have bombastic ideas that will not materialize but could be very costly. The mind should not be allowed to jump to conclusions but should rather listen to good advice. Trouble at work, with machinery or when entering into contracts or agreements, are bound to occur. Difficulties with money belonging to others, as defined by the 8th house, can prove costly. The health and nervous system may be affected. At this time, the mind needs control and discipline to function properly. Social diseases maybe contracted that will affect the reputation and health.

491 ☿ □ ♆ The mind is muddled and occupied with fantasies and day dreaming. Mental confusion, unpractical ideas and deception of mind, occur. Secrets may pressure the mind and will be divulged unintentionally. Abuse of alcohol and drugs may affect, not only the mind, but also cause illness. During this confusing state, no contracts or agreements should be entered into. Avoid misunderstandings.

492 ☿ □ ♇ An interest in investigation, mental coercion or being nosy and using sarcastic, domineering speech, are all engaged in as a means to assert power over others. Business and personal relationships will be disturbed. Involvement in joint finances or other people's money will run into problems. Contracts and agreements should not be signed during this transit. Power struggle and disagreements over sex will lead to break ups. Under this transit social diseases may be contracted and other germs may affect the health. The mind is forced to abandon old ideas and will change any point of view. Don't engage in arguments. Acts done in secret will be exposed. A bad time for travel and legal affairs.

493 ☿ ▲ ☉ refer to # 98.

494 ☿ ▲ ☽ refer to # 293.

495 ☿ ▲ ♀ A charming appearance, kind speech, harmonious relationships and controlled feelings are displayed. Great diplomacy is applied in all dealings with others. Enjoyment of art, music and all forms of entertainment are pursued. Relationships with neighbors may blossom at this time and provide needed cooperation. Social standings will be improved.

496 ☿ ▲ ♂ The mind controls and directs the feelings. All kinds of communications may be turned into a new enterprise. This transit produces good and skilled work performance. A good time to enter into contracts and agreements. The health could be improved through physical activity. A sharp mind and high intellect provide for sound planning and execution of goals.

497 ☿ ▲ ♃ The mind is very optimistic allowing the nerves to relax, thus, improving the overall health. This transit should be used to pursue higher education, studies and any kind of communication that will further the interests. Legal affairs fair well and job opportunities could present itself. Religious circles provide knowledge. Gain can be received through contracts, or through buying or selling or travel, undertaken for any business purpose.

498 ☿ ▲ ♄ The mind is precise, practical and efficient in all business matters. Advanced education is entered into to seek job promotions. Receiving help from an older and more established person will be rewarding by receiving guidance and counseling. Any business

communication is more serious, organized and geared to promote progress. The health will be improved by applying a more disciplined personal diet. Methodical and pain staking attendance to details in contracts will add to advancements in business.

499 ☿ ▲ ♅ The mind resorts to original and inventive thinking. Sudden ideas surface that may be advanced of its time. Goals will be pursued. Any study of astrology or related subjects will prosper. Money from the resources of others needs to be handled at this time. Intellectual discussions with friends and groups could bring new friendships or interests. The person is more intense; the mind is more awake and mentally astute, desiring more activity and new adventure.

500 ☿ ▲ ♆ The mental faculties are stimulated by communications. The mind will visualize and absorb ideas better which motivates and triggers action to implement such ideas. Any artistic profession will benefit from this transit. Work at or visits to hospitals and institutions, or religious organizations and places, will enlighten and will serve the health well. The emotions are more sensitive, relaxed and pleasant. Sympathy is shared with others.

501 ☿ ▲ ♇ The mind is strong and focused. Interests revolve around science, sex, psychology and all kinds of related study. A positive time to plan and properly execute business affairs. The health and appearance will be improved and result in social gain. A favorable time to address legal papers and to engage in social events to further understanding of society.

502 ☿ ☍ ☉ refer to # 107.

503 ☿ ☍ ☽ refer to # 302.

504 ☿ ☍ ♀ Passion and intellect clash at this time. Social, romantic and business affairs are causing disagreements and trouble. Worry and tension prevail. Lack of tact, coarse speech and an unsympathetic attitude, will be damaging. Gossip should be avoided as it damages the reputation and work efficiency. The personal attire may be sloppy. The diet may be neglected. The feelings are jumpy and hypersensitive. Remarks by others are taken the wrong way and will hurt the emotions.

505 ☿ ☍ ♂ Bitter arguments, disagreements, harsh and sarcastic speech, all will express mental tension. During this transit business

negotiations are difficult and not satisfactory. Frustration and disappointment are irritating and will affect the nerves and general health. Beware of rash acts and accidents. The feelings may reach a boiling point. A bruised ego will refuse to cooperate. Inflammatory and infectious diseases could seriously affect the health. Any aggressiveness should be curbed. Criticism should be dealt with in a calm and diplomatic manner. This is not a good time to engage in new enterprises.

506 ☿ ☍ ♃ The mind is so overly optimistic that it has trouble concentrating. Beware of unrealistic thinking. Be careful of promises and do not avoid responsibilities. Disagreements or misunderstandings will occur over education, beliefs or how to deal with problems. Dealings with foreigners or long distance communications could lead to disappointments as the original terms of the agreement are not kept. Ill health, due to internal tension, may severely affect the person, especially the mental faculties. Pay attention to details to avoid legal confrontations.

507 ☿ ☍ ♄ Intense worry occurs under this transit. The mind is slow, depressed and negative. People in position of power and authority are not agreeing with the projects presented. Criticism will be harsh and cooperation is withheld. The mental stage can deplete the vitality, thus, affecting the health and well being. Legal difficulties may have to be dealt with. A bad time to enter into contracts and agreements. It is better to let this transit pass before making any important decisions. Severe depression may lead to estrangements. Avoid a negative attitude. This transit brings loneliness, a seriousness and gloom. If at all possible, refrain from business and travel transactions and activities.

508 ☿ ☍ ♅ The mind is way out, irritable, nervous, confused and disrupted by eccentric ideas. Getting involved with unreliable or crazy characters should be avoided. Trouble with handling the resources of others may emerge now. Mechanical problems can occur. Accidents may happen. Communications with others are confused. Health problems of the nerves and circulation will affect the body. Keep the mind in check, avoid rapid communications and be disciplined. Avoid entering into any kind of contract or agreement during this transit.

509 ☿ ☍ ♆ The mind is aloof, unrealistic and prone to day dreaming and fantasizing. Problems in communications will arise. The reality may be distorted. Mental problems will surface. Confusion will interfer with efficiency at work. Contracts and agreements should not be entered into during this transit. Avoid alcohol and drugs as misuse is possible, but at the very least, it will further distort the mind. The emotions are very sensitive and subject to peculiar changes. The mind is not focused, is subject to unrealistic expectations and misunderstandings. The nerves need a rest at this time.

510 ☿ ☍ ♇ The ego turns the speech sarcastic. The mind is suspicious, radical and may revert to coercion. Something got to give at this time. Cooperation is required to see any project progressing. Intrigues may cause harm. This is not a time to enter into contracts. Taxes, insurance, inheritance or other sources of money may dry up or create disagreement. Smoldering conflicts and involvement in legal matters should be avoided. Sexual promiscuity may lead to disease.

☿ PROGRESSED

511 ☿ ☌ ☉ refer to # 118.

512 ☿ ☌ ☽ refer to # 328.

513 ☿ ☌ ♀ The mind is bright and cheerful creating benefits in many ways, especially from a social and mental standpoint. Benefits will come through the help of friends, or partners, or those who are associated with the person in the domestic sphere. There will be contacts with musical and artistic people. Many social advantages may be gained. Depending on the lunar aspects in force at the time it might bring the good it promises, otherwise it may pass with only minor benefits.

514 ☿ ☌ ♂ The mental conditions are either very practical or dogmatic. Somewhat severe, shrewd and alert, the mind is inclined to over-estimate and to be too expectant, with a tendency to commit acts of indiscretion or to give way to impulsive conduct. Care is necessary to avoid going to extremes, or giving way to strong passion and desires. Hasty speech and a tendency to be bitter and

sarcastic, especially where writing, correspondence, or literary work is concerned, should be avoided. This conjunction excites and over-stimulates the whole nervous system, it is therefore necessary to act cautiously during this period. It is not a good time to travel or to deal with literary persons.

515 ☿ ☌ ♃ A very favorable and fortunate position, instilling good judgment, sound reasons and a powerful mental ability. Gain could be reaped from travel, publishing and foreign affairs. The general health and nervous system will be balanced. The person feels more confident and capable of managing all affairs to his advantage, provided no negative aspects inflict any change.

516 ☿ ☌ ♄ The mind is very careful and considers its own interests but otherwise it is rather suspicious and apprehensive. When depressed it will incline to melancholia and despondency. This aspect is bad for the health as it will impede the circulation, chill the blood and affect the nervous system. This could give rise to neuralgia or some form of congestion. Mental disappointments and suffering may occur at the hands of elders, or those having some power or authority.

517 ☿ ☌ ♅ The mind is acute, ingenious and original but there could be a tendency to become abrupt, nervous and irritable. Quick changes in the attitude towards others are denoted. There will be a complete alteration of previous opinions and beliefs. Strangers will influence and impress the person. Sudden journeys or travel may take place. The mind should be kept under control and flights of fancy should be avoided.

518 ☿ ☌ ♆ Involvement in some kind of scheming or mental illusion is possible. Strange and vivid dreams may be experienced.

519 ☿ ☌ ♇ The mind concentrates on every detail. This is a good period to conduct research and investigative work.

520 ☿ * ☉ refer to # 118.

521 ☿ * ☽ refer to # 329.

522 ☿ * ♀ Social advantages will help to express the self more successfully. Financial gain maybe obtained from friends or those in the domestic circle. A good time for travel, pleasant changes, happiness and receiving help to realize some hopes and wishes.

Attachments or beneficial engagements, that will expand the feelings and emotions, may occur.

523 ☿ * ♂ The mind will be very keen, bright, sharp and active and will gain through mental pursuits, through travel, writings, correspondence, and all matters wherein papers and literature are concerned. This aspect is good to deal with agents, solicitors, clerks, or any person who can act for or be of service in any way. A period in which much activity and mental force may be used to greatly benefit and bring success to hopes and wishes.

524 ☿ * ♃ The mind will expand, become hopeful, bright and intelligent. There is an excellent judgment and willpower to arrange the affairs to a satisfactory outcome. Gain will be received through all affairs where writing or correspondence is required and financial benefits will result. Profitable journeys or travel for gain and pleasure bring meetings with those whose influence upon the life will be helpful and peaceful. This aspect brings successful engagements and attachments that have a very lasting and positive effect. With a good lunar aspect, it will cause the native to deal with others, such as to make ties and friendships, that will not easily be broken.

525 ☿ * ♄ The mind is thoughtful, careful, prudent and acts with great discretion and order. The person behaves wisely and acts systematically towards the improvement of a position through honor and credit. All dealings with agents, elders and those who are serious minded would be satisfactory, and all things will tend to go smoothly and well. Long journeys may be taken and good relationships with kindred are formed. It is a good aspect for contracts and engagements.

526 ☿ * ♅ The mind is original, thoughtful, ingenious, inventive and fertile in construction, expressing original plans, good ideas, and the ability to put them into practice. Romantic attachments may be formed and contacts are made with those who will attract on a mental level. The mind will expand and progress with a strong desire to reform and improve existing methods. This good aspect will bring success in travel and will enable the native to get on well with kindred and relatives. It will also favor the forming of attachments of a unique and uncommon character.

527 ☿ * ♆ Poetic, mystical and humorous inventions will flow into the consciousness. Lasting benefits from the exercise of literary or artistic skills may be reaped. Otherwise, pleasant journeys, friendships, religious, mystical or strange experiences connected with the sea, may develop.

528 ☿ * ♇ The mind loves mystery, solving of difficult puzzles or problems and strives on analysis, examination and improvement of conditions, while teaching others. Decisions made during this time are solid, built on foundations and will be beneficial.

529 ☿ □ ☉ refer to # 119.

530 ☿ □ ☽ refer to # 330.

531 ☿ □ ♀ The feelings are at war with fixed habits of thought, and artistic enlightenment. Words may be used against loved ones, creating mistrust.

532 ☿ □ ♂ The mind is too impulsive, inclined to act rashly and without consideration regarding the outcome of those actions. Errors in speech, to say much more than it is wise to say, inclination to be unkind and cutting in speech, are all primary faults under this progress. Care is required in all dealings with those intimately connected, and also with inferiors or those who can affect the honor and reputation. This is a bad time to sign papers, write or engage in correspondence, or to deal with lawyers or agents. Guard against fraud or imposition by others is necessary. A tendency to uncontrolled speech may bring trouble.

533 ☿ □ ♃ Grave errors of judgment and other mistakes could be made that will produce much worry and anxiety. Hypocrisy, deceit, fraud and treachery may be involved. Care must be taken in regards to all papers or correspondence. Trouble through writings or through speech is possible, as well as a liability to legal involvement. Promises made, but also caution upon the promises of others, should be guarded against. Lots of anxiety, especially if unwise speech has been allowed to occur for this influence often causes libel or scandal, in which one's good name is likely to be imperiled.

534 ☿ □ ♄ Delay or hindrance to progress is experienced. The mind will be warped and suspicious. The native will be inclined to fret, worry and look upon the dark side of things. This is a bad time to

sign papers or enter into any correspondence with others, also to deal with elders, agents, lawyers, or those who have power to injure in any way. Disagreements with friends and family will cause grief and sorrow. A period full of mental disappointments and worry. The honor and reputation should be guarded. Care should be exercised in all actions. A liability to scandal or slander, to suffer in discredit or reputation, is possible if the mind is uncontrolled.

535 ☿ □ ♅ Sudden and unexpected changes, also strange and peculiar episodes in connection with any attachment or friendship that may have been formed, is threatened. The mind will not be peaceful or harmonious, and a temper, with a sarcastic turn of speech, will produce trouble. Great care in speech is needed and signing papers or entering into any contract should be avoided as it is likely to bring discredit or dishonor. All dealing with others should be done very carefully and cautiously, especially with those in the domestic sphere. The nervous system will now be in a state of extreme tension.

536 ☿ □ ♆ This is a very unfortunate and somewhat perilous aspect. The mind is obscured by vague and undetermined fears, longings or aspirations, so much so, that in extreme cases the moral senses may become quite perverted. The person may achieve an unenviable notoriety through some evil deed. Otherwise, fraud and deception of some kind or a disease or hypochondria will be likely to cause sorrow.

537 ☿ □ ♇ Do not argue or force an opinion onto others. Do not engage in verbal power games. This aspect is unfavorable for travel and legal matters.

538 ☿ ▲ ☉ refer to # 118.

539 ☿ ▲ ☽ refer to # 329.

☿ ▲ ♀ This aspect cannot be formed during a normal life span.

540 ☿ ▲ ♂ The person has a sharp mentality that is eager to learn and gain experience. A very keen, shrewd and practical approach to intellectual matters is present. This aspect is positive for enterprising, aspiring, and speculative matters. The mind will be able to observe matters accurately and quickly. A superior time for travel, writing, correspondence and dealings with lawyers and agents. This is positive for the nervous system, and also for the

general health. With good lunar influences this aspect will make a good period for general improvement and bring an ability to take advantage of opportunities.

541 ☿ ▲ ♃ The mind becomes intuitive, sound in judgment and is full of common sense. There is gain by investment, speculation or commercial enterprise and also by travel. Ties will be formed and attachments of permanent and very beneficial character are indicated. The nervous system will be in good order and dealings with inferiors will be profitable. Writing, correspondence, matters concerned with papers and legal transactions, will be successful.

542 ☿ ▲ ♄ The mind will be very steady, sincere, honest and responsible. This is a good time to invest money or to so arrange affairs for future gain that benefits result from the exercise of care and forethought. A good time for important correspondence and for signing papers.

543 ☿ ▲ ♅ Sudden, unexpected benefits, very original attachments and gain in some quite unexpected way, by speculation or investment, may be experienced. A good time for the study of astrology or kindred subjects and also for literary work. Dealing directly with others, where magnetic conditions are able to influence them, bring benefits. The person is very original in thought and likes to pursue all forms of movements connected with humanitarian principles.

544 ☿ ▲ ♆ The mind is in a pleasant state and all things signified by ☿ run well and smoothly.

545 ☿ ▲ ♇ Sorting out problems, investigations, research and thorough intellectual thinking aids the person. These are times to learn new things, dive into mystery, and engage in communications. A positive time for signing any legal documents.

546 ☿ ☍ ☉ refer to # 119.

547 ☿ ☍ ☽ refer to # 330.

☿ ☍ ♀ This aspect cannot be formed during a normal life span.

548 ☿ ☍ ♂ Much trouble and opposition is indicated. Suffering through fraud, deception and indiscretion is possible. Being guarded and careful in dealing with others is necessary as the mind will be upset and worry a great deal. During this period no papers should

be signed and if it cannot be avoided, outmost care should be exercised when signing documents or dealing with lawyers or agents. The person may be subject to scandal, libel or ill-repute, and in the extreme, be threatened with litigation or suffer attacks upon the reputation. Separation from friends or relatives and serious quarrels or disputes with others, may occur. It is not a good time to travel or to begin any new undertaking. It may cause accidents or inflammatory diseases if the lunar aspect is also adverse at the time.

549 ☿ ☍ ♃ Impairment of judgment causes errors and mistakes either through speech or in writing and correspondence. Separation, also a liability to suffer through litigation or legal trouble, is possible. Neither lend money nor become surety for anyone. Great care will be necessary with regards to finances for expenditure will tend to exceed receipts. All acts undertaken should be done very discretely for there is a liability to offend others. Separation from others may occur either through misunderstandings or through conditions arising from outside matters, which will cause unpleasantness or problems. Trouble and anxiety may result.

550 ☿ ☍ ♄ The person will suffer from deception, fraud, treachery, depression, and be despondent and look upon the dark side of life. Separation and estrangement will result. Those in whom trust has been placed will prove untrue to one's interests. It is not a good time to attend to signing of documents, writings or correspondence or to study or incline the mind to serious thought. Dealings with others must be carefully scrutinized. Avoid the law or serious disputes for all affairs will tend to go wrong under this aspect, especially if the lunar aspect is also adverse.

551 ☿ ☍ ♅ The mind becomes unreasonable or is expressed in very extreme views. A liability to serious and persistent opinions will be decidedly hurtful. Be careful when placing any trust in others for some disappointment will come along. Charges or accusations will be made and be difficult to refute. Eccentricity should be avoided. These extraordinary influences bring sudden and quite unexpected events into the life. Many romantic and other very strange episodes follow this aspect.

552 ☿ ☍ ♆ This aspect is evil. The person will find himself deserted by those whom he has trusted in, deceived in his speculations, and disappointed in his hopes.

553 ☿ ☍ ♇ Mental conflicts with others may develop. Be careful of any communications, especially in connection with contracts and legal matters. There will be suspicion and a harsh attitude as well as an obsession with ideas that may not be practical.

BABY CHART

☿ ☌ ☉ = travels close to the ☉, there are no aspects between them at birth.

554 ☿ ☌ ☽ The emotions are openly displayed and communicated with others. Depending on the sign and house position involved the emotional energy and expression of feelings may be copied from the mother's behavior.

555 ☿ ☌ ♀ Great family communications encouraging the child to talk about everything. Sometimes the child turns into a chatterbox.

556 ☿ ☌ ♂ A quick mind, forceful speaking, impulsive speech, harsh words and jumping to conclusion are inherent with this position. Restlessness and lack of patience may lead to a learning disability as the mind wanders off before it can grasp the issue. An unwillingness to listen leads to disagreements.

557 ☿ ☌ ♃ A joy of communication is given, which sometimes, however, indicates one who talks profusely.

558 ☿ ☌ ♄ The father may inhibit the child's expression and restricts any communications. A learning disability may be present. Words come with difficulties or harshness as the child perceives talking to others as a risk of rejection. The need to express the self must be learned.

559 ☿ ☌ ♅ The family environment, especially on a mental level, is in a chaotic state. Erratic and undisciplined behavior, talking without making sense and a restricted learning ability subject the child to an erratic adult life. The mental faculties must be trained to be coherent and to follow a thought through to completion.

560 ☿ ☌ ♆ Spiritual involvement is practiced by the parents, at times, however, in an unorthodox way. A lot of dreaming and wishful

thinking makes communications rather vague and incomplete. Halting a conversation in mid-sentence, forgetting or abandoning its conclusion or jumping from one subject to the next creates psychological aberration. If the energy is channeled and used correctly the mind may become very creative.

561 ☿ ☌ ♇ From the parents the child may have picked up an uncontrolled speech, or the speech is controlled to manipulate. Manipulating words may be used to control jobs and relationships. Speech is never spontaneous but always calculated to gain.

562 ☿ * ☽ The person has immense feelings and talent in the art of communications. The mother encourages the child to openly express feelings.

563 ☿ * ♀ Shyness, being introvert and a talent for the arts and communications, is indicated. The child easily communicates with the mother.

564 ☿ * ♂ The child acts with reasons and foresight. Problems are analyzed and communicated to find proper solutions.

565 ☿ * ♃ This indicates a well developed mind. Excellent expression of communications with proper training will serve the person well.

566 ☿ * ♄ A serious attitude with restricted communication is practiced within the family.

567 ☿ * ♅ A talent for creative, unusual and innovative communications is indicated. The parents instill a sense of productivity.

568 ☿ * ♆ This aspect gives an interest in spiritual development, in religious groups and creative communications. Writing and/or speaking ability on spiritual subjects may be of interest and should be developed.

569 ☿ * ♇ The child is cooperative and communicates well with people and institutions.

570 ☿ □ ☽ The mother does not communicate her feelings often but when she does, it comes out in anger and suppression. The child absorbs this behavior as normal and imitates it later in life. This creates relationship problems. The person remains misunderstood due to the inability to openly and coherently express, feelings. As the years go on the person becomes angry, negative and has

problems to communicate with the mother. Depending on the sign, expressing communications in a normal way seems impossible, hence, preventing inner peace.

571 ☿ □ ♂ The mind is quick but improperly used. The mind is confused and unable to focus properly. Lack of communication in childhood inhibits full and controlled expression of thoughts, hence creating misunderstandings and a jumping to conclusions. Disagreement with or disapproval of others, as well as a refusal to listen, confuse the mind. There is a trend to believe only people who look the part but reject others that don't fit into the concept. Lack of consideration may disturb relationships.

572 ☿ □ ♃ The family is not supportive of each other. Words are used harshly and communication is difficult. There is a need to lean to share feelings and ideas. A refusal to communicate on an honest level and to expand the consciousness creates difficulties in relationships.

573 ☿ □ ♄ The father impedes the ability to communicate and share feelings. The father instills a certain fear into the child that blocked any open exchange of feelings and communicating. The self-expression is hampered or suppressed. Words are harsh, authoritarian and designed to offend rather then to please. This aspect interferes with harmonious relationships. The development of the self-worth needs attending.

574 ☿ □ ♅ The mind is bright, witty and quick but suffers from confusion which prevents a throughout consideration of matters prior to any communication. Speech and thinking may be eccentric, erratic and willfully designed to hurt others.

575 ☿ □ ♆ The family was unfocused creating misunderstandings. The child needs to understand spiritual development. The family may have been adverse to religion. The child is intuitive and may resort to a life of fantasy, day dreaming, alcoholism and drugs. A desire for strange lands and people may fascinate the child. Incomplete thoughts create problems in communications. A disconnection to others may occur. The mind needs to be focused, kept stable and trained to develop continuos thoughts in order to use the constructive energy to the fullest.

576 ☿ □ ♇ Cooperation and communications are never learned and understood. Control and sadistic humor is used instead of kindness and diplomacy. Words come out in anger, through obsession and without consideration of its consequences. This behavior often overwhelms others and inhibits the forming of lasting relationships as the thoughts are not shared but forced onto others.

577 ☿ ▲ ☽ From the mother the child learns creative and positive expressions of feelings and communications.

578 ☿ ▲ ♂ The mind is organized and geared for action. However, if this aspect is not developed it may lead to procrastination.

579 ☿ ▲ ♃ The parents encourage the mental development of the child. The child learns to enjoy communication and listens well.

580 ☿ ▲ ♄ The father instills the need for serious conversations and a sense of responsibility, which helps the child being organized and have a well functioning mind.

581 ☿ ▲ ♅ If developed, this aspect may produce a brilliant mind. Ideas come easily and develop into unusual and creative concepts. The pursuit of creative endeavors will focus the energy into productivity.

582 ☿ ▲ ♆ The mind is focused on spiritual development. The danger lies in the child accepting fantasy and illusion as facts that prevent growth and maturity.

583 ☿ ▲ ♇ The mind will develop towards communications that affect the masses.

584 ☿ ☍ ☽ There is a disturbance between the feelings and communications, which is instilled by the mother who has been withholding an honest self-expression in the child. The result may be suppressed feelings and anger or a chatterbox that is overly opinionated, depending on the sign and the house in which this opposition occurs. A balance to listen and to communicate must be achieved.

585 ☿ ☍ ♂ Communication is harsh and insulting. Compromises must be achieved to control the undesired outburst of ♂. There is a need to learn that listening precedes any reply.

586 ☿ ☍ ♃ No one in the family is able to relate to each other. There is a poor choice of words creating tension and conflict. This creates resentment. When bestowed on others, it will bring conflict. The

sign affected will point to the basic behavior that must be changed to overcome bad aspects from this opposition.

587 ☿ ☍ ♄ The father restricts communications. This creates an atmosphere of coldness or is used to quiet the child by disapproving in silence. The child does not get the opportunity to express feelings. This creates later learning and communication problems. If the self-worth is also underdeveloped communications may be harsh and disturbing.

588 ☿ ☍ ♅ The family does not communicate open and constructively. Desires and eccentricity rule decisions. Decisions are made without discussions. Later this creates relationships and professional problems as a kind of power play takes place where decisions are willfully made and enforced, even if wrong. Minds may be changed constantly creating erratic conversations that prevent a positive result.

589 ☿ ☍ ♆ The mind is undirected and delusional. In extreme cases a mental disturbance may be present. The spiritual concept and understanding of religion may be so vague or unacceptable that the mind creates facts instead of accepting facts in order to understand. The communication of ideas is not fully functioning resulting in incomplete sentences or conversations. The mental concept needs channeling and understanding to avoid delusion and misunderstandings.

590 ☿ ☍ ♇ The family atmosphere is subject to constant manipulation. Words are used to control rather than to communicate. Relationships may be difficult, as there is no spontaneous exchange of ideas and conversations. Words are used to control not to share. A flow of mind is needed to stop the urge to control.

☿ TRANSIT OR PROGRESSION TO A (Ascendant)

591 ☿ ☌ A. A well developed intelligence provides for very clear and logical thinking. The nerves may be strained but always seek to advance the knowledge. During transit it presents a good time for negotiations, entering into contracts and correspondence. Work will be performed well and be gainful.

592 ☿ ∗ A A good ability to communicate allows for diplomacy and harmony in expression. During transit, travel, communications, mental exchange and business negotiations will be beneficial.

593 ☿ □ A Communicating is very difficult. The self-expression is hampered resulting in awkward behavior. Nervous disorders may become apparent. An involvement in fraud is possible. Disagreements cause strife. Be diplomatic and avoid communications and gossip until this transit has passed.

594 ☿ ▲ A The mental faculty is alert, strong and well developed. Any kind of communication is well presented. Cooperation is received. The mental health will be strong if this aspect is not otherwise afflicted. During transit, communications will be beneficial. Furtherance of education, entering into agreements and solving of problems will produce results.

595 ☿ ☍ A refer to # 593

☿ TRANSIT OR PROGRESSION TO M (Mid heaven)

596 ☿ ☌ M A talent in speech, coupled with great originality and intelligence as well as very good manners, provide for advances in an occupation connected with communications. A great ability to learn and teach is given.

597 ☿ ∗ M The self-expression is strong and precise. Business advances in any kind of communication and for the public's benefit will result. During transit correspondence, planning, negotiations and education will improve the mind and position in life.

598 ☿ □ M Professional obstacles may result from confused communications. Trouble in connection with writing, contracts and dealings with agents or lawyers or anyone who is involved in any deal-making. During transit do not engage in contracts, professional agreements or important communications. It pays to wait.

599 ☿ ▲ M The profession may require the application of a high degree of intelligence and is involved in communications. A position in public maybe desired and obtained. Detailed planning will improve work. A good time to solve problems and engage in new ventures.

600 ☿ ☍ M refer to # 598

39

♀ Venus

This planet represents beauty, sincerity, artistic talents and occupations, love, marriage and financial fortunes. A good ♀ will provide charm, attractions to a good partner and provides for financial rewards. A desire for luxury, a display of passions and gain of happiness, are all instilled in the positive aspect of ♀.

If afflicted, the good aspects are lessened or even reversed. The morals are lax, rivalry, jealousy and disturbed behavior will lead to scandal, loss of reputation and money. Disappointment in love will be experienced. In the extreme, forgery, extensive litigation, and other misdeeds will expose a questionable character. Venereal diseases may develop. Social diseases may also be contracted when ⛢ is negative with ☿ and ♇ is adverse with a ☿ *or ♀ transit. While the natal house position is activated by natal aspects and transits to other planets, ♀ transit stays in a house for only one month, thus, its effect is shorter in duration and intensity.*

♀ IN THE HOUSES

601 (1) The person is graceful, has a pleasing and friendly demeanor as well as physical beauty and happy disposition, is outgoing, pleasant and attracts lots of friends and admirer. Business, social and marital opportunities are plenty and talent in the arts is indicated. A negative ♀ signifies self-interests that may lead to manipulation.

602 ♀ (2) There is love of money, possessions, object de art and personal adornment. All representing strong motivators to actively seeking and achieving a social status. Love and money are closely tied when considering a relationship. Charm may be used to obtain an advantage.

603 ♀ (3) Literature, poetry and all kinds of communications are favored. Lots of short distant travel is indicated which might be for personal pleasure or business. Good relationships with brothers, sisters, and neighbors and other social contacts are promoted.

604 ♀ (4) There is an emotional attachment to the family and home. The desire to entertain in the home and cook for friends and lovers is strong. The home is tasteful and artistically decorated. An emotional closeness to the parents is indicated. Love of beauty and comfort, gardens and all natural beauty, is instilled in the character.

605 ♀ (5) A strong desire for pleasure, romance, love of life and a positive outlook in life is prevalent. Kindness and happiness received from and given to children and a desire for entertainment, especially in the arts, is indicated. Children may be girls rather than boys and a close relationship with them can be established. Gain through investments depends on the aspects formed to ♀.

606 ♀ (6) The person may engage in a possible love affair at work, and has a desire to perform artistic kind of work. Harmonious and friendly relationships with co-workers are established. There is an enjoyment of beautiful clothing and great affections for animals. The health may be weak and need taken care of. Irritation and anxiety may be experienced. Romance formed at work may not be enduring and causes emotional stress.

607 ♀ (7) Socially active, the person desires a happy marriage and may achieve great popularity with the public. A desire to be married and enjoy social and financial prosperity may lead to an early marriage. If lawsuits occur, they may be settled out of court.

608 ♀ (8) Financial gain will be received through marriage, business partnerships, inheritance, insurance and law suits. However, loss of inheritance or other benefits may occur. Marriage may be entirely motivated by greed. Intense emotions, jealousy and possessiveness may destroy important relationships.

609 ♀ (9) Involvement with religion, foreigners, education, law and overseas travel is indicated but more for pleasure than for business. The marriage partner may be from a different country and background and may be influenced by religious beliefs. When positive, good relations exist with in-laws.

610 ♀ (10) Strong artistic, social and business ambitions are present. Partnerships or marriage may bestow status and wealth. A position of importance or fame may be indicated in their career. However, the person may be a social climber on the back of others to achieve a desired goal. Relations maybe formed with elders to guide and gain a public career.

611 ♀ (11) There is an interest in friends and groups to seek fulfillment of hopes and wishes. Many friends among artists will be made. However, if ♀ receives negative aspects at birth friends may not be able to help even if they wanted to.

612 ♀ (12) A strong desire for solitude, secretive contacts, romance and love affairs may be entered into to overshadow shyness and romantic frustration. The emotions are motivated by unconscious habits, are easily hurt and sensitive, but there is great compassion for others.

♀ IN THE SIGNS

613 ♀ (♈) The emotional self-expression can be aggressive but also be outgoing and sparkling. A desire for the affection of others is actively pursued. An artistic talent is indicated. The person is passionate and persistent when pursuing love but due to impulsiveness, the end result may be unstable. A need for personal attention and selfishness may be prevalent. Due to a lack of refinement frustration may develop.

614 ♀ (♉) Enduring affections, emotional security and stability in love are all important. Loyal and steadfast, but possessive and jealous, unstable emotions may create problems. The person enjoys being pursued in love rather than be the initiator. Comfort, luxury, beautiful surroundings, excellent food and things of beauty are items money is easily spent on. Efforts are made in the home to create happy living conditions. A personal effort is made to improve

beauty and adorn the body with jewelry and expensive clothing. Collecting material things is a constant desire and interest. A great voice and talent as a singer may be bestowed under this aspect.

615 ♀ (♊) Variety, excitement and intellectual inspirations are required in a relationship. There is a possibility of dual relationships to keep the excitement going. Friendships are pursued and become necessary as an intellectual outlet. Social activity and travel, as well as literary endeavors, are indicated. However, fickleness, inconsistency, unreliability or superficial involvement in friendships and relationships may unravel existing partnerships.

616 ♀ (♋) The deep and sensitive feelings are easily hurt and vulnerable to the opinion of others. A strongly fluctuating mood and unpredictable acts could create havoc. Marriage is contemplated more for domestic security and to create a stable environment for their emotions, rather than for love and affection. There is a domestic tendency, such as the enjoyment of cooking and entertaining at home. In men, this aspect creates femininity and the desire to mother others. On a negative trend boredom, loneliness, over sentimentality, a tendency to sulk and unstable emotional reactions are used to cover up inadequacies. At full moon this person is emotionally oversensitive.

617 ♀ (♌) Dramatic behavior is displayed seeking center stage for affection and approval of others. Great pride and desire is extended to seek the spotlights. Throwing big parties but at times overdoing things in a desire to be the admired one and to dramatize and be flamboyant, makes the person a good actor or visual artist. Extremely outgoing and affectionate, children are liked and desired. Being very romantic, there is a craving for constant excitement and also for showing off to gain approval. Extreme possessiveness, jealousy, a strong ego, false pride, snobbishness, selfishness and addiction to sex may bring a downfall.

618 ♀ (♍) The person tends to overanalyze and organize, is critical, but at times too critical towards others. Partners are selected to share intellectual interests. The person is very picky and may never marry. Good relationships with co-workers are necessary for productive work. Cleanliness and order is preferred and jobs as

cooks, fashion designer, or nursing can be a good source of income. Great sympathy and effort is made to help others in need. On the negative side, there is social shyness and feelings of social or sexual inferiority from which coldness and retreat into seclusion may result. The affections can turn into education and be bestowed on animals rather than on people. When annoyed, mannerism can become coarse or the person avoids contact altogether.

619 ♀ (♎) Harmony in family and social relationships is very important. Beauty, art, good looks and physical beauty provide attraction and opportunities for marriage. The desires pursue romance and affection. The sharing of feelings is important for any close personal bond with friends and lovers. Being well liked and eager to please there is a desire to seek status and money through relationships. A sense of justice and fair play together with good manners makes for good judges and lawyers. Any musical ability should be expressed. Dealing with and appearances before the public will bring acclaim. A dislike of disagreements, discord or disharmony may result in mental nervousness and upset, hence affecting the health. There is a desire to avoid conflicts and arguments. A lack of integrity may affect the emotions which can be superficial. Social niceties are used solely to obtain favors.

620 ♀ (♏) Strong emotions, sexual desires and preoccupation with sex, as well as passion, jealousy, secret involvement and the eagerness for ego confrontations are floating just below the surface. If well positioned, anything will be done for the loved one but, at times, things are taken far too serious, lacking in enjoyment. An overblown pride, jealousy, resentfulness, bitterness and love turns to hate, will sever relationships, which will never be resumed. Sex may be used to gain power over others. The person likes to control and run relationships.

621 ♀ (♐)Idealistic, friendly, sociable and eager to mingle with others, is a characteristic of this influence. Always trying to blend in with society, be friendly, idealistic and ready to open the feelings to gain more friends. However, there may be a strong religious belief which dictates the relationship. To satisfy the desire to live a flamboyant life and, of course, in a style to impress, travel and

general activities are constantly engaged in. Very often marriage with a foreigner and a good education is desired and pursued. A dramatic flair and longing to be noticed, is prevalent. Blunt speech can easily offend others. Impractical idealism and a tendency to impose beliefs on others, create tension and break ups.

622 ♀ (♑) The person is pursuing wealth and status for emotional security but there is a dislike of public display of emotions and affections. Refined manners are present. At times, periods of loneliness will separate the person from society. An older and mature partner is preferred. Responsibilities in relationships are extended to friends and partners and are loyal and steadfast. Involvement in the arts may lead to income opportunities. A display of coldness and a concern over material goods may lead to depression. Calculations and ulterior motives may rule the affections. Marriage may be entered for gain not love.

623 ♀ (♒) The mind is elusive of materialism. The mannerism is impersonal but friendly. There is an interest in human values. The person is friendly, outgoing and unusual in all approaches to life. Intellectual stimulation is necessary to hold any interest. At times, a display for ingenuity, eccentricity and a willingness to explore the new, coupled with a drive for adventure, is evinced. Friends are important to the well being and a partner must be more than a lover and be willing to accept new challenges. Partners must be willing to provide mental freedom and possessiveness drives this person away. Unusual taste, an out of the ordinary opinion and an interest in unusual subjects comes with this placement. Promiscuity, sudden changes of affections and feelings could interfere with friendships. A constant desire for new experiences interferes with work and relationships. Stubborn attitudes, and an inability to see the point of others, may create friction.

624 ♀ (♓) Love and emotional security is all important. A strong and deep compassion brings emotional dependency on the partner. The person is romantic and sensitive, but feels lonely if not receiving the same deep feelings from the partner. This position is good for artists, musicians and writers. If the dependency on others for

emotional security is driven too far, disappointment may lead to dependency on religion and may lead to martyrdom. While absorbing the feelings and suffering of others, the own feelings may be taken advantage of. In the extreme, an emotional state of fear of rejection prevails, this could lead to a refusal to express the emotions at all. Suffering in silence will take over. The hypersensitivity over dependency on others, or outright laziness, may stand in the way of reality, causing problems relating to life.

♀ IN ASPECT WITH OTHER PLANETS

625 ♀ ☌ ☽ A strong artistic ability and a desire for beauty, arts and harmony, is displayed. Interest and talent in cooking and dressmaking, combined with a winning charm, will also provide for a good earning potential. Financial and emotional attachments turn lucky. Diplomacy and pleasing manners provide for popularity. Any affliction hereto can render the person to be self-indulgent, a financial waste, or the feelings may be taken advantage off by others.

626 ♀ ☌ ☿ A pleasing and graceful voice and diplomatic communications provide for talent in the arts and music and also support any literary undertaking. Friends will be easily made and help is received from others but, if this aspect is afflicted by other major planets, the mind turns fickle, is not concentrated and may turn the person into a social butterfly without a genuine purpose in life.

627 ♀ ☌ ♂ Passion, aggression and rash action will manifest as behavior leading either to artistic expressions or sexual involvement. Depending on other aspects to this conjunction, the experiences may be pleasurable or degrading, thus affecting the mind. Hasty decisions and overspending can lead to loss.

628 ♀ ☌ ♃ The person is generous, optimistic, sociable, has a cheerful disposition and is willing to cooperate and help others. Displaying artistic talents, the feelings may be loving and harmonious, provided no negative aspects are made to this conjunction. Otherwise laziness and over-expansion will occur.

629 ♀ ☌ ♄ This aspect brings talent in the arts, music and poetry. The detail oriented ♄ provides a sound foundation for the outlet of ♀ to produce fine and detailed work. A sense of loyalty provides for lasting partnerships and friendships. Afflictions to this conjunction, however, turn the mind to being a user, who is solely interested in his/her financial welfare. Others are used to satisfy deep-seated emotional needs without giving of the self. The sensitive emotions may be gripped by depression creating the feeling of being unloved or unwanted.

630 ♀ ☌ ♅ Sudden sexual attractions may occur. Being charming, popular, outgoing and sociable, however, there is a craving to be at the center of attention in social life. Events may also break up in sudden and erratic ways. The emotions are spread among many and have trouble focussing on one love, thus, making long term relationships difficult.

631 ♀ ☌ ♆ Spiritual love, harmony and the desire to help others may lead to a profession in religion or healing as the concern is to spread happiness and understanding among many. The ability to hypnotize is strongly indicated feeding a fertile imagination. This aspect will support any kind of artistic endeavor. If this aspect is negatively afflicted by other planets the person merely will be a dreamer, be impractical, unreliable, deceptive and becomes a burden to others.

632 ♀ ☌ ♇ A zest for life is present. The person is magically attracted to the opposite sex. The experience of spiritual love is strong and the emotions are forcefully expressed. Any talent in art, drama, music and poetry is bestowed under this aspect. An affliction to this conjunction will turn the person into a sexual pervert who just can't get enough and will use partners or friends for personal gain.

633 ♀ ∗ ☽ Pleasing emotions provide for a good relationship and harmonious marriage. Talent in the arts and domestic affairs, combined with a loving, sweet and graceful mannerism, bring social favors and success. Family ties are close and harmonious. A general popularity comes with this aspect.

634 ♀ ∗ ☿ The speech and mannerism is graceful and kind. Artistic endeavors and music may provide an outlet for the many talents.

635 ♀ ✶ ♂ Interested in action and adventure, the person is happy, energetic, harmonious and eager to please. Artistic talent is given and business related to the arts will do well. Popularity in society may bring wealth through marriage. At times, the person is generous to a fault.

636 ♀ ✶ ♃ Being charming, well liked, with a happy and optimistic nature will attract good fortune. Artistic abilities, when well developed, will bring social and financial rewards. Marriage and partnerships will provide financial and emotional security.

637 ♀ ✶ ♄ Artists with exceptional skills for fine details are born with this aspect. It brings loyal friends and serious relationships. Marriage may be of long duration as the interest to bring happiness to others is strongly instilled. ♄ brings good planning ability and tends to render the person frugal, thus, a growing wealth is indicated.

638 ♀ ✶ ♅ The person will be popular, have many friends and may belong to purposeful organizations. Artistic and musical talent, as well as the ability to socially shine, will be helpful in any undertaking. The emotions long for happiness and comfort. The person may fall in love suddenly, marry suddenly, or be fortunate through friendships.

639 ♀ ✶ ♆ Artistic talent and a keen imagination provide a fertile ground for compassionate expressions. The mind is occupied by thoughts of beauty, the body is graceful and the person is pursuing a search for the ideal love relationship. In an afflicted chart this may lead to self-love and a heavy reliance on the constant help of others.

640 ♀ ✶ ♇ The desire for power, although applied in a cheerful way, and the desire to be accepted by society, comes with this aspect. Creativity, a public displays of art and a belief in eternal love, is bestowed. Peace and harmony are practiced and preached.

641 ♀ □ ☽ Financial, emotional and social problems will be experienced. The affection may be bestowed unwisely, thus, they maybe abused by an attachment to the wrong person. A tendency to generously trust others will lead to disappointment and abuse. Choosing the wrong partner again and again will create disappointment. A loss of money and possession is possible through unwise partnerships.

642 ♀ □ ♂ Using others for sexual gratification or relating any emotional problems onto others for selfish reasons, will create trouble. Unbridled passion, as well as jealousy and the desire to control relationships, will create estrangements. While the person's own feelings are easily hurt there is no sensitivity for the feelings of others. Relationships are not harmonious, happy or close and subject to arguments.

643 ♀ □ ♃ Self-indulgence, overconfidence, action without foresight and hypocrisy are the main faults occurring under this square. Loss of money through marriage or business ventures or legal difficulties is possible. While the person seeks center stage the own affairs may be unattended and, at times, lie in shambles. Waste and lack of appreciation, together with loose moral values, may bring disagreement and trouble.

644 ♀ □ ♄ Depression, melancholia and easily hurt feelings are characteristically for this aspect. Stiffness, shyness, lack of affection, unfulfilled romance and lack of details may bring misfortune. The attitude and acts toward others will alienate from friends and family and prevent business success. The person may purely calculate any gains or use existing wealth to attract and control others, thus, leading to unhappiness. Sometimes, this aspect is associated with hardships, unhappiness and emotional oppression. If disillusions set in the mind can turn mean, bitter, sarcastic, jealous and unable to appreciate others.

645 ♀ □ ♅ This combination brings sudden but brief attractions and possible sexual involvement, however, this will not be lasting and the emotions may fall in and out of love at the drop of a hat. The person wants emotional gratification at all cost and may become a social butterfly, having difficulties to produce stability in any relationship. The desire for freedom, represented by ♅ could override ♀ desire for stability and harmony. Divorce may happen, even more than once. The mind and the sexual feelings are irritated, always looking for something new while unappreciative of what exists.

646 ♀ □ ♆ Emotional and sexual problems may surface which the person tries to escape by resorting to drug and alcohol consumption. The mind is encased in dreams and wishful thinking.

The person engages in unhealthy relationships, particularly by bestowing affections unwisely, or getting involved in unwise financial ventures, leading to loss. Secret involvement in sexual acts may be engaged in. Any dishonest behavior may lead to loss. If the sexual passion is very strong the mind becomes ruthless in its desire to gratify the imaginations, which could lead to homosexuality. Lack of discipline and continuation and overly sensitive feelings, as well as laziness and disorderly behavior, may involve the person in schemes that will be financially and romantically disappointing and costly.

647 ♀ □ ♇ The passions may be out of control. Intense emotional and sexual involvement may have devastating results. It also indicates giving up any interest in the opposite sex to produce amazing business success, as all the energy is redirected. Emotional fulfillment, happiness and gratification of the senses may be disappointing in the long run and be replaced by the desire for material wealth. The desire for financial security may taint any relationship or marriage. Secret love affairs may be entertained while the person is presented as being single in public. A strong desire to obtain fame and success occupies the mind.

648 ♀ ▲ ☽ Femininity, grace, beauty and harmonious manners are bestowed under this aspect. Calm behavior allows for sympathy and progress with the help from others, especially from women. A talent for the arts, for music and domestic affairs is given and social advances will be gained.

649 ♀ ▲ ♂ Relationships with the opposite sex fare well. The person is full of energy, outgoing and sexually attractive. Harmony and happiness in relationships and marriage is indicated by this trine. Talent in arts, music, drama and poetry should be developed.

650 ♀ ▲ ♃ A happy and optimistic character who is inclined to engage in artistic or religious enterprises who has good taste and many opportunities for financial gain. The person may be very talented as a singer, be graceful and popular. Any major affliction hereto renders the person lazy and a social parasite.

651 ♀ ▲ ♄ The artistic talent of ♀ combined with the organized, efficient and responsible attitude of ♄ will produce fortunate results. Willing to cooperate and help the underdog, the person

will make loyal friends and form lasting relationships. If a tendency to being overly serious and stern can be avoided, good luck will follow.

652 ♀ ▲ ⛢ Relationships and marriage may be entered into spontaneously but a great cheerfulness may help make them last in the long run. Financial fortune may be obtained and events, especially when involving the opposite sex, will happen suddenly, unexpectedly and be fruitful. The person's happiness is contagious, thus attracting others from whom benefits will be derived.

653 ♀ ▲ ♆ Extreme romantic desires seek an outlet for the refined feelings. Talent may be bestowed in the arts, music, drama and poetry. What may be lacking is practicality all around, leaving the emotions open to control by others. Spiritually, the person is at ease and seeks to spread peace and happiness.

654 ♀ ▲ ♇ Love centers life. The emotions are absorbed in close relationships, which are all important for the well being. A strong sex drive needs an outlet of expression. Close relationships or marriage may improve the character and circumstances in life.

655 ♀ ☍ ☽ The emotions are oversensitive and fragile which may lead to decisions that result in domestic and financial problems. The person feels unloved and unwanted and may turn to material possessions if emotional satisfaction is not forthcoming. When depressed, the feelings may overcompensate by engaging in excessive sexual activity or plunge into food, thus overloading the body's system.

656 ♀ ☍ ♂ The emotions are very sensitive and disagreement in sexual relationships will give reason for hurt. Marriage problems may develop as the partner is not on the same level and may have entered the marriage solely for sexual gratification. Disagreements over emotional, sexual and financial issues bring discontent and separation.

657 ♀ ☍ ♃ The person tries to cover up feelings of insecurity by being overly sweet and engaging in meaningless niceties. Self-indulgence, laziness and heavy reliance on others is used to avoid any responsibility. The desire for attention and craving of luxury may lead to problems and depletion of resources.

658 ♀ ☍ ♄ A bleak outlook on life brings depression, frustration and financial hardships as well as limitations. Due to disappointments in love and business, the mind is turning to unhappiness and may consider marriage only for financial considerations, while being unable to respond to love and joy. Experiences with employers also do not develop well as the job may be despised, paying little, or the person is subject to a miserly and dictatorial boss. Relationships and friendships with older people may be subject to strife and stress. Under some circumstances marriage may never be entered into due to a lack of opportunities and unpopularity. The behavior of the parents towards the child will determine the severity of this aspect.

659 ♀ ☍ ♅ The emotions are unstable, undergoing sudden and, at times, radical changes without consideration of any consequences. Marriage and friendships are subject to sudden termination as the mind is strangely and suddenly attracted to new infatuations leaving existing relationships in chaos. However, no change will endure for long as the mind engages in never ending desires for new and more opportunities. Impulsive behavior with friends and money will drain the resources and lead to separation and estrangements. The erratic and willful desire for freedom, and to forge ahead regardless of the consequences, will lead to disaster by which the person may lose any gain previously made. Unfortunate relations may be entered into that lead to loss and ultimately loneliness as friends and associations are not of enduring character.

660 ♀ ☍ ♆ The person may be his/her own worst enemy by destroying what had been carefully built over a long period of time. The mind is plagued by wishful fantasies removing any logic and reality from consideration. The person may be lazy, leaching onto others, or distort reality by escaping through drugs and alcohol. Financially, the person will be plagued by losses due to bad considerations or involvement in schemes or excessive pleasure. Secret romance may bring scandal and disappointment. Homosexual tendencies are possible. Marriage and unhealthy relationships will fall apart.

661 ♀ ☍ ♇ Involvement in intense and sometimes traumatic sexual relationships could bring trauma. Due to the inability to control the passion relationships and marriage are formed with undesirable

characters, especially when prostitution or crime involvement occurs. This will be degrading and of karmic consequences. Dictatorial behaviour by all involved may lead to violence. Financial problems, especially with other people's money, may bring a downfall. If disappointment through love and life is too great, the person may resort to suicide.

TRANSITS

662 ♀ ☌ ☉ refer to # 72.

663 ♀ ☌ ☽ refer to # 267.

664 ♀ ☌ ☿ refer to # 468.

665 ♀ ☌ ♂ An increased interest in romance and partnership, together with a desire for artistic expression, surface during this transit. Business activities could increase resulting in financial gain. If negatively aspected, a lack of sensitivity towards others and a forceful approach to sex will create quarrel, so will a hasty temper. If badly aspected, the person is inclined to favor the company of the lower side of society. Emotional sensitivity, quarrelsome behavior and too much emphasis on sex could bring disagreements.

666 ♀ ☌ ♃ A happy, cheerful and optimistic time with increased popularity. Artistic endeavors, higher education, religious involvement and the pursuit of romance will improve life. Interactions with foreigners or travel to a foreign country are possible. An excellent time for marriage and new undertakings. Beware, however, of excessive pleasure and cravings for luxury, which may require costly spending.

667 ♀ ☌ ♄ Romance or friendships with older or mature individuals are desired. The manners are reserved and cautious. Business dealings could bring financial gain. For existing relationships it could spell the end of it or serious problems will be overcome to secure the continuance of the union. Old friends or acquaintances may reappear while this transit lasts. If negatively aspected, loneliness may render the person miserable. Responsibilities regarding loved ones or business activities may require extra consideration. Extreme financial problems lead to mental depression. Sacrifices are required at this time.

668 ♀ ☌ ♅ Harmonious relationships with friends and lovers will be enjoyed. New friendships and affairs will be forthcoming under good aspects. Unexpected rewards and opportunities may present itself. The mind is content and seeks adventure. Business affairs will prosper. This is excellent for public relations and furtherance of causes. When afflicted, business, financial and social affairs will be met with discontent. As the desire for sex and romance can overwhelm the person, care is advised in choosing one's company. Love affairs that began during afflicted times will dissolve suddenly and unexpectedly, leaving behind hurt feelings. The temperament is irritated as unexpected circumstances interrupt the flow of life.

669 ♀ ☌ ♆ The mind and the imaginations are stimulated. An excellent time for creative and artistic endeavors. Photographers and especially writers will advance their craft. Travel for pleasure may be undertaken. However, beware of involvement in secret business and sexual affairs, which, in the end will not bring the desired advances. Visits to hospitals, institutions and retreats will be beneficial. If afflicted, deception of the mind is possible. Confusion and distortion of romantic and financial expectations will cause grief. Day dreaming may divert paying proper attention.

670 ♀ ☌ ♇ The emotions are intense, powerful, possessive and crave for sexual experiences. Existing relationships will be transformed. If unfavorable, extreme jealousy may grip the mind. Finances of others may be delusive and subject to arguments. Old romantic concepts may end. New relationships, formed at this time, may be only of a temporary nature.

671 ♀ ✱ ☉ refer to # 81.

672 ♀ ✱ ☽ refer to # 276.

673 ♀ ✱ ☿ refer to # 477.

674 ♀ ✱ ♂ Action is taken regarding social, romantic and business affairs. The mind is in harmony with the emotions. This may be a positive time to get pregnant. Social activities are engaged in to satisfy the desires, or to socialize. Beware of rash acts. Success needs to be pursued.

675 ♀ ✱ ♃ The mind is at ease, is happy, optimistic and content. Social activities will bring progress and honor. Getting romantically involved with foreigners or educational trips to foreign countries

can take place. This is a good time to marry and favorable to reap financial gain. Benefits could be derived from involvement in education and publishing.

676 ♀ ✱ ♄ A more formal manner is displayed. Business and financial matters will progress well. Support will come from authorities in power. Personal affairs may be formed with older co-workers. Legal matters fair well. The mind is calm and focussed but can be somewhat shy. Financial gain through relationships is possible. Be disciplined and focus on gain.

677 ♀ ✱ ♅ Unexpected and unusual business, social and private affairs bring excitement and change. Social ability and joining of groups bring benefits. Ideas may be new, inventive, original and lead to improved financial conditions. New romantic partners will be attracted.

678 ♀ ✱ ♆ The mind is harmonious. The imaginations are activated and urge to engage in artistic endeavors. The ability to visualize will promote creative affairs. Sympathy is extended toward the feelings of others. A favorable time to seek treatment in hospitals. Romantic interests are heightened. Spiritual enlightenment may affect the soul.

679 ♀ ✱ ♇ Private and social relationships are harmonious. The ego is calm and friendly without the urge to dominate. Sexual relationships are invited and could develop into lasting unions. The feelings will undergo intensity to the point of receiving extra vigor, thus, enhancing life.

680 ♀ □ ☉ refer to # 90.

681 ♀ □ ☽ refer to # 285.

682 ♀ □ ☿ refer to # 486.

683 ♀ □ ♂ Intense jealousy in romantic and business relationships disturb the affairs. Making openly sexual demands creates disagreements and estrangements. Financial problems come up. Avoid extravagance in spending. Enterprises don't perform well. Quarrels must be avoided, as well as seeking out prostitutes or other from of sexual exploits with undesirable individuals. An overall disharmony prevails. Curb the temperament to avoid misunderstandings and trouble. Relationships entered into, at this time, will not be of lasting value.

684 ♀ □ ♃ A reliance on others, laziness, self-indulgence and meaningless chatter applies to this transit. Procrastination and inattentiveness to responsibilities bring financial loss. Overspending out of emotional frustration should be avoided. Problems with foreigners or foreign travel may turn costly. Beware of overeating and drinking to drown the sorrows. Sudden impulses should be curbed. Love affairs may not be seen realistically and may be subject to later dissappointment.

685 ♀ □ ♄ Disappointment in all affairs will be experienced. Lack of sympathy for others, distant feelings and emotional coldness, will all lead to separations. Losses on all levels, especially financially, will be part of this transit. Authorities will disagree and hinder progress. Legal matters will experience set backs. Misunderstandings will lead to conflict. Loneliness and depression could prevail if allowed to get the upper hand. Don't neglect important responsibilities.

686 ♀ □ ♅ Attachments made, at this time, will not last. Sudden unwanted changes will have to be dealt with. Excessive demands for luxury and pleasure lead to impulsive spending. Verbal disagreements with friends, family and lovers could result in estrangements. Watch any changes in behavior that could be detrimental to progress. No cooperation is received. Love affairs entered into during this transit end in bitterness and dispute.

687 ♀ □ ♆ Emotional confusion, deception in love affairs, unrealistic expectations and hypersensitivity all bring disappointment and confrontations. Secret love affairs will drain the emotions and do not proceed as expected. Abuse of alcohol and drugs bring health problems and alienation from society. Day dreaming may replace reality. Do not get involved in any fast money schemes or it will lead to loss. Deception will be experienced. Be prepared for delusions and disappointments. Extra care needs to be applied.

688 ♀ □ ♇ Extreme jealousy, sexual aggressiveness and running with the wrong crowd, will bring disappointment and loss. The desire to remake others, as well as bully behavior in relationships, will bring breakdowns and resentments. Joint resources bring strife and loss. An expected inheritance may not materialize. Any

involvement in the criminal underworld or questionable schemes must be avoided. Financial losses must be expected.

689 ♀ ▲ ☉ refer to # 99.

690 ♀ ▲ ☽ refer to # 294.

691 ♀ ▲ ☿ refer to # 495.

692 ♀ ▲ ♂ The sexual urges awake. Romance and sexual attractions are foremost on the mind. A good time to get pregnant. Any artistic undertaking will progress and bring financial rewards. Carefully entered investments may profit. A good time to initiate new friendships that can be enduring. An increased social life will be experienced.

693 ♀ ▲ ♃ Optimistic, happy, loving and caring emotions bring advances. Romantic relationships develop well. Artistic enterprises will blossom and may deserve recognition. All social activities bring benefits. Agreements with lovers create an harmonious atmosphere allowing goals to be pursued to completion. A perfect time to study, go on vacation or deal with legal issues. Financial gain is indicated. Well planned investments will increase.

694 ♀ ▲ ♄ Serious business will be conducted in a friendly and organized manner. Partnerships will be appreciated and will be beneficial. Old Relationships may be renewed at this time. Responsibilities are accepted and executed with more ease. Financial rewards could be forthcoming. Older, or mature persons in positions of authority, will provide valuable cooperation. Benefits are received through loyal contacts. Climbing into a higher role in society is possible.

695 ♀ ▲ ♅ Especially artists and writers enjoy a boost of inspirations. Sudden opportunities will present itself. Help from friends and groups will be received. New romantic attractions and savvy business deals bring happy surprises. Financial rewards are indicated. New engagements, however, need to be scrutinized, as they may not be of long duration.

696 ♀ ▲ ♆ Enhanced imagination, spiritual and creative urges to produce a product of beauty, will emerge. There is harmony in relationships and with business partners. Depending on the natal position, this could bring the perfect love affair, that is satisfactory,

not only on the sexual level but also on a mental level. Secret finances may emerge or be provided by the lover.

697 ♀ ▲♇ An interest in entertainment and relationships is heightened Financial affairs may improve by using old work or renewing previously discarded items for profit. Resources of others will be beneficial. A possible inheritance could materialize. The partner may be generous with finances. Strong sexual affections may be of enduring effect. The sensuality is increased.

698 ♀ ☍ ☉ refer to # 108.

699 ♀ ☍ ☽ refer to # 303.

700 ♀ ☍ ☿ refer to # 504.

701 ♀ ☍ ♂ Hasty, extreme and emotional actions cause regret. Jealousy, sexual aggressiveness and lack of sensitivity could lead to resentment and separation. Emotional and financial extravagance will be costly. Business and relationships will suffer. The sexual energy needs controlling to avoid bitterness. Don't be selfish.

702 ♀ ☍ ♃ The optimism exceeds reality. Emotional and financial extravagance will be costly. Gain of weight is indicated as the mind lacks discipline for a sensible diet. Laziness and procrastination should not be allowed to gain the upper hand. Engagement in religious activities may not turn out as expected. Cooperation is needed in all actions. Do not avoid responsibilities. Strife, lawsuits, imprudent decisions and foolish acts may all cause disappointment and trouble. Keep the emotions in check.

703 ♀ ☍ ♄ Depression, bouts of melancholia, feelings of loneliness, all create disappointment. Unwanted separations may have to be endured. Professional activities cause dissatisfaction and lack fulfillment. Trouble will ensue. A lack of confidence can have undesired consequences. No cooperation is received from authorities. Financial loss may occur due to poor management or emotional spending. The emotions are cool and unresponsive causing disharmony in relationships.

704 ♀ ☍ ♅ Sudden romantic attractions will be of short duration. Unstable relationships, sexual promiscuity, personal irresponsibility and eccentric behavior will create problems in social dealings. Old friendships may cool off dramatically. A breakdown

of established business and friendships is indicated due to extreme indifference and lack of willingness to cooperate, thus, losses will occur. Care is needed in all transactions. Sudden upset will affect personal freedom, hence creating restrictions and tensions.

705 ♀ ☍ ♆ Emotional confusion, excessive fantasizing, secret affairs, delusion of expectations and unrequited love will come to the forefront during this transit. Avoid dubious financial dealings. Laziness, alcohol and drug consumption and excessive financial spending should be avoided. Be careful regarding personal relationships. Avoid day dreaming and romantic deception.

706 ♀ ☍ ♇ Don't be selfish but be sensitive to other people's emotions. A strong desire for sexual gratification will cause arguments and possibly separation. Don't get involved in extra marital affairs. Any attempt to dominate others causes resentment. Be cooperative and stay away from conflicts. Financial affairs are stressed and subject to disagreements and loss. Alimony payments are either late or subject to changes. Jealousy, guilt feelings and depressed emotions will be experienced. Avoid childish behavior.

♀ PROGRESSED

707 ♀ ☌ ☉ refer to # 120.

708 ♀ ☌ ☽ refer to # 331.

709 ♀ ☌ ☿ refer to # 513.

710 ♀ ☌ ♂ A very impulsive and expressive position that produces either 'love at first sight' or some very hasty decisions, which affect the feelings and emotions. The desires should be kept under control and away from rash and hasty actions.

711 ♀ ☌ ♃ This aspect brings peace, happiness and success, which are well disposed and will attract financial gain.

712 ♀ ☌ ♄ Disappointment, loss of honor and credit is indicated. Affections and financial affairs will not do well either. Attachments may be made to older persons, which may or may not be positive, depending on the lunar position hereto. A thrifty and careful attitude pays well during this aspect. The feelings and affections may be rather cold and limited or may cause the person to become a slave to his/her own emotions. It causes grief and tends to chasten the feelings of suffering, thus creating sorrow.

713 ♀ ☌ ♅ Premature consummation or sudden termination of attachments is found under this influence. Sudden ties affected by others, whose magnetic influence will move towards actions, will have a lasting effect upon the life. Sudden gains or losses are likely depending on the aspects operating while this conjunction lasts. The unexpected always happens while under this influence, however, the affections and emotions are often stimulated to the highest level. Usually more idealistic and imaginative, but also very susceptible to the influences of others, the person will seek to act originally and independently.

714 ♀ ☌ ♆ Remarkable and unique attachments or engagements may happen under this influence. It may produce platonic love affairs and could raise the affection to a higher level than experienced by ordinary people. Under normal circumstances it may bring social and financial benefits. If the natal position of these planets to each other was not positive emotional disappointment may be experienced.

715 ♀ ☌ ♇ Relationships may be karmic and extremely passionate. Strong sexual attractions are experienced and the dramatic side of the personality is enhanced. Any negative aspect hereto results in perverted passion, used as a power play for personal gain.

716 ♀ ✱ ☉ refer to # 121.

717 ♀ ✱ ☽ refer to # 332.

718 ♀ ✱ ☿ refer to # 522.

719 ♀ ✱ ♂ Personal feelings and desires will play a prominent part in life. If the ♀ influence be the stronger, then the mind will become more artistic, will give great mental energy and will raise the feelings into a higher expression in which the soul will express a purer and fuller love. This will enable the person to form good and lasting attachments. Any attachment will have a lasting effect that will be binding on all involved.

720 ♀ ✱ ♃ Very pleasant dealings with kindred or relatives and with those who will benefit socially and financially, will be experienced. Pleasures and all things tend to go evenly and smoothly while this harmonious influence is operating. It will act very beneficially in conjunction with other aspects. When the lunar aspects hereto

are good its influence will be most powerful. This is a good time for travel and for making binding and lasting attachments, which will be beneficial from the financial standpoint and also socially, hence, increasing the honor and standing in life.

721 ♀ ∗ ♄ Benefits will be obtained by forming very favorable attachments, which in turn will lead to success and fruitful unions. Gain, honor or an increase in reputation may be achieved. This aspect denotes a steady period of improvement and progress that also strengthens the character. When the lunar aspects are good, this will be a very good and prosperous period in which the foundation for future benefits can be established.

722 ♀ ∗ ♅ A very favorable aspect but, in some cases, the good that comes from it may end unfavorably. It brings strange attachments in which the feelings and emotions are very much affected. This aspect is good for social pleasures, entertainment and social involvement. The person is magnetically drawn towards others and inclined to act freely and independently. A strange link with others may be formed. Unexpected feelings or creative impulses may act and if not very discreetly handled, or if others be permitted to take advantage of the person, may ultimately create suffering. A good time to express inventive abilities and also to reap financial gain.

723 ♀ ∗ ♆ This is a very harmonious influence, which provides happiness and joy. Some friendships and attachments may be of a rather peculiar character with something secretive and mysterious about them. For those involved in religion it may be a period of seclusion and reflection but for others, a period of happiness and accomplishment will be experienced.

724 ♀ ∗ ♇ This presents a positive person who has great empathy for the problems of others, who is loyal to friends and liked by society. A strong interest in sex is possible.

725 ♀ □ ☉ refer to # 122.

726 ♀ □ ☽ refer to # 333.

727 ♀ □ ☿ refer to # 531.

728 ♀ □ ♂ This aspect denotes a conflict between the soul and the senses. The person either gains according to the attitude toward

the circumstances involved, or if ♂ is stronger, acts of indiscretion and impulsive acts, without any forethought, will bring out extreme feelings on the passionate side, hence producing havoc. A lot of temptation will occur that brings disappointment and pain. This is not a good time, neither financially nor socially. Great care will be required to avoid disgrace and dishonor, which may cause regrets and repent of some actions taken. Discreet action is required during this period as the feelings and emotions must be kept under control.

729 ♀ □ ♃ Losses in travel, dealing with religious people and financial losses, will be harmful. Conflict with superiors and the law should be avoided, as this could be a losing proposition. This aspect is not good for domestic affairs or for any new attachments as difficulties and loss will result. Separations may happen during this time.

730 ♀ □ ♄ An evil time concerning the affection. It tends to bring very intense emotions, which cause grief, sorrow and disappointment. Loss through the feelings, financial losses and forming of new attachments or engagement in social affairs, will be harmful. It affects the morals and tends to make the person careless and lacking in self-control. Deception and fraud should be avoided. One should not trust others too much as dishonor or general ill-repute may be harvested. Depending on the lunar influence, if this affliction is supported by other influences, the result will be very bad. Forethought and discretion should be exercised.

731 ♀ □ ♅ Domestic troubles, sudden estrangements or unfavorable family conditions may cause irritation and dispute. This aspect often leads to notoriety or encourages eccentricity, especially in regards to the expression of feelings. Care should be taken not to get involved in scandals or hurting situations as one could easily be offended. Erratic actions, based on peculiar feelings, may cause attachments or connections that will not be favorable. Events arising out of such connections will tend to injure the honor and thwart hopes and wishes. Financial loss may occur by the actions of others. No removal or changes should be made while under this influence.

732 ♀ □ ♆ Very strange and peculiar attachments cause the feelings to be affected by conditions quite out of the ordinary. All individuals

who exercise strange influences should be avoided and all dealings should be conducted under strict honesty and fair dealings. The person must act very discreetly to avoid trouble. Financial affairs and attachments should be very closely watched while this influence operates.

733 ♀ □ ♇ Jealousy, possessiveness and attachments to the wrong kind of people bring trouble, loneliness and emotional disappointments. A strong sex drive may lead to uncontrolled lust but furthers an inability to express feelings of love. Society may reject the person and loss of finances have to be dealt with.

734 ♀ ▲ ☉ refer to # 121.

735 ♀ ▲ ☽ refer to # 332.

736 ♀ ▲ ☿ This aspect cannot be formed during a normal life span.

737 ♀ ▲ ♂ This aspect is harmonious and peaceful in character. It will bring fruitful attachments, satisfaction to the feelings and emotions. Permanent ties or unions will be successful and fortunate. Hopes and wishes can be realized. Social advantages and financial gain may be indicated. It will bring joy into the life, according to the ability to respond to its vibration, but if allowing the feelings to go to extremes, suffering through excess of emotions will result.

738 ♀ ▲ ♃ This aspect will bring many financial benefits, for all things tend to go well. Social advantages can be made through making lasting attachments, as well as building helpful and profitable relationships. The affections will expand creating feelings of generosity and kindness, which in turn, attract others who are helpful in assisting to make life happy and prosperous.

739 ♀ ▲ ♄ This is a very steady period for the feelings and emotions. Faithful attention from others will be received bringing a thoughtful, sincere and thrifty attitude. The moral character will undergo improvements. Financial gain, either through judicious and careful investment, or by the advice of friends, will be reaped. This is a good time for strengthening the health and for the enjoyment of social pleasures and entertainment. It tends to form lasting attachments that will be enduring. It brings credit, honor and help to establish monetary affairs upon a sound basis, thus, helping improve future endeavors.

740 ♀ ▲ ⛢ Financial, emotional and social success is indicated. Some sudden gain and possible benefit through speculation and investment can be made. Fresh engagements or attachments are formed which will influence the person. This is a good time for travel and friendships. The mind is imaginative or idealistic and will have opportunities to experience new friendships or romantic attachments. This aspect is good for occult, astrology or any other study of higher thoughts.

741 ♀ ▲ ♆ It denotes a joyful period. Unless contrary conditions exist the person will experience a period of complete satisfaction. Financial matters will prosper. Material and spiritual gain could be achieved.

742 ♀ ▲ ♇ refer to # 724.

743 ♀ ☍ ☉ refer to # 122.

744 ♀ ☍ ☽ refer to # 333.

745 ♀ ☍ ☿ This aspect cannot be formed during a normal life span.

746 ♀ ☍ ♂ A struggle is taking place between the soul and the senses. Much will depend upon the attitude of either as to how this influence can be conquered. Much opposition and suffering of disappointment in love affairs will be felt. The will and desire are at cross-purpose and will severely be tried and tempted by the emotions. Some financial losses, social troubles and disadvantages are indicated. This is a very bad time to make engagements, to bind one self to others, or to allow the feelings and emotions to be drawn out in any way towards sensation or passion. The person should act very discreetly and be careful in whom any trust is placed, especially when the lunar aspects are unfavorable.

747 ♀ ☍ ♃ A very unfavorable time for social affairs, for travel and for monetary affairs. All waste should be avoided Money should be spent wisely. Money should not be lend to anyone. No surety for others should be given, as there is liability to be involved in heavy losses or in pecuniary embarrassments. Money and love affairs are not going well at this time. Legal trouble may be threatened. Much opposition will be experienced, therefore it is prudent to take great care and avoid risks, especially where money is concerned. It is unfavorable for religious matters and for dealing with those who are proud and aristocratic.

748 ♀ ☍ ♄ This position is likely to bring much trouble and anxiety and the experience of disappointment in all attachments, feelings and emotions by suffering the consequences of wrong actions. It denotes separation, bereavement and sorrow, also financial losses and general money trouble. A bad time to attach oneself to elderly persons or authority as it threatens scandal and a liability to be secretly attacked and slandered. Discretion is the answer to this aspect until is has passed.

749 ♀ ☍ ♅ This will bring separation and estrangements from loved ones and cause sorrow and pain. The feelings and emotions are at high tension and easily affected. Care should be taken when choosing new attachments. Guarding against sensations or of becoming too susceptible to the influences of others, is necessary. It is a bad time for legal affairs and monetary matters, especially in regards to speculations and investments. The native must be careful in all love affairs and make no unwise changes or handle things abruptly and suddenly.

750 ♀ ☍ ♆ A denial of success at the last moment is indicated. To people who are driven mostly by their feelings it produces extreme sorrows, even involving secrecy. To the person in control of their emotions it may involve fraud and misrepresentation, hence demanding a constant guard in all business matters.

751 ♀ ☍ ♇ refer to # 733.

BABY CHART

752 ♀ ☌ ☉ refer to # 143.

753 ♀ ☌ ☽ refer to # 353.

754 ♀ ☌ ☿ refer to # 555.

755 ♀ ☌ ♂ The concept of love and sex is confused and may lead to any sexual dysfunction. Any sexual involvement may be perceived as difficult or will be unsatisfactory affecting relationships and causing tension and insecurity. People may become obsessed with or have severe crushes on others and desire to marry them before a relationship has even developed. The mother affects the sexual behavior of the child and may even turn her son into a homosexual as the child has problems relating to women or has a loyalty complex

to mother that is disturbed by being sexually involved with women.

756 ♀ ☌ ♃ Lucky in love, having many suitors available but the positive energy must be channeled or the person merely becomes selfish and does not know what is wanted to satisfy the mind.

757 ♀ ☌ ♄ The father restricted the understanding of love and affection by placing limitations on the child's concept of love, thus creating a feeling of loss. This could create a feeling of pessimistic attitude when viewing love relationships. A marriage will be consumed not out of love but someone who will logically make a good partner. When the child is involved in a love relationship he may break it up or create a hate or hurt relationship as he cannot deal with the flow, trust and understanding of love. The fact that there is no guarantee in love, but that understanding and trust must be created and earned, may not be understood. The person is unable to give of the self and always feels that the grass is greener on the other side. The lesson here is to learn how to give, not how to buy someone.

758 ♀ ☌ ⛢ The erratic behavior of the parents confuses the child. The concept of love may need to be channeled and understood or constant breakups will occur. In later life the lack of consideration before actions are taken may cause pain to others and undermines relationships. The concept of love may be very unstable and undergoes constant changes. The concept of communicating with loved ones is disturbed. Relationships are ended without a warning, creating a shock to the partner with possible emotional trauma.

759 ♀ ☌ ♆ Love and the ability to relate or express affection and share feelings and communications are clouded and distorted. A deluded and unrealistic spiritual concept of emotions may develop into some kind of phobia that, at times, will prevent enjoying sexual relationships or any closeness to others. A person may be attracted to a homosexual partner in order to avoid physical love, or the partner may be an alcoholic or drug addict that constantly needs someone. The result is a strong sense of loneliness, as well as physical and emotional deprivation of needs. Secret or hidden relationships or family problem and lies may prevent an honest

and open assessment of the problems. Sometimes the real parents are not known.

760 ♀ ☌ ♇ The mother uses her womanhood to control her surroundings which instills in the child a desire to control everyone. Relationships may suffer from obsession and manipulation, thus creating unhappiness. The child may resent the mother and a battle of wills could develop. To escape this aspect, the will must be redirected to lessen the control freak factor.

761 ♀ ✱ ☉ refer to # 152.

762 ♀ ✱ ☽ refer to # 361.

763 ♀ ✱ ☿ refer to # 563.

764 ♀ ✱ ♂ The mother instills a healthy attitude towards sex and emotional relationships so that both can be enjoyed.

765 ♀ ✱ ♃ Able to reach out, obtain and enjoy the needs of life, this aspect instills confidence to pursue goals.

766 ♀ ✱ ♄ The childhood is mainly serious but also produces great steadiness of purpose and steadfast co-operation in work and love relationships.

767 ♀ ✱ ♅ The mother is eccentric but teaches the child how to love and be appreciated, providing uplifting energy and talent for creative expression.

768 ♀ ✱ ♆ A great ability and interest in the arts, in creative expressions and spiritual development is present. However, the talent needs developing.

769 ♀ ✱ ♇ Loved by the masses and together with an in-depth understanding what motivates people, make cooperation with groups very beneficial.

770 ♀ □ ☉ refer to # 161.

771 ♀ □ ☽ refer to # 369.

772 ♀ □ ☿ This aspect does not happen at birth due to the planets close proximity to each other.

773 ♀ □ ♂ A possible guilt complex in love relationships may have been adopted in childhood from the mother creating frustration on the concept of love. The physical need for sex and the emotional satisfaction of love may not harmonize. This may cause the person to be like a bee flying from flower to flower in hope of finding satisfaction of all desires.

774 ♀ □ ♃ The concept of how to relate to others may be underdeveloped or too excessive, creating constant changes in search of perfection. Falling in and out of love or obsessive overreaction may destroy a relationship. Lack of self-worth may be covered up by excessive overreaction to everything.

775 ♀ □ ♄ The self-worth is underdeveloped. The concept of masculine and feminine principles is at odds with each other creating emotional confusion in the child. The lack of expressing affection constricts the child to be apprehensive in later relationships. Role playing and acting out Mom and Dad instead of sharing emotions creates frustrations against the partner. Loneliness, pessimism, lack of giving and receiving love, may hinder happiness and contentment in life.

776 ♀ □ ♅ The mother's unpredictability prevents the child later from forming stable relationships. Expressing and sharing feelings must be learned to break the circle adopted at birth. Sudden unexplained breaking off of relationships can create havoc and hurt the feelings of all involved.

777 ♀ □ ♆ The concept of love is nebulous. Giving, sharing and receiving love is a concept not understood by the child. The desire for love, without knowing what it means, may lead to involvement in strange religious cults. Cults may perceive sex as dirty and teach celibacy and force their sense of morality onto others. A need to develop spiritually and, for each to follow their own path, is necessary.

778 ♀ □ ♇ Mother's constant control and manipulation may drain the family of emotions. The child may have accepted such behavior and later on repeats it thereby draining the energy that could be used for valuable achievements. Money and power cannot provide a warm and caring relationship.

779 ♀ ▲ ☉ refer to # 170.

780 ♀ ▲ ☽ refer to # 377.

781 ♀ ▲ ☿ refer to # 772.

782 ♀ ▲ ♂ The parents had a positive influence over the child's psychological development, thus, creating expressions for wants, desires, appreciation and accomplishment.

783 ♀ ▲ ♃ The child learns to give, to receive love and relate to others. Artistic expressions are indicated that may attract likewise.

784 ♀ ▲ ♄ The parents express a good balance of feelings onto the child as they understand their personal and sexual role in society. The child will be somewhat serious but very reliable.

785 ♀ ▲ ♅ The child is sharing, caring and supportive of others. Unusual talent and a teaching ability may be present. Love relationships are unusual, unorthodox, but sincere.

786 ♀ ▲ ♆ The child learns creativity from the mother and appreciates art. The understanding of the concept of sex and love and how they are to be combined needs developing.

787 ♀ ▲ ♇ Cooperation with people of all walks of life is beneficial. Combined with a sense of appreciation, the person will thrive if not too materialistic.

788 ♀ ☍ ☉ refer to # 179.

789 ♀ ☍ ☽ refer to # 385.

790 ♀ ☍ ☿ refer to # 772.

791 ♀ ☍ ♂ The ability to love is hampered by the mother's behavior creating fear, apprehension or feelings of self–disgust and discomfort towards love, sharing of emotions and physical needs. Love cannot be applied to sexual emotions creating confusion about the wants of the person and how to relate to both in a relationship.

792 ♀ ☍ ♃ The concept of accepting the self creates conflict in the child. Extravagance and excessiveness are present when forming any relationship just to lose interest soon thereafter. Lack of appreciation of the self and others needs understanding in order to be resolved. A selfishness of instant gratification may turn into problems.

793 ♀ ☍ ♄ The concept of male and female has not developed as the parents are at odds with their own sexuality. A parent may be absent from the home. The ability to love may be underdeveloped and any authority may be rejected. A lack of self-esteem causes later relationship problems.

794 ♀ ☍ ♅ The mother displays erratic and eccentric behaviors toward the child diminishing the child's understanding of loving and caring.

In later life, the child jumps in and out of love unsure as to how to deal with these emotions. Constant changes of the mind create instability. Mistrust of relationships has been instilled by the mother's behavior creating an abrupt turnover of relationships.

795 ♀ ☍ ♆ Some kind of separation from the mother is indicated. The child has difficulties to express wants, wishes, love and affection and has not developed a caring attitude as none was provided during childhood.

796 ♀ ☍ ♇ The mother's overwhelming personality may have smothered the child. Control and manipulation are instilled which make it later difficult for the child to have a caring and sharing relationship. The child needs to learn to let go rather than stay in a relationship to manipulate or be manipulated.

♀ TRANSIT OR PROGRESSION TO A (Ascendant)

797 ♀ ☌ **A** Great beauty, diplomacy and tact is instilled. If not otherwise negatively aspected, this position may bring much pleasure and wealth. If unfavorably aspected, narcissistic tendencies and a strong self-interest may develop. During transit new love relationships and expressions of affection will improve the social standing.

798 ♀ ∗ **A** If not otherwise negatively aspected, this aspect provides for social grace, receiving of public favors and fortunes, also through a successful marriage. In general, there is a cheerful disposition. Artistic talents are instilled. During transit socializing will be favorable. Disputes can be settled and new relationships can be formed.

799 ♀ □ **A** Losses through extravagance, trouble with the affections and health problems with the generative system. The self-expression may be hampered by society. There is trouble relating to others. During transit any acts in excess will cause trouble. Control any mood and spending and avoid any dispute.

800 ♀ ▲ **A** Grace, charm and a pleasant personality attract benefits from the public. A favorable position that increased stamina and health. During transit all forms of entertainment and socializing will be enjoyed. Financial rewards can be reaped.

801 ♀ ☍ **A** refer to # 799.

♀ TRANSIT OR PROGRESSION TO M (Mid heaven)

802 ♀ ☌ **M** A career in the public eye is certain. An abundance of charm promotes the desires and social ambitions. Acquiring wealth, or the prospect of a wealthy marriage, are indicated. During transit new love relationships may be formed that involve business, profession or social contacts.

803 ♀ ✱ **M** Harmonious business and private affairs are indicated. A good and even public marriage, or a marriage into the upper society, is possible if there are no negative influences present. General prosperity could be obtained. During transit offers of help are forthcoming. A helpful attitude will bring rewards.

804 ♀ □ **M** Trouble through attachments, the public and any involvement in business affairs. Attacks on the honor and reputation may occur. Emotional unhappiness is indicated. Over possessiveness, jealousy and emotionally unbalanced behavior will lead to disputes and estrangements.

805 ♀ ▲ **M** Charm, grace and ambitions are used to further any interests. The popularity increases and provides for a favorable marriage and business engagement. During transit improvement of the home, artistic endeavors and love of beauty finds fulfillment. Affections are displayed and promote diplomacy.

806 ♀ ☍ **M** refer to # 804.

40

♂ Mars

This planet symbolizes strength, courage, energy, ambitions and actions. It provides endurance, athletic built and never ending resourcefulness. Fond of and passionate about sexual matters, attractions are actively initiated for company and emotional outlets.

When afflicted it means rashness, loss of temper, quarrelsome, harsh speech, aggressive in sex and addicted to alcohol, gambling or other bad habits. The morals are diminished. Lack of trust is indicated. A liar who is possibly involved in crimes. A very bad ♂ to ♀ may indicate an abortion. Accidents, fever, infections, high blood pressure and liability to accidents are ruled by this planet. During its transit of about 1 ½ months through each house, depending on the size of the house, the temper, ambitions and physical energy emerge. A weak ♂ may hinder a person to forge ahead. Too strong a ♂ may engage the person in constant quarrels.

♂ IN THE HOUSES

807 ♂ (1) The person is aggressive, impulsive and outgoing with lots of energy and is always ready to get involved in life. The body is usually strong, muscular and rugged. A need to think before one acts is required to avoid disappointment. An indulgence in all kinds of sports provides for great stamina. An intense restlessness should be curbed.

If afflicted, the person is egotistical, bully, headstrong and eager to get things done in his/her way. Any interference from others will not be tolerated. This may involve disregards for the rights and feelings of others. Anger and violence, as well as rash acts lead to emotional impulsiveness. Illness could result from high fever, scars, inflammations and rushes, particularly on the face. Men may lose their hair early.

808 ♂ (2) The desire for money and material goods is strong. Being an easy spender any savings may be quickly depleted. A desire to be boss, a very competitive attitude and a will to fight to protect personal property, is instilled. Giving, however, is done more to win favors or make good impressions.

If afflicted, material gain could become an obsession. Dishonesty and unlawfulness may be pursued to acquire possessions and feed the desire to be important. A harsh temper brings trouble and disputes over money.

809 ♂ (3) The intellect is used aggressively. Quick thinking will be applied but a tendency to jump to conclusions before all the facts are known may lead to disappointments. The speech is direct and, at times, caustic, and mostly aggressive in all communications. Short term traveling, combined with all kinds of communications, can be a source of income.

If afflicted, the person may become reckless, bully, and suffers from instant flashes of anger. Sarcasm or engaging in argumentative confrontations and trouble with contracts, publications, communications, brothers, sisters and neighbors, may occur.

810 ♂ (4) There is a strong interest in the home and family but also a desire to dominate here. Working constantly to improve the home by repairing and changing it, engages the person. There is an interest in the environment. A strong constitution is given, even in old age.

If afflicted, there is conflict inside the home environment, within the family and especially with the parents. Strong self-control is needed to avoid quarrels. Property may be a source of trouble. The home could be endangered by acts of nature or by criminal elements or excessive taxes.

811 ♂ (5) Pleasure and love are aggressively pursued. A strong sexual drive needs controlling. A good but stern relationship with children may be formed. Investments must be addressed with caution to avoid rash acts and misunderstandings.

If afflicted, impatience, sexual aggressiveness to the point of violence, or out of wedlock pregnancy, is possible. Trouble with children, even accidents or death of children, could occur. Dictatorial attitudes toward others create strife. Gambling addictions may become ruinous.

812 ♂ (6) The energy is expressed through hard work. Mechanical and engineering work is preferred. There is little patience with people who are not as driven in their desires and execution of goals. The person is generally well organized and efficient in job performance.

If afflicted, injuries, irritability, ill health with sharp pain, or accidents due to rashness, may be experienced. Involvement in work disputes and conflicts with co-workers and employers is possible. Being overly concerned with details can distract from the real issue and lead to uncompleted projects.

813 ♂ (7) Partnerships and work may involve the public. The person and/or the marriage partner is likely to be aggressive and impulsive.

If afflicted, disagreements with associates, marriage partners or the public could lead to divorce and disintegration of partnerships. Matters of joint business and finances are subject to dispute. A lack of tact and diplomacy or interaction for purely selfish reasons, may lead to trouble.

814 ♂ (8) The emotional and financial security is a prime motivator. Aggressiveness is indicated regarding other people's money, insurance, inheritance or corporate finances. A strong sex drive is leading the emotions. A violent and sudden death could be the result of war or other mass conflict.

If afflicted, criminal tendencies could be evinced. Actions are conducted in secret to avoid confrontations. Conflict over taxes, joint finances, insurance money, inheritances and partners spending will ensue.

815 ♂ (9) An interest in sport, outdoors, travel, religion, law and educational institutions, is strong. A desire for social reform and

an interest in social causes may lead to long distant travel and contact with foreigners.

If afflicted, a tendency to revolutions, extreme adventures, interest in the military or religious fanatics, may develop. A severe narrow mindedness or fanatical outlook can lead to conflict. A tendency to promote only ones own point of view, and an overblown sense of self-importance and guru worship, create friction.

816 ♂ (10) Fame, status and fortune are prime motivators. The desire to reach the top, especially in politics, corporate management, engineering, military and other powerful and authoritarian positions, is strong.

If afflicted, unfair means will be used to gain power or position. The reputation may suffer and reversal of fortune occurs after wrongdoings are exposed. The desire for money and power may be so consuming that human values are ignored.

817 ♂ (11) Friendship and group activities are developed to achieve hopes and wishes. Friends of masculine character and physique are preferred.

If afflicted, conflicts with friends and groups develop. A strong desire exists to change social conditions to one's own point of view. Impulsive behavior may lead to injury or death to self, friends and groups.

818 ♂ (12) Unconscious desires rule the mind. Work may be carried out in seclusion, in secret or behind the scene in institutions and hospitals. Secret sexual involvement may be entertained.

If afflicted, involvement in secret plots, having secret enemies or suffering from possible incarceration or confinement in hospitals, will bring reversals. During transit, a loss of wealth or extreme expenses may curb the social position.

♂ IN THE SIGNS

819 ♂ (♈) Bursts of energy, aggressiveness, courage, headstrong behavior, a drive for independence and impulsive acts, all run the emotions. There is a strong drive for accomplishment, to succeed and be first. However, the person may abandon a goal for lack of staying power. Opposition and interference is despised. A need to

think before any acts are taken is necessary as the emotions override any logic. Engagements in competitive games require strength and courage. When ill there will be high fever. Head injuries often happen but there is also a strong power of recuperation.

If afflicted, egotism, aggressiveness, anger, bully and violent temper will rule the emotions.

820 ♂ (♉) The energy is expanded to obtain money and possessions, which may be limited, or obtained only after overcoming obstacles. Slow to act, the person is very stubborn but possesses great determination, perseverance and will power to complete a chosen path. Good ability for craftsmen work is indicated.

If afflicted, sexual desires and an excessive drive for money and possession, or jealousy and violence in sexual situation, are possible. The desire to act this way is to dominate and cover up feelings of inferiority.

821 ♂ (♊) The mental capacity is engaged in education and acts aggressively. The person can be critical to a fault, loves debates and intellectually inspired conversations. Any position that produces reporters, critics and jobs that require mental stress and quick thinking, is suitable.

If afflicted, the person may be argumentative, irritable, suffer from sarcasm, rudeness and has many job changes or several jobs running simultaneously, as constant confrontations take place.

822 ♂ (♋) The mind is ruled by emotions creating moodiness, frustration and anger. When aggressive, there will always be an emotional argument.

If the anger is suppressed psychological disorders, ulcers and other internal illnesses will result. Much aggressiveness is displayed that must be channeled into physical work to find an outlet.

823 ♂ (♌) Tremendous willpower, creativity and a desire for leadership exist. The person loves to be at the center of attention and likes to win at all costs. Beliefs and opinions are strongly expressed and turn bully if others disagree. Desires, especially sexually, are strong but may be ruled by possessiveness and jealousy.

Men may lose their hair early. Egotism, as well as dominating and overbearing behavior, may create a believing in one's own infallibility.

824 ♂ (♍) Organizational talent and practical skills in work, coupled with systematic execution of plans, prevent rush actions without practical reasons. Attention to details and a desire for perfection may rule the mind.

Fussiness and highly critical attitudes can lead to frictions. Disagreements with co-workers, employers, or other authority may jeopardize job security. Accidents at work, due to carelessness, nervousness and irritable temperament, are possible.

825 ♂ (♎) An interest in dealing with the public leads to an abundance of social activities. The person likes to be appreciated, noticed and is willing to work in partnerships. A strong desire exists to marry for emotional gratification and security. Aggressive and energetic partners are desired. Social grace and discipline are used to help further any interest.

If afflicted, anger and great concern with morality, or a tendency to strictness and adherence to social rules, arguments and conflicts of will in relationships, all create discontent and problems.

826 ♂ (♏) Powerful emotions drive and lead to courage and execution of plans. Resourcefulness and an abundance of energy can help lead the way out of any difficult situation. Danger may be faced without being frightened. The strong will pursues any goal. Even if that means fighting to the bitter end. A powerful sex drive, possessiveness and intense jealousy, together with an all-or-nothing attitude, may lead to difficulties. The point of view is rarely changed. Acts done in secret may make enemies by insisting on going it alone.

If afflicted, the powerful sex drive, coarseness, bluntness, bully, anger, resentment, and ability to hold grudges, makes for dangerous enemies. All kinds of wrong characters will be attracted leading into bigger trouble. This person has a tendency to dominate and control others emotionally and requires servitude of others.

827 ♂ (♐) Intense feelings for foreigners, law, religion and philosophy are expressed. A strong belief to convert others to one's own dogmatic belief and a strong feeling of patriotism is likely. There is

fondness of parades and displays and a strong desire to travel, engage in sports, and outdoor activities. A desire to be a leader in religious matters and a constant drive for higher education, follows an interest in foreign lands.

If afflicted, the speech is caustic. There is lack of diplomacy, an inability to accept the opinions of others, querulous behavior and an utter demand for one's own freedom at all costs. The desire to be in charge and to be always right may lead to underhanded tactics for power by disregarding rules and laws.

828 ♂ (♑) Strong financial and professional ambitions, together with a desire for recognition and status, is intense and calculating. A practical reasoning compels the person to act. Great self-control and severe discipline make for good employees.

If afflicted, there is a tendency to leach on others. Laziness is displayed, and people are used solely for gain. Sometimes the desire for money overrides human and social values and creates total disregard of others. Cold, calculating, selfish and materialistic behavior will drive the person to the top but will lead to disappointment and trouble.

829 ♂ (♒) Independence, menial freedom, a desire for adventure and unorthodox actions are instilled. An interest in humanitarian organization and teamwork could lead to a business in these fields. The person is very original, logically, practical and desires to work alone and does not thrive well under authority.

If afflicted, there is a desire to overthrow old rules and this position can make the 'blood boil' with anger.

830 ♂ (♓) The emotions are ruled by the unconscious mind. Resentment, repressed anger and unhappiness may lead to neurosis and other ailments. Emotional sensitivity can undermine the self confidence and delay decisions. Actions are taken in secret to avoid emotional confrontations. The person is easily brought to tears. Periods of solitude are needed to regain emotional strength. Work is best done behind the scene. An artistic talent is strongly indicated and should be developed.

If afflicted, emotional dependency on others will turn into dominating them or the emotional problems are unloaded onto others hoping to gain pitty by smothering others with their problems.

♂ IN ASPECT WITH OTHER PLANETS

831 ♂ ☌ ☉ refer to # 28

832 ♂ ☌ ☽ refer to # 223

833 ♂ ☌ ☿ refer to # 428

834 ♂ ☌ ♀ refer to # 627

835 ♂ ☌ ♃ An increased self-confidence, higher energy, enthusiasm, optimism and a desire for action is indicated. Favors may be received that will increase business and finances. If this aspect is negatively affected a "know-it-all" attitude may produce unpopularity and disagreements.

836 ♂ ☌ ♄ This aspect instills an ability for hard work and gives responsibility even in the face of adversary. Life requires sacrifices and, at times, provides for a bumpy ride. If negatively afflicted, the person may display lingering feelings of anger and malice, resenting other's, who's life is more easy and successful. At the worst, self-destructive tendencies will result through sudden, uncontrolled actions, outbursts of anger and hasty decisions, all leading to more difficulties.

837 ♂ ☌ ♅ Sudden, erratic and impulsive action, coupled with a strong desire for adventure, is bestowed by this aspect. The person is rebellious, ready to do drastic and life altering changes that sometimes lack prudence and foresight. This applies to business, finances and sexual engagements. The energy expressed by ♂ needs an outlet to be transformed into positive directions. Any kind of sport, requiring physical strain, will work out the energy stored by this aspect. If this conjunction is afflicted, the person may thrive on danger, be reckless, prone to accidents and experience all kinds of mechanical trouble. Sexual aggressiveness, as well as arguments with friends and family, should be avoided.

838 ♂ ☌ ♆ The spiritual development may be led by a blind following of occult and mystical organizations. Actions taken could be unprepared, impractical, unrealistic and misguided. Any romantic involvement may be one sided, secretive and fueled by strange

desires. Drugs and alcohol create problems if this conjunction is negatively aspected by other planets.

839 ♂ ☌ ♇ The willpower is extremely strong, coupled with endurance and a fearless attitude it will help accomplish even difficult tasks. If this conjunction is negatively affected involvement in crime, dishonesty and destructive violence will be detrimental. The desires are hard to control. The person may either achieve a goal or incur destruction. Accidents may happen due to inconsequent and rash acts.

840 ♂ ∗ ☉ refer to # 37.

841 ♂ ∗ ☽ refer to # 232.

842 ♂ ∗ ☿ refer to # 436.

843 ♂ ∗ ♀ refer to # 635.

844 ♂ ∗ ♃ The energy is high, so is the optimism, enthusiasm and the desire for self-improvement. Success will follow if the path chosen is well planned and executed. A good aspect for legal matters.

845 ♂ ∗ ♄ Perfection in work, great discipline and endurance come with this aspect. The person is very competent, however, an expression of coldness and sternness emanates from the personality.

846 ♂ ∗ ♅ The willpower is strong so is the desire for quick action. The nervous energy needs an outlet for achievement.

847 ♂ ∗ ♆ A desire to carry out actions in secret, or to plot and plan to achieve results, may not receive the approval of others. A certain involvement in military action is indicated.

848 ♂ ∗ ♇ The desire for power, action and accomplishment is overwhelming and leads to relentlessly pursuing any goal.

849 ♂ □ ☉ refer to # 46.

850 ♂ □ ☽ refer to # 241.

851 ♂ □ ☿ refer to # 444.

852 ♂ □ ♀ refer to # 642.

853 ♂ □ ♃ The desires are overwhelming, destructive and used solely for self-aggrandizement, regardless of the feelings of others. The "holier-than-thou" attitude makes for fanatical beliefs and extreme behavior, which could lead the person down the path of ruin and disaster. A constant restlessness and change of course

will render the person unreliable and unpopular. Hypocrisy may occur. In extreme cases, and depending on any negative aspect hereto, this will lead to arrest and possible incarceration.

854 ♂ □ ♄ An enormous amount of frustration, due to obstacles and continuous hard work, renders the person depressed, negative and produces melancholia. A conflict in relating to others, due to an overly rigid attitude and behavior, creates difficulties and unpopularity. To achieve any form of success requires tremendous hardship and perseverance. Only after pursuing all opportunities and not giving in, may success be obtained. There is an air of danger attached to the person's life, which either is related to an occupation or general circumstances in life. If there is a tendency towards selfishness, this aspect makes for unpopularity and creates harsh attitudes toward others.

855 ♂ □ ♅ Impulsiveness, uncontrolled, erratic desires and actions are likely to bring disagreements or outright danger into the life. Accidents may occur due to hastiness. Involvement in thrill-seeking activities is dangerous. Eccentricity and a desire to force one's will onto others, bring unpopularity or lead to legal trouble. Any lack of cooperation or bully tactics will create friction.

856 ♂ □ ♆ Deep seated neurosis and hurtful emotions could lead to sexual attacks or drugs and alcohol consumption. The mind has no purpose, is muddled, confused and may act in secret to avoid confrontations. There is a possibility of deceit by or against the person. In extreme cases sexual perversity could manifest. The imaginations may be far out and removed from reality. However, the emotions may tune in to the feelings and sensations of others.

857 ♂ □ ♇ Lack of diplomacy, a strong, dictatorial will, and a desire for power will all lead down the wrong path. Foolish and unconsidered actions, if taken, will lead to trouble. The nerves are high strung, the temper is violent and criminal tendencies may manifest. The person is sexually aggressive and has uncontrolled and undirected desires. If other negative aspects affect this square, a death by violence is possible. The will and the desire are in conflict and need direction for any achievement to occur.

858 ♂ ▲ ☉ refer to # 55.

859 ♂ ▲ ☽ refer to # 250.

860 ♂ ▲ ☿ refer to # 452.

861 ♂ ▲ ♀ refer to # 649.

862 ♂ ▲ ♃ Optimism and energy combined with the desire for action may lead to fulfillment of ambitions. The person is very helpful to the less fortunate and thrives in all kinds of social, religious and psychological occupations.

863 ♂ ▲ ♄ Hard work, precise action, serious and responsible execution are the main assets of this aspect. There is a display of tremendous willpower and energy to seek projects through to completion. All occupations involving machinery, surgical and engineering skills are favored. Mental strength and an application for endurance will provide the stamina to overcome all obstacles and hardships.

864 ♂ ▲ ♅ Willpower, originality, inventive ideas and the successful execution of them, will provide for achievement. The person is outspoken, full of energy, independent and knowledgeable in occult laws. Travel, adventure and any kind of unusual experience are favored to satisfy the high nervous energy level.

865 ♂ ▲ ♆ The senses are in tune with society. Occult, astrology and healing practices may support the person. Acting in secret to avoid interference from others could result in some kind of seclusion, as the sensitivity of the emotions will absorb the feelings of others.

866 ♂ ▲ ♇ There is a desire for power, a strong will and stamina and the ability to regenerate life through decisive actions. An interest in science, physics and social aspects may be developed. The person is fearless and willing to go all the way for a worthwhile cause.

867 ♂ ☍ ☉ refer to # 64.

868 ♂ ☍ ☽ refer to # 259.

869 ♂ ☍ ☿ refer to # 460.

870 ♂ ☍ ♀ refer to # 656.

871 ♂ ☍ ♃ Over-optimism, extravagance and a high self-interest could lead to unpopularity. Outspoken and always promoting ones own point of view for the desire to actively seek fame and fortune. Lot's of travel, restlessness, extreme wanderlust and a constant desire for adventure makes the person unsteady, unreliable and subject to constant changes in life. Any involvement in lawsuits should

be avoided as well as dishonesty, speculation and ill-considered rash decisions, as they will bring loss.

872 ♂ ☍ ♄ A sternness, being resentful, depressive, frustrated and a possibility of violence may be displayed. Rash and ill-considered acts lead to loss. As ♄ represents the slow and hindering process in life, the desire to rash, as displayed by ♂, may act in the disinterest of ♄. Misfortune will occur. Any relationships with authority figures could create argument and disagreement. If anger is allowed to prevail, distraction will follow. Finances may not do well. Any joint resources are subject to dispute. The unwillingness to cooperate or to be helpful may result in being shunned by others. Such a behavior may also be displayed toward the person. If this opposition receives more unfavorable aspects from others planets, violence, crime or participation in war, is possible.

873 ♂ ☍ ♅ The mind is bitter, ready to quarrel and throw irritable tantrums. An immense desire for independence renders the person unsuitable for any long-term routine job. There is a lack of sustained effort and discipline, which makes it hard to deal with the person. Reckless behavior or involvement in dangerous situations or violence could result in death. The life becomes unstable and is subject to dangerous situations. The unwillingness to cooperate, combined with an unpredictable behavior, renders any involvement difficult.

874 ♂ ☍ ♆ Aggressiveness, anger, hate and sometimes violence is instilled into the personality. Deceiving others and being deceived comes with this aspect. The emotions are unstable and out of control. The function between the desires and any reasoning are out of balance leading to ill considered acts. Secret and underhanded tactics lead to self-undoing. Relationships and sexual desires may turn perverted, damaging the person's reputation. The use of drugs and alcohol presents a real danger as the mind is not subject to conscious control. Neurosis and other mental illnesses can develop due to the unbalanced feelings, which constantly long for something unobtainable. The mental state may become a physical ailment. Involvement in religion may be fueled by unrealistic expectations and turn to disappointment when the

feelings remain unsatisfied. Dishonesty or dealing with likewise characters or schemes should be avoided as they will lead to loss.

875 ♂ ☍ ♇ The willpower and the desire for glory and forceful actions are fueled by this aspect. Participation in dangerous and violent situations could lead to death The concept of desire and will is unbalanced leading to ill-considered rash acts. The person is tempted to use personal powers and violence instead of diplomacy, thus resulting in dangerous situations. At the very least, the person is out for revenge, displays hate and bitterness, thus making for a dangerous enemy. The desire to remake others causes disagreements and separations. An active involvement in criminal activity or dealings with the underworld in some way could turn dangerous.

TRANSITS

876 ♂ ☌ ☉ refer to # 73.

877 ♂ ☌ ☽ refer to # 268.

878 ♂ ☌ ☿ refer to # 469.

879 ♂ ☌ ♀ refer to # 665.

880 ♂ ☌ ♃ There is a great amount of energy and enthusiasm to forge ahead. New undertakings, foreign travel, legal affairs, joined finances and the furtherance of education can be handled well at this time. Physical exercise will shape body and mind. Financial benefits can be obtained through prudent business transactions. Good health is indicated.

881 ♂ ☌ ♄ Hard and arduous work needs performing. Anger, irritation, resentment and depression will affect the mind. Heavy responsibilities have to be dealt with. Better be organized to handle it all. Conflict and disagreements arise with superiors or other authority figures. Strong determinations will push ahead. If afflicted, there could be a death in the family, loss of money or conflict. Beware of fraud. Don't act destructively. Beware of accidents. While the energy is greatly increased during this transit, a total collapse and need for rest may follow as soon as the transit has passed.

882 ♂ ☌ ♅ A desire for freedom above all else is strongly expressed. Aggressive behavior to push ahead is displayed but may cause

conflict. Sudden disruptive events have to be handled swiftly. A sudden death of a friend may occur. An interest in the study of astrology develops. If afflicted, accidents, loss of temper or conflicts and violence may be experienced. Beware of inconsistent and rash behavior. Cooperation with others is absolutely necessary. The inner tension will affect the health. Avoid erratic behavior and impulsive decisions.

883 ♂ ☌ ♆ Secret acts, quarrels and emotional confusion will surface. Artists will find stimulation from this transit. Caution should be used in all financial transactions and dealings. This is not a good time to seek treatment in hospitals as there is a chance of receiving the wrong medication. Strange feelings will prevail. Avoid feelings of inferiority, dominating attitudes and acts guided by delusion. Don't start anything new. Take care of the health, relax, avoid fever and infections. Stay away from alcohol and drugs. The body maybe attacked by severe infections and needs extra care as the overall physical and mental conditions tends to be low and stagnating.

884 ♂ ☌ ♇ Any bully behavior, attempts to dominate others, aggressive actions and willful display of superiority should be avoided. Stay clear of dangerous situations. If afflicted, quarrel, injury, accidents and involvement in social unrest will lead to disturbing events. Old conditions will forcefully end to make room for the new. Keep the emotions under tight control. Physical activities could ease the body's tension.

885 ♂ * ☉ refer to # 82.

886 ♂ * ☽ refer to # 277.

887 ♂ * ☿ refer to # 478.

888 ♂ * ♀ refer to # 674.

889 ♂ * ♃ This transit is excellent for legal affairs. There is progress in business. Social and educational advances will be made. The health will improve by outdoor activities and travel. Physical exercise will calm the mind. A positive time to forge ahead and make advances.

890 ♂ * ♄ Professional activities will be addressed in an organized and efficient manner. Advice from an older and more mature person

will be beneficial. Be diligent and patient when working toward a goal.

891 ♂ ⚹ ♅ Desires for freedom and independence are expressed. Precise action are taken to advance any objectives. A good time to deal with the resources of others. The study of astrology is favored. Restlessness and impatience need curbing. Sudden urges for change should be scrutinized. New friends can be made. Keep an open and relaxed mind.

892 ♂ ⚹ ♆ Secret actions are performed. Hospitals and institutions will provide valuable services. Artistic and musical talents should be utilized for valuable work. Helpful to friends, the person will enjoy company. A good time to relax and meditate. A good time to clear and quiet the mind.

893 ♂ ⚹ ♇ Desire for power and action is displayed. Business affairs and issues of money, belonging to others, will come up for consideration. The body is strong and needs physical exercise. A good time to pursue well crafted goals. Cooperation will advance plans to completion.

894 ♂ □ ☉ refer to # 91.

895 ♂ □ ☽ refer to # 286.

896 ♂ □ ☿ refer to # 487.

897 ♂ □ ♀ refer to # 683.

898 ♂ □ ♃ Inconsistent behavior due to over-confidence and a tendency to display an inflated sense of self-importance, result in conflicts with friends and business partners. Mental reliance on overly broad and religious beliefs could affect the self-confidence. Trying to cut corners should be avoided. Business, financial and legal affairs create problems. If involved in criminal activities this may be the time where arrest are imminent. Involvement in foreign conflicts could cause trouble, loss and even death. Guard against accidents. Travel plans may not materialize.

899 ♂ □ ♄ Hard work, depression and frustration of plans will bring on negative outlooks. Responsibilities will increase and become burdensome. Health problems develop from the mind's unhappy state. Legal battles will need extra effort to handle. Business and

financial matters will be subject to trouble and disagreements. Beware of accidents or physical confrontations. Avoid injuries from falls or poisoning or severe illness may drain the vitality. If intense depression prevail suicide could be contemplated and lead to an untimely death. Be careful, act cautiously and prudent at this time. Disagreements with superiors and authorities will disturb the mind. Avoid irritability and enraged attitudes. A period of great caution.

900 ♂ □ ♅ The temper is subject to outbursts and explosive actions. Ego-centered, argumentative, disagreements and quarrel with friends, family and business associates, will affect the reputation and finances. Don't start anything new at this time, it is bound to suffer. Sudden accidents could happen. Pay extra attention, take extra care. The mind is restless and impulsive. This leads to constantly changing conditions. Disruptions in life will occur. Keep your anger at bay.

901 ♂ □ ♆ Secret affairs, secret intrigues, secret actions and investigations will affect the person. Boiling anger, abnormal behavior and excessive abuses, will all have negative effects on the personality and reputation. Sudden intense illnesses may surface. Treatment in hospitals may lead to wrong diagnoses that endanger the health. Business and financial affairs have to deal with problems and loss. Beware of deception and fraud. Avoid all confrontations. Take care of the health and don't engage in abnormal behavior of any kind.

902 ♂ □ ♇ Power struggles, a desire to control others and sudden rash acts all lead to conflict that will be damaging. The mind is aggressive, unbending and hungry for success. Trouble and disagreements arise over money, sexual demands and jealousy. Avoid crime, dangerous situations, accidents and social conflicts, otherwise injury, even death, could occur. Avoid chemicals, radiation or excessive medication as it could alter the tissue and cells in the body. Avoid opposition, deception and underhanded action as this could lead to destruction.

903 ♂ ▲ ☉ refer to # 100.

904 ♂ ▲ ☽ refer to # 295.

905 ♂ ▲ ☿ refer to # 496.

906 ♂ ▲ ♀ refer to # 692.

907 ♂ ▲ ♃ Great confidence, energy and desire for expansion, will emerge. A desire for adventure and foreign travel may bring interesting experiences. A good time to handle legal and business affairs. Outdoor activities are pursued and improve the health. An excellent transit to improve financial conditions and enter institutions of higher learning.

908 ♂ ▲ ♄ A strong will to succeed is instilled despite hardship experiences and obstacles in life. Authorities will be supportive. The mind confers patience and will execute all necessary work in a well organized manner on a step by step basis until completed.

909 ♂ ▲ ♅ The desire for freedom and adventure is increased. Exploring new ideas and inventions will be beneficial for business affairs. New friends can be made through sport events and professional meetings. Astrology is a suitable subject for study. Personal growth will be supported by this transit.

910 ♂ ▲ ♆ The creative energy will be displayed and should be used for artistic achievements. A good time to discipline the mind. Research, investigating and secret undertakings may be necessary at this time. Religious, occult and other institutions may become places of interest. Treatments in hospitals will go well. Financial advances can be made during this transit. Cooperation is received from others. A good time to improve the health.

911 ♂ ▲ ♇ The will power is strong and positive. An increase in energy should be used to further any business and personal interests. New kinds of physical exercises will be taken up to improve the health. This transit is excellent for self-improvement by finding new directions in life.

912 ♂ ☍ ☉ refer to # 109.

913 ♂ ☍ ☽ refer to # 304.

914 ♂ ☍ ☿ refer to # 505.

915 ♂ ☍ ♀ refer to # 701.

916 ♂ ☍ ♃ Dangerous over-optimism, extravagance and over-expansion can invite loss. Be realistic, plan and execute well to avoid disappointments. Trouble with foreigners or incidents in foreign countries could lead to difficulties. Lawsuits may arise, as

well as difficulties with institutions of learning. Beware of rash and foolish actions. Avoid accidents due to rashness and lack of caution.

917 ♂ ☍ ♄ The body and mind are overstrained and subject to hard work. Accidents can easily happen as caution is not adhered to. Conflicts with authorities are likely. Dictatorial attitudes should be avoided. Frustration, depression and negative attitudes will create problems in relationships and business affairs. Beware of legal trouble. Avoid irritable temper and ill-considered actions. The health should be guarded.

918 ♂ ☍ ♅ Conflicts, opposition and disagreements take place with friends, family and business. There is danger through accidents. Avoid revolutionary tendencies. Impulsive behavior will disrupt goals, thus leading to destruction. Conflicts over the resources of others will ensue. Do not avoid duties and responsibilities. Tension will build in the system and affect the health. Estrangements could occur.

919 ♂ ☍ ♆ Working against the self will bring loss. Secret intrigues, love affairs, internal anger and the desire to plot against others, should be avoided. This transit produces extreme internal tension which leads to illness that also will affect the mental health. Infectious diseases, due to a lessened resistance, will affect the body. Drugs and alcohol should be avoided as it will affect the ability to judge reality. This is a bad time to seek treatment in hospitals. Private, business and general affairs will be fraught with problems. Fraud and deception are likely and could affect the financial well being. Anybody's loyalty should be questioned at this time and is subject to caution. Misunderstandings will affect the efficiency at work. This is a time in which one should wait out without being to concerned with results.

920 ♂ ☍ ♇ The ultimate power struggle will now ensue. Autocratic, aggressive behavior, especially when in public, will have undesired effects. Don't control others and vice versa. Be calm and realistic. Conflict over taxes, insurance, inheritance or partner's resources will bring loss. Accidents and other injuries may result in death.

Do not engage in any criminal activity or associate with underworld figures. Avoid chemicals and radiation as that will negatively affect the health. Sexual aggressiveness will lead to separation. Opposition from others will be experienced. Keep control of desires and actions. Avoid any violence.

♂ PROGRESSED

921 ♂ ☌ ☉ refer to # 123.

922 ♂ ☌ ☽ refer to # 334.

923 ♂ ☌ ☿ refer to # 514.

924 ♂ ☌ ♀ refer to # 710.

925 ♂ ☌ ♃ Pride, extravagance and overconfidence should be guarded against. Overconfidence and acting without care and foresight may involve the person in affairs that result in litigation and loss of finances. Depending on the present lunar aspect the person could gain or lose under this aspect. To those who lack self-confidence, it may bring out a tendency to frivolity and giddiness and requires lots of prudence.

926 ♂ ☌ ♄ This aspect stirs up the passion resulting in rash acts which, when wrongly applied, may give reasons to repentance later on. The temper must be kept under control. If the lunar position is also bad, a critical period may result.

927 ♂ ☌ ♅ Sudden unexpected events occur and bring peculiar and strange results. It increases the desire to study clairvoyance, astrology and mystical things. However, it is not a good time for travel, making constructive changes or new friends and acquaintances. While the nervous system is on high tension, care and forethought is required.

928 ♂ ☌ ♆ It either denotes a wealth of creativity and temperament or, if afflicted, imposes despair, dishonorable deeds or the person becomes the victim of fraud and deceit.

929 ♂ ☌ ♇ A very aggressive behavior and intensified willpower is used to seek control of others. Any involvement in secret affairs, crime, or underworld connections brings dangerous situations. A fight for survival may ensue. In the extreme, death by accident or through crime, is possible.

930 ♂ * ☉ refer to # 124.
931 ♂ * ☽ refer to # 335.
932 ♂ * ☿ refer to # 523.
933 ♂ * ♀ refer to # 719.
934 ♂ * ♃ The person is generous and liberal but with a tendency to go to extremes, which could result in monetary losses. It brings social advantages and calls for improvements of conditions. While the feelings are easily excited under this influence, impulsiveness should be avoided or rash acts will end unfavorably.
935 ♂ * ♄ Courageous, venturesome and blunt desires and actions are taken to carry out plans to fruition and success. A good lunar aspect will support this aspect.
936 ♂ * ♅ Increased energy, sudden inventive thoughts, quick perceptiveness and sound judgments should be utilized to make acquaintances that may be helpful and promote any interest. Travelling and business will be beneficial to the person.
937 ♂ * ♆ Promise of prosperity and benefits from business and relationships increase the feeling of joy. Outgoing and well liked, the health will be good and the spirit is upbeat. Possible interest in religious matters and sharing of emotions is indicated.
938 ♂ * ♇ Tremendous energy, courage and willpower is applied and may result in beneficial changes. Good dealings with society is indicated.
939 ♂ □ ☉ refer to # 125.
940 ♂ □ ☽ refer to # 336.
941 ♂ □ ☿ refer to # 532.
942 ♂ □ ♀ refer to # 728.
943 ♂ □ ♃ Heavy financial losses, extravagance in spending money or too lavish in giving, creates waste and losses. The person must avoid litigation as adverse decisions may result therefrom. Sometimes this means false imprisonment, confinement or other conditions tending to deprivation of liberty. This aspect is bad for social affairs, religious matters and it creates over-enthusiasm. Excess of feelings, involvement with finances, religion and travel should be avoided during this progression.
944 ♂ □ ♄ An outburst of temper or very hasty and rash conduct will bring trouble. Dishonor and disgrace may be experienced and

caution must be exercised to avoid ruin. Avoid all quarrels, disputes and confrontations with others. Control any over-enthusiastic and extreme behavior.

945 ♂ □ ♅ Extreme rashness and unexpected trouble will bring the feelings under enormous stress. The tension requires great self control or ruin may be faced. Beware of accidents, stay calm and keep a good attitude until this aspect has passed.

946 ♂ □ ♆ Strong turbulent desires, unexplained attractions, eroticism and impulsive affections or religious dependency will hurry the persons actions into a direction that later on will be repent. Physical or emotional violence will either be suffered or received.

947 ♂ □ ♇ Destruction will bring disintegration and annihilation when feelings of revenge boil over. The passionate side is out of control. An attempt is made to take advantage of those in a weaker position. Deliberate enmity will be created. Family interest and friendships will be disrupted. Dislike of children will be expressed. This progression creates a liability for accidents.

948 ♂ ▲ ☉ refer to # 124.

949 ♂ ▲ ☽ refer to # 335.

950 ♂ ▲ ☿ refer to # 540.

951 ♂ ▲ ♀ refer to # 737.

952 ♂ ▲ ♃ Good for speculations, investments and social affairs relating to finances, however, over estimation and excess must be curbed. It will make the person daring and if prudent, success will follow.

953 ♂ ▲ ♄ Feelings of courage, steadiness and enthusiasm are activated. An increase in authority, successful ambitions and an active interest in enterprises will help receive favorable outcomes if supported by a good lunar position.

954 ♂ ▲ ♅ The mental activity is stimulated seeking greater opportunity. Travel, dealing with strangers, friends and society at large, will bring benefits and advancement. If other strong aspects are also good at the same time, the person may bring forth the powers of genius.

955 ♂ ▲ ♆ Good for travel, adventure, religion, speculation, investments, and also emigration. An increased vigor, abundant

ideas and schemes from which profit could be reaped, will guide this aspect.

956 ♂ ▲ ♇ A strongly developed willpower will guide decisive and constructive action. Able to fight for any cause, the person is persistent and will not be intimidated. It is possible that old and discarded matter can be resurrected to a successful conclusion.

957 ♂ ☍ ☉ refer to # 125.

958 ♂ ☍ ☽ refer to # 336.

959 ♂ ☍ ☿ refer to # 548.

960 ♂ ☍ ♀ refer to # 746.

961 ♂ ☍ ♃ Extreme caution is required especially with money. Otherwise through extravagance, waste or litigation, heavy losses will be incurred. If the person is too egotistical, losses will occur. When the feelings are allowed to be carried away, dangerous situations may result. It will mark a very critical state in the career and could mean shipwreck or utter ruin if the lunar position is also bad at the same time. It serves to be very careful. Any careful consideration, before making any decisions, will pay off later.

962 ♂ ☍ ♄ There is a liability to accidents due to impulsiveness. Flaring up of bad temper, foolhardiness and involvement in crimes, must all be avoided during this aspect. Anger will burst up easily. The nerves are irritated and some violence or lack of self control, regarding the desires, my spell trouble. Depending on the lunar aspect this may be a very bad period or it will pass just as an irritation, if nerves are kept calm and controlled. However, separations and estrangements may occur under this aspect.

963 ♂ ☍ ♅ A complete breakdown of existing conditions will occur based on moral, mental or physical conditions. Bad endings to love affairs, affections and feelings will bring violence and in the extreme, uncontrolled passion or grief.

964 ♂ ☍ ♆ A trying time when impulsive and explosive acts cause trouble. Rash acts should be avoided. Guard should be up against being taken advantage off by others.

965 ♂ ☍ ♇ The will is in conflict with actions and desires, therefore creating disagreements within social circles. An abuse of power,

selfish aggrandizement and ill considered rash acts may have far-reaching consequences. There is a possibility of involvement in war, crime or violence. The person could be the perpetrator or victim of these acts. The desire to rule and remake others leads to disputes and separation.

BABY CHART

966 ♂ ☌ ☉ refer to # 144.

967 ♂ ☌ ☽ refer to # 354.

968 ♂ ☌ ☿ refer to # 556.

969 ♂ ☌ ♀ refer to # 755.

970 ♂ ☌ ♃ Over-sensibility, aggressiveness in personal expression and sexual relationships will lead to trouble. The mind jumps to conclusions or overreacts before knowing all the facts. The child needs to learn to think before action is taken.

971 ♂ ☌ ♄ Influences by the father have placed restrictions and limitations on how to act and express sexual energy. Expressions may be harsh or aggressive. Occupations in the defense forces or police work are sought that require a degree of forcefulness. On a sexual level, either overindulgence or frigidity may be chosen to deal with sexual energy. Sexual acts may be performed without being attracted to the partner. A certain guilt complex will develop that needs addressing before healthy and happy relationships can be achieved.

972 ♂ ☌ ♅ A short temper, as well as eccentric and erratic behavior may create havoc. While the energy level is up it must be channeled in thoughtful expression or it will be disruptive. The sexual energy may turn perverse. Impulsive acts attract unusual and eccentric partners. Calmness and logical thinking must be learned.

973 ♂ ☌ ♆ The mind may be erratic, uncontrolled and subject to delusion. The mind delves on sexual fantasies and has a distorted self-image. If this aspect is under control and positively aspected, it may be an indication of brilliance. When growing up the child needs to learn what it is that is actually desired and not rely on fantasies.

974 ♂ ☌ ♇ Actions are controlled, manipulated and directed by anger against the self or others. Emotional possessiveness and a desire

to control mentally and sexually will disturb any relationship. Sexual violence may hurt the self or others and may be practiced through masochistic acts or indicates a rapist who will do anything to hurt to please his own desires. The parents or immediate society has had an impact on the child's thinking.

975 ♂ ∗ ☉ refer to # 153.

976 ♂ ∗ ☽ refer to # 362.

977 ♂ ∗ ☿ refer to # 564.

978 ♂ ∗ ♀ refer to # 764.

979 ♂ ∗ ♃ The child learned through the parents how to relate, to positively address and enjoy sex and to have positive energy regarding work.

980 ♂ ∗ ♄ The father instilled seriousness, careful planning and a realization of sexual responsibility which adds seriousness and understanding to a relationship.

981 ♂ ∗ ♅ There is a desire to be different and express the will but in an organized and thoughtful way.

982 ♂ ∗ ♆ The parents instill dreams and fantasies to create and express the mental ability. However, an overly optimistic attitude may create illusions. Think before you act is well advised with this aspect.

983 ♂ ∗ ♇ Actions are taken by being involved with the population. Cooperation has been instilled by the parents allowing for good communication through mass media, politics, films and any kind of media.

984 ♂ □ ☉ refer to # 162.

985 ♂ □ ☽ refer to # 370.

986 ♂ □ ☿ refer to # 571.

987 ♂ □ ♀ refer to # 773.

988 ♂ □ ♃ The child has not learned how to make a determination of reasons prior to action and may give out a wrong expression that offends others. Understanding responsibility may be difficult as the sensitive side is disturbed by rash and uncontrolled actions. A tendency to overdue actions, especially uncontrolled sexual desires, will lead to confusion and problems. Sex may be separate from relationships and the emotional side suffers.

989 ♂ □ ♄ Mistrust, fear and rash acts are instilled by the father's influence on the child. Problems develop in accepting authority figures, which are seen as stifling, creating rebel like behavior, which in turn leads to disturbances. The sexuality may not be developed causing sexual disappointments. The problems adopted from the father need solving to permit the person to be loyal and serious about any commitment and relationship.

990 ♂ □ ♅ Erratic and impulsive behavior may lead to self-destruction. The parents may have abused the child in some way, thereby creating uncontrolled anger and impulses. Relationships are built on anger, possessive behavior and sometimes on violence. Learning the need to be responsible for one's own action is necessary.

991 ♂ □ ♆ Too much fantasy, delusion and imagination is inappropriate and leads to disorganized actions. Drugs and alcohol may be used to avoid coping with reality. Sexual fantasies may produce a guilt complex that will negatively influence relationships. There is a need to learn a healthy attitude about sex, religion and relating to others emotionally.

992 ♂ □ ♇ Indecisiveness, too much attention for control, and an excessive pride may stand in the way of positive achievements. Anger may be acted out either sexually or by engaging in control and power games. This may lead to frustration and blind, intense rage, that surge up from the unconscious and control the person. Either exploding or imploding the anger affects the person. The need to understand the feelings and reasoning is required to channel the anger into active creativity.

993 ♂ ▲ ☉ refer to # 171.

994 ♂ ▲ ☽ refer to # 378.

995 ♂ ▲ ☿ refer to # 578.

996 ♂ ▲ ♀ refer to # 782.

997 ♂ ▲ ♃ Positive and constructive actions were encouraged by the parents and are well expressed by the child.

998 ♂ ▲ ♄ A seriousness and maturity gained early in life permits for careful decisions, well organized actions and loyalty in later life.

Relationships are only entered into after careful considerations. Goals are carefully planned prior to its execution and a good deal of responsibility is assumed in any working or personal relationship.

999 ♂ ▲ ⛢ This may indicate the mind of a genius. Actions and unconventional behavior bring up new ideas that may benefit many. The person must learn to express its creativity positively in order to be constructive and not just merely be different with no goals to express.

1000 ♂ ▲ ♆ Creative abilities must be developed to the fullest extent in order to gain great advantages from this aspect.

1001 ♂ ▲ ♇ Great energy, action and cooperation is bestowed under this aspect. If properly utilized it will advance a career in the public eye.

1002 ♂ ☍ ☉ refer to # 180.

1003 ♂ ☍ ☽ refer to # 386.

1004 ♂ ☍ ☿ refer to # 585.

1005 ♂ ☍ ♀ refer to # 791.

1006 ♂ ☍ ♃ Absorbed from the parent's behavior is an excessive attitude to have one's own way, to overreact, to take excessive risk or to compromise feelings and needs for the desire to belong. A poor judgment in personal and career choices and jumping in and out of love, is indicated. A need to consider a situation prior to acting on it is required and a reality check may help channel the energy into less destructive decisions.

1007 ♂ ☍ ♄ A tendency exists to rebel against society, authority or restrictions. Problems with sexual expressions may make it difficult to establish long lasting relationships. In any occupation excessive worry, trouble to handle a crisis, or an inability to act out of fear, may bring trouble. The father's negative influence needs to be overcome in order to become a careful planner, decision maker and emotionally secured person who is able to hold on to relationships.

1008 ♂ ☍ ⛢ There are problems of relating to others through a strong self will, erratic actions and lack of cooperation. Anger and even violence may erupt when threatened. The parents were unpredictable. Their behavior tends to indulge in instant gratification, expressing to the child to take what it can get at any moment without consideration of others or consequences to the self. Internal anger and frustration closes off the mind to consider all details before acting on an idea, thus, leading to unproductive existence, self-blame, or wrongly laying blame on others, creating a destructive energy. The child may harbor resentments toward the parents. The possibility of abuse by the parents may have taken place, thus, inflicting guilt onto the child that blocks any positive and creative release of energy.

1009 ♂ ☍ ♆ Actions may be confused or muddled and not directed specifically. Sexual expression may be confused with spirituality. Sexuality can be perceived as something dirty that one has to be ashamed of. Fantasies may fill in for reality, thus making the forming of relationships difficult and disappointing. Imaginations may replace reality. Alcohol and drugs may be a substitute for the real world, which is perceived as being too harsh.

1010 ♂ ☍ ♇ There may be a lack of cooperation, an avoidance of crowds, claustrophobia or fear of losing power and control. Anger and the inability to act and react may go out of control. The anger needs controlling and understanding as it is generated out of hurt and fear.

♂ TRANSIT OR PROGRESSION TO A (Ascendant)

1011 ♂ ☌ **A** The personality is forceful and very impulsive. The body is rugged and displays muscle. A high degree of aggressiveness may lead to actions without consideration of the consequences. Being bully and attempting careless acts could lead to accidents and ill health. During transit the mind becomes quarrelsome, bossy, obstinate and creates conflict. Cooperation is needed to avoid health problems and accidents.

1012 ♂ ✱ **A** A positive attitude brings opportunity to further any ambitions. The health is robust. Any sports activity will improve the body. Personal efficiency is improved. A favorable period during transit to be cooperative, disciplined and ready for gain.

1013 ♂ □ **A** Aggressive actions and demands may create great difficulties and unpopularity. Accidents may happen due to haste that will leave scars and affect the health. The character could be bully and forceful in its expressions. The fighter per se, whether physically or through arguments. During transit agreements and contracts should not be entered into and calmness should be practiced.

1014 ♂ ▲ **A** A strong body and mind is ruled by a strong willpower resorting to quick action. The physical constitution is well built. Any sports activity will increase the stamina and health. Cooperation with others bring gain. The health and physical strength will improve.

1015 ♂ ☍ **A** Conflict and confrontations with enemies or loved ones bring sorrow. A power struggle will ensue. Danger of illness is denoted. Be calm and careful during any transit that could enhance the natal position.

♂ TRANSIT OR PROGRESSION TO M (Mid heaven)

1016 ♂ ☌ **M** Great ambitions and desires to engage in business enterprises will lead to completion of goals. Occupations involving machinery, engineering or the military may be favored. During transit impulsive behavior should be curbed and careful planning maybe rewarded.

1017 ♂ * **M** Career advancements which improve the home and reputation will be offered. Constructive involvement in business may lead to public favors. During transit the self-confidence will improve. While independent and self-reliant, any help given to others will improve plans and work in progress.

1018 ♂ □ **M** Disagreements with authorities create strife. Conflict, as well as quarrels bring unpopularity and loss. Being headstrong will be damaging to honor and reputation. Aggressive behavior brings conflict and disputes, especially with superiors or other authority. Avoid haste and stay calm.

1019 ♂ ▲ **M** The ambitions and desires for success are strongly expressed. A dominance in the public sphere is possible and will further any ambitions. During transit this a good time to work towards a goal and achievements.

1020 ♂ ☍ **M** Oppositions in business, profession and social life bring strife and disappointment. The temper needs controlling. Arguments create serious tension that affect the health and social standings.

41

♃ Jupiter

A positive and lucky ♃ denotes generosity, an interest in law, in education, religion and the likes. Long journeys are undertaken, sometimes more for business than pleasure. It signifies success in a foreign country if found in the 9th house. Good fortune and success will be provided for in life.

If afflicted, over-optimism to the point of being gullible, extravagance and careless or by engaging in misjudgments, could provide loss in a big style. Lawsuits will bring loss.

♃ IN THE HOUSES

1021 ♃ (1) The person is optimistic, honest, friendly and full of self-confidence, has a sociable personality and is well liked. A strong drive and desire for leadership and to be recognized by others exists. Being very fortunate includes always relying on and receiving help from others. Religious and moral convictions are strong and may be openly expressed.

If afflicted, there is gaining of excessive weight, self-indulgence and an exaggerated sense of self-importance. To promise more than the person is able to deliver may come from this position.

1022 ♃ (2) Bestowed with an extensive business ability and good fortune, income is obtained easily. The expectations for money are good but caution should be applied to not indulge in extravagance due to over-optimism.

If afflicted, money will quickly disappear. Too much is taken for granted and things are expected just to come along easily. Overreaching oneself and ignoring of problems to come, may lead to loss and heavy debts.

1023 ♃ (3) There is optimism, an increased interest in education and all kinds of communications, to expand the mind. Short distant travel will be undertaken. The mind adjusts to prevailing trends and good relationships are kept with brothers, sisters and neighbors.

If afflicted, there is danger of accidents while traveling. Recklessness, overconfidence and quarrel with siblings and neighbors result in estrangements and loss.

1024 ♃ (4) A closeness to the home and family is indicated. The person desires comfort in the home and may inherit from other family members. Religious beliefs are adopted from parents and possibly be practiced. Money is spent on home improvements and gain may come from real estate ventures.

If afflicted, there is an urge and possible a need to move to try someplace else. The parents may become a burden or impose rigid religious beliefs on the person.

1025 ♃ (5) The person is very active in arts, sports, education and involvement with children. Their own children may be well adjusted and fortunate in their lives. Happiness in romance and luck in speculation comes when this house is positively aspected by other planets.

If afflicted, financial losses through speculation and trouble with children or having children will bring disappointment.

1026 ♃ (6) Any work in service or an interest in health and physical well being may lead to employment in healing, religion, missions, medical massage, homeopathy or related fields. Good relations and friendships exist among co-workers and employers. A sensitive diet should be followed to avoid weight gain. A closeness to animals maybe expressed.

If afflicted, there is trouble at work, with the health, and also by overreaching the self or laziness, with an attitude, of 'let others do it'. The health may suffer from overindulgence resulting in malfunctioning of internal organs.

1027 ♃ (7) Friendships, relationships, partnerships, honesty and fairness do well in public relations. Morally well adjusted, the person may form a lasting marriage. Wealth and high standing through marriage and good judgment in choosing associates bring prosperous business. A selfless love and understanding for the well being of others is expressed through all kinds of work in public relations.

If afflicted, the person takes too much for granted, has too high an expectation and is being taken in by business partners and marriage partners, which leads to loss.

1028 ♃ (8) Benefits through taxes, insurance, inheritance and joint finances will be received. The person is attracted to business related to funeral homes, insurance, tax accounting, corporate fund raising or family trusts and a strong interest in life after death issues exists. Death comes through natural causes. A prosperous inheritance could be forthcoming.

If afflicted, there will be litigation over taxation, inheritance and money belonging to others.

1029 ♃ (9) A love for travel, religion, education, law and all matters related to foreigners and foreign countries and cultures, is bestowed. This may lead to a job or business in a foreign country or work with foreigners will be performed. A well aspected ♃ will positively support a legal situation.

If afflicted, the person could resort to religious fanaticism, incur trouble in foreign land or with the higher courts. Laziness and indifference to social issues may cause estrangements from participating in society.

1030 ♃ (10) A position of prominence may be obtained that provides a high standing in the professional world, in politics or the entertainment field. In fact, any executive position is desired to seek out gain and acceptance in society. Ambitions, honesty and seriousness of duty, a good reputation and standing in society, together with an interest in higher education, will benefit the business or reputation. Acquisition of wealth and public standing is the goal. Prudent decisions should be made to avoid over-expansion.

If afflicted, there is an unsatisfactory home life due to a relentless pursuit of power in business. Hypocrisy and egotism may lead to disgrace and reversal of fortune.

1031 ♃ (11) Friendship and group activities will further personal interests. Advice and help is received from friends. The person has an interest in humanitarian projects. Goals maybe formed that provide for hopes and wishes.

If afflicted, false friends or friends with no power to help, are damaging or the person is receiving the wrong advise. Friends may be solely made for personal gain. Lack of responsibility and ulterior motives for friendships create problems. Friends may merely leach off the person and have no interest in helping out.

1032 ♃ (12) Meditation, a study of occult, mysticism, acting on hunches or intuition as well as giving aid to those in need, bring emotional gratification. Work is performed behind the scene in hospitals, large institutions, churches, universities or welfare systems. An ability to make friends with enemies and receive needed support in times of crisis is indicated.

If afflicted, neurotic tendencies, martyr complexes, impracticality and wishful dreams remove the mind from reality. A reliance on charitable organizations or becoming parasites of society to avoid responsibility is common. Escapes into fantasy worlds create affliction of psychological well being.

♃ IN THE SIGNS

1033 ♃ (♈) Restlessness, abundance of energy, self-confidence, courage and the ability to leadership is given. A strong ego and an attitude of self-importance is prevalent.

If afflicted, foolish desires, rash, impulsive, careless and overconfident manners, as well as an overblown ego and an attitude of self-importance will lead to loss. Impulsive and wasteful spending of money, or making investments in dubious businesses, may create unforeseen difficulties.

1034 ♃ (♉) Money and resources are spent wisely. Practicing generosity and giving back to society is a learning trend of this position. It attracts wealth and bestows good and refined taste for luxury and the good things in life. Persistence in pursuing goals will pay off. There is a desire to belong to the upper classes of society.

If afflicted, any waste of money, any self-indulgence, self-righteousness, or radical political involvement bring trouble. Any indifference to the problems of others and resentment, jealousy or physical exhaustion, may lead to illness and despair. Business ideas must be practical otherwise over-confidence will lead to loss. Spiritual values may be tainted by financial concerns and any extravagance could lead to indebtedness and loss.

1035 ♃ (♊) The study of philosophy, religion, laws or the pursuit of higher education is important. A constant desire for intellectual development renders the mind restless in search of mental inspirations. This position bestows great ability for teaching even in connection with travel, lecturing and general communication work.

If afflicted, there may be a constant change of mind, of education and point of view. Holier than thou attitudes may create an intellectual snob.

1036 ♃ (♋) A strong bond with the parents instills values and love. A friendly, harmonious, prosperous and comfortable home environment is desired. Sharing the home with others, entertaining in the home, and a liking of mothering others, makes the person a good home maker, cook and gracious host. Business interests revolve around real estate, food and all matters related to the home. Financial help is received from the parents. The latter part of life is more financially secured.

If afflicted, overeating leads to obesity and other health problems. The person could suffer from impracticality and over-confidence or resort to dreaming in an effort to escape reality. An overly need for emotional security, self-indulgence or dependence on parents, especially the mother, may create personality and social problems.

1037 ♃ (♌) There is great optimism, self-confidence, a strong energy, and a desire to be in the lime light. Admiration from others is expected. Loyalty, lavish and expensive taste will be displayed. The person resorts to drama and grandeur to gain attention. A deep seated desire exists to participate in all forms of social engagements to feel important and gain status. Leadership abilities are given. Any co-operation, self-confidence, reliability, honor and great love of children benefits teachers and business engaged in the entertainment industry.

If afflicted, any conceit, overconfidence and expansion, any egotism, arrogance and liking of gambling, stock market activity and other speculations, could lead to ruin. Disappointments will be experienced in love, with children, romantic attachments and in speculations.

1038 ♃ (♍) The person is well organized, is practical in the execution of work, and very detail oriented. Honesty, integrity and co-operation with employees create pleasant working conditions. There is an interest in service to others, in charity, hospitals and the well being of others.

If afflicted, overwork, lack of co-operation with others and too much focus on detail instead of the whole picture, creates a perfectionist to a fault, or may lead to sloppiness and disorderly behavior. Unstable employment situations, laziness and disagreement with co-workers, may lead to constant changes.

1039 ♃ (♎) A sense of justice, of moral principles and an interest in religion, education and spiritual values is strong. A sense of fair play goes beyond any sexual attractions, thus creating a mental harmony and balance. Friends, partners and social surroundings influence any social and religious beliefs. The person is popular, well liked and has an ability to deal with the public. Charm is applied to influence society.

If afflicted, the person wants to make decisions for others and meddles in their affairs. There will be more promises than the person can deliver. Expectation of favors, disloyalty, jealousy and vindictive behavior become apparent when things go awry. There is a possibility that lawsuits arise from unfulfilled promises.

1040 ♃ (♏) Involvement in large scales business, insurance, taxes, or inheritance and other peoples money is possible. An interest in occult, life after death and the supernatural, may be pursued.

If afflicted, an intense and uncompromising attitude coupled with vindictiveness, creates enemies and oppositions. Delving into secret affairs of others, while keeping the own affairs hidden, will create mistrust and destruction. Friendships are based on secret motives. Legal battles over money may ensue over belonging of others and unwise investments. There is a desire to manipulate for personal gain.

1041 ♃ (♐) Foreign travel, religion, the law and education are of interest. The person displays a strong adherence to principles. A job may be performed in a foreign country or is related to international travel. A strong interest in foreign cultures, in race and in social systems, is pursued.

If afflicted, overconfidence, religious fanaticism, trouble with the law, or trouble while traveling could be experienced. A desire to convert others to one's own point of view or strong religious affiliations may create distrust and disturbances. A narrow-minded attitude, bias, a self-righteousness and dogmatic beliefs, or too conservative and clinging to childhood beliefs, are carried on to avoid facing the unknown.

1042 ♃ (♑) The person is overly concerned with social rules. However, integrity, a good conservative outlook, adherence to moral conduct, ethics and responsibility bring promotions and high positions in business. A possible attainment of wealth through ambitions, and multiplying of resources, may bring benefits.

If afflicted, exceptional rigid behavior, lack of imagination, or a strong drive for power, may interfere with home and family. Cold and austere manners create emotional frustration and loneliness. This may result from too strong a drive for success. Using people to achieve high position, wealth and power could backfire. To adopt the attitude and value of those above to gain prominence may lead to self denial and disappointment. There will be fluctuations between miserliness and extravagance.

1043 ♃ (♒) A willingness to mix with races, classes and to share with others spiritually and materially, brings great tolerance for values and creates many friendships. There is a desire for freedom and interest in the unusual. Being pioneers in astrology and philosophy, religion and social concepts, a person is broad minded, full of ideas, and is always willing to help.

If afflicted, there is unreliability, impracticality and an unrealistic attitude. The person ignores discipline, rules and responsibility and often scatters the energy, thus having trouble reaching any goal.

1044 ♃ (♓)There is an emotional depth, together with strong feelings and a willingness to help others. At times, however, the person is gullible and too generous. Seclusion is needed and may lead to work in the field of religion, hospitals, yoga teaching and mental occupations that are related to expressing the soul.

If afflicted, the emotions can easily overflow, thus allowing others to take advantage. Too little reliance on the self creates problems. Overconfidence, egotism, guru worship and cultist, in search of finding the self, lead to waste and scattering of energy. Religious devotion may exists for lack of believing in the self and accepting responsibilities. Social parasites are common under this sign.

♃ IN ASPECT WITH OTHER PLANETS

1045 ♃ ☌ ☉ refer to # 29.

1046 ♃ ☌ ☽ refer to # 224.

1047 ♃ ☌ ☿ refer to # 429.

1048 ♃ ☌ ♀ refer to # 628.

1049 ♃ ☌ ♂ refer to # 835.

1050 ♃ ☌ ♄ Seriousness, responsibility, good organization and hard work all come with this aspect. While ♃ is connected with luck and optimism, this aspect could bring obstacles into the life, especially problems to do with money, business and the occupation. Very hard work and endless patience are needed for the achievement of any goal. While ♃ wants to expand, ♄ hinders, restricts and delays hopes and wishes. Even with a positive attitude and willingness to work hard, the person will have to deal with disappointments.

1051 ♃ ☌ ♅ The principles of expansion and optimism are pushing for unusual opportunities coming from friends and organizations. Sudden travel may occur that could increase education and be very beneficial. Involvement with occult, astrology, yoga, education and religion will bring increased knowledge and rewards. As ♅ represents the unusual, originality, ingenuity and new inventions, ♃ expansion thereto will provide progress.

1052 ♃ ☌ ♆ The imagination is positive and supportive of talents in art, music and religion. The emotional sensitivity is tuned into these talents but needs self-discipline to develop. Any affliction to this aspect produces loss of reality and encases the person in a dream and fantasy world. Unreliability and being unproductive will cause harm. At an extreme, the person may resort to leaching onto others.

1053 ♃ ☌ ♇ The willpower is strong and is improving the concentration. Achievement is sought via regeneration and improvement of current conditions. Some involvement with the law is indicated.

1054 ♃ ✱ ☉ refer to # 38.

1055 ♃ ✱ ☽ refer to # 233.

1056 ♃ ✱ ☿ refer to # 437.

1057 ♃ ✱ ♀ refer to # 636.

1058 ♃ ✱ ♂ refer to # 844.

1059 ♃ ✱ ♄ This combination with ♄ produces persistence, good organization and the ability to work hard. It also works well together with ♃ interest in expansion, honesty, integrity and support from others. The person will be helpful but will also receive help, when needed. Stability in all affairs is desired and prominence before the public may be achieved. This aspect supports lawyers, judges, politicians or any other position that deals with the public.

1060 ♃ ✱ ♅ Unusual and new inventions are supported by the principle of good will and expansion. The mind is able to grasp new and exciting ideas. There will be opportunities for advancement. The person has great foresight and is especially talented as an astrologer. Optimism and luck make a good combination to realize hopes and wishes.

1061 ♃ ✱ ♆ A fertile imagination, talents in the arts, music and religion, are expressed by this aspect. However, unless strongly supported by other positive aspects, the person may lack discipline, common sense and endurance to express the talents. Helpful by nature, the person also receives help from friends and family. If negatively aspected, the person may seek seclusion from society or is encased in a dream world.

1062 ♃ ✱ ♇ A desire to regenerate the mind and spirit is expressed. Prayers and meditation will support the self-expression and provide insides into the spiritual world.

1063 ♃ □ ☉ refer to # 47.

1064 ♃ □ ☽ refer to # 242.

1065 ♃ □ ☿ refer to # 445.

1066 ♃ □ ♀ refer to # 643.

1067 ♃ □ ♂ refer to # 853.

1068 ♃ □ ♄ The person will suffer in business, jobs, legal and money affairs, either by not grasping opportunities or generally by affairs going wrong. Planning and execution of projects may be faulty or ill-timed, resulting in loss mainly due to lack of experience or discipline to see the project through to completion. Despite the optimism provided by ♃ a strong ♄ will bring depression and melancholia.

1069 ♃ □ ♅ The person acts impulsively, hoping for the best, or may be even going overboard with any ideas just to find loss or running out of steam and abandon their lavish schemes, altogether. Any attempt to gamble or speculate may deplete their entire fortune. The mind, at times, is so overconfident without regards to reality, which may lead to a blindly following of some guru or master until disillusion sets in. A strong restlessness and unreliability is bestowed under this aspect.

1070 ♃ □ ♆ The mind is under full control of the emotions and displays impracticality, unfounded idealism and builds castles in the air while the daily affairs are messy and in shambles. The restless mind craves for constant adventure and out of the ordinary experiences. The person is involved in aimless travel without a concrete idea of its purpose. The mind is expressed in an unrealistic way, encased in fantasy ideas that gets the person involved in all kinds of schemes and fraud as there is more promised than can be delivered. A degree of laziness and self-indulgence is found, especially in wealthy people with this aspect, who may live a life of non-fulfillment and meaningless activity.

1071 ♃ □ ♇ A bully attitude, a rebellious mind and a desire to change the existing society, will bring unpopularity. The desire for greatness and leadership, especially in religion, may stand in the way of living a happy and content life. The desire to reform others to one's own point of view must be curbed.

1072 ♃ ▲ ☉ refer to # 56.

1073 ♃ ▲ ☽ refer to # 251.

1074 ♃ ▲ ☿ refer to # 453.

1075 ♃ ▲ ♀ refer to # 650.

1076 ♃ ▲ ♂ refer to # 862.

1077 ♃ ▲ ♄ The person is responsible, honest, has integrity, common sense, stability and an ability to organize, which brings results through hard work. This aspect supports a steady rise in business, politics or any occupation that deals with the public. Any occupation as lawyer, judge, mediator or government employee, is very suitable.

1078 ♃ ▲ ♅ Through ♅ the mind is unusual, eccentric, inventive and eager to be creative. ♃ bestows the fortune needed to become successful. Great opportunities will be presented which could involve far away travel or contact with foreigners. The person enjoys popularity and has ambitions for politics, religious undertakings and astrology, by sensing the trends and feelings of others. If this aspect is positively supported by the ☉ and ☿, the person may be a genius.

1079 ♃ ▲ ♆ The spiritual senses are highly activated but if not controlled may resort to pompousness. The emotions are easily swept away in search of some guru or master. There is a danger of deception with this aspect. The person is generous to a fault and loves to mother the world. The mind is calmed when living near water. Jobs may be found in institutions, hospitals, educational forums or religious retreats. A strong wanderlust comes with this aspect. The imaginations are fruitful and when developed, bring exceptional talent in the arts, music and any field of entertainment. If this aspect received negative influences the person may be lazy, give way to self-indulgence and may leach onto others while their own affairs are in disarray.

1080 ♃ ▲♇ The will is strong and the mind is ready to act. A high degree of concentration gives creative powers that can be used to transform the life of the person.

1081 ♃ ☍ ☉ refer to # 65.

1082 ♃ ☍ ☽ refer to # 260.

1083 ♃ ☍ ☿ refer to # 461.

1084 ♃ ☍ ♀ refer to # 657.

1085 ♃ ☍ ♂ refer to # 871.

1086 ♃ ☍ ♄ Severe problems in the professional world, in domestic affairs, religion and legal conflicts are represented by this aspect. A lack of foresight and organization may bring disappointments. The mind is too rigid, too conservative and too set in its ways, thus lacking the ability to spot opportunities when presented. The weight of heavy work and responsibilities deplete the energy, thus creating unhappiness and depression. At times, it is hard for the person to see the light at the end of the tunnel. Hardships and disappointments may be experienced under this aspect, which affects the mind and emotions, rendering them narrow-minded and prone to depression. Obtaining higher education may be an obstacle, as well as legal difficulties, as any lawsuit may end with a loss.

1087 ♃ ☍ ♅ Over-optimism and unwise attempts to gain from financial or social situations may require more investments than owned by the person and subsequently lead to loss. Sudden unforeseen difficulties will be experienced. New undertakings should be avoided or, at the very least, be well prepared and planned out before getting involved to avoid massive losses. If ♂ is also negative to this aspect the outcome could be outright disastrous. No get-rich-quick schemes should be entered into and the overconfidence displayed may lead the mind to overlook problems that will later destroy the desired enterprise. The mind visualizes more than is obtainable. Any involvement in religious organizations may lead the person astray. Blindly following religion, due to obstinate opinions, leaves no room for reality. Legal trouble may occur causing massive losses. Restlessness and wanderlust make the person unstable and deplete the finances. Disharmony with friends is indicated and the person is either deceiving others or is deceived by them.

1088 ♃ ☍ ♆ There may be a deliberate dishonest or evasive and unreliable behavior in a delusion as to fame and fortune. When belonging to a religious group the person may be lead astray due to the mind's distortion of reality. A dream world and fantasyland will be adopted to avoid the harsh reality. Sometimes, the person is seeking strong emotional gratification to the point of annoying others or becoming an embarrassment. The mind will strongly idealizes others to overcome their own inadequacies. The desire to be special may be so overwhelming that it becomes an obsession, distorting reality of life.

1089 ♃ ☍ ♇ A bully opinion and an indulgence in power games are used to conform others to one's own point of view. Reforming others and being dogmatic creates conflict and unpopularity. The desire for power and wealth is pursued above all else, even involving schemes to gain such ends. Lack of humility and bossy attitudes may ultimately lead to the person's downfall.

TRANSITS

1090 ♃ ☌ ☉ refer to # 74.

1091 ♃ ☌ ☽ refer to # 269.

1092 ♃ ☌ ☿ refer to # 470.

1093 ♃ ☌ ♀ refer to # 666.

1094 ♃ ☌ ♂ refer to # 880.

1095 ♃ ☌ ♄ Good organization, a serious attitude and a strict adherence to prudence and plans will be beneficial to any long term goals. Depending on the natural aspect, this is a time of reaping or a time of weeping. Rewards will only come if eared through hard work. Business, legal and educational affairs will develop. Travel may be undertaken more for business or educational purpose than for personal pleasure. Personal growth is anticipated and increased responsibilities are handled well. If afflicted, break ups and health problems will manifest. Beware of over-extension.

1096 ♃ ☌ ♅ Interests in unusual educational institutions on scientific, or astrological subjects, or way out religious groups, may arise.

Sudden financial gain, travel or opportunity for higher learning could develop. New friendships will be made. An interest in law, or meeting with people in a profession related to law, is possible. The mental faculties are stimulated during this transit. An increased desire for personal freedom emerges.

1097 ♃ ☌ ♆ Happiness is on the horizon. An increased interest in religious groups now surfaces. Possible job opportunities may be forthcoming in hospitals, institutions or religious groups. The mind desires inspiration through long distant travel. Artistic expressions will do well at this time. If afflicted, however, abuses of all kinds will affect the mind and may render reality nebulous. Help will be offered by others. This is not a good time to invest, or follow suggestions of others, as the mind may be mislead. Common sense needs to prevail.

1098 ♃ ☌ ♇ The finding of the self is foremost on the mind during this transit. Possible financial benefits through the resources of others could materialize. Legal and business affairs may develop well. If afflicted, a possible retreat from society may occur if the desired power is not received. Conflicts with authority may result. Keep your ambitions grounded.

1099 ♃ * ☉ refer to # 83.

1100 ♃ * ☽ refer to # 278.

1101 ♃ * ☿ refer to # 479.

1102 ♃ * ♀ refer to # 675.

1103 ♃ * ♂ refer to # 889.

1104 ♃ * ♄ An optimistic pursuit of goals will result in progress. Recognition due for hard work may be received at this time. A judgment of fairness is instilled. Relationships with an older person and prudent business decisions will bring gain. A time of expansion and growth if not negatively aspected in the natal chart.

1105 ♃ * ♅ Optimism and progress, coupled with a desire to invent, bring new and helpful associations and friends. This is an excellent transit for the study of astrology. Travel, more for the opportunity to learn than as a means of vacationing, will be undertaken. Financial benefits through the resources of others may become available. A desire for change emerges.

1106 ♃ ✱ ♆ A spiritual enlightenment, intense mental harmony and an advancement of the soul will be triggered during this transit. Beware of excessive emotional urges and stay grounded.

1107 ♃ ✱ ♇ A desire to belong to society and fit in is strongly displayed. Self-improvement is undertaken through furtherance of studies in fields of the unusual, the clairvoyant and other phenomena. Psychology may be a subject to study. An interest in law, higher education, religion and travel is indicated. To reform social institutions is of interest. A good time to remold life by making creative changes. Avoid selfish behavior.

1108 ♃ □ ☉ refer to # 92.

1109 ♃ □ ☽ refer to # 287.

1110 ♃ □ ☿ refer to # 488.

1111 ♃ □ ♀ refer to # 684.

1112 ♃ □ ♂ refer to # 898.

1113 ♃ □ ♄ Business, legal and financial affairs will not do well at this time. Loss in lawsuits, unemployment, investments, and even domestic affairs, are subject to conflict. Pessimism and despair may alternate with undue overconfidence. Support from people in power is not forthcoming. The reputation and honor could be subject to reversal. Separations are possible. Internal tension through worry will affect the health. Feelings of uncertainty will prevail for the duration of this transit. Avoid expenses and be careful in making any decisions.

1114 ♃ □ ♅ Common sense is in short supply due to overconfidence. The mind is erratic, unfocussed and bound to jump to conclusions. Responsibilities are shunned or delayed due to an unrealistic attitude or to plain bouts of laziness. Travel without a purpose in mind may bring difficulties and drain the finances. Eccentricity should be avoided. Religious causes may not be what they claim to stand for. Trouble with lawsuits, investments, business, taxes or other sources, will be costly. Avoid bickering or separation will occur.

1115 ♃ □ ♆ Confusion, fantasizing, day dreaming, unrealistic expectations and escape of reality, by abuse of drugs and alcohol, are common under this transit. Ideas about beliefs, belonging and reality are misplaced or far out to the point of causing mental distortion and loss. Matters may not turn out as expected, creating disillusion. Financial schemes could back fire and devastate the person. It is ♆ trade of bringing self-undoing if the mind is not kept under control and the thinking is not related to reality. Promises turn out to be foolish or delusional. Laziness and false optimism demand their price.

1116 ♃ □ ♇ A strong willpower is displayed. The use of coercion and dominance to control others will have negative results. The desire to reform others to one's own point of view must be avoided. Attitudes will undergo drastic changes due to enforced circumstances. Criminal schemes and association with underworld figures, as well as using dishonesty to gain from others, if practiced, will backfire. Conflict will arise over the resources of others. The ego needs to be held in place to avoid arrogance and social whiplash. Sexual perversity, obsession and strange occult practices must be avoided. Rebuilding will be necessary as some of the old life will break down and disappear. Legal conflicts may arise. Enormous tension will lead to restlessness and nervous illness.

1117 ♃ ▲ ☉ refer to # 101.

1118 ♃ ▲ ☽ refer to # 296.

1119 ♃ ▲ ☿ refer to # 497.

1120 ♃ ▲ ♀ refer to # 693.

1121 ♃ ▲ ♂ refer to # 907.

1122 ♃ ▲ ♄ Progress in legal affairs, in business enterprises and working conditions will be made at this time. Travel, especially for business, will be successful. A good time to change working conditions or the occupation. Authorities may be helpful and supportive. Well organized and executed endeavors provide for later rewards. The person is responsible, honest and serious about life. A good transit for expansion.

1123 ♃ ▲ ♅ Sudden unexpected gain through the resources of others will be reaped. Interesting and adventuresome travel will be undertaken. New friendships with unusual persons will be made. This is an excellent transit for the study of astrology. The mind is open to all new, exiting and daring ideas. Greater talent may emerge. A period that is good for financial gain.

1124 ♃ ▲ ♆ The mind and feelings are in harmony. Meditation will increase the concentration. A good time to seek hospital treatments. Spiritual awakening may occur.

1125 ♃ ▲ ♇ An improvement of the self and standing in society is desired. The emotions are strong but not overpowering. Benefits are obtained through the resources of others. A good time to progress in life and start something new. Business travel will be profitable. If the planets are positive in the natal chart, this may elevate the person into a good position in politics.

1126 ♃ ☍ ☉ refer to # 110.

1127 ♃ ☍ ☽ refer to # 305.

1128 ♃ ☍ ☿ refer to # 506.

1129 ♃ ☍ ♀ refer to # 702.

1130 ♃ ☍ ♂ refer to # 916.

1131 ♃ ☍ ♄ Business, legal, travel and domestic affairs are subject to dispute and disappointment. Unfavourable rulings in court, or lack of support from authorities, create loss and depression. A financial crisis could occur. During this transit nothing new should be started. Existing issues should be handled with care to completion. Heavy responsibilities burden the person. Separations may occur that affect the status in life. Obstacles need overcoming. A trying time to make any kind of decision as the affairs tend to go wrong. Severe restlessness, moodiness, unhappiness and lack of confidence will all bring down the energy level. Illness may result from worry and overwork.

1132 ♃ ☍ ♅ Unreliable, unstable and eccentric friendships formed bring disappointment. Excessive spending, show of luxury to impress others, and uncertainty of income, will drain the finances. The mind suffers from restlessness. Jumping from one idea to another brings unstable conditions, all of which create tension and affect the nervous system and overall health. Plan and execute well at this time to avoid unexpected loss. Be careful when investing money. Estrangements and disruptive events will occur.

1133 ♃ ☍ ♆ The mind is confused and driven by unrealistic beliefs. Blindly following some guru will fall under this transit. Any involvement in financial schemes will end in disaster. Do not blindly believe others. Don't lose track of reality. Avoid day dreaming, make believe and distortion of reality to befit the mood of the day. Abuse of alcohol and drugs can have severe health and emotional effects. The imaginations run astray and distort the mind. Beware of financial ruin. Be careful in investment deals as they may not bring the return previously promised.

1134 ♃ ☍ ♇ The ego may overstep control and damage the reputation. A force of will leads to separation. Beware of fraud and deception. Lawsuits may follow. Grandiose attempts to prove the self should be avoided. Take extra care in financial dealings. Avoid any kind of extreme behavior. Let this transit pass before resorting to making new deals.

♃ PROGRESSED

1135 ♃ ☌ ☉ refer to # 126.

1136 ♃ ☌ ☽ refer to # 337.

1137 ♃ ☌ ☿ refer to # 515.

1138 ♃ ☌ ♀ refer to # 711.

1139 ♃ ☌ ♂ refer to # 925.

1140 ♃ ☌ ♄ Both planets progress so slowly that a ☌ has to be there in the natal chart that may, by progression, just come either more towards perfection (within 1 degree) or separate more to dilute a conjunction effect.

1141 ♃ ☌ ♅ refer to # 1140.

1142 ♃ ☌ ♆ refer to # 1140.

1143 ♃ ☌ ♇ refer to # 1140.

1144 ♃ * ☉ refer to # 127.

1145 ♃ * ☽ refer to # 338.

1146 ♃ * ☿ refer to # 524.

1147 ♃ * ♀ refer to # 720.

1148 ♃ * ♂ refer to # 934.

1149 ♃ * ♄ Both planets progress so slowly that a * has to be there in the natal chart that may, by progression, just come either more towards perfection (within 1 degree) or separate more to dilute a sextile effect.

1150 ♃ * ♅ refer to # 1149.

1151 ♃ ✱ ♆ refer to # 1149.

1152 ♃ ✱ ♇ refer to # 1149.

1153 ♃ □ ☉ refer to # 128.

1154 ♃ □ ☽ refer to # 339.

1155 ♃ □ ☿ refer to # 533.

1156 ♃ □ ♀ refer to # 729.

1157 ♃ □ ♂ refer to # 943.

1158 ♃ □ ♄ Both planets progress so slowly that a □ has to be there in the natal chart that may, by progression, just come either more towards perfection (within 1 degree) or separate more to dilute a square effect. (see # 1068)

1159 ♃ □ ♅ refer to # 1069.

1160 ♃ □ ♆ refer to # 1070.

1161 ♃ □ ♇ refer to # 1071.

1162 ♃ ▲ ☉ refer to # 127.

1163 ♃ ▲ ☽ refer to # 338.

1164 ♃ ▲ ☿ refer to # 541.

1165 ♃ ▲ ♀ refer to # 738.

1166 ♃ ▲ ♂ refer to # 952.

1167 ♃ ▲ ♄ Both planets progress so slowly that a **s** has to be there in the natal chart that may, by progression, just come either more towards perfection (within 1 degree) or separate more to dilute a triangle effect.

1168 ♃ ▲ ♅ refer to # 1167.

1169 ♃ ▲ ♆ refer to # 1167.

1170 ♃ ▲ ♇ refer to # 1167.

1171 ♃ ☍ ☉ refer to # 128.

1172 ♃ ☍ ☽ refer to # 339.

1173 ♃ ☍ ☿ refer to # 549.

1174 ♃ ☍ ♀ refer to # 747.

1175 ♃ ☍ ♂ refer to # 961.

1176 ♃ ☍ ♄ Both planets progress so slowly that a ☍ has to be there in the natal chart that may, by progression, just come either more towards perfection (within 1 degree) or separate more to dilute an opposing effect.

1177 ♃ ☍ ♅ refer to # 1176.

1178 ♃ ☍ ♆ refer to # 1176.

1179 ♃ ☍ ♇ refer to # 1176.

BABY CHART

1180 ♃ ☌ ☉ refer to # 145.

1181 ♃ ☌ ☽ refer to # 355.

1182 ♃ ☌ ☿ refer to # 557.

1183 ♃ ☌ ♀ refer to # 756.

1184 ♃ ☌ ♂ refer to # 970.

1185 ♃ ☌ ♄ The father had restricted the child's ability to relate, which instilled fear of authorities. The child becomes very sensitive in its expression and retains feelings in fear of expressing them, because it expects an opposition. Seriousness and reliability are present but should be curbed to permit room for happiness and joy. Facing fear and limitations, as instilled by the father, the child must develop a way to relate and share with others to open up the restrictions imposed by the father.

1186 ♃ ☌ ♅ Unusual relationships require considerations of any consequences if such relationships are expected to survive. The great confidence of ♃ must be utilized but also channeled into reality to meet the eccentricity imposed by ♅.

1187 ♃ ☌ ♆ The idea of love may be universal and perceived as a lofty spiritual expectation that is removed from reality. The rose-colored-glasses approach is common. A need to relate to the fellow man must be constructive by leaving the feet on the ground.

1188 ♃ ☌ ♇ There is a need to control and manipulate all relationships. Caution and care are used in order to stay in control. Sensitivity about relationships may lead to over-analysis of any situation, making it difficult to reach a conclusion.

1189 ♃ ✱ ☉ refer to # 154.

1190 ♃ ✱ ☽ refer to # 363.

1191 ♃ ✱ ☿ refer to # 565.

1192 ♃ ✱ ♀ refer to # 765.

1193 ♃ ✱ ♂ refer to # 979.

1194 ♃ ✱ ♄ The father's influence helped the child to reach out and to relate well, even to authority figures.

1195 ♃ ✱ ♅ Innovations, new concepts of relating to others and positive development of relationships, benefit the child.

1196 ♃ ✱ ♆ Encouragement and creativity provide for artistic talent and beneficial relationships.

1197 ♃ ✱ ♇ Working well with groups and an interest in the development of the generation will affect the child on a larger scale.

1198 ♃ □ ☉ refer to # 163.

1199 ♃ □ ☽ refer to # 371.

1200 ♃ □ ☿ refer to # 572.

1201 ♃ □ ♀ refer to # 774.

1202 ♃ □ ♂ refer to # 988.

1203 ♃ □ ♄ The father's influence creates problems of relating and expressing toward others which are adopted by the child. Seriousness creates restrictions to openly express the self. A fear of the new, lack of confidence, and an uneasiness to accept a new job or a new relationship, places restrictions that hinder progress in life. The child avoids dealing with people and draws either inferior types or is unable to emotionally love someone. The child needs to learn to take responsibility and express more feelings in relationships.

1204 ♃ □ ♅ Excess of an unused energy causes eccentricity, unreliability and sudden changes of mind. The person may feel of not fitting in, or may be selfish and displays abrupt behavior or tries to enforce the will onto others. Cooperation and understanding are required to negate the negative influences.

1205 ♃ □ ♆ Over-optimism leads to frustration in the real world. Cloudy and nebulous expectations make any relationship difficult. Responsibility, self-awareness and conscious understanding of what is real, needs developing.

1206 ♃ □ ♇ There is a strong need to control any relationship which prevents real sharing and relating to any partner. Sometimes the need to control turns into an obsession and a desire to win at all cost. The subsequent fear of being controlled may destroy any relationship. Sharing the self needs to be learned to avoid any obsessive behavior.

1207 ♃ ▲ ☉ refer to # 172.

1208 ♃ ▲ ☽ refer to # 379.

1209 ♃ ▲ ☿ refer to # 579.

1210 ♃ ▲ ♀ refer to # 783.

1211 ♃ ▲ ♂ refer to # 997.

1212 ♃ ▲ ♄ The parents are supportive and help the child learn to think before making any commitment. Relationships will be serious and responsible. There is a steady growth and maturity. The child will later understand the full relationship it has had with the father.

1213 ♃ ▲ ♅ Unusual ideas and concepts help form interesting relationships. If the partner's ♃ lends good aspect hereto a close, but unusual, relationship may be formed.

1214 ♃ ▲ ♆ The child may search for the perfect spiritual relationship. Sometimes, there is fantasy coupled with the will to discover the perfect and ideal situation by ignoring the real world. Following the rules of society may, at times, be difficult. To gain fulfillment, the person must face reality, listen and relate more to others.

1215 ♃ ▲ ♇ The person enjoys relating to the masses. Traditional concepts are adopted but if not adhered to, the person will succumb to any new fad and fashion just to satisfy the feeling of belonging. It's very important what the "others" have, just to copy from them. However, the own value system needs developing to bring out the individual within the masses.

1216 ♃ ☍ ☉ refer to # 181.

1217 ♃ ☍ ☽ refer to # 387.

1218 ♃ ☍ ☿ refer to # 586.

1219 ♃ ☍ ♀ refer to # 792.

1220 ♃ ☍ ♂ refer to # 1006.

1221 ♃ ☍ ♄ The father restricted the child in reaching out and exploring the new, thus, instilling fear and apprehension into the child to open up and relate to authority figures. The child may turn emotions from friendly to cold without understanding the reason for doing so. The concept of responsibility and relationships may cause fear and withdrawal as the child has never learned how to deal with it. Self-confidence and self-assurance must be learned.

1222 ♃ ☍ ♅ The opposition between the freedom of the will and the desire to belong, creates conflicting energies. Relationships are either formed immediately on impulse, without consideration of feelings and wants, or the child hesitates, feels uncomfortable and cannot decide to commit. The child lacks the understanding that it needs two to tango and feels uncomfortable to listen and to share.

1223 ♃ ☍ ♆ The process of thinking and considering before action is taken is nebulous and lacks realism. Relationships are entered into without considering the compatibility of the parties and feelings are hurt when there is nothing in common that could sustain a relationship.

1224 ♃ ☍ ♇ A desire to control and manipulate any relationship in order to protect feelings and avoid hurting, is creating an atmosphere of mistrust. The energy of caring for others should be more developed to take away from the self-centered power-games, played by ♇. If respect is not received the control game will start again instead of sharing hurt feelings.

♃ TRANSIT OR PROGRESSION TO A (Ascendant)

1225 ♃ ☌ **A** If not negatively aspected elsewhere, success, prosperity,optimism and a pleasing and much liked personality emerges. During transit favors will be received. Optimism will prevail and the health will improve. However, care should be exercised in the diet to avoid weight gain. Travel maybe undertaken to expand the business.

1226 ♃ ✱ **A** The personality is pleasing and draws popularity. Being fortunate in marriage and general enterprises will bring enthusiasm and happiness. The emotions are well balanced. The person possesses great optimism. During transit, fortunate social contacts and working with groups will be bcneficial.

1227 ♃ □ **A** The desires are hindered by the inability to express the emotions in a pleasing manner. Pompous and righteous behavior will create unpopularity and loss. Without an ability to stick to a goal nothing of substance may develop. Don't be selfish. Attractions maybe important but require scrutinizing. Try to stay harmonious in all relationships.

1228 ♃ ▲ **A** The mind is very optimistic, enthusiastic and ready to cooperate. The pleasing disposition brings happiness and marriage and business success. Growth and expansion will attract help and optimistic views that further happiness and good relationships.

1229 ♃ ☍ **A** refer to # 1227.

♃ TRANSIT OR PROGRESSION TO M (Mid heaven)

1230 ♃ ☌ **M** Prominence and fame before the public may catapult the person into the spot light. A good character, honesty and good social skills will improve the standing in society. A public and well respected occupation is indicated and draws favors. Any negative affliction hereto may lead to overconfidence and a desire for self-importance. During transit matters will be handled with confidence and help expand and bring recognition through government and superiors. Progress is indicated.

1231 ♃ * **M** A good indication for public popularity. Any leadership of religious organizations could lead to mass popularity. Good fortune is indicated. The study of law and medicine will be of interest. Great confidence will benefit any progress.

1232 ♃ □ **M** Overblown opinions and ideas may drain the finances and emotions. Unrealistic expectations could bring disappointment. During transit, any overestimation of self, any afflicted ego and arrogance, could lead to loss. Be careful and plan wisely.

1233 ♃ ▲ **M** A rise to the top is possible through the optimistic, honest and graceful attitude. Help will be received to further any ambitions. An occupation in law, politics or religion could bring fame. During transit, help will be received and will further confidence and success. Financial gain and even fame may arrive, especially when the natal position between ♃ and **M** was positive.

1234 ♃ ☍ **M** refer to # 1232.

42

♄ Saturn

The planet of Karma has limits and restrictions as its chief purpose of keeping in check, to guide and change, and if necessary, will apply life altering experiences. It is concerned with the application of discipline and perfection. Another of nature's tasks to induce progress. Struggle will be necessary to conform to its demands. Any attempt to fight ♄ influences will bring enormous struggle and delays. The mind is hindered in any progress until the direction, the planet had intended for the person, has been chosen and applied.

If not aspected at all in the natal chart it subjects man to a life of idleness, rendering him unable to choose any direction.

Badly aspected, it will subject the person to strife and ongoing struggle. Servitude, dependency, excessive worry and fear will result. Association with undesirable characters and health problems will manifest itself. Deceitful acts, a melancholic mind and ongoing depressions, as well as obstacles, will befall the person.

♄ IN THE NATAL HOUSES

1235 ♄ (1) The person is serious minded, responsible, a hard working personality and may only speak when there is a real purpose, hence, comes across as cold, unfriendly, superficial and distant. A good sense of justice and an ability to carry great responsibility is present but sometimes indicates a lack of humor. Cooperation with others may provide personal fulfillment and happiness.

If afflicted: limitations, hardships, obstacles, selfishness and especially in early life, drudgery and struggle may result. Materialism, overly ambitious projects, intense independence, mistrust and interest only in one's own gain may create alienation from others. Scheming and plotting may result in self-undoing. Physical disabilities may create a life of hardship, especially when the ☋ of the moon is also placed herein.

1236 ♄ (2) Money, possessions and status are obtained through hard work, shrewd business and good investments. Acquiring money may come easier later in life. Prudence, farsightedness and acquisition of land and property provide for lasting values. Material gain may be obtained through the father, elders, employers or authority and through government contracts in mining and construction.

If afflicted: the person is stingy and may have trouble parting with money for expenditures. If money is not kept fluid, stagnation occurs. Amassing of great wealth, because of fear of poverty, may occupy the mind. There could be hard work for very little gain and an intense possessiveness of money could turn into an obsession.

1237 ♄ (3) Mental discipline, practicality, deliberate speech and patience give strength to the personality. Work may be performed in publishing or all kinds of communications but care is needed when signing contracts and exercising agreements. Travel happens more for business than for personal enjoyment.

If afflicted: there are difficulties with brothers, sisters, neighbors, as well as negative thinking, excessive worry and faultfinding. Career disappointments, lack of education and training may be experienced.

1238 ♄ (4) Heavy responsibilities could be imposed through the family and home. Strict and overbearing parents may create a feeling of isolation. There is a struggle to maintain a family and home. Business and work may be created and executed from home or is related to real estate, such as managing property, farming and products needed in the home. Later years are more easy and peaceful. The last years are lived as recluse or the person could be home bound due to lingering illness.

1239 ♄(5) Children and their responsibility, speculation, art, and schools are a matter of concern. If positioned well ♄ will help gain with investments. A romantic involvement with an older person may impose heavy obligations.

If afflicted: financial losses through speculations, lack of romantic opportunity and disappointment in love, may be experienced. The self-consciousness may block any happiness. There is a need to express in a more loving, openly and warm way to find happiness. An inability to relate to children, excessive strictness, or coldness, an inability to love or trouble with children, as well as physical and mental restrictions, may burden the person.

1240 ♄ (6) There is an ability to work hard with a serious attitude, with efficiency and with specialized skills, precision and knowledge. Heavy responsibilities are incurred through work or service and the mind works carefully and steadily. Good co-operation with co-workers and bosses is indicated.

If afflicted: chronic health problems, low vitality, worry, overwork and lack of opportunity to advance may create impediments. Bad relationships with employees and employers may result.

1241 ♄ (7) The person adheres to responsibility, dependency, justice in relationships and public dealings. Marriage may only occur late in life and to a serious, mature or career involved person. Partnerships in business may fare well and lead to better opportunities.

If afflicted: marriage problems may occur, or the person may never marry at all. Partnerships can be troubling. A critical attitude, negative, cold, unloving and uncooperative behavior may lead to lawsuits over partnerships. All relationships entail a high degree of responsibility.

1242 ♄ (8) A strong responsibility and involvement with finances belonging to taxes, insurance, partner's finances, inheritance or corporations, is evinced. The person is accountable for the resources of others.

If afflicted: the person will be involved in litigation over money belonging to others. In case of divorce, losses will be suffered and heavy taxation may be imposed. Death will come after a long term illness. The marriage could be a financial burden while an inheritance may be denied. Distressing dreams could have a disturbing psychological effect.

1243 ♄ (9) The person displays a serious interest in religion, philosophy, publishing and higher education, as well as higher law and foreign affairs. A position of power, distinction and achievement is sought out. The moral reputation is guarded. An official position at universities or other institutions of education may attract the person's interest. Long journeys are taken but more for business than pleasure.

If afflicted: narrow minded authoritarian attitudes, religious fanatics and morality problems, as well as trouble with foreigners or in foreign countries, are possible.

1244 ♄ (10) The person has a strong career ambition, a drive for status, power and wealth, engages in hard work and desires a position of authority, wealth and leadership.

If afflicted: unfair means are used for personal gain that eventually may lead to reversal of fortune, public disgrace and fall from position. Obstacles and disappointments may be experienced that bring lack of opportunity in business, and trouble with authorities.

1245 ♄ (11) Friendships and group associations are important. There is a desire of meeting with the right people to advance one's own interest. Loyalty and help from friends are gained and friendships with elders and those in authority, will be made.

If afflicted: friends are solely used for personal gain. Hopes and wishes are delayed or foreclosed altogether.

1246 ♄ (12) The person prefers to work in seclusion, behind the scene in large institutions, universities, hospitals, corporations or government agencies. It will be hard to obtain recognition even for hard work performed.

If afflicted: loneliness, depression, secret actions, mental illness and confinement in hospitals, prison, or other detention places, could result. The person may cause his/her own downfall.

♄ IN THE SIGNS

1247 ♄ (♈) Patience, self-reliance, resourcefulness, mental creativity, strength and persistence are required to provide recourses in life.

If afflicted: a lack of understanding social boundaries and rights of others. An inability to see the consequences of their actions, may be present. ♈ is the beginning state and the person needs to learn a lot about life. Defensive acts, opposition from and against others, difficult communications and cooperation, may be experienced. Self-centeredness, impulsive self-justification, a desire to push ahead at all costs, could all place limitations on success. The desire is to go it alone, be the boss and be headstrong. Suffering from severe headache will create obstacles and trouble.

1248 ♄ (♉) Discipline and hard work are needed to gain in life. Financial and emotional securities are the prime motivators. Endurance, reliability and patience are eventually paying off, especially in business. Banking, investment, insurance and management are suitable occupations. Sometimes a person will be frugal seeking maximum value for their money. Saving for emergency and old age is typical. This person requires a nest egg for a rainy day.

If afflicted: obstinacy, an excessive desire for money and possession, miserly with funds or hoarding of possession may impede happiness.

1249 ♄ (♊) Well disciplined with logical thinking, being well educated and willing to solve problems, the person is suitable for all kinds of mental work that require mental challenge, as well as constant and continued education. The person is very organized, detail oriented and displays clarity in contracts and agreements. Honesty and dependability is present. Secretaries, bookkeepers, accountants, writers, teachers and researchers fare well with this position.

If afflicted: there is a severe doubt about the self. Suspicion, shyness and critical attitude bring misunderstandings that prevent happiness and won't allow the mind to be at ease.

1250 ♄ (♋) The emotions rule any kind of work. Family responsibilities are serious business. There is a need for balanced emotions. Deep emotions are often hidden from the public. Insecurity or a desperate need for approval may estrange the person from relationships.

If afflicted: there can be estrangement from the family, emotional isolation and neurotic problems. There may be a cold and austere relationship and a constant worry about problems. Difficulty in stability and security in home life may result. Health problems, particularly of sluggish digestion and metabolism, are triggered by any emotional instability. Emotional hypersensitivity, defensiveness and a mind that is overly concerned with materialism, may create isolation.

1251 ♄ (♌) A need for importance, recognition and control of the environment is displayed. The person strives for a position of power and leadership. Entertainment industry, politics, investments and public business, are all worth considering.

If afflicted: dictatorial attitudes, egotism, stubbornness, rigidity and a desire to constantly control others, will manifest. Disappointment in love, problems with children, and heavy losses through financial speculations, could be experienced.

1252 ♄ (♍) Practical at work and concerned with details, the person strives for accuracy, precision and efficiency. Bookkeeping, research, health, medicine and library work is suitable.

If afflicted: perfectionism may stand in the way of achievement. Strict adherence to rules and regulations may create difficulties to get along. A strong drive to work and perform may be exhausting. Becoming gloomy and depressed when overworked can lead to health problems, especially in the nervous system and with digestion.

1253 ♄ (♎) There is an understanding and also cooperation with others. Human relationships require mutual commitment to succeed. Lawyers, judges and mediators are common under this sign. Contracts and agreements must be kept. Business arrangements, planning and legal arrangements are part of the work routine, as well as a strong ability to plan and organize. Marriage may only happen later in life and may interfere with business or become burdensome. When tactful, reliable and patience, this aspect may provide wealth and high a position.

If afflicted: there is a tendency to be driven at work, to be rigid, to lack the feeling of love, of forgiveness and responsibility towards others. False ambitions may scatter energy and remain fruitless.

1254 ♄ (♏) Responsibility will develop towards money from inheritance, taxes, insurance, business relationship or partner and joint finances. Any business activity is likely to deal with these issues. The person

is a perfectionist at work, thrives for constant improvement, has a strong ambition and drive to succeed.
If afflicted: trouble in the financial area and losses through litigation will be experienced. The person may be too driven and dictatorial, has little patience with others and always demands a high energy from others. Emotional intensity may boil over at times and there is a possibility of using unfair means to obtain a goal. When hurt, the person displays deep resentment. Scheming, plotting and a desire for revenge, coupled with an inability to forget the past, may turn into trouble.

1255 ♄ (♐) The person is serious in religion, educational matters, the law and things related to travel and understanding foreign cultures. There is an adherence to a strict moral code. By using the intellectual faculties more depth of concentration is gained. A strong desire exists to be an authority in some profession.
If afflicted: there is a fear of rejection, disapproval and damage of reputation. Being self-righteous and trying to impose the will on others, will disturb relationships.

1256 ♄ (♑) A strong ambition for power and possession is inherent to this sign. A need to succeed and attain prominence may make the person appear cold and distanced. There could be an overly strict obedience to authority. The early life may be beset by struggle for security and self-sufficiency. This may be overcome by a strong will to achieve. There is a strong pride and honor for the family.
If afflicted: any wealth, position and property may be used to control others. If born wealthy, there can be a lack of understanding for others in need. Things of one's own interest may be seen in a more favorable light. If the desire for wealth is carried too far it will stifle any spiritual values. Unscrupulous means may be used to achieve wealth and power, leading to dictatorship, public disgrace and a fall from power.

1257 ♄ (♒) Being well organized, there is a sharp mental concentration, and a desire to adhere to the truth. Mental concentration requires meditation to sharpen the mind, which may lead to inventions and discoveries. A strong sense of justice and responsibility, loyalty, level headedness and understanding of the universal laws, is displayed.

If afflicted: the person is selfish and domineering and desires to advance through others, for personal gain. Coldness and emotional insensitivity in personal relationships, together with a display of intellectual pride, may hinder advancement in life.

1258 ♄ (♓) The mind is trapped in past memories creating overactive and fearful imagination, which can lead to neuroses and anxieties. Humility and the willingness to work hard and help those in need, is present. Quiet and solitude is needed to recharge the energy and mind. Participating in the world's affairs should not be avoided by retreating from it altogether. Work may be done behind the scene in large institutions.

If afflicted: paranoia, worry, fretfulness, regrets and a neurotic tendency may be leading to institutionalization. Physical illness may result from a stressed state of mind. Any self-pity may become overwhelming. Regretting what happened in the past may become a serious concern that will shut off future growth and happiness.

♄ IN ASPECT WITH OTHER PLANETS

1259 ♄ ☌ ☉ Burdensome restrictions and delays imposed by ♄ create limitations of the self-expression and prevent or severely limit the healthy development of the ego. Throughout life extremely hard work and perseverance is required to reap any gain. If negatively aspected by other planets, the mind could turn to a restless and gloomy state and suffer from depression.

1260 ♄ ☌ ☽ Work may be performed from the home. The mind is serene and serious while dwelling on business opportunities, which may involve food, farming or real estate. Business ventures involving women may be considered. If this aspect is not afflicted by other planets such a business may prosper. If afflicted, however, all dealings with women need scrutinizing and care must be taken when dealing with common mankind as misfortune, losses and association with the wrong people will drag the person down.

1261 ♄ ☌ ☿ The mind is controlled, efficient, precise and difficult work is possible under this aspect. Business revolves around all kinds of communications and the person may experience a heavy workload. Suffering from overwork, or worry and depression, fear may result in a negative attitude that would prevent any positive development. Dealings with older people, or authority figures, are indicated. Serious agreements can be contemplated and entered into, however, said contracts need to be carefully scrutinized to avoid later disagreements. Any affliction hereto will turn the mind bitter, pessimistic and creates an interest in cheating others. Addictions to licentious pleasures create disagreements and possible loss. This aspect afflicts the nervous system. The speech and any kind of written communication should only be undertaken with care to avoid critical, nagging and bitter outlooks that depress the mind. Care must be taken not to overlook important details, thus, setting the person up for failure.

1262 ♄ ☌ ♀ Reserved social manners are evinced and the person may enter into romantic and/or business relationships with elders. A strong desire for emotional and financial security develops. Existing relationships either brake up or will be strengthened or old romantic or business relationships are renewed. A sense of loneliness may develop when things are not turning out as planned. Business and financial responsibilities may interfere with happiness. If afflicted, loneliness, depression and worry will result. The emotions and any relationship will undergo a time of testing and re-examination. Sacrifices may be necessary, as well as a period of withdrawing from others, to resolve the tension that has developed.

1263 ♄ ☌ ♂ Any rashness or hasty actions, or suppressed anger and resentment, may drive the person to frustration and a wrong kind of behavior. Heavy work and responsibility create a mental burden or at times, a hard, unsympathetic attitude, which leads to conflict. Disagreements or confrontations with authority figures should be avoided. An involvement in lawsuits is possible. Uncontrolled rashness may lead to accidents. The mind is argumentative and will not find any peace.

1264 ♄ ☌ ♃ The mind is optimistic but serious, if not afflicted. This is a good position to handle business, political and legal affairs. New business or educational matters may develop and will prosper. A job or business may involve the necessity of travel. The restlessness and impatience must be curbed. Restrictions may create discomfort. Strife with children must be avoided. Changes of job and/or residence may be made. The natal position of ♃ will determine the outcome.

1265 ♄ ☌ ♅ Original and inventive ideas are applied in a constructive and practical way. The slowness, responsibility and throughout planning of ♄ supports ♅ to forge ahead by applying a reality check on the outcome. The ability to systematically investigate, discover and apply knowledge provides for good scientific work, as well as for astrology and occultism. Any affliction to this conjunction provides obstinacy, autocratic attitudes and overbearing righteousness which will result in estrangements. The mind may long to entertain unrealistic ideas, which lead to loss and pessimistic outlook, if followed through. Hastiness may bring on accidents or business loss.

1266 ♄ ☌ ♆ The mind is slow but steady and has full power of concentration if this conjunction is well aspected. It gives the ability to work behind the scene, in secrecy and on long term projects that need careful planning and execution. If afflicted by other planets, foul play and deliberate deceit may be involved giving rise to anxiety and depression. Drugs and alcohol should be avoided as they present a danger to lead the mind astray.

1267 ♄ ☌ ♇ The person may simply suffer from a depressed power complex or presents him/herself to he world, by having a transforming effect upon the masses (Arnold Schwarzenegger is born with this conjunction) Acts are often performed in secret. A wide range of power over society and the environment is desired. Any affliction hereto involves the person in corruption, intrigue, selfish motives and insatiable desires for power, hence, creating secret enemies that will ultimately bring a downfall from power.

1268 ♄ ✶ ☉ A well developed discipline and good organization, as well as any methodical application of logic, will provide for a steady success. Good character traits, such as honesty, integrity and cooperation, will further any plans. The ability to take on burdensome responsibilities may provide for a position in authority. The physical health is strong and has the power of recuperation.

1269 ♄ ✱ ☽ Domestic issues are attended to in details. The emotions are controlled and the mind attends to serious work and study. Friendships can be established with older, mature individuals, especially women, and authority figures. Financial help may be obtained from the mother or other mature women. This can make the person fearful, suspicious and changeable, if afflictions apply.

1270 ♄ ✱ ☿ The mind is logical, realistic and attends to serious study, work, or long range planning. Any work involving communications and writings, is favored. This is a good time to begin any serious study.

1271 ♄ ✱ ♀ A kind demeanor is displayed. The person will seek and receive financial considerations from an older and established person. Business opportunities will present themselves as well as romantic opportunities. Legal matters may now fare well. Involvement in artistic projects could lead to the development of a business. Romantic attachments may be connected to business and may be driven by a desire to gain through them.

1272 ♄ ✱ ♂ Discipline, organization and efficiency are applied to constructively perform work. Business may involve those who hold a position of authority and power. Contracts and agreements regarding business may be entered into. Professions involving machinery, engineering, construction or any work that involves precision, is suitable. As long as the actions are controlled, reasonable, practical hard work and good planning will pay off.

1273 ♄ ✱ ♃ The energy is directed towards career achievements. Help and recognition from people in authority and power may be received. Advancements can be made by steadily and systematically following a path, thereby adhering to honesty and applying responsibility. The mind is serious, optimistic and willing to consider step after step necessary for success. Lawyers, politicians, administrators and businessmen do well under this aspect. Opportunities for advancement will arise.

1274 ♄ ✱ ♅ Responsibility, self-discipline, steady planning and execution of even original or unusual undertakings is bound to lead to success. Loyalty and honesty toward others bring reliable and enduring friendships.

1275 ♄ ✱ ♆ The disciplined and throughout application of ♄ brings steadiness of purpose and focuses the imagination so that any plans, open or secret, can be carried out. Suitable for any kind of research projects, the mind is willing to consider even the smallest, minute detail for information.

1276 ♄ ✱ ♇ The will is organized and controlled. Hard work is not seen as an obstacle, but will be accepted to bring changes into the life.

1277 ♄ □ ☉ This indicates a life of hardship with many obstacle littering the way to the top. Frequent changes in jobs and unstable relationships, especially with authority figures, could lead to frustration and depression. If willing to fight and overcome this aspect, a stronger character will emerge. Diplomacy, optimism and a more happy outlook in life may help overcome this stern position. The health may not be very strong and is subject to prolonged illness. Trouble with the bone structure, the teeth or accidents due to a fall, may bring misery or death.

1278 ♄ □ ☽ Worry, anxiety and even physical ailments may be experienced. Persistency is needed to overcome this aspect. Feelings of apprehension over affairs and depressed attitudes may interfere with every day life. Emotional upsets, especially when older people or authority figures are involved, may confuse the person.

1279 ♄ □ ☿ Delays, mental agitation, heavy responsibilities and loss of concentration will be experienced due to worry and anxiety. Loss of intellectual interests, annoyance with routine tasks and depression will hinder progress. This is difficult for communications and serious conflicts may develop with the family as well as in business relationships.

1280 ♄ □ ♀ Emotional depression and loss of finances will occur. Social affairs and personal attachment will be delayed causing mental aggravation. The ability to earn income can be interfered with by unpleasant circumstances. The person may experience a lack of sympathy from others. A lust for the wrong person may invite ruin by running with the infamous. Love relationships may break off and financial losses will be incurred.

1281 ♄ □ ♂ Irritation and frustration about work and responsibilities, as well as disagreements, anger and rage, especially disagreements with older authority figures, will be felt. The overall harmony is disturbed. Anxiety and worry will prevail making the person susceptible to accidents, especially through falls. Any aggressive feelings should be curbed. Any tendency to be bitter, antagonistic and allowing unexpected outbursts of anger, directed at others to win a situation, should be avoided.

1282 ♄ □ ♃ Obstruction, difficulties and disappointment are felt. Interruptions regarding business and money may lead to serious problems. Lawsuits may be filed against the person, especially when the seventh house is involved. The same applies to ♂ □ ♃.

1283 ♄ □ ♅ The slow and prodding characteristics of ♄ clash with the inventive, eccentric and sometimes radical ideals of ♅. The person either opposes any change and wants to continue with the way things were, or becomes so radical and sudden in any action that the outcome may be costly. This aspect could bring dictatorial tendencies, unreliability and disagreements with friends and groups. Lack of common sense and an unwillingness to cooperate may lead to a downfall, to accidents and others misfortunes.

1284 ♄ □ ♆ The mind is absorbed by anxiety, fear, neuroses and phobias. Any skeleton in the closet may be exposed by this aspect. Drugs and alcohol use may bring the person down. The mind is not strong enough to overcome temptations due to inadequacy of the character and the desire to escape all responsibilities. Very often confused, the person may lack efficiency at work or use devious and deceitful methods to get ahead. Scandal and intrigue may tarnish the reputation. Any kind of religious belief may be too extreme or unrealistic to be accepted by others. Loneliness may ultimately lead to mental illness.

1285 ♄ □ ♇ All plans seem to fizzle out. Nothing will develop and never ending changes bring unstable and undesired conditions into the life. Through ♇ there may be danger of plots, schemes and involvement with the underworld that leads to destruction. The will is overly strong, at times dictatorial, controlling and willing to remake others, to satisfy the ambitions.

1286 ♄ ▲ ☉ A steady, conservative and good character is focused on a steady rise. The ability to be well organized, to concentrate on even minute details, a willingness to apply hard work and careful planning for the future, will all help improve the circumstances in life. Relationships with authority figures will be beneficial.

1287 ♄ ▲ ☽ The mind is stable and well controlled. The emotions are reserved and cautiously applied. Dealings with older, mature and established people, especially with women, may develop and become beneficial. Business, finances and interactions with the family are disciplined and bring financial rewards. Real Estate transactions and any business relating to women can be successfully completed.

1288 ♄ ▲ ☿ The mind is alert, practical and engages in good organization and planning. Study, advanced education and furtherance in the career, will be pursued. Older, mature and established people will be of help. All kinds of communications are beneficial and the person may be teaching others. Architects, designers, teachers and technicians benefit from this aspect.

1289 ♄ ▲ ♀ The person displays a pleasant but serious demeanor. Work and interest in the arts or music are favored. Close personal relationships may deepen and old friendships are renewed and may be long lasting. There is a strong sense of responsibility towards others. Business and financial interests may develop favorably. If this is a natal position the person may find romance in or through business. If not in youth it will occur at the latest, by the time ♄ transits this position again in 29 years and no afflictions exist. A love and business partnership could develop that will be of financial benefit to both parties, or the person may be romantically involved with a superior or older person through work.

1290 ♄ ▲ ♂ The will is expressed with a determination to succeed. Hard work and good organization serve the person well. Managers and administrators, engineers, architects, builders, as well as police or military positions are suitable as an occupation. This aspect is favorable when dealing with authority or lawsuits. This aspect is favorable for any kind of work, which requires precision and concentration.

1291 ♄ ▲ ♃ Good progress will be made in business, especially when related to law, politics, travel and religion. New undertakings in work and business bring financial rewards. Legal affairs and all dealings with government and authority will be favorable. Cooperation is received from others. An optimistic and responsible attitude helps achieve any goal.

1292 ♄ ▲ ♅ The mind is able to transform the imaginations into practical results. Cooperation, executive ability and good relations with the public promote any undertakings in politics, religion or any large organization where leadership is required.

1293 ♄ ▲ ♆ Work done in secret or behind the scene is favored promoting all kinds of business connected with research, investigation, photography and all forms of visual entertainment. Favors will be received from older people or persons in authority.

1294 ♄ ▲ ♇ A good organizational ability, responsibility and methodical thinking instilled by ♄ finds a good outlet in occult, astrology or related fields. The will power provides support to achieve any goal. Good leadership, coupled with a willingness to cooperate and engagement in hard work will provide gain. This allows for positive changes in life and for the general population.

1295 ♄ ☍ ☉ The effect is similar as described in the square aspect. The self-expression and ability to cooperate in a harmonious way is restricted and creates disharmony and strife. Relationships and work conditions are subject to disagreements and will dissolve. A lack of confidence may be the source of the problem. Any unwillingness to work hard and overcome obstacles will render the person without support and will subject the personality to misery and despair.

1296 ♄ ☍ ☽ Mental depression, health problems especially with the nerves and digestive system, a lower vitality, feelings of loneliness and of being unwanted, rule the mind. Relationships lack emotional warmth and understanding for each other. Dealings with authority and women will not work well and there is disharmony within the family. A lack of self-confidence may hamper any program. Work or business will be beset with difficulties. A need to learn a more optimistic and logical behavior to override the severely depressed emotions, is necessary.

1297 ♄ ☍ ☿ A lot of worry and a closed mind create obstacles that prevent any progress in life. The person may be criticized by authority and burdened with a heavy work load and receive no cooperation from others. Ill health could result from the mental state of depression and unhappiness. There may be teeth, skin, bone and intestine problems due to the cramped up state of the mind. Business problems and legal difficulties will affect the mind, thus, setting the body into a position of anger that affects all organs negatively. The signing of any contract and agreement or implementing any important decision should only be made after careful consideration of all factors involved to avoid further unfavorable developments. Decisions to be made should be postponed, if possible while a negative transit affects this aspect, as this may lead to permanent estrangements from others.

1298 ♄ ☍ ♀ The mind feels lost and alone. Desired relationships either do not develop or break up leading to disappointment and unrequited love. Certain coldness in behavior may cause separation. Business and financial affairs may cause frustration, or delays or may not develop altogether. Tension, conflict, separation and bickering will cause difficulties.

1299 ♄ ☍ ♂ The body's physical capacity is overstrained leading to injury and illness. Actions may be frustrated by uncooperative authority figures or due to an inflated ego and dictatorial attitudes. Favors and cooperation will not be forthcoming. At the extreme, the person may be subject to arrest if the 12th house is involved. No important changes should be made. Legal difficulties and involvement in lawsuits may occur. Opposition will be experienced. If the person is revengeful by nature, rash acts may lead to action that may later give reason to repent.

1300 ♄ ☍ ♃ Professional and business affairs are subject to wrong decisions and poor timing. Questionable or underhanded tactics may lead to loss. No cooperation is received. Cold and stiff mannerism prevent receiving needed support. Legal difficulties and severe financial problems may hinder any advancement. Education, the law, travel and social activities are stifled preventing happiness and furtherance of goals. This negative aspect impacts on the family, especially on children, on relationships and business affairs. Any ulterior motive regarding money, status and advancement may create a breakdown of relationships. A balance between optimism and pessimism is needed to avoid going overboard either way.

1301 ♄ ☍ ⛢ A strong will power, dictatorial attitudes, inconsistency and unreliability occur with this opposition. The desire to control and remake others will lead to estrangements. Relationships with superiors and authorities are not harmonious but give way to strife, arguments and disagreement, which will ultimately lead to loss. The financial affairs fluctuate greatly in life and there may be times where all security is swept away. Lacking humility and understanding, one is being ruled by ever changing moods. The person may not have the planning and foresight to achieve success.

1302 ♄ ☍ ♆ The person is mistrustful, morbid, confused and absorbed in dreams and fantasies. Irrational fears, anxiety, acting in secret, being cunning and deceitful, will all create trouble and separation. Getting involved in schemes or other illegal activity could unravel and all skeletons in the closed will be exposed. Scandal may follow. In extreme cases, any mental problems will result in institutionalization.

1303 ♄ ☍ ♇ ♄ represents karma over the person and may create many problems under this aspect. The person may be subjected to or be involved in harsh treatment, crime, cruelty or intense power struggle, which will bring unwanted changes into the life. A string of misfortune may be experienced resulting in extreme hardship and possibly involving the person in war or even incarceration. Extreme hard work, as well as improvement of the self-expression and self-appreciation is needed to overcome this aspect.

♄ IN TRANSIT THROUGH THE HOUSES

This planet is very powerful and, even by transit, has an enormous effect on our daily life. ♄ is associated with Karma and is responsible for reaching into our life, forcing us to face changes. Destruction will occur for unhealthy conditions that need changing to make room for future progress. It often reveals, through events, what must be done to resolve stale and unhealthy conditions by forcing us to move on even when we are fearful of changes. Inner pressure will enforce changes in order to let us escape limitations and frustration, thus promoting new growth. Whatever resembles excessiveness in one's life in regards to ego, attachments, dependency, activity or faith, is bound to be readjusted. As ♄ transit through the houses has a powerful effect on life the author has especially addressed this issue herein in detail.

1304 **HOUSE 1:** When ♄ transits through this house it reflects a new beginning after all was dissolved during the transit through the 12th house of Karma. After conjunction with the **A** the person is brought down to earth, realizing the result of previous actions and past habits and why they have produced certain results. Outer circumstances will compel the person to see action and reaction and force some realization of their own faults and the actual truth of the matter, which was previously rejected. Being more realistic and acknowledging an honest self-appraisal, allowing for more seriousness and truthfulness which will be applied to life. The personality needs to regain structure and purpose for future development.

Physical changes may include losing weight, sometimes to the point of emaciation. The energy level is low, tiredness, poor digestion and feelings of depression may occur. This is part of the effort to rebuild body and soul. The lifestyle, particularly as it concerns the diets and health, should be improved to give the body and mind the energy needed to spread out for something new. Karma wants to mold us into the person we need to be. This transit through the 1st house is a period of building a new character by paying attention to the own wants and needs and retreat from the outer world until the changes are completed and firmly in place. New goals and interests will develop and the person seems guided toward new types of work even if those professions were previously not considered.

1305 **HOUSE 2:** The urge to be productive and make money surfaces. This is a time where a new business is opened or some new kind of practical training and education is pursued in the quest for higher earnings. The push for survival makes the person inventive, frugal and driven to reap material benefits.

1306 **HOUSE 3:** The energy is placed into new learning that will enhance the professional skills and further ideas. Private research, education involving writing and all kinds of communications, may be pursued. The skills learned may not be used into the distant future but the new knowledge and background will be helpful in assessing ones experience and level of intelligence. Friendships within the family and neighbors may be restructured to befit new ideas. When negatively aspected, depression and negative thinking could temporarily halt any advances made.

1307 **HOUSE 4:** Order and structure in the home environment are redefined at this time. Either additions, or alterations to an existing home or relocation of the residence are contemplated. Family obligations become more real and urgent. Long term planning should be considered regarding the job, the family and the home. Involvement in real estate ventures and relationships with elders may be beneficial.

1308 **HOUSE 5:** The acts of love, joy and entertainment may be drastically reduced at this time leaving feelings of depression, of being unloved and unappreciated, thus, forcing the person to confront all fears or restricting habits. Greater responsibility and disputes re: children, spending and investing money and engaging in love affairs come forth for consideration. Emotional stability needs encouraging to avoid attractions and attachments to older persons simply out of fear and insecurity. A man from the past may re-enter your life. Love affairs may stabilize or break up during this transit. Attachments should not be entered into merely to escape the feelings of loneliness. If inclined to creative art this is the time to let the energy flow. This house also deals with any hobbies that the person may have or wants to take up. Any overwork, by trying to cramp it in all at once, may result in fatigue. If the energy is properly applied a previous hobby may develop into a growing enterprise.

1309 **HOUSE 6:** Work and health habits undergo adjustments and changes. More organization and discipline is applied. Misunderstandings at work may cause stress. Job changes are made to escape stifling, restricting and limiting conditions. Health problems need to be taken care off. Depression may appear after realization how people feel about us and may have been permitted to abuse our generosity for too long. A self-purification is needed. Toxic has accumulated in the body particularly due to stress and mental unhappiness and a wrong diet. Adjustments in the diet and attitude toward work and service must be made during this transit. Any problems with health and/or the work situation must be addressed and changed to accommodate progress.

1310 **HOUSE 7:** Relationships formed are more serious and subject to greater responsibility. The need, limitations and duties of any relationship will be stressed. Whatever isn't working should be dealt with realistically. Changes must be made to clear the way for progress. A certain coldness and reserved attitude or withdrawal from partner is normal at this time to get an objective and detached perspective of any relationship. If a relationship survives this transit it will emerge stronger and more determined.

1311 **HOUSE 8:** Old habits are terminated. The emotions and desires need to be adjusted, structured and disciplined to ease pressure and frustration. Desires and power over others may be questioned by deep suffering as a soul searching is taking place. Financial, sexual or emotional security may be taken away to promote a different growth. Sexual energy needs channeling and be more disciplined to allow this energy to be expressed other than through physical means. Cutting off previously experienced sexual outlets to retain the forces within one self may balance the desires for a more constructive purpose. Occult study and spiritual practices may be pursued at this time. New life ideals will be formed and emerge at the end of this transit.

1312 **HOUSE 9:** New religious studies, long distance travel and new academic training are contemplated when this transit begins. A great desire for self-improvement is expressed. An interest in teaching others develops, as well as a strong desire for education. Foreign travel will be undertaken more for business than pleasure. A feeling of loss may prevail during this transit.

1313 **HOUSE 10:** Serious concerns about the career, the reputation and ambitions of desires must be dealt with. Frustration, anxiety, hard work and tiring duties affect the career. If the ambitions have not been achieved at this time frustration and depression will occur. Only by executing better goals and pursuing them relentlessly will positive changes be made. Important past mistakes may now bring a downfall and affect the reputation and standing in society.

1314 **HOUSE 11:** How one functions in society and interacts with others will be brought to the forefront. A time to concentrate on friendships or group associations. Any friendship that has not work out or has not been important will fade out. Old friendships may now be totally severed and new, more meaningful friendships, will develop. An older person may become very valuable and may act as a mentor.

1315 **HOUSE 12:** Being now in the house of karma ♄ forces the reflection on the results of past thoughts, action, desires and undertakings as engaged in previously. It represents the end of an old cycle and hence, confusion, discontent, disorientation and a confinement of the emotions and expressions emerge as the old dissolves completely. What once gave meaning is no longer of interest and will dissolve. New values and interests need to be adopted and a more refined attitude towards life and its meanings will emerge. The spirit needs a new purpose and orientation. ♄ will provide guidance into a new cycle by destruction of the old. In the 12th house, ♄ imposes a kind of isolation to prepare the mind to look within at what has been missing and is now creating an emotional prison that forces the isolation from the outer world. If this is not done voluntarily situations will arise enforcing new circumstances. The resulting acts are unavoidable. One cannot set a clock back in life. A force is in place that will propel the person forward, even at times of resistance to new situations. Secret affairs which seldom last, may be initiated. Skeletons can come out of the closet and turn self-destructive. If the health is not taken care off confinement in a hospital or institution may become necessary. The physical energy is low and the emotional energy and willpower feels drained. This is a period in which a person should question old behavior and habit pattern, make necessary changes and prepare for ♄ entrance into the first house upon which the changes will manifest.

♄ TRANSIT

1316 ♄ ☌ ☉ refer to # 75

1317 ♄ ☌ ☽ refer to # 270

1318 ♄ ☌ ☿ refer to # 471

1319 ♄ ☌ ♀ refer to # 667

1320 ♄ ☌ ♂ refer to # 881

1321 ♄ ☌ ♃ refer to # 1095

1322 ♄ ☌ ♅ The person will be burdened with extra responsibilities. The eccentric side of ♅ may interfere with the organized ♄ that can confuse or delay any goal. Depending on other aspects this may be make or break season. Karma will dish out what has been earned. Mental tension will develop and affect the health. In the desire for the new and exciting sudden break ups may proceed any progress. Play fair and work hard.

1323 ♄ ☌ ♆ Artistic talents may surface. This is a good time to meditate and clear the mind. Goals may now be revised. Worry and depression will lower the vitality. Anxiety and fear may grip the mind and severely stifle the ability to think and to move. In the extreme, institutionalization could become necessary. A time of uncertainty in all affairs, especially in business. Any afflictions hereto could lead to lawsuits, deceptions in business, emotional separations from family and friends and scandal could follow. Avoid intrigue, beware of secret acts. Don't allow negative thinking to take over. Self-doubt, uncertainty and mental illness need attention. It is imperative to attend to the health as this transit could trigger chronic illnesses that could turn malignant.

1324 ♄ ☌ ♇ Business affairs could undergo drastic changes. Something old has to give before anything new can develop. The reputation could be tested. Intrigues and power struggles may develop. The resources of others, also taxes and inheritance, could all be the subject of problems. Responsibilities weigh heavy on the person. Life and death issues may occur. The element of danger could be present during this transit. Financial problems will impose a heavy burden. Authorities may not be supportive.

1325 ♄ ✱ ☉ refer to # 84

1326 ♄ ✱ ☽ refer to # 279

1327 ♄ ✱ ☿ refer to # 480

1328 ♄ ✱ ♀ refer to # 676

1329 ♄ ✱ ♂ refer to # 890

1330 ♄ ✱ ♃ refer to # 1104

1331 ♄ ✱ ♅ Friends are made through business affairs. Older, mature individuals, who also have power of authority, will be helpful, thus, progress will excel. The restless and erratic mind is kept focused by ♄.

1332 ♄ ✱ ♆ The memory is enhanced. Creative imaginations surface and together with ♄ ability to steady, concentrated and organized work, this will advance the person. Business matters will improve. A good time to study and enhance the mind. Don't let worry or fear enter into any new challenge.

1333 ♄ ✱ ♇ The ego is subdued, more organized, more concentrated, which allows for disciplined studies. New opportunities could open up that, if followed, bring accomplishment and honor in the long run.

1334 ♄ □ ☉ refer to # 93

1335 ♄ □ ☽ refer to # 288

1336 ♄ □ ☿ refer to # 489

1337 ♄ □ ♀ refer to # 685

1338 ♄ □ ♂ refer to # 899

1339 ♄ □ ♃ refer to # 1113

1340 ♄ □ ♅ Sudden, unexpected obstacles and challenges appear. ♄ power of karma may punish the person for selfish acts taken in the past. Frustration, worry, depression and feelings of being lost, will surface. Mistrust, loss of a job, legal difficulties and health problems can be a part of this transit. This can be a very upsetting time, full of tension, as plans will not work out to satisfaction. Beware of accidents. Disagreement and separation will happen.

1341 ♄ □ ♆ Deep seated fears and phobias float to the top. Anxiety about life, relationships and work will depress the mind. In extreme cases the mind is subject to illness, confusion and paranoia. Drugs and alcohol consumption must be avoided or it will aggravate any problems. Slander and libel may damage the reputation. Long hidden secrets may surface and will damage any social standing. Because the mind is so muddled during this transit, not much will be achieved. Many disappointments will follow. During this transit it is better to preserve the status quo and not to engage in new ideas or plans as they will not ripen to fruition.

1342 ♄ □ ♇ A desire for power, coercion and control comes with this transit. The lack of sensitivity towards the feelings of others will bring difficult circumstances that bring disappointment and loss. A confrontation with undesirable or even criminal elements may involve blackmail, threats, violence and corruption, all of which will be detrimental to the person. Any desire to cut corners and to use dishonorable means will lead to disaster. Business affairs, as well as personal relationships, will suffer. The person may have to fight for survival and protect the reputation. Don't be ambitious at this time. Avoid spending. Take care of the health. Breakdowns and separations will occur before this transit is over. Sexual problems may interfere with relationships.

1343 ♄ ▲ ☉ refer to # 102

1344 ♄ ▲ ☽ refer to # 297

1345 ♄ ▲ ☿ refer to # 498

1346 ♄ ▲ ♀ refer to # 694

1347 ♄ ▲ ♂ refer to # 908

1348 ♄ ▲ ♃ refer to # 1122

1349 ♄ ▲ ♅ This influence keeps the erratic ♅ in check and helps focus to bring a goal to fruition. Good progress can be made. New friendships with older, wiser and connected people will develop and bring advancement. An excellent time to study astrology and related subjects. New ideas bring improvement. A good time to seek and receive favors and induce changes.

1350 ♄ ▲ ♆ The imaginations are applied well bringing beneficial results. Secrets may surface and benefit the person. This is a favorable time for spiritual advancement. If disciplined, this transit brings mental stability and progress. Self-understanding will occur. A good time to study yoga, metaphysics and other movements.

1351 ♄ ▲ ♇ The mind is more focussed and concentrated. The ego is in check and able to relate better to society. This is a positive transit to activate plans and engage in endeavors that will further the talent, mind, body and profession. An excellent time to handle legal affairs, investigations and contracts. Ambitions and efficiency are increased. If willing to work hard advances will be made. Help is received, particularly from older and more established individuals. The personality grows and more self-assurance improves efficient execution of goals.

1352 ♄ ☍ ☉ refer to # 111

1353 ♄ ☍ ☽ refer to # 306

1354 ♄ ☍ ☿ refer to # 507

1355 ♄ ☍ ♀ refer to # 703

1356 ♄ ☍ ♂ refer to # 917

1357 ♄ ☍ ♃ refer to # 1131

1358 ♄ ☍ ♅ Rebellious and eccentric behaviors bring confrontations with the elder or authority figures. Relationships may suffer and break up all together due to irrational attitudes and behavior. Conflicts will arise in friendships and business. Finances, expected from others, may not materialize. The sudden and unexpected is bound to happen and could create havoc in life. Lawsuits over financial issues may arise. A very upsetting period during which trouble on all four corners is to be expected. Stay calm and disciplined.

1359 ♄ ☍ ♆ Neurotic behavior interferes with social relations. Emotional depression, fantasies, day dreaming, mistrust and secret acts will undermine the reputation and standing in life. Family and relationship obligations create anxiety, fear and self-doubt and could be severely disturbed due to mental illness. Avoidance and fear of performing responsibilities may be a sign of trouble to come. Any abuse of alcohol and drugs will negatively affect the senses and the mind. Secret affairs, dishonesty, as well as unsound and underhanded dealings will surface and affect the reputation, business and social standing. This is not a good time to seek treatment in hospitals. Inner conflicts and tension will add to health problems, especially on a mental level. Disappointment and depression, remorse and irrational fears, will last throughout this transit.

1360 ♄ ☍ ♇ A stubborn, plotting and power hungry mind will engage in dishonest and sometimes even secret criminal activity or people of sinister character have to be dealt with. Great emotional or financial loss has to be endured through coercive acts of others. The internal tension is unbearable and will affect the health. The old will break down and has to be let go off. Participating in lawsuits, power struggle or business ventures are all subject to struggle and disappointment. A time where fighting on all levels may be necessary to avoid a total loss. Physical strain and extremely hard work are required if one intends to hold on to belongings or defend from attacks of others. Nothing new should be undertaken. The health may suffer to the point of serious illness or even death.

♄ PROGRESSED

While ♄, ♅, ♆, and ♇ progress so little over a life time the natal position will not change much, as any progression of ♄ brings life altering events its effects are explained here in more details.

1361 ♄ ☌ ☉ A critical time during which the affairs tend to develop contrary to any plans. The mind turns bitter. Excessive responsibilities bring anxiety and depression. The health may suffer. Any positive influences hereto will stabilize conditions, strengthens the character, and give great ability to persevere towards the goal.

1362 ♄ ☌ ☽ Any progress is retarded by ♄ which limits the action, affects the emotions, and brings depression and sorrow. Nothing new should be started while this progress lasts. Dealings with the elderly, or people in authority, should be postponed. The entire nervous system is sensitive. Ill health may result due to the restrictive flow of all fluids in the body. Social affairs will not develop well. Negative changes will result therefrom if any action is taken during this period.

1363 ♄ ☌ ☿ The mind is hindered from being fully expressed, making the person rather suspicious and apprehensive, even to the point of developing melancholia and despondency. The health is affected by impeding of the circulation, which affects the nervous system in the form of neuralgia or congestion or intestinal trouble. The person may be subject to heavy and responsible work, mental disappointments and disagreements with people in power and authority over him. An overly critical or fault finding attitude should not be developed. The emotions should stay calm until this progress has passed.

1364 ♄ ☌ ♀ The person must be careful not to do anything that causes disappointment, loss of honor and credit. Financial affairs will suffer. Social affairs will not turn out as planned. Attachments to older persons may occur, but unless well aspected in the natal chart, this will not endure or remain happy. The emotions are restrained, remain unfulfilled and are subject to suffering. If the ☽ is in an unfavorable position at the same time, this progress may be extremely painful.

1365 ♄ ☌ ♂ Any anger and passion may be stirred up. Acting rashly without consideration of the outcome will bring trouble. The desires and temper must be curbed in order to avoid dangerous and destructive situations. Be aware of any rash acts and do not say or do things that will give rise to later regrets. If at the same time the ☽ is also in a negative position, the person will be overcome by emotions leading to destructive acts.

1366 ♄ ☌ ♃ The optimism is dampened. Heavy responsibilities are imposed and obstacles must be overcome. Financial problems need patience and careful planning to avoid losses. The person needs to work extra hard and long to gain even a little. Disappointment can weigh heavily on the mind and dampen any optimism. While ♃ tries to expand ♄ restricts and delays. Important plans should be left for a later time.

1367 ♄ ☌ ♅ The mind tends to be original, but combined with ♄ careful planning abilities, this aspect could support the self-discipline by keeping any eccentricity in check. The mind is creative and well suited for the study of astrology, mathematics, science and may discover new and better ways of handling things. A good aspect hereto will support successful undertakings. Any afflictions hereto subject the person to accidents, loss of security, stubborn obstinacy, pessimism and unrealistic thinking.

1368 ♄ ☌ ♆ Under very positive aspects the person may develop a high concentration and may use clairvoyant talents. Any latent talent in music or art may be developed at this time. Activities may be performed in secret to avoid opposition. Should there be an affliction to this aspect, deceit and fraud will be engaged in or experienced. Depression, anxiety or wild running imagination could cause problems. At an extreme, this may lead to institutionalization, especially if this aspect affects or takes place in the 12th house. No drugs and/or alcohol should be used. No engagement in psychic or religious influences should be permitted as that would weaken the mind and make the person susceptible to the control of others.

1369 ♄ ☌ ♇ A strong desire for power and leadership is displayed. Ideas may have a great effect upon others. Seriousness and acting in secret comes with this aspect. Any negative influences to this aspect produces selfishness, intrigue and an overwhelming desire for power. Hard work and persistence are required to succeed.

1370 ♄ * ☉ A strengthened character will accept more responsibility. Progress can be made through friends and acquaintances. This is a good time to increase the honor and reputation through deeds and good planning.

1371 ♄ * ☽ Gain from hard work is indicated. Stability and security can be obtained. The mind becomes more serious, more persevering and frugal in order to reach a goal. This is a good time to put all affairs in order. Entering into new and lasting friendships will be beneficial. Said friendships will involve women. Advancement in life is indicated if this aspect is free from negative influences.

1372 ♄ * ☿ The mind becomes careful and prudent. Affairs are attended to in a wisely manner and brought to a conclusion. Increased responsibility may improve the honor and standing. All dealings with elderly and authorities will go well and be satisfactory. Relationships will be improved. Entering into contracts, agreements and engagements, will be favorable.

1373 ♄ * ♀ Financial improvement will be achieved. Help will be received and favorable attachments bring honor and gain and may elevate the person into a better position in life. Steady progress is indicated if the ☽ is positive at the same time. Advantage should be taken of this progress.

1374 ♄ ✱ ♂ The will and the desire are in better harmony to each other, allowing for clear-headed, precise decisions to accomplish goals. Again, the ☽ aspect hereto will determine if this aspect acts favorable or merely calms the person down.

1375 ♄ ✱ ♃ The mind is optimistic, cautious, prudent and well organized. Plans will be executed precisely and successfully. Help will be given and also received. A good period to make plans and execute them wisely.

1376 ♄ ✱ ♅ Due to the slow movement of both planets the natal position will not differ by any progression.

1377 ♄ ✱ ♆ refer to # 1376

1378 ♄ ✱ ♇ see refer to # 1376

1379 ♄ □ ☉ This aspect is unfortunate. Sorrow and grief may be experienced, especially in the domestic circle. Death could occur. This is not a good time to make any changes. Due to nervous tension and depression the health will suffer. Chronic disorders may develop if despondency is permitted to prevail.

1380 ♄ □ ☽ A very critical time during which the person must be careful in all dealings with others, especially in domestic and family circles. Worry and financial trouble may result. This is not a good time to make any changes or starting anything new. It will not progress well. The general health, circulation and vitality will be affected while the power of recuperation is slow. Great care is necessary to prevent affairs from going wrong. Sorrow and grief and, possibly a death of a female figure, may happen during this influence.

1381 ♄ □ ☿ Much delay and hindrance in all affairs will be experienced. The mind is depressed, worried, suspicious and warped, preventing a logical and clear decision. It is a very bad time to deal with authorities and lawyers or engage in the signing of contracts and agreements. Grievous losses may occur and general disappointment will be experienced. The honor and reputation may be attacked creating liability to scandal and slander.

1382 ♄ □ ♀ The emotions and affections will experience grief and sorrow. Financial loss will occur. Any new attachment will cause great disappointment. If this aspect affects the morals the person may act rashly, carelessly and lacks self-control. Deception and fraud should be avoided. Care should be taken as to whom one trusts and confides in as the danger of ill repute and dishonor looms over all affairs. Dealings with others should be minimized and forethought, discretion and care should be applied to avoid remorse over wrong actions.

1383 ♄ □ ♂ Any progress is hindered and delayed. Any outburst of temper and very rash and hasty conduct will bring trouble. Dishonor, disgrace, even ruin, could follow. Any dispute, quarrel or friction should be avoided as it may have serious consequences. Again, if the ☽ is also unfavorable at the same time, great caution should be exercised.

1384 ♄ □ ♃ Difficulties in business and financial affairs are indicated. Misfortune or lack of opportunity will hinder many plans made. Financial affairs may be purely structured, leading to loss. Jumping ahead without proper planning and considerations, as well as lacking any discipline or just bad timing, will hinder any development. The mind either wallows in overconfidence or plunges into depression. Careful planning is needed to combat this negative influence.

1385 ♄ □ ♅ refer to # 1376

1386 ♄ □ ♆ refer to # 1376

1387 ♄ □ ♇ refer to # 1376

1388 ♄ ▲ ☉ While this position does not denote the reaping of much material benefits it will, however, improve the honor and reputation. Based on past actions it could bring progression of plans and greater permanency into the life. Careful investments will materialize into greater benefits.

1389 ♄ ▲ ☽ Steadiness, seriousness and careful planning will bring promotions and improvements. Thrifty and prudent execution of plans will be beneficial. Elderly, as well as people in authority and women, will become friends and be supportive. This is an excellent time to arrange all affairs and plan for the future.

1390 ♄ ▲ ☿ A well balanced mind is willing to take on detailed responsibilities that are serious and require faithful discharge of duties. This is a good time to invest and arrange affairs for the future and engage in study to further the intellect. Important correspondence, entering into contract and agreements, dealing with lawyers and authority figures, all bring permanent results. A positive ☽ position will guarantee a satisfactory outcome of all undertakings.

1391 ♄ ▲ ♀ The feelings and emotions are steady and help gain by business, investments, finances and through friends. The health is improving. Social activities develop well and could bring lasting attachments of great mutual benefit. Honor and credit will help improve the status in life. Together with a good ☽, this will be a prosperous time.

1392 ♄ ▲ ♂ The will increases thereby lending spirit to more enthusiasm, courage and enterprise as diplomacy and skills will be carefully applied. Acting out authority and ambition, the person may get involved in risky enterprises. The outcome thereon depends on other aspects to this trine.

1393 ♄ ▲ ♃ Business, financial affairs and friendships will fare well. The ability to plan ahead and the capability to coordinate and cooperate, permits for the execution of difficult work and may place the person before the public. Dealings with the law will be favorable. An interest in religion or travel may develop for the purpose of going into business.

1394 ♄ ▲ ♅ refer to # 1376

1395 ♄ ▲ ♆ refer to # 1376

1396 ♄ ▲ ♇ refer to # 1376

1397 ♄ ☍ ☉ Suffering in business, reputation and health, as well as obstacles and opposition will be experienced. Loss, not only on a financial basis but also emotionally by death and other sorrows, may lead to despair. A deep depression may affect the well being. The severity of this aspect depends on the lunar position in effect at the same time.

1398 ♄ ☍ ☽ Delays, hindrance and disappointment will prevent any progress. The mind turns depressed and morbid. This is a critical period in which affairs and health will suffer. Financial trouble and a general state of unfavorable affairs, will cause great anxiety. The person should not trust others and not rely on elders opinion or have any dealings with any authority. Sorrow and grief may enter the family circle. Extreme care is necessary while this aspect last.

1399 ♄ ☍ ☿ The person may meet with deception, fraud and treachery. Separations and estrangements will result and by trusting the wrong person, undesirable results will happen. Correspondence and signings of papers should, if at all possible, be avoided, as well as involvement in law, or serious disputes will develop. All affairs may turn adverse if not carefully monitored.

1400 ♄ ☍ ♀ Disappointment, trouble and anxiety will be suffered. Separation may be faced, also bereavement and sorrow which affects the monetary side. Dealings with elderly or authority figures should be avoided, as well as serious disputes, as it may affect the honor and reputation. This is a time where serious caution needs to be exercised on all levels.

1401 ♄ ☍ ♂ A liability to accidents may arise as the emotions are stirred up and impulses could be uncontrolled. It may have fatal results. The mind is easily irritated, filled with anger and the person could get involved in violence. If the ☽ is also bad at this time the word 'dangerous' is in operation. Separation and estrangements will occur if the person does not exercise a strong self-control.

1402 ♄ ☍ ♃ Any kind of relationship will be negatively affected. Financial, professional and legal problems are sure to arise. The optimistic side of ♃ is severely suppressed by the rigid ♄ creating unhappiness and hardship. Obstacles in higher education and disagreements over studies can develop. The person may suffer from depression and intolerance and have problems in foreign countries or during travel.

1403 ♄ ☍ ♅ refer to # 1376

1404 ♄ ☍ ♆ refer to # 1376

1405 ♄ ☍ ♇ refer to # 1376

BABY CHART

1406 ♄ ☌ ☉ refer to # 146, however keep in mind that in this position ♄ is stronger as when the ☉ is the leading planet. The effects of the father's behavior toward the child are therefore intensified.

1407 ♄ ☌ ☽ The childhood was rigid and mostly unhappy. The child either suffered from prolonged illness or emotional deprivation.

Mother and child may have been depressed in their expressions by the father. The father, who puts down the mother's friends and stifles her emotionally, restricts the atmosphere in the home. The mother may be depressed, emotionally unfulfilled and unhappy, such vibes are absorbed by the child. The relationship between the parents is disturbed and does not function on any emotional level. Emotional deprivations become the norm for the child and this attitude carries over into later adult relationships. The circle of emotional deprivation must be broken or chronic ailments will manifest.

1408 ♄ ☌ ☿ Daddy inhibits the child's verbal expression. Later, this inhibits communications, as the child feels guilty of speaking up. The learning ability may also be restricted, as the child, out of fear, does not want to participate with the teacher and answer questions. The mind is bending under pressure making it difficult for the child to follow directions. The child may have difficulties with words. Conversations may be harsh and cold. Any demand to communicate feelings may meet with resentment. There is a need to learn to express the self and communicate feelings without fear of being restricted or ignored.

1409 ♄ ☌ ♀ The child may be prevented from obtaining guidance and love while the parents were restrictive and would not give much to the child. This creates later a pessimistic outlook on love and giving and causes friction in a relationship. There is no guarantee in love. When the ability to give, including of the self, is underdeveloped nothing is satisfactory. No relationship will be good enough as there looms a constant desire for something better to have. The habit of not sharing the self with others must be undone in order to overcome this strong aspect.

1410 ♄ ☌ ♂ This ☌ places a restriction on the ability to act but the strong desire under ♂ to act and do it rashly, may create a cross-purpose inviting frustration. If ♄ is the stronger planet the sexual energy may be inhibited and frigid. If ♂ is the stronger aspect the sexual energy may be expressed forcefully and inappropriately. There is no sexual harmony in the child, creating guilt and apprehension in the adult.

1411 ♄ ☌ ♃ The father imposed restrictions on the optimistic expression of the child, hence, creating a confusion as to the child's attitude and relation with authority figures. Relating to others, without fear of restrictions, must be learned.

1412 ♄ ☌ ♅ The father behaved erratic and unpredictable while the child grew up. The child may becomes unruly and has trouble to accept facts even after the own beliefs have been proven wrong. The child has trouble accepting authority. It may be stubborn and insisting always to be right, at all costs. As an adult the person may be extremely self-centered and unable to accept others point of view. The harshness expressed is used to cover up hurt feelings and fear. Emotional apprehension needs to be dealt with.

1413 ♄ ☌ ♆ The connection to the father is nebulous. There may be delusion about the family history creating illusions about the father and authority figures in general.

1414 ♄ ☌ ♇ The person tries to take the law into his own hands and manipulates everything. Not taking criticism well, criticizing others will be practiced.

1415 ♄ ∗ ☉ refer to #155, however keep in mind that in this position ♄ is stronger as when the ☉ is the leading planet. The effects of the father's behavior toward the child are therefore intensified.

1416 ♄ ∗ ☽ The child adopts a seriousness from the father and a control of the emotions from the mother. This enables the child in later life to take emotional commitments serious and act in a responsible manner.

1417 ♄ ∗ ☿ The mind is of a rather serious character but is precise and thorough.

1418 ♄ ∗ ♀ This aspect instills steadiness and a somewhat serious person. Later on love relationships will be taken serious and may be lasting due to the person's commitment. Work will be related to art somehow and one of the parents could be artistically inclined.

1419 ♄ ∗ ♂ The father instilled caution and seriousness into the child. In later life, the child will plan very carefully and may become a leader of a group or business. As an adult, the person displays responsibility.

1420 ♄ ∗ ♃ The father encouraged the child to reach out, be open and positive. The child therefore sees authority figures as a role model and is able to relate well to them. A degree of maturity is instilled in the child.

1421 ♄ ✱ ♅ A serious attitude, as instilled by the father, will provide for good working conditions with groups, friends and large corporations.

1422 ♄ ✱ ♆ The child is connected to the family tradition and keeps a good relationship with the father. Business talents to occupations connected with art, music and religion may be developed.

1423 ♄ ✱ ♇ An ability exists to relate well to groups without the urge to control. Public connections will further the career and relationships.

1424 ♄ □ ☉ refer to #164, however keep in mind that in this position ♄ is stronger as when the ☉ is the leading planet. The effects of the father's behavior toward the child are therefore intensified.

1425 ♄ □ ☽ The father held down the mother's desire for a personal expression to establish his own desire for ultimate authority. Mother and child are not free to express themselves. In later years, the child has trouble developing a personal relationship for fear of hurt. If the later adult opens up to some degree he may thereafter retreat and close up to protect his emotions from being hurt. The child needs to learn to trust and express feelings or the mom/dad relationships will be attracted and replayed again.

1426 ♄ □ ☿ The father is introverted, thus, impeding the child's ability to communicate well, to find the right words and to deal with authority. The child's self-expression is underdeveloped because of dad's inability to express himself. The words come out harshly and offensively, creating annoyance rather than understanding.

1427 ♄ □ ♀ A lack of self-worth exists due to the undeveloped understanding of the masculine and feminine principle. There was no connection and understanding between mom and dad. The child therefore is not sure as to the role either had played as a parent. It lacks the ability to extend feelings and affection on others. As mom and dad acted against each other, so will the child act in a later relationship. In marriage the partners merely live together but don't share emotions. The feelings of loneliness, pessimism and an inability to get close to a partner will disturb any relationship even on a friendship level. The child needs to learn how to give and how to receive in order to overcome this aspect.

1428 ♄ □ ♂ The father may have instilled an anti-authority attitude in the child. A negative attitude and opposition to established norms will get the child into trouble throughout life. Subconscious fears rule the child's behavior. Trouble with sexual compatibility and the general attitude of aggression towards sex, may render the act unpleasing and unsatisfactory.

1429 ♄ □ ♃ The self is inhibited and restricted and prevents the child to open up to contacts and communicating with others. There may be fear and apprehension of anything new that requires relating to the yet unknown. If this problem is not solved as an adult, the person attracts the same kind of inferior behavior to his/her own relationships creating apprehension and unhappiness. Responsibility in life is what the child needs to learn.

1430 ♄ □ ♅ The child will become a kind of rebel against established authorities and norms. Again, responsibility for the self and others in society, needs to be learned and applied.

1431 ♄ □ ♆ The father may live in his own world or dreams about things that may never happen, thus, instilling into the child an unrealistic view of the world. Creativity may remain unexpressed. People will be found disappointing and the family may stifle progress and openness. To move away from the family and see the world from another point of view may be necessary for any achievement in the future.

1432 ♄ □ ♇ A strong will to control, as learned from the father, may become overbearing. He just wants to control and manipulate all. The child learns little respect for authority. While great attention is focused on the power game, the personal expression of emotions is stifled and remains unexpressed, or turns into obsession.

1433 ♄ ▲ ☉ refer to #173, however keep in mind that in this position ♄ is stronger as when the ☉ is the leading planet. The effects of the father's behavior toward the child are therefore intensified.

1434 ♄ ▲☽The parents cooperate with each other and instill serious attitudes and balanced emotions in the child. The child will think and plan carefully and execute all actions in a reasonable manner.

1435 ♄ ▲ ☿ The father is serious but communicates well with the child. The child will be detail oriented and goes on well with authorities.

1436 ♄ ▲ ♀ The parents cooperation provides a feeling of self-worth in the child. Life is taken seriously. Confidence and strong and lasting relationships are build.

1437 ♄ ▲ ♂ Actions are carefully planned and not hastily entered into. The child will think and organize before action is taken. Relationships are considered and tested before a commitment is made. In later years the person is loyal, steadfast and very responsible in a relationship.

1438 ♄ ▲ ♃ The parents will support the child, financially and emotionally. This instills trust for authority in later life. Relationships will be taken very serious and are allowed to grow with a sense of responsibility.

1439 ♄ ▲ ♅ The father cooperated with others and allowed the child the freedom to develop. Maturity is instilled, which will help the child grow into adulthood.

1440 ♄ ▲ ♆ The father teaches the child about tradition and beliefs. The child will need to further such teaching into creative actions and later form his/her own spiritual path.

1441 ♄ ▲ ♇ Cooperation is learned early on in life allowing the child to deal constructively with society at large.

1442 ♄ ☍ ☉ refer to #182, however keep in mind that in this position ♄ is stronger as when the ☉ is the leading planet. The effects of the father's behavior toward the child are therefore intensified.

1443 ♄ ☍ ☽ The parents suffer from depression and melancholia. The child may lose a parent due to death or separation. The father restricts the mother's emotions and desires leaving the child unaware of the feelings of love and caring. The father's restriction on the mother may be so stifling that her unexpressed longings and desires be so repressed that the child never learns those emotions and in later life is emotional unavailable or afraid to give emotionally to others, causing coldness and disagreements. The concept of love is underdeveloped in the child leading later to purely sexual encounters devoid of any love.

1444 ♄ ☍ ☿ The parents do not communicate with each other. The father puts a lid on everybody's desire to communicate and prevents a healthy development of the mind. This creates an atmosphere of coldness and resentment. The child fears to speak up as rejection and disapproval have been received from the father. This creates learning impairment for fear of participating at school. The sense of self-worth is stifled and needs developing. Words used are harsh, cutting and offensive to others. As an adult he/she comes across as power hungry and arrogant as any communication is not attempted in a diplomatic and caring way.

1445 ♄ ☍ ♀ The parents have no understanding for each other. One parent may leave the child behind, thus instilling a sense of abandonment, or the father maybe very ill and is emotionally unavailable to the child. This creates confusion as to how to treat a partner in a relationship. Love relationships develop into sad or miserable union as the person does not know how to care and feel emotionally about the other. The sense of love, caring and understanding the partner was never instilled by the parents and must be learned in later life. As the mother did not value herself and merely performed her tasks, no love and self value was instilled in the child. Later, relationships are seen as unsure and a demand is made onto the partner, for some kind of love assurance, which, of course, is unattainable. The person does not trust himself therefore others are to be mistrusted too. There may be only an ability to give materially but not of himself in a relationship.

1446 ♄ ☍ ♂ The child learned from the father to rebel and therefore forces issues rather than discussing them. Long lasting relationships may be difficult because of personal behavior and a destructive trend coming from the ♂ energy that is not controlled.

1447 ♄ ☍ ♃ The father may suppress and disapprove of the child's attempt to reach out to others. He restricts the child's self-development, thus, creating later difficulties in life. The concept of relating in a warm, harmonious, caring and open manner needs to be learned. The child may eventually reject the father in an effort to move on in life.

1448 ♄ ☍ ⛢ Rebellious, unorthodox and willful behavior may be experienced from the father which is instilled in the child as an attitude of eccentricity, later causing problems with authorities. The person may refuse to listen and enforce the will rather than to cooperate with others.

1449 ♄ ☍ ♆ The harsh and restrictive father may have stifled the child's dreams and desires. Developments of creativity may never materialize. The child's frustration may create neurotic problems.

1450 ♄ ☍ ♇ A fear of failure and suppression of the feelings may have been absorbed from the father. There may be a mental hold of the father on the child, which creates later obsession or hate. In order to break with obsession and manipulation, the child must develop its own courage to learn and experience, without fear of failure.

♄ TRANSIT OR PROGRESSION TO A (Ascendant)

1451 ♄ ☌ **A** A strong sense of responsibility coupled with seriousness is instilled into the personality. Extreme sternness may be interpreted as coldness and being unresponsive. Unpopularity may result. If not otherwise positively aspected, it may produce a life of hardship and problems. Prone to accidents and ill health, especially to colds and lingering disorders, affairs may give reason to worry. Authority figures may not be cooperative. During transit the work load will increase leaving little time for other tasks. New projects should not be started but old ones should be completed. Unsound relationships will deteriorate and dissolve. Struggle is indicated.

1452 ♄ ✱ **A** A seriousness prevails. However, honesty, integrity and reliability make up for the sternness. Gain through inheritance and property brings prosperity. Take advice from older people but do not accept things at face value. Don't becomc overly serious but proceed with discipline and diplomacy as this transit will have an affect for several years.

1453 ♄ □ **A** Coldness and an unwillingness to cooperate will create unpopularity. Social problems hinder any progress. Trouble with the health, honor and reputation will arise. Relationships will be tested creating a feeling of loneliness and loss as no support is forthcoming.

1454 ♄ ▲ **A** Responsible and conservative manners permit precise planning prior to executing any task. Stability is a trait of character.

Disciplined and reliable action find solution to problems. Be cautious of relationships during this transit. Older people will be beneficial. Concealed help maybe received to further any goal.

1455 ħ ☍ A A very critical time where hard work is required. Fear, anxiety and loss will affect the flow of life. A critical time when health and progress will be affected.

ħ TRANSIT OR PROGRESSION TO M (Mid heaven)

1456 ħ ☌ M Hard work and perseverance is the way to slowly reach the top. A position of responsibility may bring benefits and advances. Gain could come from benefits through elders. During transit duties and responsibilities will demand hard work. Take care of the health. Take your duties seriously and work steadily. Any shortcut will make you suffer. A job maybe left for it becomes to stifling, or the pink slip arrived, as conditions at work have deteriorated. In short, if changes are not made they will be enforced by circumstances. Past good deeds will be rewarded with opportunities.

1457 ħ * M Discipline and perseverance bring success in the long run. Reliability is greatly appreciated in the work environment. General improvements are indicated. Use your energy and be a willing worker to achieve material gain.

1458 ħ □ M Refusal to cooperate and adhere to any routine bring trouble and many job changes. Responsibilities may be overwhelming or will be rejected. Legal trouble, liability to dishonor and disgrace, and other damaging events will be experienced. During transit, feelings of loneliness will be experienced. Worry, anxiety and fear will bring productivity to a halt. Be careful and avoid opposition from others.

1459 ħ ▲ M Good education and a steady climb to the top will pay off. Good organizational and managerial abilities are helpful. Nonetheless, ħ still demands hard and persistent work before any gain is obtained. During transit, help will be received to accomplish a goal. Changes will be enforced that bring benefits in the long run.

1460 ħ ☍ M This transit will create a break up period in your life. Relationships in personal, business and domestic circles will end.

Family and property issues may become subject to strife. After this transit has passed new conditions will emerge that require hard work to be established.

43

♅ Uranus

This is the planet of sudden surprises, eccentric actions, unexplained behavior and erratic changes, which could turn into outright disasters. But it also provides for adventure, inventions and discoveries.

If negatively aspected, sudden changes will be enforced even if they are not in the person's best interest. Those primarily ruled by this planet certainly have a different drummer in life, where the unusual is the norm.

♅ IN THE HOUSES

1461 ♅ (1) A strong drive for freedom and an eccentric display of intuitive talent exists but there is little concern for conventional behavior. Unusual friendships, leaderships, adventures and interests are indicated. New inventions are sought out. An intense intelligence and foresight, which at times is far ahead of the average mankind, can produce a genius who will make important discoveries. Under transits the unexpected will happen suddenly. *If afflicted, there is unreasonable obstinacy, a lack of common sense, extreme eccentricity and a desire for personal freedom at all costs. Restlessness, a desire for constant changes or leaving one idea for another to gain more excitement, as well as unreliability and disdain for any routine, will affect the security. Lack of moderation is instilled in and expressed through unpredictable behavior.*

1462 ♅ (2) The finances are unsettled. Any impulsive spending, any gain and losses in a rapid succession, may render the finances unpredictable. Unusual talent is indicated if ♅ is well aspected. Very often conventional values are disregarded for advanced thinking.

If afflicted, any venture could be impractical and money may run through the fingers forcing the person to borrow heavily to make up for losses, thus creating conflicts over debts.

1463 ♅ (3) The unusual and intuitive mind creates opinions that are based on experiences and scientific facts and not formed on opinions of others. The person is open to new ideas, is inventive, involved in travel and communications with siblings and neighbors, and is open to intellectual friendships and activities, to further the mental stimulation. Writers, Astrologers or scientific interests and all kinds of communications with radio, television and internet, are favored.

If afflicted, there is a possibility of being restless, unreliable, impractical, or jumping to conclusions. Constant changing of opinions may be used to obtain personal gain.

1464 ♅ (4) There is an unusual home and family life. The parents may be eccentric and demanding but are willing to provide personal freedom. Friends are easily accepted as members of the extended family. Sudden changes in residence and in family and relationships are very common.

If afflicted, relationships with family and friends are difficult. Break up of conditions in the home will lead to constant changes of residence and environment.

1465 ♅ (5) The person may form sudden, unusual and romantic attachments which, after being formed, also break off as suddenly. The partners chosen may be even more eccentric and unconventional. The sexual morality may be very low. Gambling, stock market activity and investments may bring a sudden gain or loss depending on the chart's overall picture. Children may be very talented and successful, especially in all forms of art. During transits love affairs may bloom but will not endure the test of time.

If afflicted, promiscuity will result in children out of wedlock or the children may be neglected. Children will have peculiar problems, psychological disorders or physical abnormalities. Antisocial behavior and unhealthy forms of excitement and pleasures are pursued. Extra marital love affairs and an unstable romantic life create disturbing relationships with friends, family and children.

1466 ♅ (6) Work of an unusual nature, such as an interest in homeopathic medicine, spiritual development and all unconventional forms of healing may be pursued. Work with advanced technology or new techniques are favored. Inventiveness for a better work product and the possibility of great mathematical ability and good co-operation with employees and employers, bring gain and success.

If afflicted, there is an inability to go on with others, due to a demand for personal freedom at all costs, creating discord with labor unions or rules of employment. Change of jobs for lack of satisfaction, a disdain for routine, coupled with a nervousness, restlessness and irritability, may affect the health and the position in life.

1467 ♅ (7) A strong desire for freedom in partnerships and in dealing with the public is instilled. Marriage may occur suddenly. The chosen partner may be brilliant or an unreliable eccentric who is subject to illness. During transits sudden attraction may occur that will, however, not be of long duration. Partnerships may be formed on the spur of the moment but need more to be enduring.

If afflicted, relationships will end in divorce. The desire for freedom at all costs will undermine the commitment to the partner. There is a rapid turnover of friends and acquaintances, a danger of loss in lawsuits, a bad rapport with the public and an unwillingness to cooperate. Sudden mood swings, attitudes, opinions or change of promises made, leave others confused and disappointed. Any unpredictability, if carried too far, will cause severe difficulties. It would be a critical time for any partnership or relationship.

1468 ♅ (8) There is a concern with death and other people's money, with the spending habits of the partner and sudden changes in fortune may occur through inheritance, taxes, insurance, corporate finances or partner's resources. During transit unexpected financial gain or loss may occur.

If afflicted, a sudden death, possibly by accident involving an intuition of death, may be occurring. Too much attachment to wealth and sex brings unhappiness and lack of inner harmony.

1469 ♅ (9) Unusual ideas about religion, foreigners, education, the law and philosophy are entertained. Advanced ideas may or may not be practical. A great interest in travel and adventure exists, especially for remote and far distant places. Any interest in astrology could result in publishing on that subject. During transits the urge to travel and learn, or changes of spiritual beliefs, may be pursued.

If afflicted, fanatical adherence to cults, religion, political institutions, as well as a restless search for the unknown is prevalent in the person.

1470 ♅ (10) Unusual professional participation and a reputation for leadership in humanitarian courses, astrology, scientific or occult fields, will all create a strong will that is leading to great ambitions. Changes in fortune and reputation are happening suddenly and unexpectedly. Controlling ones own career or business is favored. During transits, sudden changes occur that will alter your life. Older people may lend support in business matters.

If afflicted, there are revolutionary tendencies or unhealthy involvement in politics, which are ruthlessly pursued. This will create an inability to get along with any authority. Scandal and a sudden fall from grace may follow a previous rise to prominence. Routine responsibilities are irritating and will be avoided. Business loss and damages to the reputation may follow.

1471 ♅ (11) Unconventional behavior, rejection of traditions and an interest in humanitarian courses with people from all walks of life may bring many unusual friendships for mental stimulation. The emotions are spread more among friends rather than on any personal relationships. During transit, changes in your social circles will affect your hopes and wishes.

If afflicted, unstable friendships and unreliability to commitments with friends or groups are indicated. Friendships are exploited for personal gain. Social ideas and activities may be irresponsible and impractical.

1472 ♅ (12) A search for the unknown, the unconscious or any spiritual identity, as well as an interest in yoga, meditation or astrology, are embraced together with all forms of mysticism. The person is a keeper of secrets or gets involved with secret organizations. Work behind the scene, to further humanitarian causes, may be of interest. During transits, clandestine affairs may be entered into which are not of long duration.

If afflicted, there are illusionary goals, neurotic motivations, misuse of occult, confusions, delusions and unobtainable goals and ideas. Long kept secrets may surface.

♅ IN THE SIGNS

1473 ♅ (♈) A demand for freedom to act on one's own terms is coupled with courage, initiatives, resourcefulness and enterprising ideas, to create the character of this person.

If afflicted, there can be an explosive temper, impulsive, fanatic, violent, blunt and outspoken behavior.

1474 ♅ (♉) New original ideas to make money can be initiated, as well as reforming of business. These are executed in practical and original ways.

If afflicted the person is stubborn and demands freedom at all costs. There is a relentless desire for material things.

1475 ♅ (♊) The mind is original, inventive and able to pioneer new concepts. Travel and exchange of new ideas and concepts with others is required for the development of a healthy mind.

If afflicted, there is extreme restlessness and ideas are abandoned halfway before completion. A strong discipline is needed. The thinking can be unreliable, extreme, distorted, eccentric and impractical. There is danger of accidents due to a lack of attention. Trouble and disagreement with siblings and neighbors may lead to estrangements.

1476 ♅ (♋) The emotions and expressions are subject of tremendous excitement. Ideas can be unorthodox and independent. Friendly relations with parents are kept. The person is unsure as to where to find emotional security. A taste for modern gadgets, architecture and décor is present but the person suffers from insecurity and prefers community living or living with friends, for emotional assurance. An interest in occult is given.

If afflicted, an erratic temperament, mood swings and unreliability make it hard for the person to keep friendships and relationships.

1477 ♅ (♌) Freedom of expression, freedom in love, sex and romance, together with a strong desire to lead, is instilled by this aspect. Creative and dramatic expressions in art, music and endeavors, which involve the public at large, are favored.

If afflicted, ego problems, over dramatic display of emotions and stubbornness to the point of having difficulties to compromise or cooperate with others, will create disagreements.

1478 ♅ (♍) The person is practical, well organized and meticulous in any work and is able to develop revolutionary concepts. Unusual talent for business, through resourcefulness and determination, will strongly manifest.

If afflicted, disruption of employment, erratic health problems, laziness and a disinterest in work, all lead to loss and constant changes.

1479 ♅ (♎) Interesting and new ideas about partnerships, relationships and social rules are entertained. Freedom and friendships are most important in relationships. New concepts of justice and human relationships may be enforced.

If afflicted, unreliability and difficulties getting along with others in any kind of relationship, will undermine the standing.

1480 ♅ (♏) Death, destruction and changes in society will occur under this sign. Great social upheavals will change the human civilization. Strong, powerful emotions and a demand for decisive actions are expressed.

If afflicted, violent temper and destructive actions can lead to a downfall.

1481 ♅ (♐) New ideas for religion, education, philosophy and foreign travel, as well as a strong interest in the occult, astrology and mental telepathy, as well as adventure and foreign cultures, is entertained in life.

If afflicted, there is dogmatic belief, religious fanaticism and sudden trouble with traveling or with people, especially with foreigners, or while being in a foreign country.

1482 ♅ (♑) Changes in government, business structures and social concepts are contemplated, as well as the wish to change the present status and to advance society in a more practical way. Original ideas and strong ambitions to succeed are present.

If afflicted, the person is overly ambitious, expresses extreme desires to change but lacks the patience to pursue said changes.

1483 ♅ (♒) Intuitive insight into the future is given. Understanding of spiritual energy, religious and scientific concepts, coupled with a strong will for independence and a desire for the truth is instilled. Direct experience and observation in life is used for constructive change. An interest into the good for humanity and dignity of man engages the person in society, reform society or form organizations to that effect.

If afflicted, the person could have an extreme desire for freedom at all cost, display stubbornness, is impractical, eccentric, unreasonable and unwilling to follow any rules or discipline.

1484 ♅ (♓)An interest exists to discover the working of the intuitive mind. Interest in religion and social forms that promise emotional security and a desire to escape the past, together with letting go of too much materialism as it hinders the spiritual development, are avenues of mental satisfaction.

If afflicted, impracticality and a strong desire for material goods, an unreliability, deceptiveness and the avoiding of facing unpleasant situations will all lead the person into confrontations or hinder advances in life.

♅ IN ASPECT WITH OTHER PLANETS

1485 ♅ ☌ ☉ refer to # 31

1486 ♅ ☌ ☽ refer to # 226

1487 ♅ ☌ ☿ refer to # 431

1488 ♅ ☌ ♀ refer to # 630

1489 ♅ ☌ ♂ refer to # 837

1490 ♅ ☌ ♃ refer to # 1051

1491 ♅ ☌ ♄ refer to # 1265

1492 ♅ ☌ ♆ This aspect primarily influences an entire generation instead of just any individual. The person may display original and inventive imaginations. The senses and feelings are subject to sudden changes. Involvement in a secret affair or in secret projects is of interest.

1493 ♅ ☌ ♇ Again, this is another conjunction, the effect of which is primarily felt by society at large, rather then by any individual. The person may engage in action that is original and will make positive changes, which will affect an entire generation. However, before any changes can be implemented, the old needs to be let go off to make room for the new.

1494 ♅ ✶ ☉ refer to # 40

1495 ♅ ✶ ☽ refer to # 235

1496 ♅ ✶ ☿ refer to # 439

1497 ♅ ✶ ♀ refer to # 638

1498 ♅ ✶ ♂ refer to # 846

1499 ♅ ✶ ♃ refer to # 1060

1500 ♅ ✶ ♄ refer to # 1274

1501 ♅ ✶ ♆ The person is interested in and gifted to pursue occult and astrology interests and may write on these subjects to educate the masses.

1502 ♅ ✶ ♇ The person may be involved in scientific or physics discoveries for the benefit of the masses.

1503 ♅ □ ☉ refer to # 49

1504 ♅ □ ☽ refer to # 244

1505 ♅ □ ☿ refer to # 447

1506 ♅ □ ♀ refer to # 645

1507 ♅ □ ♂ refer to # 855

1508 ♅ □ ♃ refer to # 1069

1509 ♅ □ ♄ refer to # 1283

1510 ♅ □ ♆ An entire generation is affected by social turmoil. An individual will be merely affected by confusion, self-doubt and sudden upsetting events. Involvement in secret society, intrigues and inharmonious relationships may present disappointment and trouble.

1511 ♅ □ ♇ War, revolution, a downward spiraling economy or natural disasters disrupt people's lives. A person may display a bad temper, a strong desire for power, eccentricity and radial views. There is a strong desire to reform others. Sexual confusion or abuse and a deep-seated feeling of insecurity, are instilled by this square. *See Ephemeris 2008, world map* ♅ **24** ♓ □ ♇ **27** ♐ shows the beginning of a bad economy. This aspect endures on and off the important degrees until about 2016.

1512 ♅ ▲ ☉ refer to # 58

1513 ♅ ▲ ☽ refer to # 253

1514 ♅ ▲ ☿ refer to # 455

1515 ♅ ▲ ♀ refer to # 652

1516 ♅ ▲ ♂ refer to # 864

1517 ♅ ▲ ♃ refer to # 1078

1518 ♅ ▲ ♄ refer to # 1292

1519 ♅ ▲ ♆ This is another aspect affecting an entire generation rather than any individual. This will be a time when astrology, occult, yoga and all spiritual enhancements will be in favor and be practiced.

1520 ♅ ▲ ♇ A generation of people show an active interest in reform and will implement profound changes.

1521 ♅ ☍ ☉ refer to # 67

1522 ♅ ☍ ☽ refer to # 262

1523 ♅ ☍ ☿ refer to # 463

1524 ♅ ☍ ♀ refer to # 659

1525 ♅ ☍ ♂ refer to # 873

1526 ♅ ☍ ♃ refer to # 1087

1527 ♅ ☍ ♄ refer to # 1301

1528 ♅ ☍ ♆ Social unrest, sensitivity to large institutions, neurotic tendencies, possible abnormal sexual activity and increased drug and alcohol consumption, identify with this aspect. Rigid attitudes and fanatic attitudes may involve large parts of society in opposition to established power.

1529 ♅ ☍ ♇ A generation of people experiencing social and political unrest, war, revolution, violence and crime. Fanatical ideas beset the population. An individual can get caught up in the wave of destruction.

♅ TRANSITS

1530 ♅ ☌ ☉ refer to # 76

1531 ♅ ☌ ☽ refer to # 271

1532 ♅ ☌ ☿ refer to # 472

1533 ♅ ☌ ♀ refer to # 668

1534 ♅ ☌ ♂ refer to # 882

1535 ♅ ☌ ♃ refer to # 1096

1536 ♅ ☌ ♄ refer to # 1322

1537 ♅ ☌ ♆ Sudden enhanced imaginations will help achieve goals and further artistic talents. New friendships with talented, unusual people can be made at this time. Involvement in secret investigations or relationships may occur. Peculiar circumstances may arise regarding the financial resources of others which could become subject of any profit or loss. The self-confidence is improved. However, if the ego is overblown and unrealistic, losses have to be taken financially due to the standing in society. Don't act on hunches, wait to learn the facts. Don't subject the mind to erratic thinking as tension will affect the health. Extreme fatigue and drowsiness could be experienced during this transit. Desires should be realistic.

1538 ♅ ☌ ♇ A strong desire for change prevails. Old conditions need breaking down to make room for the new. Reality should be applied to avoid making wrong decisions. Old relationships and friendships may end as the person has outgrown its prior habits. A need for new and advanced companionship emerges. Events will happen rather unexpected and not always planed. If afflicted, dangerous situations may arise. Financial expectations may turn to disappointment. Radical changes will bring tension to the emotions and health problems may follow. If enforced changes are resisted this may be a time of danger and difficulties. In the end, the changes, although not welcomed, will prevail.

1539 ♅ ✱ ☉ refer to # 85

1540 ♅ ✱ ☽ refer to # 280

1541 ♅ ✱ ☿ refer to # 481

1542 ♅ ✱ ♀ refer to # 677

1543 ♅ ✱ ♂ refer to # 891

1544 ♅ ✶ ♃ refer to # 1105

1545 ♅ ✶ ♄ refer to # 1331

1546 ♅ ✶ ♆ The emotions and intuitions awake with excitement. Artists profit from this transit. Unusual ideas and works of art will be produced. Rewards may come forward at this time. A deep interest in religion or any similar interest will emerge. Enlightenment, higher consciousness and sudden insight into mysticism are possible.

1547 ♅ ✶ ♇ Important changes are initiated. New and unusual social projects are contemplated. A desire for improvement for the self and social institutions is strong. Financial rewards due to the resources of others, may be received. Changes may include values, habits and choosing better company.

1548 ♅ □ ☉ refer to # 94

1549 ♅ □ ☽ refer to # 289

1550 ♅ □ ☿ refer to # 490

1551 ♅ □ ♀ refer to # 686

1552 ♅ □ ♂ refer to # 900

1553 ♅ □ ♃ refer to # 1114

1554 ♅ □ ♄ refer to # 1340

1555 ♅ □ ♆ Fantasies, day dreaming and non-productive attempts on creating work and a strong desire to escape all responsibilities are destructive at this time. Extreme confusion renders reality obscure. Fears and phobias may unleash, rendering the emotions a basket case. Delusions, hallucinations and lack of a sense of directions will deny progress. A person can't escape the self. Facing reality is always the best answer: Financial affairs may be in a state of disarray and subject to deception. A strong and clear mind is needed to avoid the effect of this transit. Drugs and alcohol consumption will increase the problems.

1556 ♅ □ ♇ Life is undergoing drastic and sudden changes. Even if not desired, changes will occur. Any attempt to resist changes will result in difficult situations, which in the end, will not deter changes. Dangerous situations could occur that might endanger the life. Old associates, friendships and relationships are subject to break ups or transformation or separation could happen by death. If progress is desired, changes should be supported and taken for what they are, although painful, they will eventually result in progress.

1557 ♅ ▲ ☉ refer to # 103

1558 ♅ ▲ ☽ refer to # 298

1559 ♅ ▲ ☿ refer to # 499

1560 ♅ ▲ ♀ refer to # 695

1561 ♅ ▲ ♂ refer to # 909

1562 ♅ ▲ ♃ refer to # 1123

1563 ♅ ▲ ♄ refer to # 1349

1564 ♅ ▲ ♆ The imaginations are stimulated to produce better unusual and artistic work. A good time to meditate and attend to psychology or related subjects. The study of astrology will be promoted under this transit. Dreams can be analyzed and positively applied. Teachers, writers and travelers do well under this transit. Old acquaintances may be renewed and help further set goals. The spiritual side will be investigated. A more content time in life may develop.

1565 ♅ ▲ ♇ The ego is under control. Ideas for improvement in life will be developed and applied. Old and worn conditions in life come to an end as those circumstances stand in the way of future developments. A good time to learn about astrology. Gain may come from inheritance, taxes or resources of others. This transit will press evolution forward, creating new conditions in life.

1566 ♅ ☍ ☉ refer to # 112

1567 ♅ ☍ ☽ refer to # 307

1568 ♅ ☍ ☿ refer to # 508

1569 ♅ ☍ ♀ refer to # 704

1570 ♅ ☍ ♂ refer to # 918

1571 ♅ ☍ ♃ refer to # 1132

1572 ♅ ☍ ♄ refer to # 1358

1573 ♅ ☍ ♆ Erratic behavior, power hungry acts and confusion in dealing with society are the identities of this transit. Nightmares, confusion and retreat from social contact, all create unhappiness. Abuse of drugs and alcohol will lead the mind astray and affect the health. Fraud may be experienced or committed with dire results. The flow of life is disrupted by forces above the person's control.

Friendships will suffer from misunderstandings or envy and jealousy. Materialistic attitudes will have to be adjusted. This transit represents a sustained period of confusion and disappointments.

1574 ♅ ☍ ♇ Old conditions in life will suddenly end and be replaced by a period of uncertainty. Goals need revision or progress will be blocked. Utterly unfamiliar conditions will push the mind to extreme tension. It will take a while until a new direction becomes recognizable. Social conflicts, natural disasters, economic downturns and sudden losses will be very upsetting. In extreme cases the person's life is in danger or a close friend or family member will unexpectedly die. A power struggle will ensue. Sweeping changes will be enforced that could bring a new direction in life. Don't fight the changes, which will eventually lead your way into a new life.

♅ PROGRESSED

1575 ♅ ☌ ☉ refer to # 132
1576 ♅ ☌ ☽ refer to # 343
1577 ♅ ☌ ☿ refer to # 517
1578 ♅ ☌ ♀ refer to # 713
1579 ♅ ☌ ♂ refer to # 927
1580 ♅ ☌ ♃ refer to # 1140
1581 ♅ ☌ ♄ refer to # 1367
1582 ♅ ☌ ♆ Due to the slow movement of both planets the natal position will not differ by any progression
1583 ♅ ☌ ♇ refer to # 1582
1584 ♅ * ☉ refer to # 133
1585 ♅ * ☽ refer to # 344
1586 ♅ * ☿ refer to # 526
1587 ♅ * ♀ refer to # 722
1588 ♅ * ♂ refer to # 936
1589 ♅ * ♃ refer to # 1149
1590 ♅ * ♄ refer to # 1376
1591 ♅ * ♆ refer to # 1582
1592 ♅ * ♇ refer to # 1582

1593 ♅ □ O refer to # 134
1594 ♅ □ ☽ refer to # 345
1595 ♅ □ ☿ refer to # 535
1596 ♅ □ ♀ refer to # 731
1597 ♅ □ ♂ refer to # 945
1598 ♅ □ ♃ refer to # 1069
1599 ♅ □ ♄ refer to # 1376
1600 ♅ □ ♆ refer to # 1582
1601 ♅ □ ♇ refer to # 1582
1602 ♅ ▲ O refer to # 133
1603 ♅ ▲ ☽ refer to # 344
1604 ♅ ▲ ☿ refer to # 543
1605 ♅ ▲ ♀ refer to # 740
1606 ♅ ▲ ♂ refer to # 954
1607 ♅ ▲ ♃ refer to # 1167
1608 ♅ ▲ ♄ refer to # 1376
1609 ♅ ▲ ♆ refer to # 1582
1610 ♅ ▲ ♇ refer to # 1582
1611 ♅ ☍ O refer to # 134
1612 ♅ ☍ ☽ refer to # 345
1613 ♅ ☍ ☿ refer to # 551
1614 ♅ ☍ ♀ refer to # 749
1615 ♅ ☍ ♂ refer to # 963
1616 ♅ ☍ ♃ refer to # 1176
1617 ♅ ☍ ♄ refer to # 1376
1618 ♅ ☍ ♆ refer to # 1582
1619 ♅ ☍ ♇ refer to # 1582

♅ BABY CHART

1620 ♅ ☌ O refer to # 147
1621 ♅ ☌ ☽ refer to # 357
1622 ♅ ☌ ☿ refer to # 559
1623 ♅ ☌ ♀ refer to # 758
1624 ♅ ☌ ♂ refer to # 972
1625 ♅ ☌ ♃ refer to # 1186
1626 ♅ ☌ ♄ refer to # 1412

1627 ♅ ☌ ♆ An aspect that may give personal creativity but is, in general, an aspect that affects a generation more than any individual.

1628 ♅ ☌ ♇ Eccentricity is expressed by the masses, as well as desires for freedom and expression of individuality. A desire to be eccentric surfaces and demands are made to make changes in society.

1629 ♅ ✱ ☉ refer to # 156

1630 ♅ ✱ ☽ refer to # 365

1631 ♅ ✱ ☿ refer to # 567

1632 ♅ ✱ ♀ refer to # 767

1633 ♅ ✱ ♂ refer to # 981

1634 ♅ ✱ ♃ refer to # 1195

1635 ♅ ✱ ♄ refer to # 1421

1636 ♅ ✱ ♆ Individualistic dreams, unusual goals and strong desires are present but without developing the personal energy, the person will remain unproductive.

1637 ♅ ✱ ♇ Learning cooperation and being supportive, beside a strong desire for individual freedom, is beneficial.

1638 ♅ □ ☉ refer to # 165

1639 ♅ □ ☽ refer to # 373

1640 ♅ □ ☿ refer to # 574

1641 ♅ □ ♀ refer to # 776

1642 ♅ □ ♂ refer to # 990

1643 ♅ □ ♃ refer to # 1204

1644 ♅ □ ♄ refer to # 1430

1645 ♅ □ ♆ The personal desire for freedom is dwarfed by ♆ uncertainty and illusion. Frustration will result when the energy of both planets will work against each other. Peculiar conditions may be attached to the parents, creating delusions in the child as to responsibility and heredity. The child may act in a willful, eccentric and uncontrolled manner.

1646 ♅ □ ♇ The child learns a strong desire to control and manipulate through erratic behavior.

1647 ♅ ▲ ☉ refer to # 174

1648 ♅ ▲ ☽ refer to # 381

1649 ♅ ▲ ☿ refer to # 581

1650 ♅ ▲ ♀ refer to # 785

1651 ♅ ▲ ♂ refer to # 999

1652 ♅ ▲ ♃ refer to # 1213

1653 ♅ ▲ ♄ refer to # 1439

1654 ♅ ▲ ♆ Love and understanding, an interest in yoga, meditation and spiritual development, is learned. Merely dreaming away must be avoided and the energy needs expressions in a controlled way.

1655 ♅ ▲ ♇ The person is interested in raising consciousness and desires to make changes in the community.

1656 ♅ ☍ ☉ refer to # 183

1657 ♅ ☍ ☽ refer to # 389

1658 ♅ ☍ ☿ refer to # 588

1659 ♅ ☍ ♀ refer to # 794

1660 ♅ ☍ ♂ refer to # 1008

1661 ♅ ☍ ♃ refer to # 1222

1662 ♅ ☍ ♄ refer to # 1448

1663 ♅ ☍ ♆ The person is overwhelmed by illusions and has a constant change in spiritual values. There are delusions as to the groups or friends that the person wants to belong to.

1664 ♅ ☍ ♇ Eccentric and obsessive behaviors and display of willpower, expressed by the use of coercion, leads to a fierce battle to control others.

♅ TRANSIT OR PROGRESSION TO A (Ascendant)

1665 ♅ ☌ A Creates a very individualistic personality which may be far ahead of its time. Extensive knowledge and insight into life on earth makes this person talented for the study of astrology. The mind is usually quick, the nervous tension is high, and the unusual and out of the ordinary will attract the mind. A life full of adventure is required to satisfy the curious mind. If negatively aspected, eccentricity, arrogance and a superior complex destroy hard earned gains. Breaks in relationships occur due to a restless desire for independence and change. Bickering, arguments and rebellious behavior will bring separation and loss. During transits, a change of personality occurs. Nervousness, sudden change in moods and dissatisfaction with work, demand change. The life style may undergo reconstruction and relationships and domicile could change to accommodate different directions and desires. At the end of this transit, an altered personality will emerge that is ready to tackle a new direction in life. Care and prudence should be used.

1666 ♅ ✶ **A** Sudden popularity could be gained through unusual events and actions. Travel can occur and new contacts will be made, however, they may not survive past this transit. Good cooperation brings benefits. Events will occur suddenly and sometimes very unexpectedly. Opportunity arises through new groups and relationships. It will guide the personality and bring new pursuits of study and interests.

1667 ♅ □ **A** Sudden disruptions occur. Due to an extremely eccentric and independent behavior disagreements may lead to divorce or rejection by friends, the public and social circles. New friendships will be of short duration. Unstable affairs will be unpredictable and not very beneficial. The flow of life will be disrupted and troublesome.

1668 ♅ ▲ **A** refer to # 1666

1669 ♅ ☍ **A** refer to # 1667

♅ TRANSIT OR PROGRESSION TO M (Mid heaven)

1670 ♅ ☌ **M** Sudden and unexpected events may bring trouble and loss if this conjunction is not favorably aspected by other planets. Unusual conditions and events are sure to happen that may involve the public per se. Sudden changes, for good or bad, influence the life. This position makes it hard to stay in any routine job or be the underdog in a profession. Leadership could be acquired when positive aspects prevail. Tension will rule the nervous system and losses through enemies and the public will be sudden and also affect the reputation. During transits, unexpected opportunities may support the desire for change.

1671 ♅ ✶ **M** The nerves are calmer and successful attachments could be made that involve the unusual and unorthodox. Support from groups and friends will lead to fulfillment of dreams. If positively aspected by other planets, a career in politic may be successful. A change of job may bring improvement and gain.

1672 ♅ □ **M** A lack for and dislike of any kind of routine will interrupt the flow of life. Frequent changes of jobs and residence or goals will leave any work unfinished and unable to provide gain. Loss through government, business and profession, will disrupt the life.

1673 ♅ ▲ **M** Unusual occupations and the work performed herein may be noticed by the public and could lead to fame. Especially the precise knowledge of astrology will attract the public and bring acclaim.

1674 ♅ ☍ **M** Opposition from others brings changes to personal, family and life per se. Old things will pass away, dramatic changes in relationships and domestic circles will bring new circumstances into the life. During transits, sudden transformations occur. Do not resist these changes otherwise circumstances will enforce them with damaging results.

44

♆ Neptune

This planet attends to the feelings, emotions and spiritual side of life. It provides inspirations, artistic, musical and psychic abilities. Clairvoyant senses, or an ability to absorb the feelings of others, is possible. Any religious involvement or spiritual development is guided by this planet. It allows the visualization of ideas, induces imaginations and influences the dreams. Involvement in love affairs can be extreme and emotionally all consuming, or secretive and unhealthy. Attractions to strange and weird characters could occur.

If afflicted, the person is unreliable, mentally unavailable, confused, and addicted to alcohol and drugs. Even sadistic crimes are possible. The entire nervous system is strongly affected. In the extreme, insanity leads to hospitalization.

♆ IN THE HOUSES

1675 ♆ (1) Being sensitive, intuitive and absorbing the feelings of others can instill clairvoyant abilities. The senses are highly developed and easily influenced. The use of alcohol and drugs can take over the mind and lead to fantasies and imaginations. Artistic talents, especially in music and peculiar relationships, will develop. During transits, the mind becomes confused, spacey and withdrawn. The imagination replace reality and may blow issues out of proportions. *If afflicted, self-delusion, unreliability, confusion, alcoholism, drug dependencies, loose living and aimless drifting through life, may lead the person astray.*

1676 ♆ (2) The person is very idealistic about money and possessions. Generous to a fault, money can come and go through unusual and sometimes hidden circumstances. If there is any sign of extravagance the resources will be depleted fast. During transits, loans should not be made and get-rich-quick schemes should be avoided. Love affairs may drain the finances without having a future.

If afflicted, impracticality, financial and mental muddle, laziness and unreliability, all bring trouble. The person may take advantage of others or is used by others. In the extreme the person becomes a parasite of society.

1677 ♆ (3) Intuition, senses and feelings are creating great ideas. An idealistic approach to life with telepathic communications is possible. The study of occult, mystical subjects, and working through mass media by channeling the energy and knowledge, can be pursued. Practical thinking and applying discipline and control of the emotions will bring benefits. Harmonious working relationships are created. Work behind the scene in large institutions, especially in the field of health care, will benefit. During transits, avoid a head in the cloud attitude as dreams and wishful thinking may interfere with reality.

If afflicted, unemployment, unreliability, unsatisfactory working conditions, and unhappy relationships will be experienced.

1678 ♆ (4) There are strong emotional ties to the home and family with possible karmic ties to prior lives, which involve family secrets and mysteries. Psychic abilities may be present and intuitive feelings can predict the future. Living next to or near water is preferred. During transits, a home maybe purchased near the water. A water related problem, such as flooding, may occur.

If afflicted, the family affairs are confused, unhealthy and at times outright chaotic. The desire to 'mother the world' may lead to take in strangers or get involved in stranger's affairs. Nervous disorders are likely to develop and the emotional state will affect the general health, especially the mental faculties. Neurotic problems may exist within the family.

1679 ♆ (5) The desire to love and to be appreciated is needed to create a healthy self-expression. Artistic talents could be instilled in children, creating a strong love of the theatre and related entertainment fields. Romantic attachment may be expressed in secret. Secret affairs may be pursued. During transits, some undeserved idealization of others may cloud a real judgment.

If afflicted, engagement to and relationships with the wrong kind of people, secret love affairs, disappointment in love and trouble relating to children, cause grief. Losses in investments and speculations may deplete the resources. The children may adopt from the parents any emotional problems and become difficult to deal with. Children may be adopted or given up for adoption or may be neglected or may be born out of wedlock. Broken families with mental problem may result if ♆ is severely afflicted.

1680 ♆ (6) Work and services require a spiritual path. Sacrifices are to be made to obtain a balance of mind. Good relationships are kept with employees and employers. There is an interest in small pets and an ability to connect on a psychological level with animals. Homeopathy, health food and other natural remedies are preferred and will be accepted by the body rather than conventional medicine. During transits, illness appears that maybe difficult to diagnose and the wrong medication could be prescribed. Deception among employees or robberies and treachery could occur at the business. The mind may wander and become either very creative or refuses to attend to work and problems.

If afflicted, mental illness, infections, hypochondria, drug abuse, alcohol abuse, or a tendency to be unreliable about work and relationships with co-workers, will manifest into unemployment.

1681 ♆ (7) There could be Karmic ties to the marriage partner or to a business partnership. Connections to the public through partnerships are likely. The person is able to absorb the moods and feelings of others and provide unselfish love and understanding through spiritual connections. Artistic talents, especially in music, should be developed. During transits, there can be deception in marriage or relationships. A partnership or marriage may reveal the wrong motivations causing disappointment. Only when the mental aspects are good and a transit herein is positive could a marriage or partnership be all fulfilling and prosperous.

If afflicted, there are difficulties in marriage, through emotional arguments and others may mislead the person. Unreliability in relationships and a deliberate deceiving others or being deceived by the partner, to the point of public scandal and involvement in lawsuits.

1682 ♆ (8) There is a strong desire to communicate with the dead. Secret deceptive or unusual circumstances may develop regarding inheritance, taxes, insurance, corporate money or the partner's resources or the way money is spent. During transits, financial decisions could be confusing or misleading. In case of divorce or break up of partnerships, lying about and hiding assets could be a source of strife. Deceit could be experienced when claiming an inheritance. Outcome of lawsuits maybe tainted with fraud. The sexual desires and energy may increase or be turned off altogether whereby the energy is turned inward and expressed more through the mind than on a physical level.

If afflicted, losses, bizarre and strange problems with money belonging to others or problems with filing and paying taxes, falsifying documents or ways to obtain money belonging to others by means of fraud, may manifest and create big problems.

1683 ♆ (9) Intense religious cults, yoga and meditation interests, even prophetic visions and beliefs may be followed. The intuition supports the mind and can lead others. During transits, religious involvement may intensify or turn to disillusion. Travel via water is preferred and used to clear the mind. Education maybe advanced which furthers the spiritual level of the soul.

If afflicted, there is a fanatical adherence to cults, blind worships of spiritual leaders or falsely believing to be the chosen one of god to teach and guide others, creating a self proclaimed prophet. Education and the way of obtaining it may be impractical or be neglected, leading to loss as the job requirements cannot be met. Trouble with in-laws is possible.

1684 ♆ (10) A career may be pursued as actor, musician, minister, psychologist, psychiatrist, or astrologer. Clairvoyant ability may be present. The career could involve secret acts or acting behind the scene. Bizarre surroundings with the career, honor and achievement may demand sacrifices. During transits, a total career change maybe necessary to bring out a profession that pleases the senses and mind. Artistic careers are favored under this transit. However, a clouded mind may believe in abilities the person does not have, thus, new ventures may turn into disasters. Deception, loss of status and reputation, whether deserved or not, may lead to self-undoing or false accusations. The mind should not be permitted to dwell on wishful thinking.

If afflicted, the person is impractical, unable to get along or has trouble holding a position or make advances at a job. Scandal, loss of reputation, unreliability or dishonesty bring misfortune when a selfish motivation is involved.

1685 ♆ (11) The person is generous with friends. Spiritual guidance will be given and received. Help will come forward and friends will be made with others within their religious circles. Humanitarian groups that advance set goals, are frequented. During transits, a turnover of friends maybe experienced. Through undefined goals disillusion sets in when nothing is forthcoming. A more realistic approach to life is needed.

If afflicted, unreliability, deception in friendship, secret enemies, self-undoing through trusting wrong groups and friends or adopting bad habits from friends, such as alcoholism and drug use, create loss and disappointment. Discrimination in the choice of friends and acquaintances should be exercised.

1686 ♆ (12) Neptune is at home here and fosters strong religious or mystical practices allowing the mind to retreat into seclusion to seek inner spirits. Recalling past lives may lead to clairvoyance and healing professions. During transits, fear, self-doubt or paranoia may turn the mind to worry. Artists may use this transit to produce exceptional work of art.

If afflicted, neurotic tendencies create imaginary problems, negative expressions, misleading attitudes and mental confusion, which may lead into a world of dreams and imaginations. Prone to fears, neurotic problems emanating from the unconscious mind could create mental havoc. Bad dreams and nightmares should be analyzed to locate the fear factor.

♆ IN THE SIGNS

1687 ♆ (♈) It denotes the beginning of new religious concepts, spiritual creativity and regeneration, which are sought by the public.
If afflicted, an overly strong pride and a display of egotism will lead to estrangements.

1688 ♆ (♉) The use of money and resources will be foremost on the mind. There is a demand for practicality.
If afflicted, there is an obsessive preoccupation with money and possessions.

1689 ♆ (♊) There is an interest in the development of the creative mind, especially through literature, poetry and all forms of education.
If afflicted, this is the aspect of those rose colored classes. The mind is encased in a dream world, has superficial values and is confused in thinking and communications, due to a distorted mind.

1690 ♆ (♋) Strong emotional and sensitive ties to the home and family, and an attachment and guidance through religion, is guiding the person. A good Neptune will instill clairvoyant abilities.
If afflicted, the person is overly emotional, has an emotional dependency on the home and family or is excessive in his/her beliefs.

1691 ♆ (♌) Very strong artistic talents, especially for the theater, the performing arts, and music, is instilled. Romantic and idealistic love relationships could be formed.
If afflicted, self-delusion, extravagance, extreme desire for pleasure or trouble with or through children and financial ruin through speculations could result.

1692 ♆ (♍)The person may experience some adverse or difficult financial circumstances in life, is confused about the economic system, or lacks employment opportunity.
If very afflicted, psychosomatic illnesses, excessive emotional preoccupation with trivialities and dependency on others, as well as unwise dietary habits, will lead to actual illness.

1693 ♆ (♎) There is an awareness of social relationships, cooperation and social responsibility, based upon the spirit of law.

If afflicted, there is confusion about relationships. Blinding abeyance to others, by sacrificing the own opinion, can lead to disregard for the law and other problems.

1694 ♆ (♏) Exploitation of man's natural resources, of sex, drugs and morality affect the person in life.

If strongly afflicted, sexual diseases, drug abuse and mental aberrations, as well as mental confusion and emotional escape through extreme music or drug abuse, will subject the person to the lower class of society.

1695 ♆ (♐) An interest in religion will find expressions. God will become the center of the emotions and people desire to be part of the larger social order. Much travel for belief and emotional security will be undertaken. Occults and guru worship may be practiced.

If afflicted, there is aimless wandering, misguided or even fanatical religious beliefs, false prophets and guru worship. In general, the mind is lost and without a purpose in life.

1696 ♆ (♑) The world governments may be in chaos. Anarchy by the people will result and bring chaos and suffering to change the system. This will cost many lives. Survival becomes a means of seeking practical changes in the unworkable and abused system.

If strongly afflicted, martyr syndrome, chaos and even death will be experienced before a new system can emerge into being.

1697 ♆ (♒) New Civilizations will be born creating a new form of energy to dissolve the remains of the previous chaos.

1698 ♆ (♓) Opportunities are presented to acquire spiritual developments over materialism. Music, arts, and healing interests will prevail to induce peace of mind.

♆ IN ASPECT WITH OTHER PLANETS

1699 ♆ ☌ ☉ refer to # 32

1700 ♆ ☌ ☽ refer to # 227

1701 ♆ ☌ ☿ refer to # 432

1702 ♆ ☌ ♀ refer to # 631

1703 ♆ ☌ ♂ refer to # 838

1704 ♆ ☌ ♃ refer to # 1052

1705 ♆ ☌ ♄ refer to # 1266

1706 ♆ ☌ ♅ refer to # 1492

1707 ♆ ☌ ♇ This aspect deals more with society per se than with any individual person. The rise and fall of nations, cultures and social concepts are controlled by this aspect. If experienced by an individual, this conjunction brings changes so subtle that they may not even be noticed but are more prevalent in the surroundings of the person.

1708 ♆ * ☉ refer to # 41

1709 ♆ * ☽ refer to # 236

1710 ♆ * ☿ refer to # 440

1711 ♆ * ♀ refer to # 639

1712 ♆ * ♂ refer to # 847

1713 ♆ * ♃ refer to # 1061

1714 ♆ * ♄ refer to # 1275

1715 ♆ * ♅ refer to # 1501

1716 ♆ * ♇ Again, this aspect affects world karma rather than any individual. It holds to infuse spiritual advancement and the opportunity for positive change or else the destruction of civilization may occur. *See Ephemeris 2008* **♆ 24 ♒ * ♇ 27 ♐**

1717 ♆ □ ☉ refer to # 50

1718 ♆ □ ☽ refer to # 245

1719 ♆ □ ☿ refer to # 448

1720 ♆ □ ♀ refer to # 646

1721 ♆ □ ♂ refer to # 856

1722 ♆ □ ♃ refer to # 1070

1723 ♆ □ ♄ refer to # 1284

1724 ♆ □ ♅ refer to # 1510

1725 ♆ □ ♇ A period of social turmoil reflects on society at large. An individual may get swept up in social and political corruption.

1726 ♆ ▲ ☉ refer to # 59

1727 ♆ ▲ ☽ refer to # 254

1728 ♆ ▲ ☿ refer to # 456

1729 ♆ ▲ ♀ refer to # 653

1730 ♆ ▲ ♂ refer to # 865

1731 ♆ ▲ ♃ refer to # 1079

1732 ♆ ▲ ♄ refer to # 1293

1733 ♆ ▲ ♅ refer to # 1519

1734 ♆ ▲ ♇ Society at large may yearn for spiritual development. For the individual, it may signify an interest in occult or reincarnation.

1735 ♆ ☍ ☉ refer to # 68

1736 ♆ ☍ ☽ refer to # 263

1737 ♆ ☍ ☿ refer to # 464

1738 ♆ ☍ ♀ refer to # 660

1739 ♆ ☍ ♂ refer to # 874

1740 ♆ ☍ ♃ refer to # 1088

1741 ♆ ☍ ♄ refer to # 1302

1742 ♆ ☍ ♅ refer to # 1528

1743 ♆ ☍ ♇ Social stress is induced on society in which the desire and urge for power will present conflict and destruction, which may affect some people on a personal level.

♆ TRANSITS

1744 ♆ ☌ ☉ refer to # 77

1745 ♆ ☌ ☽ refer to # 272

1746 ♆ ☌ ☿ refer to # 473

1747 ♆ ☌ ♀ refer to # 669

1748 ♆ ☌ ♂ refer to # 883

1749 ♆ ☌ ♃ refer to # 1097

1750 ♆ ☌ ♄ refer to # 1323

1751 ♆ ☌ ♅ refer to # 1537

1752 ♆ ☌ ♇ This transit will seldom happen in the life of a person. Should, however, a person have the opportunity to experience it, it has a rather peculiar effect, especially on the emotions. It operates on a mental level, affects the intuitive abilities and can lead to visions and strange experiences. Secrets may be exposed in public. Strange and mysterious circumstances may enforce changes that will alter the attitude and standing in life.

1753 ♆ * ☉ refer to # 86

1754 ♆ * ☽ refer to # 281

1755 ♆ * ☿ refer to # 482

1756 ♆ * ♀ refer to # 678

1757 ♆ * ♂ refer to # 892

1758 ♆ ✱ ♃ refer to # 1106

1759 ♆ ✱ ♄ refer to # 1332

1760 ♆ ✱ ♅ refer to # 1546

1761 ♆ ✱ ♇ The mind is ready for meditation. Intuitive ideas provide insight into mystical, religious or scientific subjects. Changes in society affect the person.

1762 ♆ □ ☉ refer to # 95

1763 ♆ □ ☽ refer to # 290

1764 ♆ □ ☿ refer to # 491

1765 ♆ □ ♀ refer to # 687

1766 ♆ □ ♂ refer to # 901

1767 ♆ □ ♃ refer to # 1115

1768 ♆ □ ♄ refer to # 1341

1769 ♆ □ ♅ refer to # 1555

1770 ♆ □ ♇ The emotions clash with the desire for power. Selfishness, mental abuse of others, and making mindless promises can bring trouble. Alcohol and drug abuse may trigger hallucinations and mental illness. Deception in beliefs or financial schemes could bring heavy loss. An interruption in the flow of life is possible at this time. Internal tension will enforce changes and instill hard to diagnose illnesses.

1771 ♆ ▲ ☉ refer to # 104

1772 ♆ ▲ ☽ refer to # 299

1773 ♆ ▲ ☿ refer to # 500

1774 ♆ ▲ ♀ refer to # 696

1775 ♆ ▲ ♂ refer to # 910

1776 ♆ ▲ ♃ refer to # 1124

1777 ♆ ▲ ♄ refer to # 1350

1778 ♆ ▲ ♅ refer to # 1564

1779 ♆ ▲ ♇ An interest exists into furthering the capabilities of the mind. Working with society to regenerate and obtain progress is preferred. Spiritual enlightening is desired. Travel for education and religious purposes is undertaken.

1780 ♆ ☍ ☉ refer to # 113

1781 ♆ ☍ ☽ refer to # 308

1782 ♆ ☍ ☿ refer to # 509

1783 ♆ ☍ ♀ refer to # 705
1784 ♆ ☍ ♂ refer to # 919
1785 ♆ ☍ ♃ refer to # 1133
1786 ♆ ☍ ♄ refer to # 1359
1787 ♆ ☍ ♅ refer to # 1573
1788 ♆ ☍ ♇ Only a few will experience this transit. It requires longevity and that is not even a guarantee due to both planets slow movements. In any event, it symbolizes drastic changes in society. Social upheavals, the ending of old systems or natural disasters, could occur. The mind may be stressed and subject to weird reactions. Dreams will be depressing. Deception could occur. This is a time to wait it out without starting something new.

♆ PROGRESSED

1789 ♆ ☌ ☉ This planet progresses so slowly that it will not change its position in an ordinary life time by more than 1 or 2 degree.
1790 ♆ ☌ ☽ refer to # 1789
1791 ♆ ☌ ☿ refer to # 1789
1792 ♆ ☌ ♀ refer to # 1789
1793 ♆ ☌ ♂ refer to # 1789
1794 ♆ ☌ ♃ refer to # 1789
1795 ♆ ☌ ♄ refer to # 1789
1796 ♆ ☌ ♅ refer to # 1376
1797 ♆ ☌ ♇ refer to # 1376
1798 ♆ ✶ ☉ refer to # 1789
1799 ♆ ✶ ☽ refer to # 1789
1800 ♆ ✶ ☿ refer to # 1789
1801 ♆ ✶ ♀ refer to # 1789
1802 ♆ ✶ ♂ refer to # 1789
1803 ♆ ✶ ♃ refer to # 1789
1804 ♆ ✶ ♄ refer to # 1789
1805 ♆ ✶ ♅ refer to # 1376
1806 ♆ ✶ ♇ refer to # 1376
1807 ♆ □ ☉ refer to # 1789
1808 ♆ □ ☽ refer to # 1789
1809 ♆ □ ☿ refer to # 1789

1810 ♆ □ ♀ refer to # 1789
1811 ♆ □ ♂ refer to # 1789
1812 ♆ □ ♃ refer to # 1789
1813 ♆ □ ♄ refer to # 1789
1814 ♆ □ ♅ refer to # 1376
1815 ♆ □ ♇ refer to # 1376
1816 ♆ ▲ ○ refer to # 1789
1817 ♆ ▲ ☽ refer to # 1789
1818 ♆ ▲ ☿ refer to # 1789
1819 ♆ ▲ ♀ refer to # 1789
1820 ♆ ▲ ♂ refer to # 1789
1821 ♆ ▲ ♃ refer to # 1789
1822 ♆ ▲ ♄ refer to # 1789
1823 ♆ ▲ ♅ refer to # 1376
1824 ♆ ▲ ♇ refer to # 1376
1825 ♆ ☍ ○ refer to # 1789
1826 ♆ ☍ ☽ refer to # 1789
1827 ♆ ☍ ☿ refer to # 1789
1828 ♆ ☍ ♀ refer to # 1789
1829 ♆ ☍ ♂ refer to # 1789
1830 ♆ ☍ ♃ refer to # 1789
1831 ♆ ☍ ♄ refer to # 1789
1832 ♆ ☍ ♅ refer to # 1376
1833 ♆ ☍ ♇ refer to # 1376

BABY CHART

1834 ♆ ☌ ○ refer to # 148
1835 ♆ ☌ ☽ refer to # 358
1836 ♆ ☌ ☿ refer to # 560
1837 ♆ ☌ ♀ refer to # 759
1838 ♆ ☌ ♂ refer to # 973
1839 ♆ ☌ ♃ refer to # 1187
1840 ♆ ☌ ♄ refer to # 1413
1841 ♆ ☌ ♅ refer to # 1627
1842 ♆ ☌ ♇ This aspect represents mass unconsciousness that motivates a generation. Any aspect between the two planets

indicates great changes taking place in the world. Transformation for good or bad will affect an entire generation and not so much each individual.

1843 ♆ ✱ ☉ refer to # 157
1844 ♆ ✱ ☽ refer to # 366
1845 ♆ ✱ ☿ refer to # 568
1846 ♆ ✱ ♀ refer to # 768
1847 ♆ ✱ ♂ refer to # 982
1848 ♆ ✱ ♃ refer to # 1196
1849 ♆ ✱ ♄ refer to # 1422
1850 ♆ ✱ ♅ refer to # 1636
1851 ♆ ✱ ♇ refer to # 1842
1852 ♆ □ ☉ refer to # 166
1853 ♆ □ ☽ refer to # 374
1854 ♆ □ ☿ refer to # 575
1855 ♆ □ ♀ refer to # 777
1856 ♆ □ ♂ refer to # 991
1857 ♆ □ ♃ refer to # 1205
1858 ♆ □ ♄ refer to # 1431
1859 ♆ □ ♅ refer to # 1645
1860 ♆ □ ♇ refer to # 1842
1861 ♆ ▲ ☉ refer to # 175
1862 ♆ ▲ ☽ refer to # 382
1863 ♆ ▲ ☿ refer to # 582
1864 ♆ ▲ ♀ refer to # 786
1865 ♆ ▲ ♂ refer to # 1000
1866 ♆ ▲ ♃ refer to # 1214
1867 ♆ ▲ ♄ refer to # 1440
1868 ♆ ▲ ♅ refer to # 1654
1869 ♆ ▲ ♇ refer to # 1842
1870 ♆ ☍ ☉ refer to # 184
1871 ♆ ☍ ☽ refer to # 390
1872 ♆ ☍ ☿ refer to # 589
1873 ♆ ☍ ♀ refer to # 795
1874 ♆ ☍ ♂ refer to # 1009
1875 ♆ ☍ ♃ refer to # 1223

1876 ♆ ☍ ♄ refer to # 1449

1877 ♆ ☍ ⛢ refer to # 1663

1878 ♆ ☍ ♇ refer to # 1842

♆ TRANSIT OR PROGRESSION TO A (Ascendant)

1879 ♆ ☌ **A** The mind is encased in dreams and fantasies. If badly afflicted it is removed from reality. The person is led by instincts and unconscious behavior that is difficult and, sometimes, impossible to explain on a logical level. If positive, the imaginations may be able to produce astonishing work of art. Caution must be exercised over dealings with others as there is a possibility of getting involved in deception. During transits, the mind lingers in confusion. The energy level is affected rendering the mind and body tired, moody and unable to accomplish necessary tasks. Out of the nebulous state a new direction will emerge.

1880 ♆ ✱ **A** Strange and important dreams may bring visions of the future. The kind and charming personality will attract support. However, being used by others for the expressed friendliness should be avoided. The emotions are extremely sensitive and subject to clairvoyance. People will be cooperative. Religious guidance maybe received. Gain of money is denoted.

1881 ♆ □ **A** Difficult to diagnose nervous afflictions, psychological disorders, strange imaginations and a weakness for alcohol and drugs bring confusion and loss. A desire to escape reality may bring institutionalization. Beware of taking or giving advice. There is either a desire to deceive others or being deceived by them. Confusion and difficulties apply to this transit. Avoid entering into contracts and agreements and beware of trusting others. Diplomacy will be helpful. Avoid legal confrontations. New ventures should be postponed until this transit has passed. A temporary withdrawal from society may help avoid loss and disappointment.

1882 ♆ ▲ **A** refer to # 1880

1883 ♆ ☍ **A** refer to # 1881

♆ TRANSIT OR PROGRESSION TO M (Mid heaven)

1884 ♆ ☌ **M** Unless the professional interest is geared towards artistic creations and musical talents any other job will end in boredom.

The emotions may be fragile and require solitude. A feeling of loneliness may develop. If this aspect is afflicted by other planets scandal, mental aberrations and a distaste for the public may hinder success. Any use of alcohol and drugs may lead to addiction and social disgrace. Being involved in secret intrigues or any secret attachment will eventually surface and bring disgrace. Beware of depression and notice all experiences during a transit as they will later prove valuable. During transits, a kind of illusion prevails over one's image to society. The rose colored glasses need trading in for a reality check.

1885 ♆ ✱ **M** Unexpected gains may happen. Unusual and peculiar attachments may be formed. An ability to delve into hidden issues may unravel the secrets of others. The sensitive emotions may try to avoid any opposition, hence agreeing for the sake of harmony. Occupations related to the sea may be pursued as music and water have calming effects. New interests in occults and spiritual development, as well as sudden and mysterious experiences, may alter the course of life. Service to others will bring spiritual understanding.

1886 ♆ □ **M** There is a liability to suffer from fraud, wrong advice and damage to the reputation. The mind is confused, rendering the person unreliable and irresponsible towards others and the self. Excessive daydreaming will interfere with professional responsibilities. Lack of confidence may allow others to take advantage which leads to loss. An unwillingness to act may paralyze the mind and prevent taking of any action.

1887 ♆ ▲ **M** refer to # 1885

1888 ♆ ☍ **M** Jobs or professional and domestic affairs may alter course and create problems. A psychological crisis may grip the mind. A sense of meaningless prevails during this transit. Allow it to pass as changes will ultimately bring good rewards.

45

♇ Pluto

This planet relates to society at large, to crime, the underworld, secret elements of society and the dealings of power within the self and society. It destroys the old, annihilates what is no longer needed to make room for the new. It constantly transforms, breaks up and even produces death. It attempts to regenerate, transform and changes present conditions. If regenerating includes total annihilation, namely death, it will occur to further evolution. It presents a fine line between right and wrong, i.e. the right side or wrong side of society. Any attempt to avoid ♇ influences will create situations in which ♇ power is painfully enforced. It represents the ending of a cycle in favor of a new beginning.

♇ IN THE HOUSES

1889 ♇ (1) A powerful will, coupled with an intense self-awareness and a possible clairvoyant ability is present. The early environment could be burdened with hardship and entails some kind of struggle for survival. This may later form a character of a loner and a person with whom it is difficult to get along. During transits, the personality and life style will undergo changes. It either rebuilds or breaks up completely if room for the new is necessary. This internal crisis will affect both, the business and personal life.

1890 ♇ (2) The will to pursue money and possession is foremost on the mind. A positive ♇ gives the ability to be resourceful and helps obtain hidden information on how to obtain money. During transits, either gain or bankruptcy seems to be the choice. Fatal attractions involving obsession and money strain the feelings and place the nerves on edge.

If afflicted, however, greed, selfishness, involvement in lawsuits over other peoples money, over taxes, inheritance, insurance and partner's resources could result.

1891 ♇ (3) Strong opinions are over-expressed. The unwillingness to compromise and a strong will to convince friends of one's own ideas may lead to involvement in world affairs and all kinds of communications which can have serious consequences. Short distant travel, at times in secret to avoid discovery or for investigation, may result in strange experiences. During transits, there will be a change of attitude and intellectual expression.

If afflicted, scheming and plotting, as well as difficulties to go along with siblings, neighbors and co-workers, and a desire to upset the established social order, may create havoc in the person's life.

1892 ♇ (4) The home and the family may become part of a battle of wills. There is great resourcefulness to provide and maintain a home. Love of nature and social issues, along with a desire to uncover the secrets of the earth, may result in involvement in mining or geology. During transits, domestic and living conditions will undergo dramatic changes.

If afflicted, a death in the family is possible and there may be hidden issues or secrets associated with the home and family. Danger of power struggles with members of the family might occur.

1893 ♇ (5) Talents in creative activities and involvement in the arts, and/or with children are developed. The own children will have artistic talent. Investments maybe made and the birth of a child could alter the course of life.

If afflicted, there may be sexual excess and promiscuity leading to self-degradation. The person or a partner may be dominant resulting in a battle of wills. Speculations could lead to ruin. Obsessive love affairs could control the life.

1894 ♇ (6) Employment and health issues will be subject to change which are influenced by society. A positive ♇ provides work that salvages and reinstates or reintroduces products or services, such as making the old attractive and usable again. The health must be taken care of. Positive thinking and spiritual healing are avenues to obtain financial gain and recognition for services rendered. During transits, workplace and health issues may become predominant. A life altering illness may change the attitude and physical conditions. Accumulated poisons and toxins come to the surface which need to be eliminated to avoid death. Psychological issues may affect, induce and intensify any illness. Accidents or illness may produce irrevocable damages. Power struggle could develop at work in which authority is rejected as the person feels threatened by superiors. A desire to improve working conditions may meet with resentment which forces a change of employment. A change in direction is desired and pursued.

If afflicted, there are constant changes of jobs. Lack of cooperation, ego and bully attitudes, as well as dishonesty, may bring retribution and a downfall. If the health is neglected, serious illnesses may result.

1895 ♇ (7) Marriage, partnership and dealing with the public will affect the life. Either strong willed or attracting a strong willed partner, cooperation is always necessary to any achievement. Lawyers and Judges may have a sense of justice if ♇ is well aspected. During transits, any relationship could be changed by death, divorce or a new passionate engagement.

If afflicted, a clash of will power may lead to disturbing relationships. Responsibility and cooperation must be learned in order to gain from this aspect.

1896 ♇ (8) The person is interested in life after death issues, in astrology, yoga, meditation and occult in general. The use of resources belonging to others, i.e. inheritance, insurance, corporate money and the partner's resources, are available and need to be managed. Business is taken serious and may be conducted in secret. Plans always include the society at large, either to gain favors or collect resources. Involvement in secret sexual or financial affairs may be pursued without the partner's knowledge.

If afflicted, serious problems with money and possessions belonging to others can arise. A power struggle over money may ensue. Temptation to use occult or other means for selfish reasons, in order to gain resources from others, may result in problems.

1897 ♇ (9) The social establishment of legal, educational, philosophical, as well as moral setting is in need for regeneration. An ability to detect and analyze problems in these fields will affect society at large. Spiritual leadership may be used to make changes affecting humanity and its institutions. Ambitions for higher education are strong. Travel to foreign countries and cultures are used to achieve higher education. If social injustice is present these people may become revolutionaries in order to turn the system around. While affected by transit, legal affairs may not have a positive outcome as the courts, especially the higher courts, are not favorably inclined towards the person. A struggle for survival over legal matters may drag the person into prolonged confrontations that will collapse their belief system. This experience will cause depression as it exposes society as it acts, not as it is supposed to function. What is actually justice will be intensely questioned. Somehow, this confrontation urges the person to engage in higher education which, eventually may lead to reformation of the broken system. Long, foreign travel may be a source of learning about society.

If afflicted, overbearing religious fanatics, lawbreakers, bullies imposing their view onto others, or antisocial behavior will manifest.

1898 ♇ (10) A strong willpower and drive to succeed is present. Politics, and all forms of bringing the person before the public, will create attraction. The desire to reform, if positive, may lead to drastic changes in society. While a climb to the top is nearly unavoidable, a fall from grace and confrontation with authorities may follow. During transits, the business, the reputation and career may undergo changes. The obsession for power and control may overstep acceptable bounds and render hardship instead. In order to regenerate, a distraction of the old has to be completed before a new direction is approached. It may even indicate leaving behind an established business or career and start anew, even to the point of embarking into different directions. Self-determination, perseverance and courage will surface and guide the person.

If afflicted, ruthlessness, dictatorial tendencies, selfish ambitions and dealings with the underworld may bring the ultimate downfall. The reputation can be destroyed and cause a distraction of earning powers, leaving chaos to rule.

1899 ♇ (11) Friends will be helpful with the rise in life. If well aspected, success may come through friends and groups that require leadership. Insight into the functioning of society may be helpful to gain a leadership position. During transits, friendships maybe broken up and will never be resumed or be extinct by death. A powerful conflict over supremacy is always on the backburner. An obsession, with ruthlessness and deceit maybe practiced, especially when sex is involved. In the end the person feels alone, unloved and isolated when the bridges have all been burned down. *If afflicted, friendships will only serve the purpose of using each other, which will lead to losses and disappointments, trouble over taxes and joint resources. Friends may suddenly disappear and ties are broken forever. Betrayal among friends is possible.*

1900 ♇ (12) Clairvoyant abilities and an interest to improve conditions of the less fortunate, is bestowed under this position. An understanding exists of mystery and occult forces. The person is capable of practicing deep meditation. Privacy and seclusion are needed to organize the mind. Secret actions for or against others may be initiated. The unconscious rules and transformation is needed and enforced. Financial gains may shrink away to bring the person back to a level from which a new direction can emerge. Transforming of outmoded institutions or confrontations with hospitals, prisons or law may occur. Periodic withdrawals from society maybe necessary to understand the inner tension created during this transit. Out of the ashes a new dawn will be rising. *If afflicted, secret and destructive actions may be undertaken. The involvement with underworld figures, an inability to get along, neurotic problems and secret enemies that are working on the person's downfall, may be the result of prior actions in society.*

♇ IN THE SIGNS

1901 ♇ (♈) Creating and beginning new civilizations.

1902 ♇ (♉) Economic expansions.

1903 ♇ (♊) Inventions and scientific discoveries.

1904 ♇ (♋) Domestic concerns and revolutions regarding agricultural techniques and ways of producing from the land.

1905 ♇ (♌) Discovery of energy, power and struggle over control.

1906 ♇ (♍) Health, work and changes to employment, medicine, business and production is made. New diseases, new means of fighting them, new ways to handle and execute work (i.e. computer revolution) fall under this aspect.

1907 ♇ (♎) The concept of justice, human relations, social expansion and the mental state of masses will undergo changes.

1908 ♇ (♏) Worldwide chaos, wars and all kinds of distraction will occur out of which a new area will emerge.

1909 ♇ (♐) New ways of religious enterprises, merging of different cultures into one melting pot and the concept of foreigners will eventually dissolve, making the world all one in the sense of absorbing all cultures.

1910 ♇ (♑) All political and economical powers, professions, as well as status and ambitions will undergo drastic changes. This is the time of anarchy, revolution and the uprising of the common man. A new principle of social, religious, political and human justice system will eventually emerge from the chaos. This is the state of our current social structure.

1911 ♇ (♒) A search for humanitarian values, a desire for real democracy and discovery of worldwide brotherhood and understanding, will be the result of this transit.

1912 ♇ (♓) A demand is made for creativity, artistic development and for cultural changes. The merging of cultures that had occurred in ♐ will now split into a new form of more spiritual insights and understanding of mankind.

♇ IN ASPECT WITH OTHER PLANETS

1913 ♇ ☌ ☉ refer to # 33

1914 ♇ ☌ ☽ refer to # 228

1915 ♇ ☌ ☿ refer to # 433

1916 ♇ ☌ ♀ refer to # 632

1917 ♇ ☌ ♂ refer to # 839
1918 ♇ ☌ ♃ refer to # 1053
1919 ♇ ☌ ♄ refer to # 1267
1920 ♇ ☌ ♅ refer to # 1493
1921 ♇ ☌ ♆ refer to # 1707
1922 ♇ ✱ ☉ refer to # 42
1923 ♇ ✱ ☽ refer to # 237
1924 ♇ ✱ ☿ refer to # 441
1925 ♇ ✱ ♀ refer to # 640
1926 ♇ ✱ ♂ refer to # 848
1927 ♇ ✱ ♃ refer to # 1062
1928 ♇ ✱ ♄ refer to # 1276
1929 ♇ ✱ ♅ refer to # 1502
1930 ♇ ✱ ♆ refer to # 1716
1931 ♇ □ ☉ refer to # 51
1932 ♇ □ ☽ refer to # 246
1933 ♇ □ ☿ refer to # 449
1934 ♇ □ ♀ refer to # 647
1935 ♇ □ ♂ refer to # 857
1936 ♇ □ ♃ refer to # 1071
1937 ♇ □ ♄ refer to # 1285
1938 ♇ □ ♅ refer to # 1511
1939 ♇ □ ♆ refer to # 1725
1940 ♇ ▲ ☉ refer to # 60
1941 ♇ ▲ ☽ refer to # 255
1942 ♇ ▲ ☿ refer to # 457
1943 ♇ ▲ ♀ refer to # 654
1944 ♇ ▲ ♂ refer to # 866
1945 ♇ ▲ ♃ refer to # 1080
1946 ♇ ▲ ♄ refer to # 1294
1947 ♇ ▲ ♅ refer to # 1520
1948 ♇ ▲ ♆ refer to # 1734
1949 ♇ ☍ ☉ refer to # 69
1950 ♇ ☍ ☽ refer to # 264
1951 ♇ ☍ ☿ refer to # 465
1952 ♇ ☍ ♀ refer to # 661

1953 ♇ ☍ ♂ refer to # 875
1954 ♇ ☍ ♃ refer to # 1089
1955 ♇ ☍ ♄ refer to # 1303
1956 ♇ ☍ ⛢ refer to # 1529
1957 ♇ ☍ ♆ refer to # 1743

♇ TRANSITS

1958 ♇ ☌ ☉ refer to # 78
1959 ♇ ☌ ☽ refer to # 273
1960 ♇ ☌ ☿ refer to # 474
1961 ♇ ☌ ♀ refer to # 670
1962 ♇ ☌ ♂ refer to # 884
1963 ♇ ☌ ♃ refer to # 1098
1964 ♇ ☌ ♄ refer to # 1324
1965 ♇ ☌ ⛢ refer to # 1538
1966 ♇ ☌ ♆ refer to # 1752
1967 ♇ ⚹ ☉ refer to # 87
1968 ♇ ⚹ ☽ refer to # 282
1969 ♇ ⚹ ☿ refer to # 483
1970 ♇ ⚹ ♀ refer to # 679
1971 ♇ ⚹ ♂ refer to # 893
1972 ♇ ⚹ ♃ refer to # 1107
1973 ♇ ⚹ ♄ refer to # 1333
1974 ♇ ⚹ ⛢ refer to # 1547
1975 ♇ ⚹ ♆ refer to # 1761
1976 ♇ □ ☉ refer to # 96
1977 ♇ □ ☽ refer to # 291
1978 ♇ □ ☿ refer to # 492
1979 ♇ □ ♀ refer to # 688
1980 ♇ □ ♂ refer to # 902
1981 ♇ □ ♃ refer to # 1116
1982 ♇ □ ♄ refer to # 1342
1983 ♇ □ ⛢ refer to # 1556
1984 ♇ □ ♆ refer to # 1770
1985 ♇ ▲ ☉ refer to # 105

1986 ♇ ▲ ☽ refer to # 300
1987 ♇ ▲ ☿ refer to # 501
1988 ♇ ▲ ♀ refer to # 697
1989 ♇ ▲ ♂ refer to # 911
1990 ♇ ▲ ♃ refer to # 1125
1991 ♇ ▲ ♄ refer to # 1351
1992 ♇ ▲ ♅ refer to # 1565
1993 ♇ ▲ ♆ refer to # 1779
1994 ♇ ☍ ☉ refer to # 114
1995 ♇ ☍ ☽ refer to # 309
1996 ♇ ☍ ☿ refer to # 510
1997 ♇ ☍ ♀ refer to # 706
1998 ♇ ☍ ♂ refer to # 920
1999 ♇ ☍ ♃ refer to # 1134
2000 ♇ ☍ ♄ refer to # 1360
2001 ♇ ☍ ♅ refer to # 1574
2002 ♇ ☍ ♆ refer to # 1788

♇ PROGRESSED

2003 ♇ ☌ ☉ The planet's progression is so slow that it will not change its position in an ordinary life span.
2004 ♇ ☌ ☽ refer to # 2003
2005 ♇ ☌ ☿ refer to # 2003
2006 ♇ ☌ ♀ refer to # 2003
2007 ♇ ☌ ♂ refer to # 2003
2008 ♇ ☌ ♃ refer to # 2003
2009 ♇ ☌ ♄ refer to # 2003
2010 ♇ ☌ ♅ refer to # 2003
2011 ♇ ☌ ♆ refer to # 2003
2012 ♇ ✱ ☉ refer to # 2003
2013 ♇ ✱ ☽ refer to # 2003
2014 ♇ ✱ ☿ refer to # 2003
2015 ♇ ✱ ♀ refer to # 2003
2016 ♇ ✱ ♂ refer to # 2003
2017 ♇ ✱ ♃ refer to # 2003

2018 ♇ ⚹ ♄ refer to # 2003
2019 ♇ ⚹ ♅ refer to # 2003
2020 ♇ ⚹ ♆ refer to # 2003
2021 ♇ □ ☉ refer to # 2003
2022 ♇ □ ☽ refer to # 2003
2023 ♇ □ ☿ refer to # 2003
2024 ♇ □ ♀ refer to # 2003
2025 ♇ □ ♂ refer to # 2003
2026 ♇ □ ♃ refer to # 2003
2027 ♇ □ ♄ refer to # 2003
2028 ♇ □ ♅ refer to # 2003
2029 ♇ □ ♆ refer to # 2003
2030 ♇ ▲ ☉ refer to # 2003
2031 ♇ ▲ ☽ refer to # 2003
2032 ♇ ▲ ☿ refer to # 2003
2033 ♇ ▲ ♀ refer to # 2003
2034 ♇ ▲ ♂ refer to # 2003
2035 ♇ ▲ ♃ refer to # 2003
2036 ♇ ▲ ♄ refer to # 2003
2037 ♇ ▲ ♅ refer to # 2003
2038 ♇ ▲ ♆ refer to # 2003
2039 ♇ ☍ ☉ refer to # 2003
2040 ♇ ☍ ☽ refer to # 2003
2041 ♇ ☍ ☿ refer to # 2003
2042 ♇ ☍ ♀ refer to # 2003
2043 ♇ ☍ ♂ refer to # 2003
2044 ♇ ☍ ♃ refer to # 2003
2045 ♇ ☍ ♄ refer to # 2003
2046 ♇ ☍ ♅ refer to # 2003
2047 ♇ ☍ ♆ refer to # 2003

BABY CHART

2048 ♇ ☌ ☉ refer to # 149
2049 ♇ ☌ ☽ refer to # 359
2050 ♇ ☌ ☿ refer to # 561
2051 ♇ ☌ ♀ refer to # 760

2052 ♇ ☌ ♂ refer to # 974
2053 ♇ ☌ ♃ refer to # 1188
2054 ♇ ☌ ♄ refer to # 1414
2055 ♇ ☌ ♅ refer to # 1628
2056 ♇ ☌ ♆ refer to # 1842
2057 ♇ ✱ ☉ refer to # 158
2058 ♇ ✱ ☽ refer to # 367
2059 ♇ ✱ ☿ refer to # 569
2060 ♇ ✱ ♀ refer to # 769
2061 ♇ ✱ ♂ refer to # 983
2062 ♇ ✱ ♃ refer to # 1197
2063 ♇ ✱ ♄ refer to # 1423
2064 ♇ ✱ ♅ refer to # 1637
2065 ♇ ✱ ♆ refer to # 1842
2066 ♇ □ ☉ refer to # 167
2067 ♇ □ ☽ refer to # 375
2068 ♇ □ ☿ refer to # 576
2069 ♇ □ ♀ refer to # 778
2070 ♇ □ ♂ refer to # 992
2071 ♇ □ ♃ refer to # 1206
2072 ♇ □ ♄ refer to # 1432
2073 ♇ □ ♅ refer to # 1646
2074 ♇ □ ♆ refer to # 1842
2075 ♇ ▲ ☉ refer to # 176
2076 ♇ ▲ ☽ refer to # 383
2077 ♇ ▲ ☿ refer to # 583
2078 ♇ ▲ ♀ refer to # 787
2079 ♇ ▲ ♂ refer to # 1001
2080 ♇ ▲ ♃ refer to # 1215
2081 ♇ ▲ ♄ refer to # 1441
2082 ♇ ▲ ♅ refer to # 1655
2083 ♇ ▲ ♆ refer to # 1842
2084 ♇ ☍ ☉ refer to # 185
2085 ♇ ☍ ☽ refer to # 391
2086 ♇ ☍ ☿ refer to # 590
2087 ♇ ☍ ♀ refer to # 796

2088 ♇ ☍ ♂ refer to # 1010
2089 ♇ ☍ ♃ refer to # 1224
2090 ♇ ☍ ♄ refer to # 1450
2091 ♇ ☍ ♅ refer to # 1664
2092 ♇ ☍ ♆ refer to # 1842

♇ TRANSIT OR PROGRESSION TO A (Ascendant)

2093 ♇ ☌ **A** A strong will power and endurance is used to reach a goal. This drive may be used for social purposes or utter selfishness. It represents the power of the will to proceed and induce changes. If negatively afflicted or any negative planet is in the house or sign of ♏ an extreme desire to get ahead at all costs will bring confrontations. Any stress level created by the strong will affects the health. It denotes a time of crisis where changes will be enforced. During transits, internal crisis affect both the business and personal life. The career interest will change. The present approach to business will no longer work. It seems that nothing works anymore and results cannot be achieved. Internal anger surfaces. Beware of accidents due to a lack of attention. The system feels as being under pressure. A feeling of being out of control manifests. Rage and anger develop. A new approach to handle life needs to be implemented.

2094 ♇ ✱ **A** Important relationships may be entered into that will affect the consciousness of society at large. The power given is applied for the good of the general public. The power provided should be used for improvement of social issues and not only be concentrated on personal gain. A time to make arrangements for reform.

2095 ♇ □ **A** Any power given is abused by righteousness and aggressive behavior leading to loss and separations. The desire to reform and dominate on one's own terms could bring lawsuits and unanticipated results. Existing relationships are subject to upheaval and drastic changes.

2096 ♇ ▲ **A** Personal power, when used constructively, will bring good influences from society.

2097 ♇ ☍ **A** refer to # 2095

♇ TRANSIT OR PROGRESSION TO M (Mid heaven)

2098 ♇ ☌ **M** The professional and public standing is subject to repeated changes. This transit will affect the entire course and direction of life. The circle of breaking down and rebuilding will have to be addressed. If an interest is developed for the public and not for the self, great inventions could be brought on for the benefit of the general public. The person may reach the top, however, if selfish motives are pursued and engagements in criminal activities are permitted, the end of the power reign will occur. During this transit people connected with the past may disappear to make room for new and beneficial connections. An effect will be felt in regards to the public image, honor and reputation of our work. Changes in career will steer the energy into another direction. All efforts will be made to accelerate speedy into a new job or profession. Any short cut or engagement with people from the underworld should be avoided. Adopt to changes, they will be necessary to excel in life.

2099 ♇ ✱ **M** Skills and knowledge are used for improvements that affect the public. Gain of power can be achieved which will greatly benefit the professional ambitions.

2100 ♇ □ **M** The desire to reform others, as well as professional conditions, will end up dissolving important affairs and relationships. Dictatorial behavior creates arguments and separations. Domestic changes will be enforced even if not desired. Personal relationships undergo drastic changes and may pass away altogether. Resisting such alterations of life will increase the force of destruction as the changes will occur anyway.

2101 ♇ ▲ **M** refer to # 2099

2102 ♇ ☍ **M** refer to # 2100

46

Transiting Planets in Aspect to Themselves

While the ☉, ☽, ☿, ♀ or ♂ transit over its own place is but fleeting, the slower planets influences during transit over the natal position can be felt when combined with other aspects. When forming an aspect to its own natal place via transit a planet will have an effect in which attributing properties are enhanced in a person's life.

♃

☌ = This conjunction will happen about every 12 years and produces growth and progress unless ♃ was badly aspected at birth.

∗ ▲ = Gain and growth is indicated. Legal affairs may turn favorable. Travel and education will further goals.

□ ☍ = Be careful about finances. Don't be over-confident or disappointment will follow. Avoid self-indulgence. It will deplete the finances and add body weight. Opposition will be experienced.

♄

☌ = Great changes will take place. After the first 29 years there will be endings in relationships, jobs or residence. After the second circle, around 58 years of age, retirement or a new direction in life is pursued. It represents a time of endings and new beginnings.

✱ ▲ = Good planning will now give good results. Dealings with authority will run smoothly and business improvements should be undertaken.

□ ☍ = A time of tension and crisis and disagreements. Difficulties in business and with authority is indicated. Avoid conflicts and arguments. Hard work is required to overcome obstacles. During the ☍ old relationships, jobs or business ventures may fade out or requiring a reinvention. It maybe very difficult to achieve any gain during this period.

⛢

☌ = If ⛢ was retrograde at birth or became retrograde after birth, thus forming this aspect, it disrupts the childhood conditions forcing sudden changes of environment and personal freedom. If it occurs around the end of life (approximately 84 years of age) it may bring changing conditions towards the close of life.

✱ ▲ = It improves personal freedom and independence and provides for new directions that bring changes to the lifestyle. It allows for greater self-assurance.

□ ☍ = Major changes take place due to the mind's rebellious attitude. Avoid making breaks just for the sake of it or valuable reliance on people and resources will disappear. Projects maybe abandoned due to extreme restlessness.

♆

☌ = A conjunction that, with very few exceptions, may not take place in a normal life time.

✱ ▲ = Mental awakenings and understandings will be experienced. Help will be received as the soul advances.

□ ☍ = It could be called the midlife crisis. Mental confusion about wants and distortion of reasons will affect decision making. Nothing permanent will develop during this transit. The past may be discarded and will no longer be of any interest.

♇

☌ = A conjunction will not take place in a normal life time.

✱ ▲ = Tranquillity and stability maybe achieved under this transit if ♇ is not badly aspected at birth.

□ ☍ = A time where old problems come up for renewal and demand solving. Society is not supportive and endings will be experienced. If very old age is reached and the ☍ is occurring, it may coincide with death.

47

Using Numerology to Support Findings in Astrology

A brief mentioning of numerology may be adequate and appreciated. One of the masters on this subject was CHEIRO who left behind a wealth of information. For the purpose of this book the author will address some aspects of numerology that can be used to support astrological findings.

This book will concentrate on the numbers 1-9 only and address all meanings in regards to the birth date and birth year of a person, as used in the astrological chart.

A person born on April 4, 1979 is guided in life by the number 7. Life will provide resources which is set out by calculating April (4) + day (4) = 8, which indicates the ability to make money.

If we now add the number 8 (representing day and month of birth) and also add the year 1979. This year brings 1 + 9 + 7 + 9 = number 26, when reduced to a single digit 2 + 6 = 8. If we now add the 8 (from day and month) and add the 8 (from the year) we arrive at 16, this reduced to a single number is 7. This number 7 symbolizes the life path of the person.

The concept of life is called evolution. Everything is directed to propel a matter forward. This is evinced by astrology as much as by numerology.

The following is a brief example of the general meanings of numbers as they relate to a person's birth date. *(birth date and month and year = added together then reduced to a single digit)*

Number 1

An independent attitude is geared to reach the top. Ambitions will be strengthened and pursued. Leadership abilities are instilled. It represents the beginning of a climb to the top.

Number 2

This number is better suited to accept work for others or share with others. If number 2 is aimed at the yearly calculation it presents a halt to progress. If there is any indication that number 2 controls the next 2 years, nothing will really materialize during this period.

Number 3

This number symbolizes social grace and a liking in the community. Not being a very strong personality, the person may float through life needing the support of others. If the year calculated reveals a 3 and 6 combination period the number 3 years are filled with more obstacles while the number 6 periods are more prosperous. In any event, a gradual climb to the top is indicated.

Example year 1956
21 = 3
1977
24 = 6
2001
3
2004

Number 4

This number demands hard work, patience and a willingness to take on challenges. During the birth year circle, a number 4 circle is filled with hard, tiring work and rough times. However, a number 22, when appearing through the birth year, should not be reduced to a single digit. It has added benefits of providing opportunities. When applying hard work thereto, progress can be achieved.

Number 5

Travel, moving around or changing jobs, will occur. In short, a very changeable time that requires extra energy. Restlessness may propel the person forward. However, during a number 5 period not much peace and quiet can be expected.

Number 6

Domestic issues, the family and marriage, are of main concern. A birth date added across and resulting in a life number 6 represents the need to be married. If applied in the birth year calculation it brings a prosperous time that is geared to advance many interests.

Number 7

This number surely represents an emotional time. It may bring death and despair. Relationships may be formed during a birth year period, however, the union may not last and ends, not necessarily by divorce or abandonment, but by the death of either party. Hurtful periods will have to be endured. If a relationship develops when the year (date, month, current year) adds to a number 7 but no other number 7 appears in the natal calculation, an intense relationship maybe in store that involves deep seated emotions.

Number 8

Money and possessions are of prime interest and will be pursued. An executive ability is instilled. When seen through the birth year circle, it produces a time when, with good planning, the finances may be improved as number 8 is the number of money.

Number 9

This number symbolizes continuous changes. Nothing will last. Everything is subject to never ending changes. Taken by the birth year circle a number 9 means changes as soon as the end of the circle is near. (every 9 years) However, it must be taken into consideration, when working with a double digit number, that a number 18 has a different effect than a number 27, although both form a single digit of the number 9. For instance, if the birth year is 1944 the calculation goes as follows:

$$\begin{array}{r} 1944 \\ \underline{18 = 9} \\ 1962 \end{array}$$

18 = 9

1980

18 = 9

1998

27 = 9

2025

The circle of number 18 represented by a 1 (improvement) and a number 8 (money) will give success on a steady rise. Lots of opportunities will be presented to the person. However, under a number 27 (represented by a 2 (things will not work out well) and a number 7 (emotional periods with trouble) matters, which have not been fully established at that time, will not come to fruition.

Going back to our example of the person born on 4/4/1979 and concentrating entirely on the birth year only, we arrive at a general meaning of the steps provided for in life. Here we concentrate on double digit numbers unless we want to establish events for a particular year.

1979 added across is

26 = 8

2005

7

2012

5

2017

This indicates that the first 26 years will be financially prosperous. As of 2005 the number 7 rules. The number 7, as a guide in life, represents trauma and emotional disappointments. Very often, this event is also connected to the person's own death or the death of a person with whom a close relationship had been enjoyed.

About 2012 the life is influenced by the number 5. A change of residence or extensive travel will be experienced. This number does not provide for a settled period but indicates a restless time. Sadly, the person born on the day, as used for this example, did not survive the double 7 period. *(number 7 life path and number 7 birth year)* After falling in love (a trend of the 7 period) he had a child. However the relationship did not survive and he was separated from his child. He died in early 2008.

This very basic concept of numerology is simple and easy and can be used to quickly determine a good and prosperous or negative and struggling period. Good advice will help reap benefits and advert troubling events. As the saying goes "fore-warned is fore-planned". Just a quick note on the subject of fame. Whenever the number 22 appears, as either the birth date or added across as the life number, the astrology chart should be reviewed for the prospect of fame. Number 22 represents center stage and, unless a very bad aspect prevents such a fame, it will happen in life. However, circumstances may limit the fame to a certain time period as the fine line between fame and notoriety is fragile at best. For people who have a strongly aspected ♇ at birth a pattern may emerge whereby the birth year, when added together with the number 12, will represent endings in life.

Example born 1949:

12
1961
12
1973
12
1985
12
1997
12
2009

In hindsight, the person may recall that every year which resulted from an added number 12 represented a year where a phase of life came to an end and something new developed that concluded in the next 12 years. Please note that the year reached is not based on the exact calendar year and may vary to a time prior to or after the date calculated.

48

Sample Chart I

Analyzing and Forecasting Without Making A Chart

The Ephemeris is an almanac of any planet's place for any certain day of the year. This permits forecasting of any desired day in the future as the position of the planets, at that particular day and year, will induce a certain event into a person's life. This marvelous book is an indispensable tool in setting up a chart, obtaining the progressed position of the planets, or simply analyzing and forecasting events in a person's life. Users of computer programs, however, may use their programs to obtain the same information.

Astrology explains the relationship between the earth and other planets in the universe. It supports man in his quest to understand himself and his mission or purpose in life. It opens up an understanding as to the laws of nature, with its imposing rules that guide us all. The power of the Universe is vast but very structured. At times it seems to act at random, but in-depth analysis has exposed that there is a law of cause and effect. The will of man, however, may rule independently of that power structure so that man himself is able to shape his own life. His dependency under stellar vibrations, therefore, may be greatly diminished if the will is strongly applied.

In most cases the date of birth is known. The location and time of birth may be unknown to the person or to the astrologer if no contact with the person exists. It is possible to derive, from the Ephemeris, enough information to accurately compile a chart by just concentrating on the birth date.

Here, the author has selected a women who recently married one of the icons in show business and has become a daily fascination of the masses. Her birth date was printed in one of the nations tabloid publications, thus, the author assumes the correctness of the obtained data. If incorrect, however, this date will then apply to countless others who arrived in this world on that given day, December 18, 1978.

Beginning with the information of the planets position at birth it is necessary to check the Ephemeris for December 18, 1978. (see page 395) The planets positions and aspects are transferred into a chart on page 398. Herein the planets transits are noted as they appear in the signs. The corresponding pages explain their position. The next step involves the natal aspects (Planets and signs involved) and the corresponding pages for information as to its meaning. Thereafter, the progression is derived by counting from the day after birth, to the present age or to any other year if future events be investigated. (see page 396) The notes continue with information of the baby chart which reflects the relationship of the parents and their behavior toward the child and each other within the first three years of the child's life. The aspects will then refer to paragraph numbers explaining their meaning.

By determining these factors we have established:

1. Planets in signs represent our basic personality;
2. The Baby Chart reflects the problems or advantages that we have adopted from our parents;
3. The Natal Position determines our blue print, our direction in life;
4. The Progression will inform us about future events that will develop for us.

Finally, a reading of the planets transit from the Ephemeris on the date at which a chart is constructed will determine the influences in the life of the person, at that particular time.

5. When determining the transit of the planets and their aspects formed one must not only consider the meaning of the aspects but also the signs involved and the duration of it's effect. Some may last but a few days, others hold on for years. The duration will vary by each planet but it is save to assume that an aspect forming a

degree of 1-4 will support a precise finding. (Of course, a 1 degree aspect forms a much stronger event than one of 4 degrees) This prognosis allows to plan well into the future to avoid negative times and will benefit the most from opportunities offered in life. Not every opportunity is instantly recognizable for lack of any ready result. Life has a way of disguising the fruits of labor and only with effort may they be reaped. It is therefore important to advice of upcoming opportunities to permit the person to increase the effort and will power to reap and gain. Without sustaining any effort to gain, the opportunity may drift back into oblivion.

Constructing a chart based solely on the birth date does not permit consideration of **A** (Ascendant) and **M** (Mid heaven) as those house positions need information on time and place of birth, which are not available for our test chart.

<u>The positions found on December 18, 1978 are:</u>

☉ 25 ♐

☽ 4-14 ♌ As the time of birth is unknown this position could vary anywhere from 4-14 degrees.

☿ 6 ♐

♀ 14 ♏ Whenever a planet's position is close to the next degree (13-56) it is rounded up to the next degree.

♂ 4 ♑ (3-59)

♃ 8 ♌ **R** While ♃ is retrograde it is deprived of its full power which it will obtain in 2042.

♄ 14 ♍ (13-54)

♅ 19 ♏

♆ 18 ♐

♇ 19 ♎ (18-52)

During progression in 2008, ♄ is retrograde, which will somehow hold back on professional ambitions. A full development of the talent is delayed. The position of the ☽ could fluctuate due to an unknown birth time and all forecasts must be approximated within the possible degrees of 4-14.

Date of Transit Calculation

February 1, 2008

FEBRUARY 2008

LONGITUDE FOR 12 h

Day	Jour	S.T. h	m	s	☉ °	′	″	♀ °	′	☿ °	′	☽ °	′	″	♄ °	′	♃ °	′	♂ °	′	♅ °	′	♆ °	′	♇ °	′	☊ True °	′
F	**1**	**20**	**44**	**19**	**11 ♒**	**59**	**47**	**10 ♑**	**02**	**22 ♒R**	**38**	**06 ♐**	**52**	**41**	**06 ♍R**	**55**	**10 ♑**	**01**	**24 ♊**	**06**	**16 ♓**	**39**	**21 ♒**	**21**	**00 ♑**	**12**	**27 ♒R**	**51**
Sa	2	20	48	16	13	00	41	11	16	21	53	18	53	39	06	51	10	14	24	07	16	42	21	23	00	13	27	49
Su	3	20	52	12	14	01	35	12	30	20	59	01 ♑	04	57	06	47	10	27	24	09	16	45	21	26	00	15	27	47
M	4	20	56	09	15	02	28	13	44	19	57	13	29	34	06	42	10	39	24	12	16	48	21	28	00	17	27	45
T	5	21	00	05	16	03	20	14	58	18	50	26	09	28	06	38	10	52	24	16	16	51	21	30	00	18	27	43
W	6	21	04	02	17	04	11	16	12	17	39	09 ♒	05	37	06	34	11	04	24	21	16	54	21	33	00	20	27	42
Th	7	21	07	59	18	05	01	17	26	16	27	22	17	57	06	29	11	17	24	26	16	58	21	36	00	22	27	42
F	8	21	11	55	19	05	50	18	40	15	15	05 ♓	45	25	06	25	11	29	24	31	17	01	21	37	00	23	27 D	42
Sa	9	21	15	52	20	06	37	19	54	14	05	18	26	16	06	20	11	41	24	38	17	04	21	39	00	25	27	42
Su	10	21	19	48	21	07	22	21	08	12	59	03 ♈	18	14	06	16	11	53	24	45	17	07	21	42	00	26	27	43
M	11	21	23	45	22	08	06	22	22	11	59	17	18	50	06	11	12	05	24	53	17	10	21	44	00	28	27	43
T	12	21	27	41	23	08	49	23	36	11	05	01 ♉	25	33	06	06	12	18	25	01	17	13	21	46	00	30	27	44
W	13	21	31	38	24	09	30	24	50	10	18	15	36	01	06	02	12	30	25	10	17	17	21	48	00	31	27	44
Th	14	21	35	34	25	10	09	26	04	09	39	29	47	54	05	57	12	41	25	20	17	20	21	51	00	33	27 R	44
F	15	21	39	31	26	10	47	27	18	09	08	13 ♊	58	56	05	52	12	53	25	30	17	23	21	53	00	34	27	44
Sa	16	21	43	28	27	11	23	28	32	08	44	28	06	48	05	48	13	06	25	41	17	26	21	56	00	35	27	44
Su	17	21	47	24	28	11	57	29	46	08	29	12 ♋	09	00	05	43	13	17	25	52	17	30	21	58	00	37	27 R	44
M	18	21	51	21	29	12	29	01 ♒	01	08	21	26	03	00	05	38	13	28	26	04	17	33	22	00	00	38	27	44
T	19	21	55	17	00 ♓	13	00	02	15	08 D	20	09 ♌	46	14	05	33	13	40	26	17	17	36	22	02	00	40	27	44
W	20	21	59	14	01	13	29	03	29	08	26	23	16	21	05	29	13	51	26	30	17	40	22	04	00	41	27	44
Th	21	22	03	10	02	13	56	04	43	08	38	06 ♑	31	33	05	24	14	03	26	43	17	43	22	07	00	42	27 R	44
F	22	22	07	07	03	14	22	05	57	08	56	19	30	41	05	19	14	14	26	57	17	46	22	09	00	43	27	44
Sa	23	22	11	03	04	14	46	07	11	09	20	02 ♌	13	35	05	14	14	25	27	12	17	50	22	11	00	45	27	44
Su	24	22	15	00	05	15	08	08	25	09	49	14	41	04	05	09	14	36	27	27	17	53	22	13	00	46	27	43
M	25	22	18	56	06	15	29	09	39	10	23	26	54	58	05	04	14	47	27	42	17	56	22	16	00	47	27	42
T	26	22	22	53	07	15	49	10	54	11	02	08 ♏	58	03	05	00	14	58	27	58	18	00	22	18	00	48	27	41
W	27	22	26	50	08	16	07	12	08	11	44	20	53	53	04	55	15	09	28	15	18	03	22	20	00	49	27	40
Th	28	22	30	48	09	16	24	13	22	12	31	02 ♐	48	38	04	50	15	20	28	31	18	07	22	22	00	50	27	39
F	29	22	34	43	10 ♓	16	39	14 ♒	36	13 ♒	20	14 ♐	40	47	04 ♍R	45	15 ♑	31	28 ♊	49	18 ♓	10	22 ♒	24	00 ♑	51	27 ♒D	38

Progressed to January 18, 1979

January 1979

Day Jour		S.T. h	m	s	☉ °	'	"	☽ °	'	"	☿ °	'	♀ °	'	♂ °	'	♃ °	'	♄ °	'	♅ °	'	♆ °	'	♇ °	'	☊ True °	'
M	1	06	40	12	09 ♑	57	53	10 ♒	44	42	19 ♐	07	24 ♏	24	14 ♑	42	07 ♌R	00	13 ♍R	54	19 ♏	42	18 ♐	50	19 ♎	06	20 ♍R	04
T	2	06	44	09	10	59	04	25	37	40	20	25	25	16	15	28	06	53	13	53	19	45	18	52	19	06	19	59
W	3	06	48	06	12	00	14	10 ♓	11	28	21	45	26	08	16	15	06	47	13	52	19	47	18	54	19	07	19	57
Th	4	06	52	02	13	01	24	24	22	39	23	06	27	01	17	01	06	40	13	51	19	50	18	56	19	08	19 D	57
F	5	06	55	59	14	02	34	08 ♈	10	32	24	28	27	55	17	47	06	33	13	49	19	52	18	58	19	08	19	57
Sa	6	06	59	55	15	03	43	21	36	26	25	51	28	50	18	34	06	26	13	48	19	55	19	00	19	09	19 R	57
Su	7	07	03	52	16	04	52	04 ♉	42	51	27	15	29	45	19	20	06	19	13	47	19	57	19	03	19	10	19	55
M	8	07	07	48	17	06	01	17	32	40	28	40	00 ♐	40	20	07	06	12	13	45	20	00	19	05	19	10	19	51
T	9	07	11	45	18	07	09	00 ♊	08	41	00 ♑	05	01	37	20	53	06	04	13	44	20	02	19	07	19	11	19	44
W	10	07	15	41	19	08	17	12	33	20	01	31	02	33	21	40	05	57	13	42	20	05	19	09	19	11	19	35
Th	11	07	19	38	20	09	25	24	48	31	02	58	03	31	22	26	05	50	13	40	20	07	19	11	19	11	19	24
F	12	07	23	35	21	10	32	06 ♋	55	43	04	26	04	29	23	13	05	42	13	38	20	09	19	13	19	12	19	12
Sa	13	07	27	31	22	11	39	18	56	09	05	54	05	27	23	59	05	34	13	36	20	12	19	15	19	12	19	01
Su	14	07	31	28	23	12	45	00 ♌	51	01	07	23	06	26	24	46	05	27	13	34	20	14	19	17	19	12	18	50
M	15	07	35	24	24	13	51	12	41	43	08	53	07	25	25	33	05	19	13	32	20	16	19	19	19	13	18	42
T	16	07	39	21	25	14	57	24	30	06	10	23	08	25	26	19	05	11	13	30	20	18	19	21	19	13	18	36
W	17	07	43	17	26	16	02	06 ♍	18	38	11	53	09	25	27	06	05	03	13	27	20	20	19	22	19	13	18	33
Th	**18**	**07**	**47**	**14**	**27**	**17**	**07**	**18**	**10**	**27**	**13**	**25**	**10**	**26**	**27**	**53**	**04**	**56**	**13**	**25**	**20**	**22**	**19**	**24**	**19**	**13**	**18**	**32**
F	19	07	51	10	28	18	11	00 ♎	09	27	14	56	11	27	28	40	04	48	13	22	20	24	19	26	19	13	18 D	33
Sa	20	07	55	07	29	19	15	12	20	04	16	29	12	29	29	27	04	40	13	19	20	26	19	28	19	13	18	34
Su	21	07	59	04	00 ♒	20	19	24	47	11	18	01	13	30	00 ♒	13	04	32	13	17	20	28	19	30	19	13	18	35
M	22	08	03	00	01	21	23	07 ♏	35	38	19	35	14	33	01	00	04	24	13	14	20	30	19	32	19 R	13	18 R	35
T	23	08	06	57	02	22	26	20	49	46	21	09	15	35	01	47	04	16	13	11	20	31	19	34	19	13	18	33
W	24	08	10	53	03	23	29	04 ♐	32	38	22	43	16	38	02	34	04	08	13	08	20	33	19	35	19	13	18	30
Th	25	08	14	50	04	24	31	18	45	03	24	19	17	41	03	21	04	00	13	05	20	35	19	37	19	13	18	24
F	26	08	18	46	05	25	33	03 ♑	24	53	25	54	18	45	04	08	03	51	13	01	20	36	19	39	19	13	18	18
Sa	27	08	22	43	06	26	34	18	26	30	27	31	19	48	04	55	03	43	12	58	20	38	19	40	19	13	18	11
Su	28	08	26	40	07	27	34	03 ♒	41	12	29	08	20	53	05	42	03	35	12	55	20	39	19	42	19	13	18	05
M	29	08	30	36	08	28	34	18	58	23	00 ♒	46	21	57	06	29	03	27	12	51	20	41	19	44	19	13	18	00
T	30	08	34	33	09	29	32	04 ♓	07	22	02	24	23	02	07	**16**	03	19	12	48	20	42	19	45	19	12	17	57
W	31	08	38	29	10 ♒	30	29	18 ♓	59	07	04 ♒	03	24 ♐	06	08 ♒	**03**	03 ♌R	12	12 ♍R	44	20 ♏	44	19 ♐	47	19 ♎R	12	17 ♍D	57

We refer to page 25 and 26 in regards to the major planet's formation. Again, here is the method of calculation:

All 12 signs form a circle of 360 degrees.

☌ means that two or more planets are stationed on about the same degree, i.e. ♀ 14 ♏ ☌ ♅ 19 ♏. Although this conjunction is not perfect within 1 degree it will have some impact as ♅ is a stronger planet that operates even outside of a 4 degrees separation.

✱ means that the planets are 60 degrees apart, i.e. ♀ 14 ♏ ✱ ♄ 14 ♍ *(14 ♍ - 14 ♎ - 14 ♏ = 60 degrees)*

□ means that the planets are 90 degrees apart, i.e. ♄ 14 ♍ □ ♆ 18 ♐. Again, we give or take a 4 degrees difference away from a perfect □. *(14 ♍ - 14 ♎ - 14 ♏ - 18♐ = 90 degrees)*

▲ means that the planets are 120 degrees apart, i.e. ☿ 6 ♐ ▲ ♃ ☍ ♌ *(☍ ♌ - 6 ♍ - 6 ♎ - 6 ♏ -6 ♐ = 120 degrees)*

☍means that the planets are 180 degrees apart, or in direct opposition to each other, as in the transit chart, i.e. ♂ 24 ♊ ☍ ☉ 25 ♐. This is again most powerful as it is perfect to 1 degree. *(24 ♊ - 24 ♋ - 24 ♌ - 24 ♍ - 24 ♎ - 24 ♏ -24 ♐ = 180 degrees)*

The positions established at birth apply directly to the Baby chart. The progression is performed by determining the year of reading, i.e. progressed to 30 years of age. To arrive at that progression, start counting the day *after* the birth date until the desired new age is reached. In our example, the birth date is December 18, 1978. Counting 30 days thereafter we arrive at the date January 18, 1979. The position of the planets on this new date represent progress in life. The reading of aspects therefrom is conducted in the same manner as described under the natal process.

Jane Doe has only a few negative aspects in the natal chart, that involve ♀, ♅ against a possible ☽ position and ♄ □ ♆. These aspects deal primarily with the emotions as expressed to friends and groups, especially towards women. See # 1284 for ♄ □ ♆ which is a focus on the undecided mind, which will vacillate due to an underdeveloped personality and mind. Fear of inadequacy may trigger events that bring out the problematic side of the personality. Life's lesson will help solve this problem.

Birthdate December 18, 1978

December 1978

LONGITUDE FOR 0h

Day Jour		S.T. h	m	s	☉ °		'	"	☽ °		'	"	☿ °		'	♀ °		'	♂ °		'	♃ °		'	♄ °		'	♅ °		'	♆ °		'	♇ °		'	☊ True °		'
F	1	04	37	59	08	♐	25	54	17	♐	16	56	19	♐R	21	07	♏	27	21	♐	11	09	♌R	01	13	♑	25	18	♏	03	17	♐	41	18	♎	27	23	♑R	38
Sa	2	04	41	56	09		26	45	02	♑	00	05	18		22	07		34	21		56	09		00	13		28	18		06	17		43	18		29	23		27
Su	3	04	45	52	10		27	36	16		46	16	17		14	07		44	22		41	08		58	13		30	18		10	17		45	18		30	23		16
M	4	04	49	49	11		28	29	01	♒	27	39	15		59	07		55	23		26	08		57	13		32	18		13	17		47	18		32	23		09
T	5	04	53	45	12		29	23	15		58	02	14		38	08		09	24		11	08		55	13		35	18		17	17		50	18		34	23		04
W	6	04	57	42	13		30	17	00	♓	13	34	13		16	08		25	24		56	08		53	13		37	18		20	17		52	18		35	23		02
Th	7	05	01	39	14		31	12	14		12	39	11		53	08		42	26		41	08		51	13		39	18		24	17		54	18		37	23		02
F	8	05	05	35	15		32	07	27		56	28	10		34	09		02	26		26	08		49	13		41	18		27	17		56	18		38	23		01
Sa	9	05	09	32	16		33	03	11	♈	23	12	09		21	09		24	27		11	08		46	13		42	18		31	17		59	18		40	23		01
Su	10	05	13	28	17		34	00	24		37	28	08		15	09		47	27		56	08		44	13		44	18		34	18		01	18		41	22		58
M	11	05	17	25	18		34	58	07	♉	38	42	07		19	10		13	28		41	08		41	13		46	18		37	18		03	18		43	22		52
T	12	05	21	21	19		35	58	20		30	57	06		33	10		40	29		27	08		38	13		47	18		41	18		05	18		44	22		43
W	13	05	25	18	20		36	56	03	♊	11	43	05		59	11		09	00	♑	12	08		35	13		48	18		44	18		08	18		45	22		31
Th	14	05	29	14	21		37	55	15		42	11	05		36	11		39	00		57	08		31	13		50	18		47	18		10	18		47	22		17
F	15	05	33	11	22		38	56	28		02	27	05		24	12		11	01		43	08		27	13		51	18		51	18		12	18		48	22		02
Sa	16	05	37	08	23		39	57	10	♋	12	49	05	D	22	12		45	02		28	08		24	13		52	18		54	18		15	18		49	21		48
Su	17	05	41	04	24		40	58	22		14	09	05		30	13		19	03		14	08		20	13		53	18		57	18		17	18		51	21		35
M	**18**	**05**	**45**	**01**	**25**		**42**	**02**	**04**	♌	**08**	**06**	**05**		**47**	**13**		**56**	**03**		**59**	**08**		**15**	**13**		**54**	**19**		**00**	**18**		**19**	**18**		**52**	**21**		**25**
T	19	05	48	57	26		43	05	15		57	09	06		12	14		33	04		45	08		11	13		54	19		04	18		21	18		53	21		17
W	20	05	52	54	27		44	10	27		44	44	06		45	15		12	05		31	08		07	13		55	19		07	18		24	18		54	21		13
Th	21	05	56	50	28		45	15	09	♑	35	10	07		24	15		53	06		16	08		02	13		55	19		10	18		26	18		55	21		11
F	22	06	00	47	29		46	21	21		33	24	08		10	16		34	07		02	07		57	13		56	19		13	18		28	18		57	21		11
Sa	23	06	04	43	00	♑	47	27	03	☊	44	52	09		00	17		17	07		48	07		52	13		56	19		16	18		30	18		58	21		11
Su	24	06	08	40	01		48	35	16		15	04	09		55	18		00	08		34	07		47	13		56	19		19	18		32	18		59	21		10
M	25	06	12	37	02		49	43	29		08	08	10		54	18		45	09		20	07		41	13		56	19		22	18		35	19		00	21		07
T	26	06	16	33	03		50	51	12	♍	30	59	11		57	19		31	10		06	07		36	13		56	19		25	18		37	19		01	21		02
W	27	06	20	30	04		52	01	26		22	35	13		02	20		17	10		52	07		30	13		56	19		28	18		39	19		02	20		55
Th	28	06	24	26	06		53	11	10	♐	43	03	14		11	21		05	11		38	07		24	13		56	19		31	18		41	19		02	20		45
F	29	06	28	23	06		54	21	26		28	06	15		22	21		53	12		24	07		18	13		55	19		34	18		43	19		03	20		33
Sa	30	06	32	19	07		55	31	10	♑	30	05	16		36	22		45	13		10	07		12	13		55	19		36	18		46	19		04	20		22
Su	31	06	36	16	08	♑	56	42	25	♑	39	07	17	♐	50	23	♏	33	13	♑	56	07	♌R	06	13	♑R	54	19	♏	39	18	♐	48	19	O	05	20	♑R	12

Jane Doe born: December 18, 1978

Ref. # *Planets/signs*	*Natal*	*Progression*	*Baby*
21 ☉ (♐)	248 ☽ ▲ ☿	115 ☉ ☌ ☽	355 ☽ ☌ ♃
212 ☽ (♌)	240 ☽ □ ♀	116 ☉ ▲ ☽	369 ☽ □ ♀
422 ☿ (♐)	224 ☽ ☌ ♃	128 ☉ ☍ ♃	373 ☽ □ ♅
620 ♀ (♏)	244 ☽ □ ♅	335 ☽ ▲ ♂	382 ☽ ▲ ♆
828 ♂ (♑)	254 ☽ ▲ ♆	537 ☿ □ ♇	577 ☿ ▲ ☽
1037 ♃ (♌)	453 ☿ ▲ ♃	542 ☿ ▲ ♄	579 ☿ ▲ ♃
1252 ♄ (♍)	630 ♀ ☌ ♅	730 ♀ □ ♄	758 ♀ ☌ ♅
1480 ♅ (♏)	637 ♀ * ♄	738 ♀ ▲ ♃	766 ♀ * ♄
1695 ♆ (♐)	1284 ♄ □ ♆		1431 ♄ □ ♆
1907 ♇ (♎)	1716 ♆ * ♇		1842 ♆ * ♇

Transits on date: February 1, 2008

Transit aspect Natal

1116 ♃ 10 ♑ □ ♇ 18 ♎ = it will be exact when ♃ is on 18 ♑ (3/2008 and going into retro 6-7/2008 until it will again emerge when going direct on 11/2008, thereby, at last, revealing its full strength.

1358 ♅ 18 ♓ ☍ ♄ 13 ♍ = This aspect will end soon as ♅ will not return by retrograde motion to ♄ position.

695 ♅ 18 ♓ ▲ ♀ 14 ♏ = This aspect will end soon as ♅ will not return by retrograde motion to ♀ position.

1555 ♅ 18 ♓ □ ♆ 18 ♐ = This aspect will last until 2009.

94 ♅ 18 ♓ □ ☉ 25 ♐ = This aspect will be activated through 2008-2009

839 ♇ 00 ♑ ☌ ♂ 04 ♑ = This aspect is getting stronger in the next 3 years.

109 ♂ 24 ♊ ☍ ☉ 25 ♐ = This aspect is lasting throughout the month of February 2008.

489 ♄ 06 ♍ □ ☿ 06 ♐ = This aspect will last until about August 2008.

CHART DEFINITION

PLANETS IN THE SIGNS

21 ☉ (♐) The person loves personal freedom, is outgoing, loves to travel, seeks involvement with foreigners and prefers to deal with all in a straightforward and open manner. Generally generous and well supported by luck, the person craves center of attention and involvement in the upper society. If the harmony desired is in imbalance, the person may suffer from anxiety, becomes narrow-minded, jumps to conclusions and engages in bickering, hence incurring nervous ailments that are hard to treat. Religious fanatics may develop under this sign when the person loses his/her own identity and is swept up by the masses. The urge for creativity is strong. Many outlets are pursued to please the ego and gather rewards. Women tend not to be very domesticated due to the strong independent nature and desire to mingle in society rather than stay at home. When putting on the charm side this person will collect many friends.

212 ☽ (♌) Quick mental reactions, great instincts and an ability to grasp opportunities, is present. A desire for happiness and contentment, at home and at work, as well as in social circles, is expressed. A position that is great for friendships, especially with women. Ill considered emotional rash acts may bring setbacks. Logic should always control the feelings, which may be stacked with ego pride. A proud person, with a flair for dramatics, desiring the center of attraction and the spotlight for themselves. A desire to be admired and appreciated is displayed. Romance and affection are sought. Normally there is a strong liking of children, parties, arts and entertainment. A tendency to be self-centered, with prima donna behavior, creates estrangements. The need for dramatization should be curbed. The desire to dominate and a childish desire for self importance can be overbearing and disturb relationships. An ability for organization and self-reliance helps attain leadership positions. If positive, it bestows popularity.

422 ☿ (♐) All contact with foreigners, foreign lands, society, religion, philosophy, law and higher education, as well as social

motivations, are considered. However, if the mind is overloaded it can lose track of facts and adopt strange attitudes. Illogical thoughts can undermine any undertaking. The person may get involved in prophecy and be influential in mass karma and destiny. The speech is direct and a strong demand is made for personal freedom. Hypocrisy may develop when the moral standard is below their preaching and is ruled solely by attitude. Because there is a desire to adjust the opinion to the general popular social norm, there may not be realization that the general attitude may not be the prevailing truth. Places of social control attract such as Churches, Universities and Government to achieve intellectual authority. When negative, the person may conform to corruption or other means of winning the game while expecting from others to adhere to the truth without considering the truth of their own opinion. Lofty goals and ideals can take precedent over real facts and situations.

620 ♀ (♏) Strong emotions, sexual desires and preoccupation with sex, as well as passion, jealousy, secret involvement and the eagerness for ego confrontations are floating just below the surface. If well positioned, anything will be done for the loved one but, at times, things are taken far too seriously, lacking in enjoyment. An overblown pride, jealousy, resentfulness, bitterness and love may turn to hate and will sever relationships, which will never be resumed. Sex may be used to gain power over others. The person likes to control and run relationships.

828 ♂ (♑) Strong financial and professional ambitions, together with a desire for recognition and status, is intense and calculating. A practical reasoning compels the person to act. Great self-control and severe discipline make for good employees.

If afflicted, there is a tendency to leach on others. Laziness is displayed, and people are used solely for gain. Sometimes the desire for money overrides human and social values and creates total disregard of others. Cold, calculating, selfish and materialistic behavior will drive the person to the top but will lead to disappointment and trouble.

1037 ♃ (♌) There is great optimism, self-confidence, a strong energy, and a desire to be in the lime light. Admiration from others is expected. Loyalty and lavish and expensive taste will be displayed. The person resorts to drama and grandeur to gain attention. A deep seated desire exists to participate in all forms of social engagements to feel important and gain status. Leadership abilities are given. Any co-operation, self-confidence, reliability, honor and great love of children benefits teachers and business engaged in the entertainment industry.

If afflicted, any conceit, overconfidence and expansion, any egotism, arrogance and liking of gambling, stock market activity and other speculations, could lead to ruin. Disappointments will be experienced in love, with children, romantic attachments and in speculations.

1252 ♄ (♍) Practical at work and concerned with details, the person strives for accuracy, precision and efficiency. Bookkeeping, research, health, medicine and library work is suitable.

If afflicted: perfectionism may stand in the way of achievement. Strict adherence to rules and regulations may create difficulties to get along. A strong drive to work and perform may be exhausting. Becoming gloomy and depressed when overworked can lead to health problems, especially in the nervous system and with digestion.

1480 ♅ (♏) Death, destruction and changes in society will occur under this sign. Great social upheavals will change the human civilization. Strong, powerful emotions and a demand for decisive actions are expressed.

If afflicted, violent temper and destructive actions can lead to a downfall.

1695 ♆ (♐) An interest in religion will find expressions. God will become the center of the emotions and people desire to be part of the larger social order. Much travel for belief and emotional security will be undertaken. Occults and guru worship may be practiced.

If afflicted, there is aimless wandering, misguided or even fanatical religious beliefs, false prophets and guru worship. In general, the mind is lost and without a purpose in life.

1907 ♇ (♎) The concept of justice, human relations, social expansion and the mental state of masses will undergo changes.

NATAL CHART

224 ☽☌ ♃ Good luck, sympathy and generosity, as well as good karma may be attracted by exceptional deeds. Optimistic, trustworthy and generous, there is a desire to help others. A major affliction to this aspect brings waste, self-indulgence and pompous behavior. A good aspect provides good health and a strong emotional attachment to family and friends. It provides for popularity.

240 ☽□ ♀ Financial and social problems are created by being too trusting of others and by unwise financial and sexual involvement. Marriage may be troubled or delayed. Unhappiness and emotional stress may be manipulated for gain by others. For a man it indicates the destruction of domestic happiness by the wife. For a woman it indicates health problems, public scandals, slander and problems related to inconsistent emotions.

244 ☽□ ♅ The imagination is strong but the emotions are subject to sudden changes in mood. A relentless search for adventure may lead a person to suddenly abandon a job or relationship in hope for more excitement. Life is ruled by unstable situations. A change of residence, of work or surroundings and touchy feelings will be upsetting, creating hurt and confusion. This results from erratic changes and over-sensitivity. When intolerant of others, personal relationships will suffer and co-operation becomes very difficult. Secret affairs will result in break ups.

248 ☽▲ ☿ The memory is strong and sharp. Well delivered communications and good business sense will help with success. A talent for languages is given as well as a fondness of travel.

254 ☽▲ ♆ A good positioned ♆, free of any bad influences, renders the person extremely mediumistic and gives psychic abilities. Intuitions that guide the mind may be able to deal with psychic phenomena's and the unseen, or make connection with the deceased. Otherwise, hypersensitivity, exceptional artistic talents, dreaming and engaging in fantasies, may come under this influence.

453 ☿ ▲ A great interest is expressed in higher education, publishing, writing, religion, travel and dealings with foreigners. The mind is alert, well educated and communicates with ease and self-confidence. The vocal faculty is pleasant and well developed. It appeals to the public. If well aspected by other planets the person is honest, ethical and fair in all dealings with others. A display of generosity, harmony and an enjoyment of intellectual debates is used to broaden the horizon. Optimism and positive thinking will bring recognition and achievement.

630 ♀ ☌ ♅ Sudden sexual attractions may occur. Being charming, popular, outgoing and sociable, however, there is a craving to be at the center of attention in social life. Events may also break up in sudden and erratic ways. The emotions are spread among many and have trouble focussing on one love, thus, making long term relationships difficult.

637 ♀ ∗ ♄ Artists with exceptional skills for fine details are born with this aspect. It brings loyal friends and serious relationships. Marriage may be of long duration as the interest to bring happiness to others is strongly instilled. ♄ brings good planning ability and tends to render the person frugal, thus, a growing wealth is indicated.

1284 ♄ □ ♆ The mind is absorbed by anxiety, fear, neuroses and phobias. Any skeleton in the closet may be exposed by this aspect. Drugs and alcohol use may bring the person down. The mind is not strong enough to overcome temptations due to inadequacy of the character and the desire to escape all responsibilities. Very often confused, the person may lack efficiency at work or use devious and deceitful methods to get ahead. Scandal and intrigue may tarnish the reputation. Any kind of religious belief may be too extreme or unrealistic to be accepted by others. Loneliness may ultimately lead to mental illness.

1716 ♆ ∗ ♇ Again, this aspect affects world karma rather than any individual. It holds to infuse spiritual advancement and the opportunity for positive change or else the destruction of civilization may occur.

TRANSITS

94 ☉ □ ♅ Any desire for freedom at all costs could result in breakups and estrangements. Do or die is the motto as erratic attitudes render the person unreliable and egotistical. Sudden attractions occur but they soon resolve as there is no stability of the mind. Financial hardships could arise. Joint finances, speculations or gambling might create dramatic losses. The heart may beat irregularly and affects the health. Erratic and foolish acts may destroy hard earned gains. No changes should be made during this transit. Protect the status quo. Machinery may suddenly break down. The mind is stressed, thus travel and controversies should be avoided.

109 ☉ ☍ ♂ Ego confrontations interfere with business and other relationships. Rash, impulsive and aggressive acts cause resentment and estrangements. Difficulties with the law and authorities could lead to physical confrontations, even arrest, if the aspects in the 12th house support such a conclusion. Beware of accidents. A period of disappointments where the emotions should be kept under tied control. Any tension will induce health problems. Avoid dealing with finances or new undertakings and curb any self-centered tendencies or loss will follow.

695 ♀ ▲ ♅ Especially artists and writers enjoy a boost of inspirations. Sudden opportunities will present itself. Help from friends and groups will be received. New romantic attractions and savvy business deals bring happy surprises. Financial rewards are indicated. New engagements, however, need to be scrutinized, as they may not be of long duration.

839 ♂ ☌ ♇ The willpower is extremely strong, coupled with endurance and a fearless attitude it will help accomplish even difficult tasks. If this conjunction is negatively affected involvement in crime, dishonesty and destructive violence will be detrimental. The desires are hard to control. The person may either achieve a goal or incur destruction.

489 ☿ □ ♄ The mind is negative, depressed, pessimistic and ruled by worry and anxiety. Communication, especially with older people, superiors or other authority figures, is difficult and could lead to estrangements. Friendships may end or cool off. Lowered vitality

requires extra hard work to achieve anything. Legal difficulties or difficulties with authorities consume the mind. The health will suffer under the strain and tension. Beware of misunderstandings. Negotiating and entering into contracts should be avoided during this transit.

1116 ♃ □ ♇ A strong willpower is displayed. The use of coercion and dominance to control others will have negative results. The desire to reform others to one's own point of view must be avoided. Attitudes will undergo drastic changes due to enforced circumstances. Criminal schemes and association with underworld figures, as well as using dishonesty to gain from others, if practiced, will backfire. Conflict will arise over the resources of others. The ego needs to be held in place to avoid arrogance and social whiplash. Sexual perversity, obsession and strange occult practices must be avoided. Rebuilding will be necessary as some of the old life will break down and disappear. Legal conflicts may arise. Enormous tension will lead to restlessness and nervous illness.

1358 ♄ ☍ ♅ Rebellious and eccentric behaviors bring confrontations with the elder or authority figures. Relationships may suffer and break up all together due to irrational attitudes and behavior. Conflicts will arise in friendships and business. Finances, expected from others, may not materialize. The sudden and unexpected is bound to happen and could create havoc in life. Lawsuits over financial issues may arise. A very upsetting period during which trouble on all four corners is to be expected. Stay calm and disciplined.

1555 ♅ □ ♆ Fantasies, day dreaming and non-productive attempts on creating work and a strong desire to escape all responsibilities are destructive at this time. Extreme confusion renders reality obscure. Fears and phobias may unleash, rendering the emotions a basket case. Delusions, hallucinations and lack of a sense of directions will deny progress. A person can't escape the self. Facing reality is always the best answer. Financial affairs may be in a state of disarray and subject to deception. A strong and clear mind is needed to avoid the effect of this transit. Drugs and alcohol consumption will increase the problems.

PROGRESSION

115 ☉ ☌ ☽ Depending on the position of both planets at birth this aspect will produce change. Whether change represents advancements or indicates a critical period is dependent on the natal aspect. If the natal aspect was favorable positive domestic and honorable changes will occur. If negative, loss will be experienced. As this combustion of vital life forces will strongly influence the health and vitality, fever may result as the extra heat, generated by this aspect, permeates the body.

116 ☉ * ☽ Fortunate for wellbeing and progress this aspect makes the mind cheerful and positive. Beneficial attachments may be made and the person is able to take full advantage of all opportunities that will present itself. Positive changes may now be made for an overall improvement of the mental and physical conditions.

128 ☉ □ ☍ ♃ Trouble and difficulties will prevail affecting money, the domestic affairs, social and legal matters. Loss will be incurred and death, separation or estrangement will bring sorrow. It is necessary to guard against deception, treachery and hypocrisy. Disappointment and disagreement will result with partners and friends and trouble through them may develop. The person should neither be too expectant nor indulge in any excesses as those bring health trouble creating long and serious suffering.

335 ☽ * ▲ ♂ The person becomes courageous and adventuresome. A good time for positive changes, for travel and entering into enterprises that require free-thinking and action. Affairs can be pushed to completion. If the emotions are controlled and guided and not permitted to undue over-enthusiasm and excitement, this time means positive progress.

537 ☿ □ ♇ Do not argue or force an opinion onto others. Do not engage in verbal power games. This aspect is unfavorable for travel and legal matters.

542 ☿ ▲ ♄ The mind will be very steady, sincere, honest and responsible. This is a good time to invest money or to so arrange affairs for future gain that benefits result from the exercise of care and forethought. A good time for important correspondence and for signing papers.

738 ♀ ▲ ♃ This aspect will bring many financial benefits, for all things tend to go well. Social advantages can be made through making lasting attachments, as well as building helpful and profitable relationships. The affections will expand creating feelings of generosity and kindness, which in turn, attract others who are helpful in assisting to make life happy and prosperous.

730 ♀ □ ♄ An evil time concerning the affection. It tends to bring very intense emotions, which cause grief, sorrow and disappointment. Loss through the feelings, financial losses and forming of new attachments or engagement in social affairs, will be harmful. It affects the morals and tends to make the person careless and lacking in self-control. Deception and fraud should be avoided. One should not trust others too much as dishonor or general ill-repute may be harvested. Depending on the lunar influence, if this affliction is supported by other influences, the result will be very bad. Forethought and discretion should be exercised.

BABY CHART

355 ☽ ☌ ♃ Overindulgence, over confidence and reliance on feelings rather than logic may create a lack of foresight. In order to feel and experience everything, as mother tends to do, the child may not learn what consequences of action could mean. An extensive closeness to the mother may be chosen instead of developing its own life and responsibility.

369 ☽ □ ♀ Bottled up feelings of resentment exist to playing the role of motherhood. Inferior feelings of being a woman are instilled. The mother expresses an inability to create a loving bond with the child, as she may not want any children. A male child may develop a dislike for woman as his ability to love and care is smothered by his mother's dislike of herself.

373 ☽ □ ♅ The eccentric mother reacts abruptly, brusque and ends relationships or jobs or friendships suddenly, at times without apparent reason. Not being sure in any involvement will prevent stable and consuming relationships. Everything may end abruptly leaving others in a state of shock. Facing situations that are unpleasant and that hurt must be learned so that the situation can

be resolved rather than deserted. A crisis needs a resolution not a flight of abandonment in order to develop compassion, understanding and growth.

382 ☽ ▲ ♆ A need to be creative, to learn meditation and spiritual growth emanates from the mother to the child. However, spiritual growth should not replace a healthy life and development and should not be adopted to the point of relying on God rather than on oneself.

577 ☿ ▲ ☽ From the mother the child learns creative and positive expressions of feelings and communications.

579 ☿ ▲ ♃ The parents encourage the mental development of the child. The child learns to enjoy communications and listens well.

758 ♀ ☌ ♅ The erratic behavior of the parents confuses the child. The concept of love may need to be channeled and understood or constant breakups will occur. In later life the lack of consideration before actions are taken may cause pain to others and undermines relationships. The concept of love may be very unstable and undergoes constant changes. The concept of communicating with loved ones is disturbed. Relationships are ended without a warning, creating a shock to the partner that could leave an emotional trauma behind.

766 ♀ * ♄ The childhood is mainly serious but also produces great steadiness of purpose and steadfast co-operation in work and love relationships.

1431 ♄ □ ♆ The father may live in his own world or dreams about things that may never happen, thus, instilling into the child an unrealistic view of the world. Creativity may remain unexpressed. People will be found disappointing and the family may stifle progress and openness. To move away from the family and see the world from another point of view may be necessary for any achievement in the future.

1842 ♆ ☌ ♇ This aspect represents mass unconsciousness that motivates a generation. Any aspect between the two planets indicates great changes taking place in the world. Transformation for good or bad will affect an entire generation and not so much each individual.

JANE DOE
READING OF HER CHART

We begin by analyzing the given character by evaluating all planets and the signs they appear in, together with the results of the baby chart, which informs us of the influences that childhood had instilled on the person. The natal chart will determine the blue print or direction in life. Combine these readings and a picture of the person's personality and character will emerge.

We discover that Jane Doe is fiercely independent and cherishes her freedom. A strong desire to travel as well as a craving to be the center of attention is instilled. At times, the emotions are prone to anxiety and are easily influenced by the opinion of others. As the desire for happiness is pursued by nearly everyone, Jane Doe has coupled her desire with a quest for friendships and affections that provide for social recognition or take place while in public and when engaged in social circles. A reliance on the mother or other female figures may affect the feelings to the extend where it overrides logic, or where the opinion of others are adopted in order to belong. This may lead to engagement with others where relationships are formed for usage and gratification rather than for the purpose of a real friendship. A strong desire for sex will rule a relationship or marriage. The absence of adequate sexual satisfaction turns the mind into bickering and will engage the mind in control games. A balance needs developing to keep the physical and mental capacities on a satisfied level. At times the emotions tend to boil over, especially when physical desires are not satisfied. Although there is a strong liking of children, her own children are either smothered with love or there is little or no direct mental bonding with them. Motherhood will be accepted but may overwhelm her as it divests from her social activities. Sudden abrupt changes may occur in relationships or feelings toward children. It is important that her own feelings of insecurity are not burdened on the child. The mind should be developed spiritually without adhering to any religious fanatics as this could block any free expression of the inner harmony. Open and healthy communications should be exercised to encourage the mind to develop and explore. Professional and financial ambitions are strongly tied to the ego. Any self earned income is tied to the ability to be disciplined and the enduring execution of professional responsibilities.

This woman is outgoing, gregarious, loves to travel and enjoys being admired and adored. ♃ is positive at birth with ☿ and provides a healthy dose of optimism that furthers communications which will result in good luck. While Jane is basically a very serious person, a display of silliness and play is also common. Going out into the world on her own opens a wide opportunity to learn, be creative and take responsibility. The self-esteem and self-confidence will fluctuate depending on the emotional state. An artistic talent is instilled, however, it may not necessarily result in business progress as ambitions, at times, be stalled to pursue other fanciful ideas. A certain weakness of the mind could result when being preached to and influenced by others. While love is pursued ardently, passion is expressed and great jealousy may play a role in a relationship. As the desire for freedom and independence is very strong, clashes of will could develop in any relationship. Outbreaks of temper, if not controlled properly, will lead to arguments and estrangements. The finances may fluctuate wildly as spending is tied to the emotional side. Money is used to further cravings for attention. A desire for fame and glory, if allowed to grow out of proportion, will result in confrontations and mental misery. Loyalty to friends is expressed but in exchange, admiration and praise is expected. Emotions are publicly expressed. Great optimism will always float to the top. Due to very sensitive emotions and a dire need for attention and recognition, an involvement in religion will manifest. However, if not controlled, blind worship may be practiced and the mind will be controlled by the influences of others. A tendency to trust others blindly could result in abuse and disappointment. If the ☽ is more closely affected on negative terms, the life could be somewhat unstable and forever changeable. The character is influenced by justice and fairness and will be well received by the general public.

From the parents Jane Doe learned the ability to be confident. At times, however, over-confidence will result in unwise closeness, especially towards females.

The next step will allow us to analyze the Natal chart. This represents our Blue Print in life. It defines what is programmed into it, what is expected, what can be utilized or must be changed. It can be compared with learning to ride a bicycle. While in the beginning we are so concerned with peddling in order not to fall off, once confidence has been reached, the concentration will progress to determine a destination, a desıre to go somewhere.

Let's support our findings with a simple exercise in numerology:

December 18, 1978 provides for a life destiny of number 1. (see page 386)

Using the year 1978 the following circles arrive:

1978

25 = 7

2003

5

2008

There is an indication here that a relationship ended when the 7th circle came to a close. The reader is advised that in numerology the year does not particularly begins and ends with the calendar year. Overlapping occurs. Between 2003 and 2008 a lot of changes and extensive travels have taken place.

The love affair, that led to this woman's marriage, is indicated by perusal of her past progression. Two years ago ♀ was at 7 ♐ while ♃ reached 6 ♌, thus forming a perfect ▲ which is an indication of entering into a prosperous marriage.

READING THE NATAL ASPECTS

As the exact time of birth is unknown we have to work with a possible position of the ☽ at being around 4 – 14 degree ♌. ♃ is located at 8 degree ♌. The ☽ position, the closer to perfection it actually is, will determine the luck factor provided for at birth. If there is a conjunction within 2 degrees of both planets # 224 applies in full. A good luck factor will act in furtherance of all affairs.

The same applies to # 240 wherein ♀ is situated at 14 ♏. Again, the ☽ influence applies if it comes close to building a □.

244 applies as ♅ is at 19 ♏ and possibly is too distant from the actual position of the ☽ to have any affect on the life of the person. The same prognosis may apply to # 248 and # 254.

Due to the ☽ undetermined exact position the above reading may vary or may not apply to the person as the actual birth time and birth place is unknown but is of importance to determine the actual position of the ☽. Therefore the planets may not completely form the aspects listed hereunder.

The major planets of this person are in harmonious relations to each other and thus, producing positive events. A love for travel and an interest in foreigners, together with an open mind, provide for a good education and intelligent communication. The personality is well received and is brought before the public. A good and prosperous marriage, coupled with a thriving for happiness, is indicated.

♀ will not progress to a □ position with ♅ in this person's life time. Therefore, the aspect of ☌ may not be expressed with full force.

The influences of # 1284 maybe only a mild one. At birth, this aspect was over 4 degrees apart. Due to the progression the gap has now widened to over 6 degrees and is losing its power. Therefore, any transit thereto will lesson its impact in the years to come.

READING THE CURRENT TRANSIT

A transit represents the position of the planets for the day of the reading. (Your Ephemeris on the day of reading, see page 397) In our case, February 1, 2008. A transit must not only be determined by the aspects meaning but need also considerations of the duration of the transit and its effect upon the person. Based thereon is the interpretation, together with its duration, which will affect the life and actions taken at those specified times.

The first planet listed below represents the NATAL position, followed by the aspects of the TRANSITING planet.

94 ☉ 25 ♐ □ ♅ 18 ♓ At birth both planets formed no aspects to each other. Therefore the events triggered by the transit will not be so severe. However, a desire for ego gratification and a demand for freedom will emerge that could create friction. Money may be spent mindlessly without consideration for the need of purchased goods. In any case, the health needs attention and the emotions should be kept calm. The impact of this transit begins around 3/2008 and lasts, on and off, until approximately 12/2010.

109 ☉ 25 ♐ ☍ ♂ 18 ♓ This opposition operates presently during ♂ transit and will last until about the end of 2/2008. It represents the ego and leads to rash and ill considered acts and confrontations. There is no natal aspect between these two planets, however, in progression there exists an ☌, thus rendering this aspect intense.

695 ♀ 14 ♏ ▲ ♅ 18 ♓ ♅ transit is in effect now and will continue until 1/2009. Artistic work will get a boost and should be pursued during this time. New acquaintances and friendships may, however, not last past any mutual interest at this time.

839 ♂ 4 ♑ ☌ ♇ 00 ♑ At birth, these planets did not form a recognizable aspect. When transit ♇ ☌ ♂ its main effect will be felt 1/2009 – 1/2011 due to ♇ slow motion. During that time ♇ transits on and off over ♂ point, thus bringing out certain characteristics, such as a strong will, possibly nagging and argumentative behavior, as it is hard to control the will and see other's point of view. Danger may come in the form of accidents or attacks, or harm caused by lack of attention due to rash acts.

489 ☿ 6 ♐ □ ♄ 06 ♍ At birth ☿ □ ♄ is within 7 degrees. Upon progression it forms an exact □. Its impact is lasting until ♄ reaches at least 12 degrees ♍, which happens around 9/2008. It presents a period of worry and anxiety. The mind is under tension, which will affect the health. Associations or even friendships may lose a common interest and will fizzle out. Difficulties with people in authority may lead to depression and anxiety.

1116 ♇ 18 ♎ □ ♃ 10 ♑ At birth, no direct aspect is formed. The same applies for the progression. The effect will be an over optimistic belief that is coupled with a strong willpower to push ahead. ♃ transit will negatively affect ♇ and its desire for power and dominance will last until about 12/2008. It will trigger effects on and off while moving retrograde. Negative situations could develop that come to fruition after ♃ proceeds again in a forward motion. These actions may involve finances, as well as associations.

1358 ♄ 14 ♍ ☍ ♅ 18 ♓ This transit of ♅ is ongoing and will last until the end of 1/2009 and only mildly have any effect thereafter when being in retrograde motion outside of the 4 degree aspect. At birth and via progression, both planets form a mild ✱ to each other providing for opportunities. The opposition will bring disagreements and financial confrontations but nothing on a heavy scale.

1555 ♆ 18 ♐ □ ♅ 18 ♓ At birth and by progression, no negative aspects are formed. This □ will endure while ♆ transits until 1/

2009. A delusion of wants creates mental confusion. Money is needlessly spent as a means of trying to satisfy the emotions. There is no fixed concept of purpose that will interests the person at this time.

READING THE PROGRESSION

From the day of birth the planets move ahead forming new and different aspects. By the rules of nature nothing stands still, everything will move and evolve. The same applies to man. By its position of progression the aspects may either be more positive than previously or more negative, thus creating situations for advancement or problems that need solving.

It needs to be considered how the progression will affect the life. The progression or any transit hereto awakens the promises set forth in the natal chart. A transit activates all material events promised in the natal and progressed chart. However, the natal position determines how the progress will be activated via transit and its interpretation thereof. If the natal position is negative – any positive aspects hereto will not bring much evil as its powers have been weakened. However, if the natal position of the planets to each other is negative and the progression and transits hereto are also evil, the combined effect brings trouble, disappointment and sorrow. If two planets are positive at the same time while others are negative with each other a determination of the superior strength of the planets involved is necessary. This may result in a trade off. For example: the good aspects promise good business involving the forming of a contract. The bad aspects may prevent the forming of a contract or place obstacles to its fulfillment. In other words: 'beware of what is signed and agreed to'. On the scale of importance a conjunction (☌) of planets is the most potent aspect. Experience has proven that the square (□) is more powerful than the opposition (☍).

115 ☉ ☌ ☽ This aspect cannot be determined exactly as the position of the ☽ may vary between 4 – 14 degree. It will eventually form a conjunction with the natal ☉, however, it is difficult to determine the exact time of such an event without knowing the exact position of the ☽ at time of birth. So, this position may affect changes at this time or the effect will take place later on. The duration of the

progressed ☽ to the ☉ will endure until the ☽ has passed the aspect. The progressed ☽ travels about 1 degree per month. So, give or take a few days, it will last about 4-5 months. If it applies, it denotes changes, especially in the domestic sphere. A determination of being positive or negative depends on the natal position and any transit hereto. It involves a relationship between men and women that changes direction.

116 ☉ * ▲ ☽ refer to # 115

128 ☉ □ ☍ ♃ Presently the progression does not form any aspect as ♃ is about at 5 ♌ while the ☉ is at 27 ♑. An effect will be felt in about 4-7 years as the ☉ progresses by 1 degree per year and will reach the 4 degree within ♃ in 2011. Thereafter it will move closer to ♃. This effect may last 7-8 years. Financial affairs should be watched closely. The ego clashes with over-optimism and could lead to separation. The mind may eventually realize that things are not what they seem, resulting in disappointment.

335 ☽ * ▲ ♂☽ * ▲ ♂ refer to # 115

537 ☿ □ ♇ This square increases in power within the next 4 years. By then it will be most powerful and last for 3-4 years after full impact. Communications need controlling especially in public matters. The speech will be rash and cutting and subject to later repentance. The health must be watched as irritation affects the general well being. Contracts need scrutinizing to avoid a bad deal.

542 ☿ ▲ ♄ Well positioned now but somewhat negatively aspected at birth and by a present transit, it has reached exact aspect. Not much may be felt and if the emotions are kept under control and not be subjected to any power games, it may pass through the next 3-4 years without much aggravation.

730 ♀ □ ♄ Positively positioned at birth the progress aspect will increase and reach an exact position within 3 years. The entire aspect will last a total of about 6-7 years. It creates financial disagreements and arguments with elders or superior people. Some kind of loss will be experienced that causes sorrow and grief. New associations and friendships may prove harmful in the long run and should be entered into very carefully. The entire impact

depends on the ☽ position in progress at the same time. This period requires a time of great caution in all action.

738 ♀ ▲ ♃ The natal position is somehow unfavorable when ♀ 13 ♏ □ ♃ 8 ♌, The progression in 2008 forms about the same difference in degrees as the natal position, namely ♀ 10 ♐ ♃ 5 ♌. Any positive transit thereto will improve the finances, social relations and partnerships. Caution should be applied that the finances are not quickly depleted, or that relationship sour and partnerships entered into result in disputes.

FUTURE PROGRESSION

714 ♀ ☌ ♆ About 2017 ♀ will have progressed forming a ☌ with the natal ♆. A time of strong attachments that may provide the "soul" mate in life.

PAST PROGRESSION OF INTEREST

738 ♀ ▲ ♃ During 2003 – 2005, ♃ had formed a ▲, thus, an opportunity was provided to meet a suitable partner who will increase the financial and social position in life.

NOTES

As a matter of interest and in furtherance of education it is advisable to read magazines disclosing the birth date of known people. The lives of celebrities are front page news these days, and provide an opportunity to check any forecast arrived at for accuracy.

For the advanced in astrology obituary columns may be of interest, especially when it discloses the birth date and date of death. It allows an analysis of the person's abilities and achievements in life and often provides an indication as to the reason of demise. Old age, illness or death by accident may be determined from such a reading. The obituary itself may later be read in its entirety to compare with the astrological findings.

The few steps set forth above are simple, easy to follow and may provide adequate results that support a reading of a birthday or entire chart.

49

Sample Chart II

Represents a person whose life has ended tragically. He was an up and coming star who was blessed with immense talent. He left his native Australia to conquer Hollywood. Unfortunately, he lost himself in the quest for greatness. Born on April 4, 1979, he fathered a daughter, born on October 28, 2005. He died on January 22, 2008. These dates are obtained from public sources.

The positions found at birth are:

☉ 13 ♈

☽ 9-20 ♋ As the time of birth is unknown this position could be anywhere from 9-20 degrees.

☿ 26 ♓ **R**

♀ 7 ♓

♂ 27 ♓

♃ 29 ♋/♌ As ♃ is so close to the next sign, ♌ must be considered as well.

♄ 8 ♍ **R**

♅ 20 ♏ **R**

♆ 20 ♐ **R**

♇ 18 ♎ **R**

The first attention will be paid to the five planets in retrograde position[1]. As long as a planet is moving retro in life (it is actually at a stand-still) its full power is somewhat held back. This affects any transit to these planets. In the progressed chart we can check the planets which are still retrograde at the date of our chart. We notice that ☿ is no longer retrograde. However, four planets, ♄, ♅, ♆ and ♇ remain in retrograde position, thus, any transit thereto is hampered in its full expression. During a negative transit, it will underline negative effects.

Chart Information

John Doe born: April 4, 1979

Ref. #	*Planets/signs*	*Natal*	*Progression*	*Baby*
13	☉ (♈)	43 ☉ □ ☽	117 ☉ □ ☽	159 ☉ □ ☽
211	☽ (♋)	59 ☉ ▲ ♆	130 ☉ ▲ ♄	175 ☉ ▲ ♆
425	☿ (♓)	69 ☉ ☍ ♇	134 ☉ ☍ ♅	185 ☉ ☍ ♇
624	♀ (♓)	249 ☽ ▲ ♀	329 ☽ ▲ ☿	377 ☽ ▲ ♀
830	♂ (♓)	234 ☽ ✱ ♄	332 ☽ ▲ ♀	364 ☽ ✱ ♄
1036-72	♃ (♋/♌)	246 ☽ □ ♇	345 ☽ □ ♅	375 ☽ □ ♇
1252	♄ (♍)	428 ☿ ☌ ♂	350 ☽ ✱ ♇	556 ☿ ☌ ♂

(Contd.)

1. Retrograde = a term used to describe a planet that appears from the earth to be moving backward through the zodiac. In actual fact, the planet does not move backward but remains rather stationary prior to a new forward movement. If a planet is retrograde in the natal or progressed position it symbolizes a repetition of events instead of a constant forward flow. Unsolved problems will rotate and come up again and again. Problems of great similarity have to be dealt with throughout life, or at least during the period a planet is retrograde. Some planets never turn forward during a life time or the other option, they turn from retrograde to forward or from forward to retrograde, thus affecting the patterns of life. When a planet is retrograde during transit situations develop which bring affairs to a halt and only after the planet moves forward again will they mature or dissolve. For example: when ☿ is in transit and turns retrograde, contracts should not be entered into, but if absolutely necessary, they should be carefully scrutinized and only finalized and executed after ☿ begins its forward motion again. This will avoid misunderstandings or even fraud which may be discovered after the forward motion is proceeding. So, in short, during a retrograde motion of any planet be alert, pay extra attention and wait for the forward motion before finalizing any plans.

(Contd. Table)

1480 ♅ (♏)	453 ☿ ▲ ♃	513 ☿ ☌ ♀	579 ☿ ▲ ♃
1695 ♆ (♐)	455 ☿ ▲ ♅	514 ☿ ☌ ♂	581 ☿ ▲ ♅
1907 ♇ (♎)	448 ☿ □ ♆	544 ☿ ▲ ♆	575 ☿ □ ♆
	658 ♀ ☍ ♄	553 ☿ ☍ ♃	587 ♀ ☍ ♄
	862 ♂ ▲ ♃	733 ♀ ☍ ♇	997 ♂ ▲ ♃
	1716 ♆ * ♇	955 ♂ ▲ ♆	1842 ♆ * ♇
		1842 ♆ * ♇	587 ♀ ☍ ♄
		965 ♂ ☍ ♇	

Planets transit on date of death, 1/22/2008

☉ 02 ♒; ☽ 00-13 ♌; ♀ 27 ♐; ☿ 20 ♒; ♄ 07 ♍; ♃ 08 ♑; ♂ 24 ♊; ♅ 16 ♓; ♆ 21 ♒; ♇ 30 ♐

Transits on date: January 22, 2008	
Transit aspect Natal	
110	☉ 02 ♒ ☍ ♃ 29 ♋ = The ☉ will travel quickly on its transit, however, as we establish a chart of a person whose life ended on the day of transit we have to pay special attention to its position.
269	☽ 00 ♌ ☌ ♃ 29 ♋ = The time of death may have occurred around 2 pm, thus, the ☽ may be considered as being around 8 degree and may not be very powerful in this position.
486	♀ 27 ♐ □ ☿ 26 ♓= ♀ is travelling speedily through the signs, however, on the date of death it formed a perfect □ to ☿, which exerted its full power.
683	♀ 27 ♐ □ ♂ 27 ♓ = The same applies to ♀ □ ♂.
490	☿ 20 ♒ □ ♅ 20 ♏**R** = Again, this aspect is direct on the point, thus powerful
482	☿ 20 ♒ * ♆ 20 ♐ **R** = This aspect is directly on point.
501	☿ 20 ♒ ▲♇ 17 ♎ **R** = The effect may be somewhat mild due to the 3 degrees difference.
	♄ 07 ♍ ☌ ♄ 08 ♍ **R** = Here the planet returns to its natal position. A return of a planet to its birth place, especially with

(Contd.)

(Contd. Table)

	♄, has the effect of a 29 year circle incurring great changes. It denotes the ending of a condition in life.
703	♄ 07 ♍ ☍ ♀ 07 ♓ = This exact ☍ creates a powerful effect.
279	♄ 07 ♍ * ☽ 9-21 ♋ = Again, the exact position of the ☽ is unknown, thus, this position may only be applied in a mild form.
675	♃ 08 ♑ * ♀ 07 ♓ = Here the * happens within 1 degree and is very powerful.
92	♃ 08 ♑ □ ○ 13 ♈ = A 5 degrees difference brings only a mild confrontation.
287	♃ 08 ♑ □ ☽ 9-21 ♋ = The same applies here.
1122	♃ 08 ♑ ▲ ♄ 08 ♍ **R** = This effect is dead on and very powerful but due to ♄ being retrograde, will not bring all benefits possible. ♂ 24 ♊ □ ♂ 26 ♓ = Although, the aspects of ♂ to itself is not addressed in this book, for the purpose of this chart it needs to be mentioned that this square implies rash acts, impulsive actions, irritability and conflict. The health may suffer through illness or accidents.
919	♂ 24 ♊ ☍ ♆ 20 ♐ **R** = A 4 degree distance will still affect the person's emotions.
911	♂ 24 ♊ ▲ ♇ 17 ♎ **R** = A 7 degree difference will trigger aggressive emotions, however, the main impact has past already as ♂ is moving forward.
487	♂ 24 ♊ □ ☿ 26 ♓ = This aspect is within 2 degrees, thus, it will affect the mind in a powerful way.
1555	♅ 16 ♓ □ ♆ 20 ♐ **R** = At birth these planets did not clash with each other. ♆ retrograde motion will intensify sudden acts initiated through ♅ which is still powerful even within a 4 degrees distance.
1554	♅ 16 ♓ □ ♄ 08 ♍ **R** = The main confrontation at 8 degrees ♓ has passed as the distance is now 8 degrees past the actual impact, thus it will somewhat lessen the impact.
298	♅ 16 ♓ ▲ ☽ 9-20 ♋ = ♅ position changes only very slowly. As the exact time of birth is unknown it can be estimated that this position was effective within 3-4 degree.

(Contd.)

(Contd. Table)

1555 ♆ 21 ♒ □ ⛢ 20 ♏ **R** = Both planets travel at a very slow speed, thus making this position within 1 degree enormously powerful.

1779 ♆ 21 ♒ ▲ ♇ 17 ♎ **R** = The same applies to these planets, however, the gap of 4 degrees brings a mild effect.

1351 ♇ 30 ♐ ▲ ♄ 08 ♍ **R** = Here, an 8 degree gap has only very mild influences unless supported by other, powerful, planets.

679 ♇ 30 ♐ ✱ ♀ 07 ♓ = The 8 degrees gap applies also to this position.

902 ♇ 30 ♐ □ ♂ 27 ♓ = Even with a 3 degrees difference it is still a powerful effect.

CHART DEFINITION
PLANETS IN THE SIGNS

13 ☉ (♈) A vital strength is present which provides ample energy to defend against diseases. The personality is rather aggressive, direct, full of energy and enthusiasm and eager to dive into action. The compulsive drive to act needs support from the brain. Learning to think before barreling ahead is necessary. The short attention span of ♈ makes the person headstrong and, at times, unwilling to accept the advice of others or is unable to finish what was set out to be done. The desire to be first, seek fame, recognition and wealth, may turn into a strong drive overlooking what else lies on the road. The search for positions of authority and superiority is accompanied by aggressiveness and a willingness to use force, if necessary, thus, ignoring all rules of diplomacy. The foolish desire to make it at all cost brings trouble and defeat. But the person is always ready to go the full distance again if the reward is promising. The ability to reach out to others, cooperate with them and consider their point of view, must be cultivated or there will be dire consequences.

211 ☽ (♋) The exercise of mental discipline is necessary in order to avoid laziness and day dreaming. If laziness is permitted to take

control a personal inability to perform may manifest. There is a love to drift with the tide and only sheer necessity will force them into action. Keeping the feet on the ground will go a long way to cooperate with others. The attitude of better now than never should be adopted to promote progress. An intensity of emotions is displayed, especially at times of full moon. Strong ties exist to the mother, the family and home. There is an unwillingness to motivate change. The status quo is preferred. Domestic security is the prime motivator and influences the emotional wellbeing. Sensitivity exists to the opinion of others, which can lead to imagination of slights. If negative it instills insecurity, thus, the person easily retreats, withdraws and broods. An emotional instability and a tendency to smother others with emotions or goods in order to emotionally dominate them, will bring disappointment.

425 ☿ (♓) Vivid imaginations and photographic abilities to recall memories, is given. The mind is able to be active on the unconscious level of thinking, thus, bestowing intuitive acts, as well as the ability to absorb the thinking of others. Like a sponge, the mind absorbs the vibes of others. However, it also reacts internally to problems absorbed from others by acting less on logic, but rather on intuitions of the unconscious mind. When in a negative state, the mind distorts reality, indulges in day dreaming, in woolgathering, and suffers from neurosis. It may vacillate to the point of turning the person into a mental basket case. There is a strong desire to seclusion and secrecy. Great artistic abilities are instilled and should be developed. Increased sensitivity may result in personal criticism.

624 ♀ (♓) Love and emotional security is all important. A deep compassion creates on emotional dependency on the partner. The person is romantic and sensitive, but feels lonely if not receiving the same deep feelings from the partner. This position is good for artists, musicians and writers. If the dependency on others for emotional security is driven too far, disappointment may lead to dependency on religion and may lead to martyrdom. While absorbing the feelings and suffering of others, the own feelings may be taken advantage of. In the extreme, an emotional state of fear of rejection prevails, this could lead to a refusal to express the

emotions at all. Suffering in silence will take over. The hypersensitivity over dependency on others, or outright laziness may stand in the way of reality, causing problems relating to life.

830 ♂ (♓) Emotions are ruled by the unconscious mind. Resentments, repressed anger and unhappiness may lead to neurosis and other ailments. Emotional sensitivity can undermine the self confidence and delay decisions. Actions are taken in secret to avoid emotional confrontations. The person is easily brought to tears. Periods of solitude are needed to regain emotional strength. Work is best done behind the scene. An artistic talent is strongly indicated and should be developed.

If afflicted, emotional dependency on others will turn into dominating them or the emotional problems are unloaded onto others hoping to gain pity by smothering others with their problems.

1036 ♃ (♋) A strong bond with the parents instills values and love. A friendly, harmonious, prosperous and comfortable home environment is desired. Sharing the home with others, entertaining in the home, and a liking of mothering others, makes the person a good home maker, cook and gracious host. Business interests revolve around real estate, food and all matters related to the home. Financial help is received from the parents. The latter part of life is more financially secured.

If afflicted, overeating leads to obesity and other health problems. The person could suffer from impracticality and over-confidence or resort to dreaming in an effort to escape reality. An overly need for emotional security, self-indulgence or dependence on parents, especially the mother, may create personality and social problems.

1037 ♃ (♌) There is great optimism, self-confidence, a strong energy, and a desire to be in the lime light. Admiration from others is expected. Loyalty and lavish and expensive taste will be displayed. The person resorts to drama and grandeur to gain attention. A deep seated desire exists to participate in all forms of social engagements to feel important and gain status. Leadership abilities are given. Any co-operation, self-confidence, reliability, honor and great love of children benefits teachers and business engaged in the entertainment industry.

If afflicted, any conceit, overconfidence and expansion, any egotism, arrogance and liking of gambling, stock market activity and other speculations, could lead to ruin. Disappointments will be experienced in love, with children, romantic attachments and in speculations.

1252 ♄ (♍) Practical at work, and concerned with details, the person strives for accuracy, precision and efficiency. Bookkeeping, research, health, medicine and library work is suitable.

If afflicted: perfectionism may stand in the way of achievement. Strict adherence to rules and regulations may create difficulties to get along. A strong drive to work and perform may be exhausting. Becoming gloomy and depressed when overworked, can lead to health problems, especially in the nervous system and digestion.

1480 ♅ (♏) Death, destruction and changes in society will occur under this sign. Great social upheavals will change the human civilization. Strong, powerful emotions and a demand for decisive actions are expressed.

If afflicted, violent temper and destructive actions can lead to a downfall.

1695 ♆ (♐) An interest in religion will find expressions. God will become the center of the emotions and people desire to be part of the larger social order. Much travel for belief and emotional security will be undertaken. Occults and guru worship may be practiced.

If afflicted, there is aimless wandering, misguided or even fanatical religious beliefs, false prophets and guru worship. In general, the mind is lost and without a purpose in life.

1907 ♇ (♎) The concept of justice, human relations, social expansion and the mental state of masses will undergo changes.

NATAL CHART

43 ☉ □ ☽ Due to a lack of self-confidence and insecurity the emotions are in disharmony, especially when dealing with the opposite sex.

59 ☉ ▲ ♆ The person has talent for the arts, music and writing. Religious involvement are furthered by this aspect. The emotions

are balanced and well applied to face reality and intuitively sense new trends, which will bring benefits and advancements.

69 ☉ ☍ ♇ A strong will, as well as a big ego and a desire for power may be exercised in the quest to dictate to others the world according to them. Disagreements will follow. A need to establish diplomacy and harmony in relationships and business is required to obtain cooperation and results. Aggressiveness in all matters of life, especially in romance, but also with authorities, should be avoided.

249 ☽ ▲ ♀ Increased feminine virtues, such as beauty, charm and affection, together with artistic and musical abilities, bestow harmony and luck onto the person. All work related to home and food is favored and may result in a prosperous business. This aspect makes for a happy marriage, great attraction to the opposite sex and any engagement in pleasure. Finances will be obtained from business or relationships or marriage partner but if there is any affliction to this aspect, the finances may fluctuate throughout life.

234 ☽ * ♄ Endurance, patience, resourcefulness and practicality in professional matters, together with good organization, integrity and frugality, support a well run enterprise. Keeping financial and other matters well organized will assure a steady climb. However, often the mind tends to be too stern and too disciplined. The general outlook of life may seem rather depressing. Self-reliance, tactful and diplomatic dealings with others support a trustworthy, responsible and honorable position in life. A slow but steady persistence will, eventually, achieve the goal set out.

246 ☽ □ ♇ A desire for affection and dominance is intensified and makes others feel uneasy. The mind is abrupt, detests interference and sometimes rejects material things. Trivialities, petty details and delving on unimportant things may stand in the way of achievement. Relationships may be forced rather then entered into by agreement of all involved. Associations, especially with females, may come into the life and after a while pass out of it, and in many instances, will never be resumed. The feelings are hurt but need to understand that a condition of permanency cannot be obtained by a one sided desire.

428 ☿ ☌ ♂ The mind and energy are highly charged. Occupations requiring the gathering and assimilation of information are suitable. The speech may be harsh and aggressive and, at times, hasty to the point of becoming insulting. Being very fond of debates, the person may enter politics or get involved in controversial issues. If this conjunction is negatively afflicted the person may engage in heated arguments, hence letting the emotions override all logical reasoning.

453 ☿ ▲ ♃ A great interest is expressed in higher education, publishing, writing, religion, travel and dealings with foreigners. The mind is alert, well educated and communicates with ease and self-confidence. The vocal faculty is pleasant and well developed. It appeals to the public. If well aspected by other planets the person is honest, ethical and fair in all dealings with others. A display of generosity, harmony and an enjoyment of intellectual debates is used to broaden the horizon. Optimism and positive thinking will bring recognition and achievement.

455 ☿ ▲ ♅ A talent for research, investigation, mystery, unusual ideas and inventions comes with this aspect. The mind is especially suited for the study of astrology and is able to think ahead of the times.

448 ☿ □ ♆ The mind has trouble concentrating on details, thus, making it forgetful or confused. Keeping a secret seems impossible as the feelings boil over just to divulge what was promised to be kept hidden. Communications will be confused as the speed of the mind exceeds the ability to form those words.

658 ♀ ☍ ♄ A bleak outlook on life brings depression, frustration and financial hardships as well as limitations. Due to disappointments in love and business, the mind is turning to unhappiness and may consider marriage only for financial considerations, while being unable to respond to love and joy. Experiences with employers also do not develop well as the job may be despised, paying little, or the person is subject to a miserly and dictatorial boss. Relationships and friendships with older people may be subject to strife and stress. Under some circumstances marriage may never be entered into due to a lack of opportunities and unpopularity.

The behavior of the parents towards the child will determine the severity of this aspect.

862 ♂ ▲ ♃ Optimism and energy combined with the desire for action may lead to fulfillment of ambitions. The person is very helpful to the less fortunate and thrives in all kinds of social, religious and psychological occupations.

1716 ♆ ✶ ♇ This aspect affects world karma rather than any individual. It holds to infuse spiritual advancement and the opportunity for positive change or else the destruction of civilization may occur.

TRANSITS

110 ☉ ☍ ♃ Over-confidence, inflated self-importance, unwise action and financial depletion might occur. Expecting too much of others while neglecting their own duties and attempts to control others through display of emotions and temper may create resentment. Narrow-minded attitudes, especially on religious matters, could lead to fanaticism or abuse by others. The main issue here is going overboard with everything, getting caught up in schemes or other events that turn unfavorable. Legal difficulties may result therefrom. Disappointment will be experienced unless some mental restrain is exercised.

269 ☽ ☌ ♃ Any action in and around the residence, will be beneficial. The mind is optimistic and kind. Business and financial affairs are bound to prosper under positive transits. A great time to commence pleasure and entertainment. If afflicted, however, overindulgence and over confidence could bring undesired results.

486 ☿ □ ♀ Difficulties appear in social and romantic relationships through misunderstood communications. The emotions may be hypersensitive, reacting to every word said in a disturbing manner. Gossip may interfere with work and can change the reputation. Expenditures should be checked, as the emotions want to overindulge to compensate for being under mental tension.

683 ♀ □ ♂ Intense jealousy in romantic and business relationships disturb the affairs. Making openly sexual demands creates disagreements and estrangements. Financial problems come up. Avoid extravagance in spending. Enterprises don't perform well.

Quarrels must be avoided, as well as seeking out prostitutes or other form of sexual exploits with undesirable individuals. An overall disharmony prevails. Curb the temperament to avoid misunderstandings and trouble. Relationships entered into, at this time, will not be of lasting value.

490 ☿ □ ♅ Sudden and unstable changes, impractical decisions or erratic communications present problems and interfere at work and with relationships. Irritation, nervousness and a confused mind may give way to associations with eccentric or unreliable individuals who have bombastic ideas that will not materialize but could be very costly. The mind should not be allowed to jump to conclusions but should rather listen to good advice. Trouble at work, with machinery or when entering into contracts or agreements, are bound to occur. Difficulties with money belonging to others, as defined by the 8th house, can prove costly. The health and nervous system may be affected. At this time, the mind needs control and discipline to function properly. Social diseases maybe contracted that will affect the reputation and health.

482 ☿ ✱ ♆ The mind is sharp and willing to visualize new ideas. A good time to deal with hospitals and institutions. Creative work, such as filming, photography, writing and other artistic expressions will do very well during this transit. A very good time to study and write.

501 ☿ ▲ ♇ The mind is strong and focused. Interests revolve around science, sex, psychology and all kinds of related study. A positive time to plan and properly execute business affairs. The health and appearance will be improved and result in social gain. A favorable time to address legal papers and to engage in social events to further understanding of society.

703 ♀ ☍ ♄ Depression, bouts of melancholia, feelings of loneliness, all create disappointment. Unwanted separations may have to be endured. Professional activities cause dissatisfaction and lack fulfillment. Trouble will ensue. A lack of confidence can have undesired consequences. No cooperation is received from authorities. Financial loss may occur due to poor management or

emotional spending. The emotions are cool and unresponsive causing disharmony in relationships.

279 ☽ ✱ ♄ Increased responsibilities in domestic affairs promote stability. Serious work or education is pursued that will steadily increase the finances and provides progress toward a goal. Help is received from women, especially from more mature authority figures. Advancement is gained through persistence, stability and serious concentration. New friends can be made who have helpful connections. Old friendships are renewed with family members.

♄ ☌ ♄ Great changes will take place. After the first 29 years there will be endings in relationships, jobs or residence. After the second circle, around 58 years of age, retirement or a new direction in life is pursued. It represents a time of endings and new beginnings. (see page 383)

675 ♀ ✱ ♃ The mind is at ease, is happy, optimistic and content. Social activities will bring progress and honor. Romantic involvement with foreigners and educational trips to foreign countries can take place. This is a good time to marry and favorable to reap financial gain. Benefits could be derived from involvement in education and publishing.

92 ☉ □ ♃ Undue optimism, extravagance and an inflated sense of self-worth create conflict with others. To promise more than one can deliver may result in loss of friends or position. The body may retain excessive weight. There may be laziness and legal trouble or problems with authorities.

287 ☽ □ ♃ Over-optimism will lead the emotions astray, which hunger for excessive approval. Emotional dependency on others, especially on women, may occur. Inertia could bring life to a halt. Unrealistic expectations may lead to disappointments. Expenditures may outstrip any income. Gain of weight or through overindulgence, will strain the health. Extreme dependency on religious beliefs may remove the mind from reality. Beware of arrogance.

1122 ♃ ▲ ♄ Progress in legal affairs, in business enterprises and working conditions will be made at this time. Travel, especially for business, will be successful. A good time to change working conditions or the occupation. Authorities may be helpful and supportive. Well organized and executed endeavors provide for later rewards. The person is responsible, honest and serious about life. A good transit for expansion.

919 ♂ ☍ ♆ Working against the self will bring loss. Secret intrigues, love affairs, internal anger and the desire to plot against others, should be avoided. This transit produces extreme internal tension which leads to illness that also will affect the mental health. Infectious diseases, due to a lessened resistance, will affect the body. Drugs and alcohol should be avoided as it will affect the ability to judge reality. This is a bad time to seek treatment in hospitals. Private, business and general affairs will be fraught with problems. Fraud and deception are likely and could affect the financial well being. People's loyalty should be questioned at this time and is subject to caution. Misunderstandings will affect the efficiency at work. This is a time in which one should wait out without being to concerned with results

911 ♂ ▲ ♇ The will power is strong and positive. An increase in energy should be used to further any business and personal interests. New kinds of physical exercises will be taken up to improve the health. This transit is excellent for self-improvement by finding new directions in life.

487 ☿ □ ♂ Mental irritation, rash and sarcastic conversation, as well as expression of anger, will all create personal and business disagreements. Beware of accidents. Slow down and take care before making any decisions. Inflammatory diseases may create high fever and affect the overall health. The temperament needs controlling. All correspondence is subject to irritation and conflicts. Calm the nerves. Don't argue and avoid any sudden impulses.

1555 ⛢ □ ♆ Fantasies, day dreaming and non-productive attempts on creating work and a strong desire to escape all responsibilities are destructive at this time. Extreme confusion renders reality obscure. Fears and phobias may unleash, rendering the emotions a basket case. Delusions, hallucinations and lack of a sense of directions will deny progress. A person can't escape the self. Facing reality is always the best answer. Financial affairs may be in a state of disarray and subject to deception. A strong and clear mind is needed to avoid the effect of this transit. Drugs and alcohol consumption will increase the problems.

1340 ♄ □ ♅ Sudden, unexpected obstacles and challenges appear. ♄ power of karma may punish the person for selfish acts taken in the past. Frustration, worry, depression and feelings of being lost, will surface. Mistrust, loss of a job, legal difficulties and health problems can be a part of this transit. This can be a very upsetting time, full of tension, as plans will not work out to satisfaction. Beware of accidents. Disagreement and separation will happen.

298 ☽ ▲ ♅ The mind provides inspirations and unusual ideas. The emotions are balanced through interaction with family and friends. Interactions with women will be beneficial. A good time for pleasure and excitement. A perfect time to engage in public relations. Unexpected income from the resources of others, such as a possible inheritance from women, may all be gainful. The residence may be changed at this time and will bring new opportunities. The mind is inventive and geared for improvement. Sudden remarkable new friendships could be entered into. Gain from investments is indicated if the ☽ has a positive position.

1779 ♆ ▲ ♇ An interest exists into furthering the capabilities of the mind. Working with society to regenerate and obtain progress is preferred. Spiritual enlightening is desired. Travel for education and religious purposes is undertaken.

1351 ♄ ▲ ♇ The mind is more focussed and concentrated. The ego is in check and able to relate better to society. This is a positive transit to activate plans and engage in endeavors that will further the talent, mind, body and profession. An excellent time to handle legal affairs, investigations and contracts. Ambitions and efficiency are increased. If willing to work hard advances will be made. Help is received, particularly from older and more established individuals. The personality grows and more self-assurance improves efficient execution of goals.

679 ♀ ✱ ♇ Private and social relationships are harmonious. The ego is calm and friendly without the urge to dominate. Sexual relationships are invited and could develop into lasting unions. The feelings will

undergo intensity to the point of receiving extra vigor, thus, enhancing life.

902 ♂ □ ♇ Power struggles, a desire to control others and sudden rash acts all lead to conflict that will be damaging. The mind is aggressive, unbending and hungry for success. Trouble and disagreements arise over money, sexual demands and jealousy. Avoid crime, dangerous situations, accidents and social conflicts, otherwise injury, even death, could occur. Avoid chemicals, radiation or excessive medication as it could alter the tissue and cells in the body. Avoid opposition, deception and underhanded action as this could lead to destruction.

PROGRESSION

117 ☉ □ - ☍ ☽ The intense power of both planets may affect the general health. It brings unfortunate conditions and sorrow into the life. A death in the family may occur. Many disappointments will be experienced, leading to separation and estrangements.

130 ☉ ✶ - ▲ ♄ The person becomes more reliable, adheres to a moral character and will meet with elders or authorities who are helpful, sincere and able to benefit and may even become friends. The mind is steady, concentrated and persevering as to increase honor and reputation. A position of trust should be obtained that will serve well in the future. This influence will bring gain rather than fulfill any material desires. Sound and solid investments will improve the financial conditions in the long run.

134 ☉ □ - ☍ ♅ Sudden and severe disappointments will come into the life. Unexpected trouble will turn all plans unfavorable, creating disagreement, opposition, conflict and cause separation. The mind will turn irritable, the health will suffer, and nervous disorders will affect the mind. Any planned changes and matters of importance should be on hold until after this aspect has passed. Disagreements and disappointments with close relationships cause annoyance or even disgrace. Travel should be avoided and if the ☽ aspect is unfortunate at the same time, caution is the big word and should be adhered to otherwise trouble may occur during those critical times. Careful consideration of consequences preceding any action

may prevent major mistakes and disappointments. Any dispute, legal affairs or actions, which may lead to disgrace and ill repute, should be avoided.

329 ☽ ∗ ▲ ☿ This is the best time to enhance the intellectual faculties, broaden the horizon and engage in studies to expand the mind. All kind of communications, travel and planned changes will fare well under this influence. The stimulation of the brain will further latent talents and be fortunate. Literary undertakings will prosper if planned and executed properly. It is the will power to mentally grow that determines the outcome of this aspect.

332 ☽ ∗ ▲ ♀ A clear mind, happy emotions and a desire for affection will help form successful and beneficial unions and relationships. The pleasantness of this aspect should be utilized to the fullest advantage. Finances may increase dramatically and the person will prosper. The entire period, during which this progress applies, will be very satisfactory and profitable. If the natal aspect of the ☽ and ♀ are very good, this time indeed, will become memorable and full of opportunities.

345 ☽ □ ☍ ♅ Sudden, unexpected changes, adverse to the interest, will occur. Removals and changes, made at this time, will give reason to regret afterwards. The mind will act in an erratic and eccentric manner causing disagreements. Attractions pursued and relationships entered into at this time are not of a long duration and may bring remorse. The speech should be well guarded as any tendency to be sarcastic or insulting will have adverse reactions. A time of caution in which obstacles must be overcome and separation occurs. Existing habits undergo changes and the mind should focus on personal improvement. If possible, no travel should be considered until this aspect has passed.

350 ☽ ∗ ▲ ♇ The emotions will reach more depth and feelings than previously. Creative changes on the domestic front and personal side will be desired. Important new relationships will be formed which are far more emotional for both parties and may be part of a public display.

513 ☿ ☌ ♀ The mind is bright and cheerful creating benefits in many ways, especially from a social and mental standpoint. Benefits will come through the help of friends, or partners, or those who are

associated with the person in the domestic sphere. There will be contacts with musical and artistic people. Many social advantages may be gained. Depending on the lunar aspects in force at the time it might bring the good it promises, otherwise it may pass with only minor benefits.

514 ☿ ☌ ♂ The mental conditions are either very practical or dogmatic. Somewhat severe, shrewd and alert, the mind is inclined to over-estimate and to be too expectant, with a tendency to commit acts of indiscretion or to give way to impulsive conduct. Care is necessary to avoid going to extremes, or giving way to strong passion and desires. Hasty speech and a tendency to be bitter and sarcastic, especially where writing, correspondence, or literary work is concerned, should be avoided. This conjunction excites and over-stimulates the whole nervous system, it is therefore necessary to act cautiously during this period. It is not a good time to travel or to deal with literary persons.

544. ☿ ▲ ♆ The mind is in a pleasant state and all things signified by ☿ run well and smoothly.

553 ☿ ☍ ♇ Mental conflicts with others may develop. Be careful of any communications, especially in connection with contracts and legal matters. There will be suspicion and a harsh attitude as well as an obsession with ideas that may not be practical.

733 ♀ □ ♇ Jealousy, possessiveness and attachments to the wrong kind of people bring trouble, loneliness and emotional disappointments. A strong sex drive may lead to uncontrolled lust but furthers an inability to express feelings of love. Society may reject the person. Loss of finances may occur.

955 ♂ ▲ ♆ Good for any investment, speculation, travel, adventure, religion, and also emigration. An increased vigor, abundant ideas and schemes from which profit could be reaped, will guide this aspect.

965 ♂ ☍ ♇ The will is in conflict with actions and desires, therefore creating disagreements within social circles. An abuse of power, selfish aggrandizement and ill considered rash acts may have far-reaching consequences. There is a possibility of involvement in war, crime or violence. The person could be the perpetrator or victim of these acts. The desire to rule and remake others leads to disputes and separation.

1842 ♆ ✱ ♇ This aspect represents the mass unconsciousness that motivates a generation. Any aspect between the two planets indicates great changes taking place in the world. Transformation for good or bad will affect an entire generation and not so much each individual.

BABY CHART

159 ☉ □ ☽ This affliction indicates that mom and dad did not go along when the child was born. This will later affect the child's development of self-worth and may affect responsibilities as the feelings remain unstable.

175 ☉ ▲ ♆ The family, especially the father, displays a spiritual goal and expression. The danger is that he will expect the child to follow his path, which may not be in the child's best interest. The child's talents must be expressed and developed even if different from the father's interests. Each individual must find its own self-expression.

185 ☉ ☍ ♇ A strong psychic energy is present. Dominance, as well as manipulation and control may be executed, as adopted from the father in the home atmosphere, which seem to drain others physically and emotionally. Once the control level is reduced or removed, positive energy can flow and develop. This will involve freeing one self of the parental control.

377 ☽ ▲ ♀ The mother bestows affection and emotional awareness and warmth on the child.

364 ☽ ✱ ♄ A seriousness, slowness and emotional control is instilled by the parents. Feelings and commitments are taken seriously. The person is very responsible.

375 ☽ □ ♇ The mother is manipulating the Universe. She is in control of everything and everyone. The child adopts such a behavior and becomes obsessed with people. Especially love relationships may experience rejection instead of understanding. Helping people may be tainted by expectations of return so that friends have to be eternally grateful. The child needs to overcome its insecurity and establish a sense of self-worth to break this pattern.

556 ☿ ☌ ♂ A quick mind, forceful speaking, impulsive speech, harsh words and jumping to conclusion are inherent with this position.

Restlessness and lack of patience may lead to a learning disability as the mind wanders off before it can grasp the issue. An unwillingness to listen leads to disagreements.

579 ☿ ▲ ♃ The parents encourage the mental development of the child. The child learns to enjoy communication and listens well.

581 ☿ ▲ ♅ If developed, this aspect may produce a brilliant mind. Ideas come easily and develop into unusual and creative concepts. The pursuit of creative endeavors will focus the energy into productivity.

575 ☿ □ ♆ The family was unfocused creating misunderstandings. The child needs to understand spiritual development. The family may have been adverse to religion. The child is intuitive and may resort to a life of fantasy, day dreaming, alcoholism and drugs. A desire for strange lands and people may fascinate the child. Incomplete thoughts create problems in communications. A disconnection to others may occur. The mind needs to be focused, kept stable and trained to develop continuos thoughts in order to use the constructive energy to the fullest.

793 ♀ ☍ ♄ The concept of male and female has not developed as the parents are at odds with their own sexuality. A parent may be absent from the home. The ability to love may be underdeveloped and any authority may be rejected. A lack of self-esteem causes later relationship problems.

997 ♂ ▲ ♃ Positive and constructive actions were encouraged by the parents and are well expressed by the child.

1842 ♆ * ♇ This aspect represents a mass unconsciousness that motivates a generation. Any aspect between the two planets indicates great changes taking place in the world. Transformation for good or bad will affect an entire generation and not so much each individual.

JOHN DOE

READING OF HIS CHART

It is clear from the natal chart that this person was blessed with artistic talents. The natal chart also indicates that the emotions were overriding the mental capacity rendering the person susceptible to drugs, alcohol and unwise association. Relationships underwent estrangements and hurt due to his inability to express feelings in a calm and pleasing manner. The natal affliction of ♆ with ☿ while being retrograde and in conjunction with ♂ have rendered the ability to make clear and decisive decisions nearly impossible. Rashness, cutting words and a nebulous mind had all contributed to his personal estrangements. We know that this person found an untimely demise. The chart will, therefore, be read to establish the prevailing influences at the time of death. This requires consideration of the progression and transits in place at the day of death.

The progression held influences over the action and circumstances on January 22, 2008. As death is hardly considered a positive event an elimination of all positive progressions is permitted to crystallize the actual events, namely his death. Numbers 117, 134, 345, 514, 553, 733 and 965 apply. The unbalanced and erratic mind and intense physical tension created unfortunate conditions that lead to mistakes and undesired consequences. Associations and attachments to wrong kind of people created reasons for remorse. Ill considered rash acts had far reaching consequences.

Negative transits on January 22, 2008 involve numbers 110, 486, 683, 490, 703, 92, 287, 919, 487, 1555, 1340, 902.

Unwise actions due to overconfidence lead to trouble. The mind and emotions were in a state of unhappiness and disarray. Undesirable involvement, especially on a sexual level with eccentric and unreliable individuals, created problems. This affected the health. Unwanted separation had to be endured that furthered the feelings of loneliness, hence creating depression, bouts of melancholia and disappointment. The mind was in a state of uncontrolled emotions leading to unwise actions. Emotional dependency on women mislead the emotions. Extreme internal tension created illness. The use of drugs and alcohol affected the ability to judge reality. People's loyalty should have been questioned at this time and caution should have been exercised. Fever could have been induced due to inflammatory diseases that zapped the vitality and wellbeing. The mind was gripped by extreme confusion which rendered reality obscure. Delusions and hallucinations may have distorted reality. Drugs and alcohol consumption had increased the problem. The planet

♆ was within 1 degree of □ ⛢, thus creating a way of thinking that is removed from reality. The natal position ♆ □ ☿ (# 448) enhances the effect of mental delusion and the desire to escape reality. Excessive abuse created intense illness. In our chart here, it went all the way and ended life. All the circumstances above have lead to an overdose of pills resulting in death.

A note towards numerology. John Doe died on January **22**, 2008, representing a day where his death would become front page news. (# 22 represents fame on center stage)

Transit January 22, 2008

JANUARY 2008

Day Jour	S.T. h m s	☉ ° ' "	♀ ° '	☿ ° '	☾ ° ' "	♄ ° '	♃ ° '	♂ ° '	♅ ° '	♆ ° '	♇ ° '	☊ ° '
		LONGITUDE FOR 12h										
T 1	18 42 06	10 ♑ 26 10	02 ♐ 07	19 ♑ 05	23 ♎ 17 27	08 ♍R 25	03 ♑ 08	29 ♊R 42	15 ♓ 23	20 ♒ 16	29 ♐ 09	29 ♒R 03
W 2	18 46 02	11 27 20	03 20	20 43	05 ♏ 09 30	08 23	03 22	29 21	15 25	20 18	29 11	29 00
Th 3	18 49 59	12 28 30	04 33	22 21	17 00 03	08 22	03 35	29 00	15 27	20 20	29 14	28 55
F 4	18 53 56	13 29 41	05 45	23 58	28 53 10	08 20	03 49	28 39	15 29	20 22	29 16	28 48
Sa 5	18 57 52	14 30 51	06 58	25 36	10 ♐ 52 07	08 18	04 03	28 20	15 31	20 24	29 18	28 39
Su 6	19 01 49	15 32 02	08 11	27 14	22 59 25	08 16	04 16	28 01	15 33	20 26	29 20	28 31
M 7	19 05 45	16 33 13	09 24	28 52	05 ♑ 16 41	08 14	04 30	27 42	15 35	20 28	29 22	28 22
T 8	19 09 42	17 34 24	10 37	00 ♒ 29	17 44 52	08 12	04 44	27 24	15 37	20 30	29 24	28 15
W 9	19 13 38	18 35 35	11 50	02 06	00 ♒ 24 21	08 10	04 57	27 07	15 39	20 32	29 26	28 10
Th 10	19 17 35	19 36 45	13 04	03 43	13 15 17	08 08	05 11	26 50	15 42	20 34	29 29	28 07
F 11	19 21 31	20 37 55	14 17	05 19	26 17 43	08 05	05 24	26 34	15 44	20 36	29 31	28 06
Sa 12	19 25 28	21 39 05	15 30	06 53	09 ♓ 31 54	08 03	05 38	26 19	15 46	20 38	29 33	28 D 06
Su 13	19 29 25	22 40 13	16 43	08 27	22 58 15	08 00	05 51	26 05	15 48	20 40	29 35	28 08
M 14	19 33 21	23 41 22	17 57	09 59	06 ♈ 57 23	07 58	06 05	25 52	15 51	20 42	29 37	28 09
T 15	19 37 18	24 42 29	19 10	11 30	20 29 41	07 55	06 18	25 39	15 53	20 44	29 39	28 10
W 16	19 41 14	25 43 36	20 23	12 58	04 ♉ 35 01	07 52	06 32	25 27	15 56	20 46	29 41	28 R 10
Th 17	19 45 11	26 44 42	21 37	14 23	18 52 12	07 49	06 45	25 16	15 58	20 48	29 43	28 08
F 18	19 49 07	27 45 48	22 50	15 45	03 ♊ 18 39	07 46	06 58	25 06	16 01	20 50	29 45	28 05
Sa 19	19 53 04	28 46 52	24 04	17 03	17 50 13	07 43	07 12	24 56	16 03	20 52	29 47	28 01
Su 20	19 57 00	29 47 56	25 17	18 17	02 ♋ 21 23	07 40	07 25	24 47	16 06	20 55	29 49	27 57
M 21	20 00 57	00 ♒ 48 59	26 31	19 26	16 45 59	07 36	07 38	24 39	16 08	20 57	29 51	27 53
T 22	**20 04 54**	**01 50 01**	**27 45**	**20 28**	**00 ♌ 57 59**	**07 33**	**07 51**	**24 32**	**16 11**	**20 59**	**29 53**	**27 49**
W 23	20 08 50	02 51 03	28 58	21 24	14 52 23	07 30	08 05	24 26	16 14	21 01	29 55	27 48
Th 24	20 12 47	03 52 04	00 ♑ 12	22 12	28 25 52	07 26	08 18	24 21	16 17	21 03	29 57	27 D 47
F 25	20 16 43	04 53 04	01 26	22 52	11 ♍ 37 03	07 22	08 31	24 16	16 19	21 06	29 59	27 48
Sa 26	20 20 40	05 54 03	02 39	23 22	24 26 29	07 19	08 44	24 12	16 22	21 08	00 ♑ 01	27 49
Su 27	20 24 36	06 55 02	03 53	23 43	06 ♎ 58 21	07 15	08 57	24 09	16 25	21 10	00 02	27 51
M 28	20 28 33	07 56 00	05 07	23 52	19 10 02	07 11	09 10	24 07	16 28	21 12	00 04	27 52
T 29	20 32 29	08 56 58	06 21	23 R 50	01 ♏ 11 46	07 07	09 23	24 05	16 31	21 14	00 06	27 53
W 30	20 36 26	09 57 55	07 35	23 37	13 06 16	07 **03**	09 36	24 05	16 33	21 17	00 08	27 R 53
Th 31	20 40 23	10 ♒ 58 51	08 ♑ 48	23 ♒R 13	24 ♏ 58 20	06 ♍R 59	09 ♑ 48	24 ♊D 05	16 ♓ 36	21 ♒ 19	00 ♑ 10	27 ♒R 53

John Doe, born April 4, 1979

APRIL 1979

LONGITUDE FOR 0h

Day Jour		S.T. h	m	s	☉ °		'	"	☽ °		'	"	☿ °		'	♀ °		'	♂ °		'	♃ °		'	♄ °		'	♅ °		'	♆ °		'	♇ °		'	☊ True °		'
Su	1	12	35	02	10	♈	40	24	01	♊	01	11	27	♓R	31	03	♓	25	25	♓	17	29	♋	04	08	♑R	19	20	♏R	28	20	♐R	29	18	♋R	03	17	♑R	17
M	2	12	38	59	11		39	37	14		02	23	26		59	04		36	26		04	29		05	08		16	20		26	20		28	18		02	17		14
T	3	12	42	55	12		38	49	26		40	54	26		33	05		48	26		51	29		06	08		12	20		24	20		28	18		00	17		12
W	**4**	**12**	**46**	**52**	**13**		**37**	**58**	**09**	♌	**00**	**09**	**26**		**13**	**07**		**00**	**27**		**37**	**29**		**06**	**08**		**09**	**20**		**22**	**20**		**28**	**17**		**58**	**17**		**11**
Th	5	12	50	49	14		37	04	21		04	27	25		57	08		12	28		24	29		10	08		05	20		20	20		27	17		57	17	D	11
F	6	12	54	45	15		36	09	02		58	40	25		48	09		23	29		11	29		12	08		02	20		19	20		27	17		55	17		12
Sa	7	12	58	42	16		35	11	14		47	43	25		44	10		35	29		58	29		14	07		59	20		17	20		26	17		53	17		13
Su	8	12	02	38	17		34	10	26		36	23	25	D	45	11		47	00	♈	44	29		16	07		55	20		15	20		26	17		51	17		15
M	9	13	06	35	18		33	08	08	♑	29	03	25		52	12		59	01		31	29		19	07		52	20		13	20		25	17		50	17		16
T	10	13	10	31	19		32	03	20		29	29	26		04	14		11	02		18	29		22	07		49	20		11	20		25	17		48	17	R	17
W	11	13	14	28	20		30	56	02	♎	40	42	26		21	15		23	03		04	29		25	07		47	20		09	20		24	17		46	17		18
Th	12	13	18	24	21		29	47	15		04	55	26		43	16		35	03		51	29		28	07		44	20		07	20		23	17		45	17		13
F	13	13	22	21	22		28	36	27		43	23	27		09	17		47	04		38	29		31	07		41	20		04	20		23	17		43	17		06
Sa	14	13	26	17	23		27	23	10	♏	36	32	27		40	18		59	05		24	29		34	07		38	20		02	20		22	17		41	17		03
Su	15	13	30	14	24		26	08	23		44	01	28		15	20		11	06		10	29		38	07		36	20		00	20		21	17		40	16		57
M	16	13	34	11	25		24	52	07	♐	04	57	28		53	21		23	06		57	29		42	07		33	19		58	20		21	17		38	16		50
T	17	13	38	07	26		23	33	20		38	08	29		36	22		35	07		43	29		46	07		31	19		56	20		20	17		38	16		45
W	18	13	42	04	27		22	13	04	♑	22	21	00	♈	22	23		47	08		30	29		50	07		29	19		53	20		19	17		35	16		41
Th	19	13	46	00	28		20	51	18		16	26	01		11	24		59	09		16	29		54	07		27	19		51	20		18	17		33	16		39
F	20	13	49	57	29		19	28	02	♒	18	20	02		04	26		11	10		02	29		58	07		25	19		49	20		18	17		31	16	D	39
Sa	21	13	53	53	00	♉	18	03	16		29	54	03		00	27		23	10		49	00	♌	03	07		23	19		47	20		17	17		30	16		39
Su	22	13	57	50	01		18	36	00	♓	46	38	03		59	28		36	11		35	00		08	07		21	19		44	20		16	17		28	16		41
M	23	14	01	48	02		15	08	15		07	24	05		01	29		48	12		21	00		13	07		19	19		42	20		15	17		27	16		41
T	24	14	05	43	03		13	38	29		29	02	06		05	01	♈	00	13		07	00		18	07		17	19		39	20		14	17		25	16	R	41
W	25	14	09	40	04		12	06	13	♈	47	31	07		12	02		12	13		53	00		23	07		16	19		37	20		13	17		23	16		38
Th	26	14	13	36	05		10	33	27		58	05	08		22	03		25	14		39	00		28	07		14	19		35	20		12	17		22	16		33
F	27	14	17	33	06		08	57	11	♉	55	53	09		34	04		37	15		26	00		34	07		13	19		32	20		11	17		20	16		26
Sa	28	14	21	29	07		07	20	25		36	42	10		48	05		49	16		12	00		40	07		12	19		30	20		10	17		19	16		18
Su	29	14	25	26	08		05	41	08	♊	57	31	12		05	07		02	16		57	00		46	07		10	19		27	20		09	17		17	16		09
M	30	14	29	22	09	♉	04	01	21	♊	57	05	13	♈	24	08	♈	14	17	♈	43	00	♌	52	07	♑R	09	19	♏R	25	20	♐R	08	17	♋R	15	16	♑R	01

Progression 2008

MAY 4, 1979

LONGITUDE FOR 0h

Day	Jour	S.T. h	m	s	☉ ° ' "	☽ ° ' "	☿ ° '	♀ ° '	♂ ° '	♃ ° '	♄ ° '	♅ ° '	♆ ° '	♇ ° '	☊ True ° '
F	1	14	33	19	10 ♉ 02 18	04 ♋ 35 54	14 ♈ 45	09 ♈ 26	18 ♈ 29	00 ♌ 58	07 ♑R 08	19 ♏R 22	20 ♐ 06	17 ♎ 14	15 ♑ 48
Sa	2	14	37	15	11 00 33	16 56 11	16 08	10 39	19 15	01 04	07 08	19 20	20 05	17 12	15 45
Su	3	14	41	12	11 58 46	29 01 29	17 34	11 51	20 01	01 11	07 07	19 17	20 04	17 11	15 45
M	**4**	**14**	**45**	**09**	**12 56 57**	**10 ♌ 56 20**	**19 01**	**13 03**	**20 47**	**01 17**	**07 06**	**19 15**	**20 03**	**17 09**	**15 45**
T	5	14	49	05	13 55 06	22 45 47	20 30	14 16	21 32	01 24	07 06	19 12	20 02	17 08	15 D 45
W	6	14	56	02	14 53 13	04 ♑ 35 12	22 02	15 28	22 18	01 31	07 05	19 10	20 01	17 07	15 46
Th	7	14	26	58	15 51 18	16 28 48	23 35	16 41	23 03	01 38	07 05	19 07	19 59	17 05	15 46
F	8	15	00	55	16 49 22	28 34 26	25 10	17 53	23 49	01 45	07 05	19 06	19 58	17 04	15 45
Sa	9	15	04	51	17 47 23	10 ○ 53 13	26 48	19 06	24 35	01 52	07 05	19 02	19 57	17 02	15 42
Su	10	15	08	48	18 45 23	23 29 12	28 27	20 18	25 20	02 00	07 D 05	19 00	19 55	17 01	15 37
M	11	15	12	42	19 43 21	06 ♏ 24 09	00 ♉ 08	21 31	26 05	02 07	07 05	18 57	19 54	17 00	15 28
T	12	15	16	41	20 41 17	19 38 14	01 51	22 43	26 51	02 15	07 05	18 55	19 53	16 58	15 20
W	13	15	20	38	21 39 12	03 ♐ 10 02	03 37	23 56	27 36	02 23	07 05	18 52	19 51	16 57	15 09
Th	14	15	24	34	22 37 05	16 56 47	05 24	25 08	28 21	02 31	07 06	18 50	19 50	16 56	14 58
F	15	15	28	31	23 34 57	00 ♑ 54 47	07 13	26 21	29 07	02 39	07 06	18 47	19 49	16 54	14 48
Sa	16	15	32	27	24 32 48	15 00 04	09 04	27 33	29 52	02 47	07 07	18 45	19 47	16 53	14 42
Su	17	15	36	24	25 30 37	29 09 02	10 57	28 46	00 ♉ 37	02 55	07 07	18 42	19 46	16 52	14 37
M	18	15	40	20	26 28 25	13 ♒ 18 49	12 53	29 59	01 22	03 04	07 08	18 40	19 44	16 51	14 34
T	19	15	44	17	27 26 13	27 27 29	14 50	01 ♉ 11	02 07	03 12	07 09	18 37	19 43	16 49	14 34
W	20	15	48	13	28 23 59	11 ♓ 33 48	16 49	02 24	02 52	03 21	07 10	18 35	19 41	16 48	14 D 34
Th	21	15	52	10	29 21 43	25 36 52	18 49	03 36	03 37	03 29	07 11	18 32	19 40	16 47	14 R 34
F	22	16	56	07	00 ♊ 19 27	09 ♈ 35 38	20 52	04 49	04 22	03 38	07 13	18 30	19 38	16 46	14 32
Sa	23	16	00	03	01 17 10	23 28 36	22 56	06 02	05 06	03 47	07 14	18 27	19 37	16 45	14 27
Su	24	16	04	00	02 14 52	07 ♉ 13 39	25 02	07 14	05 51	03 56	07 15	18 25	19 35	16 44	14 20
M	25	16	07	56	03 12 32	20 48 13	27 10	08 27	06 36	04 06	07 17	18 22	19 34	16 43	14 10
T	26	16	11	53	04 10 12	04 ♊ 09 34	29 18	09 40	07 21	04 15	07 19	18 20	19 32	16 42	13 58
W	27	16	15	49	05 07 50	17 15 28	01 ♊ 28	10 53	08 06	04 24	07 20	18 18	19 31	16 41	13 45
Th	28	16	19	46	06 05 27	00 ♋ 04 31	03 39	12 05	08 50	04 34	07 22	18 15	19 29	16 40	13 33
F	29	16	23	42	07 03 02	12 36 36	05 50	13 18	09 34	04 43	07 24	18 13	19 28	16 39	13 23
Sa	30	16	27	39	08 00 37	24 52 56	08 02	14 31	10 19	04 53	07 26	18 11	19 26	16 38	13 14
Su	31	16	31	36	08 ♊ 58 10	06 ♌ 58 07	10 ♊ 14	15 ♉ 44	11 ♉ 03	05 ♌ 03	07 ♑ 28	18 ♏R 08	19 ♐ 24	16 ♎ 37	13 ♑ 08

50

Mundane Astrology for the USA

Important events in the chart of the United States of America

MUNDANE ASTROLOGY

Mundane Astrology refers to the erection of a chart for an entire nation, government or city which will affect entire populations not just a few individuals. Technically speaking it is possible to make a chart of the world at large. The 12 Mundane Houses represent:

1st House Deals with common people, public health issues, general culture and conditions of the country and home affairs. It also represents the masses and their loyalty to leaderships. It represents the ruling party in power.

2nd House Revenues, stock exchange, banks, commercial affairs, trade and all income issues in general, and the general wealth.

3rd House Railways, traffic, contracts, telephone, stocks and shares, telegraph, postal affairs and any other means of transport. It is also concerned with communications, newspapers and any form of publications.

4th House The weather, agriculture, crops, land, mining, public buildings, and the opposition party to the government. It foreshadows the termination of issues. It deals with patriotism, poverty and real estate.

5th House Theaters, music halls, places of amusements, children, education, population growth, schools, morals and gambling. Speculations, the stock market and artistry are ruled by this house.

6th House Sickness of the people, public health issues, Army and Navy, warships, the working class in general and industries providing employment to the population. The morals of the masses come under scrutiny.

7th House Foreign affairs and relations with other powers, war, international disputes, and beginning or ending of partnerships as well as involvement in world organizations.

8th House Mortality, death rate, suicide, and investments of other people or nations within the country. It deals with public debt, pension, defense and research.

9th House Higher courts, judges, the law per se, religion, trade, publishing and dealings with foreigners and foreign powers. Air travel to and from foreign countries are affected by transits through this house.

10th House The leader of a nation, the Government of the ruling power, society of the upper class or those in power and authority. Accomplishments, world opinions, the economy and national status is determined in this house.

11th House The parliament, legislation, associates or allies of the nation. Making or losing friends and show of support or the lack thereof. Rebel movements, law making policies and social issues are determined by this house.

12th House Hospitals, prisons, asylums, charitable institutions, crime, spies and secret involvement. Organized crime that will affect the masses per se.

Events are embedded in the natal chart that guide and rule America. The law of cause and effect is displayed most powerful in the events of **September 11, 2001.**

51

Astrology Chart of the United States, Assuming a Birth Date of July 4, 1776 at 3.01 a.m.

First, we peruse the chart as to the date of commencing the war with Iraq, 3/19/2003. The 7th house of war is ruled by ♃ ♐ and ♄ ♑ through which ♂ and ♇ transit. While ♂ is ready to enter the 8th house of death and destruction, ♇ begins its transit through the 7th house, which in mundane astrology represents the house of enemies and war. ♇ is directly ☍ ♂ which aggression is already activated by the transit ♄ ☌ ♂. The opposition falls within 1 degree of A as it enters the 1st house of the common people and the nations affairs. The people, at first, seem content to enter the war without considering the consequences thereof (♃ transits the 3rd house of communications bringing optimism through false promises) However, the aspect had a far reaching effect on the country as this position is bringing death and destruction.

# 920, 2095	♇ ☍ ♂, A
# 1770	♇ □ ♆
# 926, 1341	♄ ☌ ♂ □ ♆
# 1451	♄ ☌ A

By considering just the major transits a clear picture of the effect of the war is emerging that contains issues never contemplated by the government.

As we all know, the war was started in haste with hopes of earning a profit (Weren't we told that by harvesting Iraq's oil the war would pay for itself?). However, said hope has not materialized.

So, how long will it last? ♇ will transit through the natal 7th house and thereby ☍ ♀, ♃ and eventually ☍ the ☉ by around 2014. ♇ transiting through the 7th house of war will, when afflicted, produce discord, more wars and dissolve associations and partnerships.

The signs represented in the natal house 7 are ♐ and ♑ representing the enemy against whom a war, trade war or disruption of relations will occur. These countries (enemies) include Bosnia, Afghanistan, Arabia, Iraq and Iran. Current and past events confirm that war has and still is waged in these countries. While the first two countries seem clearly identified as being ruled by ♑ the identity of the ruling sign of Iraq is somewhat difficult. Iraq is a country that has a long history. Its ancient name is Mesopotamia. A review of several books on mundane astrology has produced different results as to its rising sign. The former Persian Empire of Iran is now assigned the ruling sign ♐, based on April 1, 1979, which is the day Ayatolla Khomeini proclaimed the Islamic Republic of Iran after the reign of the Shah of Persia ended.

For Iraq, the ruling sign has changed wildly since its days as the ancient Mesopotamia. The ruling sign of a country is determined by the number of Kings in succession and the years of accession of each King who has ruled for the longest period. The position of Pluto of that year, which has to be close to mid-heaven is determined by dividing the chart into 12 equal houses. The 1st house will show the Ascendant and the cusp will be determined by the latitude of the capital city of that country. This calculation can be pretty accurately verified by taken the transits of ♄, ♅, ♆ and ♇ through various houses of the chart to compare with past events of that country. Assuming that the overthrowing of the King of Iraq on July 14, 1958 at 7 p.m. in Bagdad ushered in the new Republic. This would set **A** at 19 ♑ as the ruling sign of Iraq which has been adopted.

When afflictions occur in the 7th house foreign affairs will be troublesome producing awkward and unanticipated events of a serious nature. ♇ ☍ ♀ will subject the nation to lack of favors and admiration of other countries. Involvement with members of the underworld will backfire disastrously and further erode the reputation. Friendships will suffer due to self-centered behavior patterns. Secret and unsuitable relationships are formed in hope of gain.

♇ ☍ ♃ will negatively influence the peace of the country. There is undue hope that will not materialize. The legal system will be overburdened with the unlawful subjects of society. Any overoptimistic and extreme attitude will lead to loss. A thriving for more power over the people creates resentment and opposition. A period of conflict is overloading the already strained and dysfunctional judicial system.

Around 2014 ♇ ☍ ☉, this represents a power struggle and control over the common people and afflicts the health of the community. It leads to aggressiveness and denotes the rise of a dictatorship to obtain ultimate control over its subjects. However, ultimate power leads to ultimate distraction and collapse. The eventual demise of the Roman Empire has been a prime example of such a power structure. An increase in violence and crime and an uprising against authority will disturb law and order.

During 2007 and 2008 ♆ ☌ ☽ in the 9th house. This position afflicts the legal circles and criminal proceedings denoting fraud, corruption and deception. Legal and religious circles will be rocked by scandals and fraud. Relationships with foreigners will be handled in an emotional and confused state rather than with logic and planning. A dreamy disposition will be noted. Dealings with strangers and peculiar people will result in suffering. Old foes turn enemy and dubious relationships with foreigners or foreign countries create difficulties and loss. There is a sense of self-delusion that is very destructive. A loss of ships at sea may be experienced. As the 9th house is governed by ♒ ruled by ♅, any new friendship or dissolving of friendships will happen in an irrational and sudden way. This is an indication that the countries in conflict will include the Arabic nations, as well as Russia. Any new friendship formed during this ☌ is based on a need for emotional security but will be of short duration. The presently friendly relation with Poland will soon cool off.

A peculiar and dangerous situation will develop that could be extremely costly, could result in death and, due to loss of foreign investors, collapse the financial market all together. House 8 in ♑ carries ♇ as its natal planet while under the rulership of ♄. ♇ transit over its natal position around 2022-2024 will bring a collapse of the financial system as we know it today. ♇ ☌ ♇ does not occur in a person's chart as this event only repeats itself about every 248 years. So, America was declared independent in 1776, adding hereto 248 years, we arrive at a date of 2024. Annihilation and utter destruction will change society into a new direction. As this transit also ☍ ☿ a confused state of mind will have trouble accepting changes. ☿ position in the 2nd house of ♋ will be an emotional roller coaster. Revenues fall, banks are swindled and society as a whole will be plagued with fraud, forgery and deception. The degree of fraud and theft in the financial market will be beyond the control of the law. ♇ in its own house of outcome of lawsuits and money belonging to others will activate the underworld. At the time of the transit, the nation's party leaders and political concepts will change any culture, tradition and belief as well as any deep rooted sense of belonging, which is subject to radical changes. The pendulum will swing around whereby the wealthy will exploit the poor resulting in crime and failure of law and order. Welcome to modern slavery. A race for destructive weapons and nuclear power is sped up in the zest for almighty power and control. The weapon industry will increase productivity in anticipation of more demand. The government will assert full dictatorship. War will claim many lives and attempts on the lives of head of state will be made. Communications and writings will lead to conflict and the government may be obsessed with controlling financial flows. Hidden agendas may undermine the economy. It can be said that the activation of ♇ ☌ ♇ will be the ultimate annihilation that is necessary to allow complete change to occur.

The following charts are set up for the United States of America, based on a birth date of July 4, 1776 assuming, 3:01 AM as the birth time in Philadelphia. The exact birth time is somewhat uncertain and may vary.

The progression has been advanced to 2008.

All calculations thereon were performed by Halloran Software, Los Angeles, California who has granted permission for this publication.

USA
Thursday, July 04, 1776 3:01:00 AM
Philadelphia, Pennsylvania
Time Zone: 05:00 (EST)
Longitude: 075° W 09'
Latitude: 39° N 59'

Placidus Houses
Tropical Zodiac

Natal Chart

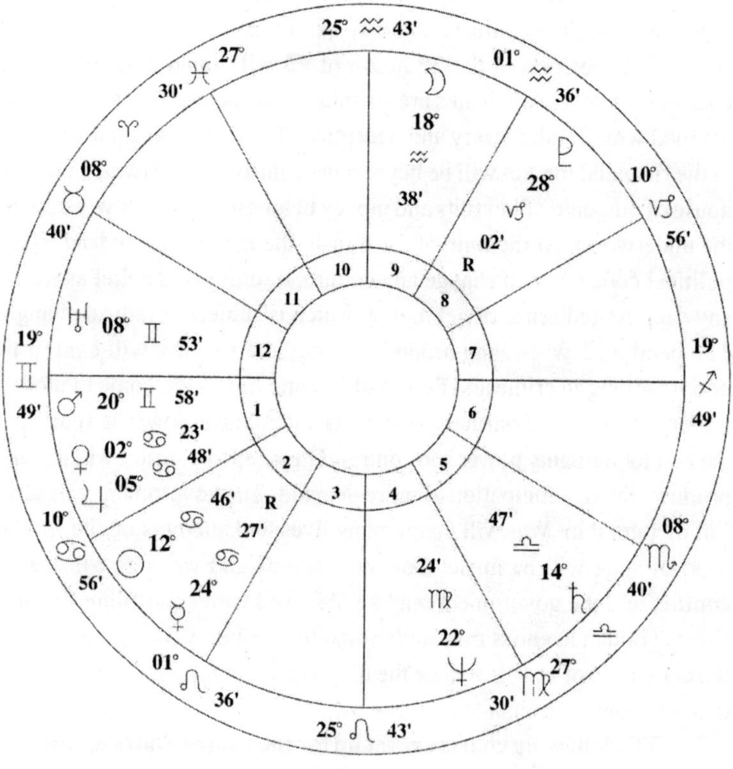

Calculations by Halloran Software, Los Angeles, California

USA
Thursday, July 04, 1776 3:01:00 AM
Philadelphia, Pennsylvania
Time Zone: 05:00 (EST)
Longitude: 075° W 09'
Latitude: 39° N 59'

Placidus Houses
Tropical Zodiac

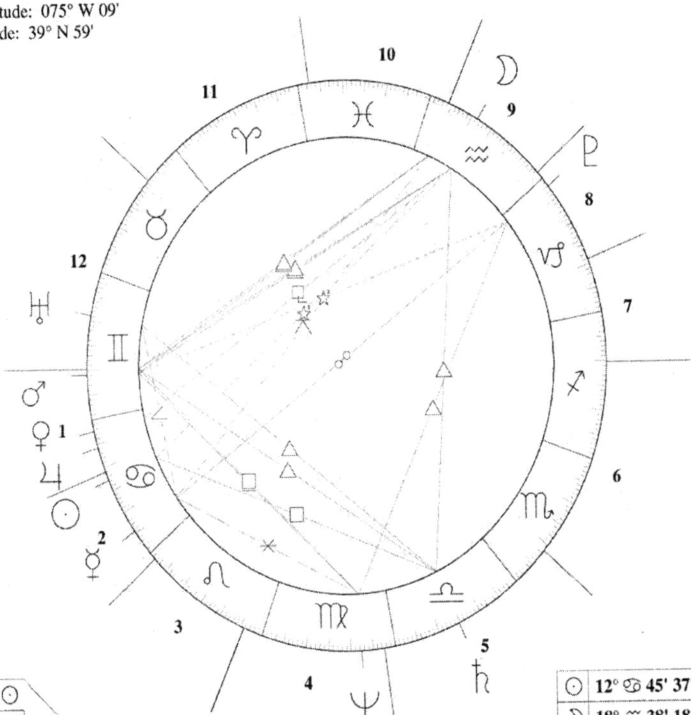

	☉	☽	☿	♀	♂	♃	♄	♅	♆	♇	A	M
☽	☆											
☿												
♀		⚼										
♂		△										
♃	☌			☌								
♄	□	△										
♅			∠				△					
♆			⚹		□							
♇			☍		☆				△			
A		△			☌		△		□			
M			⚻		△						△	

1	19° ♊ 49'
2	10° ♋ 56'
3	01° ♌ 36'
4	25° ♌ 43'
5	27° ♍ 30'
6	08° ♏ 40'
7	19° ♐ 49'
8	10° ♑ 56'
9	01° ♒ 36'
10	25° ♒ 43'
11	27° ♓ 30'
12	08° ♉ 40'

☉	12° ♋ 45' 37"
☽	18° ♒ 38' 18"
☿	24° ♋ 27' R
♀	02° ♋ 23'
♂	20° ♊ 58'
♃	05° ♋ 48'
♄	14° ♎ 47'
♅	08° ♊ 53'
♆	22° ♍ 24'
♇	28° ♑ 02' R
A	19° ♊ 49'
M	25° ♒ 43'

USA
Saturday, February 22, 1777 3:01:00 AM
Philadelphia, Pennsylvania
Time Zone: 05:00 (EST)
Longitude: 075° W 09'
Latitude: 39° N 59'

Placidus Houses
Tropical Zodiac

Progressed to 2008

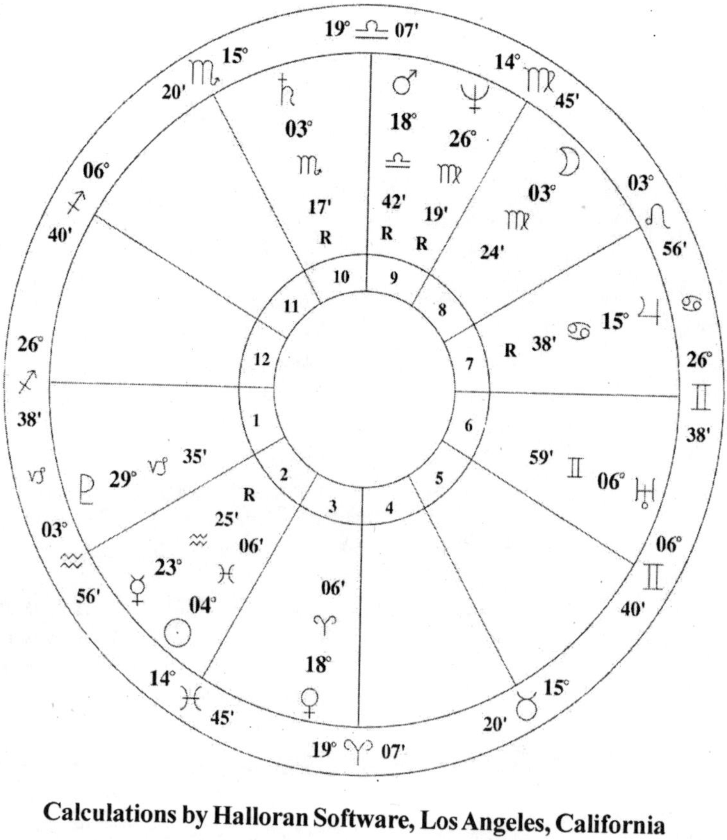

Calculations by Halloran Software, Los Angeles, California

USA
Saturday, February 22, 1777 3:01:00 AM
Philadelphia, Pennsylvania
Time Zone: 05:00 (EST)
Longitude: 075° W 09'
Latitude: 39° N 59'

Placidus Houses
Tropical Zodiac

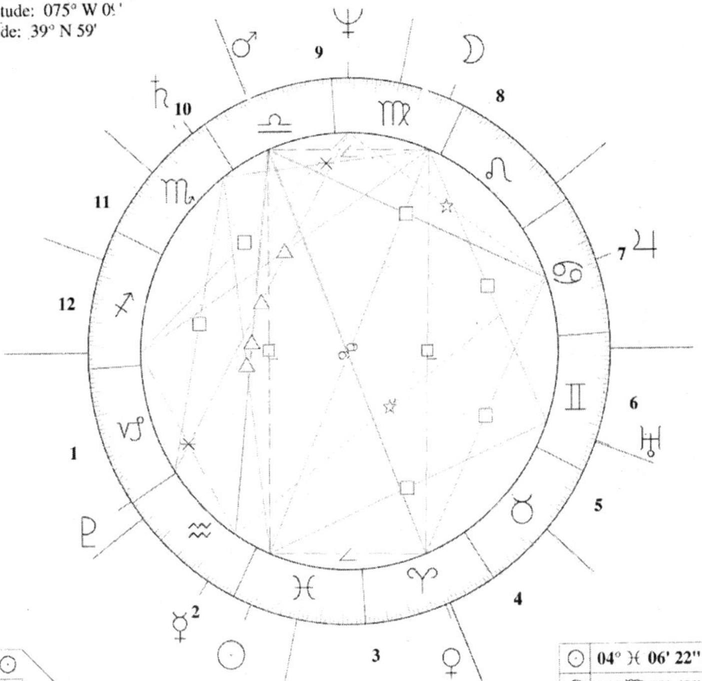

	☉	☽	☿	♀	♂	♃	♄	♅	♆	♇	A
☽	☍										
☿											
♀	∠	□									
♂	□	∠	△	☍							
♃			☆	□	□						
♄	△	⚹									
♅	□	□									
♆						☆					
♇							□		△		
A		△	⚹						□		
M	□	∠	△	☍	☌	□					

House	Cusp
1	26° ♐ 38'
2	03° ♒ 56'
3	14° ♓ 45'
4	19° ♈ 07'
5	15° ♉ 20'
6	06° ♊ 40'
7	26° ♊ 38'
8	03° ♌ 56'
9	14° ♍ 45'
10	19° ♎ 07'
11	15° ♏ 20'
12	06° ♐ 40'

☉	04° ♓ 06' 22"
☽	03° ♍ 23' 42"
☿	23° ♒ 25' R
♀	18° ♈ 06'
♂	18° ♎ 42' R
♃	15° ♋ 38' R
♄	03° ♏ 17' R
♅	06° ♊ 59'
♆	26° ♍ 19' R
♇	29° ♑ 35'
A	26° ♐ 38'
M	19° ♎ 07'

Beginning of the Irak War 3/19/2003
MARCH 2003

LONGITUDE FOR 12 h

Day Jour		S.T. h m s	☉ ° ' "	♀ ° '	☿ ° '	☾ ° ' "	♄ ° '	♃ ° '	♂ ° '	♅ ° '	♆ ° '	♇ ° '	☊ True ° '
Sa	1	22 35 31	10 ♓ 28 55	28 ♑ 47	24 ♒ 07	21 ♒ 49 44	22 ♊ 11	09 ♌R 48	27 ♐ 50	29 ♒ 28	11 ♒ 45	19 ♐ 49	03 ♊R 32
Su	2	22 39 28	11 29 10	29 58	25 44	04 ♓ 29 20	22 12	09 42	28 29	29 32	11 47	19 50	03 18
M	3	22 43 24	12 29 22	01 ♒ 09	27 22	16 57 22	22 13	09 37	29 07	29 35	11 49	19 50	03 04
T	4	22 47 21	13 29 33	02 19	29 01	29 13 55	22 14	09 31	29 45	29 39	11 51	19 51	02 51
W	5	22 51 17	14 29 41	03 30	00 ♓ 42	11 ♈ 19 44	22 15	09 26	00 ♑ 23	29 42	11 53	19 52	02 40
Th	6	22 55 14	15 29 48	04 41	02 23	23 16 24	22 17	09 20	01 02	29 45	11 55	19 52	02 31
F	7	22 59 10	16 29 53	05 52	04 05	05 ♉ 06 29	22 18	09 15	01 40	29 49	11 57	19 53	02 25
Sa	8	23 03 07	17 29 56	07 03	05 49	16 53 28	22 19	09 10	02 18	29 52	11 59	19 53	02 22
Su	9	23 07 04	18 29 57	08 14	07 34	28 41 42	22 21	09 05	02 56	29 55	12 01	19 54	02 21
M	10	23 11 00	19 29 55	09 25	09 19	10 ♊ 36 09	22 23	09 01	03 34	29 59	12 03	19 54	02 D 21
T	11	23 14 57	20 29 52	10 36	11 06	22 42 16	22 25	08 56	04 12	00 ♓ 02	12 05	19 55	02 R 21
W	12	23 18 53	21 29 46	11 47	12 54	05 ♋ 05 33	22 27	08 52	04 50	00 05	12 07	19 55	02 20
Th	13	23 22 50	22 29 38	12 59	14 44	17 51 04	22 29	08 48	05 29	00 09	12 08	19 55	02 17
F	14	23 26 46	23 29 28	14 10	16 34	01 ♌ 02 54	22 31	08 44	06 07	00 12	12 10	19 56	02 12
Sa	15	23 30 43	24 29 15	15 21	18 26	14 43 18	22 33	08 40	06 45	00 15	12 12	19 56	02 04
Su	16	23 34 39	25 29 01	16 33	20 18	28 51 59	22 36	08 37	07 23	00 18	12 14	19 56	01 55
M	17	23 38 36	26 28 44	17 44	22 12	13 ♍ 25 33	22 38	08 33	08 00	00 22	12 16	19 56	01 45
T	18	23 42 33	27 28 25	18 56	24 07	28 17 32	22 41	08 30	08 38	00 25	12 17	19 57	01 35
W	**19**	**23 46 29**	**28 28 04**	**20 07**	**26 03**	**13 ♎ 19 10**	**22 43**	**08 27**	**09 16**	**00 28**	**12 19**	**19 57**	**01 26**
Th	20	23 50 26	29 27 41	21 19	28 00	28 20 51	22 46	08 24	09 54	00 31	12 21	19 57	01 20
F	21	23 54 22	00 ♈ 27 16	22 30	29 59	13 ♏ 13 46	22 49	08 21	10 32	00 34	12 22	19 57	01 16
Sa	22	23 58 19	01 26 50	23 42	01 ♈ 58	27 51 13	22 52	08 19	11 10	00 37	12 24	19 57	01 15
Su	23	00 02 15	02 26 22	24 54	03 58	12 ♐ 09 09	22 55	08 17	11 48	00 40	12 26	19 R 57	01 D 15
M	24	00 08 12	03 25 52	26 06	05 59	26 06 03	22 59	08 14	12 25	00 43	12 27	19 57	01 16
T	25	00 10 08	04 25 21	27 18	08 00	09 ♑ 42 22	23 02	08 13	13 03	00 46	12 29	19 57	01 R 16
W	26	00 14 05	05 24 48	28 29	10 02	22 59 43	23 05	08 11	13 41	00 49	12 30	19 57	01 14
Th	27	00 18 02	06 24 13	29 41	12 04	06 ♒ 00 17	23 09	08 09	14 18	00 52	12 32	19 57	01 11
F	28	00 21 58	07 23 36	00 ♓ 53	14 06	18 46 16	23 12	08 08	14 56	00 55	12 34	19 56	01 04
Sa	29	00 25 55	08 22 57	02 05	16 08	01 ♓ 19 40	23 16	08 07	15 33	00 58	12 35	19 56	00 56
Su	30	00 29 51	09 22 16	03 17	18 09	13 42 06	23 20	08 06	16 11	01 01	12 38	19 56	00 47
M	31	00 33 48	10 ♈ 21 34	04 ♓ 29	20 ♈ 10	25 ♓ 54 53	23 ♊ 24	08 ♌R 05	16 ♑ 48	01 ♓ 04	12 ♒ 38	19 ♐R 56	00 ♊R 37

52

Manhattan, New York
September 11, 2001

On 9/11/2001 ♂ (the lord of war) transits the 7th house of war and international disputes. Therein it ☌ ♅ and brings sudden upset, rash behavior and surprising incidents. It indicates international disputes and disagreements with other powers. This involves explosions and destruction (the trades of the planet ♂) ♅ natal position in this house foreshadows unexpected complications. The sign in the 7th house indicates the enemy and is ♐ turning into ♑. This represents Arabia, Albania, Bosnia, Afghanistan and Iraq. The opposition to ♐ is the sign ♊, representing the USA.

The transit of ♂ creates vast destruction and brings upheaval of the human kind. It stands for explosions, fire and war machinery inflicting extreme damages. Any ☌ plays a very important role in a nation's existence that will have far reaching consequences.

At the same time a transiting ♇ 12 ♐ stands at the cusp of the 7th house opposing natal ♇ in house 12 within 1 degree, which creates the strongest possible impact. In the chart of a person this transit of ♇ will not occur as its transit is extremely slow. In order for this position to occur about 124 years have to pass. In mundane astrology an aspect of ♇ to itself has great impacts and deals with the destruction of the old and the forming of new conditions that will profoundly affect its citizens. In past times, Kings would employ their own private astrologer who advised the emperor on all issues from personal questions to the best and most prosperous time to engage in war. As the advice of these counselors incurred the fate of, not only the King, but all of his subjects, the knowledge of this one person held tremendous power over the outcome of important affairs.

The transit of ♅ ☌ **M** □ ♂ ☍ ☽ forms a conjunction with mid-heaven by an exact degree. Concurrently with the negative aspect to other planets this provides for sudden destruction and loss that will occur to business and the reputation. **M** □ ♂ represents acts against the people with military involvement (house 6). Such destruction will happen in Manhattan as the ☽ resides in the 4th house (home ground) which includes action towards buildings.

For the purpose of this chapter other transits will be ignored as they are not of major importance for our perusal of the September 11, 2001 event. In sum, the attack on 9/11 was well represented in Manhattan's chart.

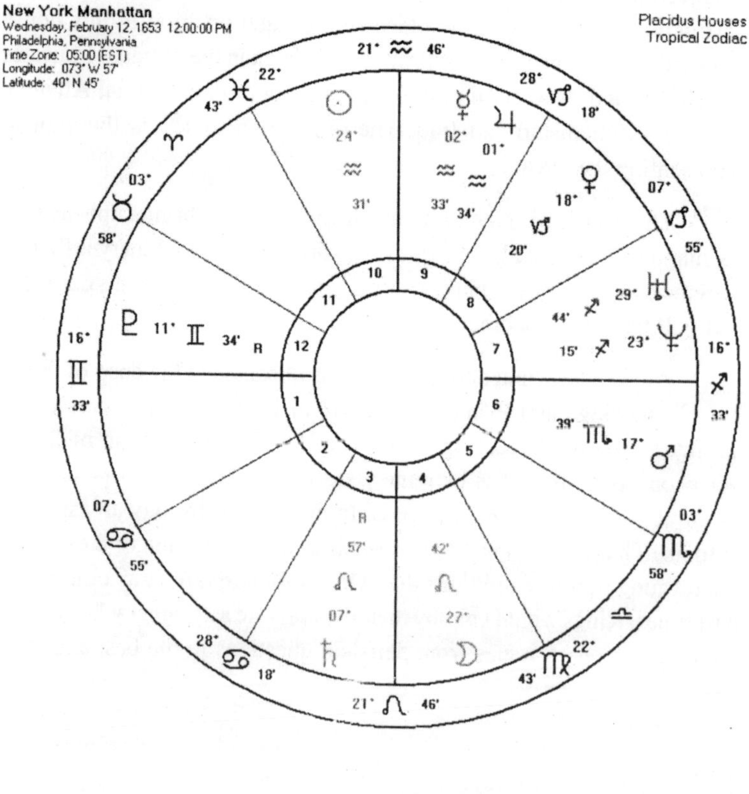

September 11, 2001
SEPTEMBER 2001

Day Jour		S.T. h	m	s	☉ °		'	"	♀ °		'	☿ °		'	☾ °		'	"	♄ °		'	♃ °		'	♂ °		'	♅ °		'	♆ °		'	♇ °		'	☊ True °		'
Sa	1	10	42	52	09	♑	06	52	06	♑	21	00	♎	42	23	♒	48	13	14	♊	23	10	♋	02	26	♐	28	22	♒R	12	06	♒R	33	12	♐	34	04	♋R	21
Su	2	10	46	48	10		04	58	07		32	02		10	05	♓	39	25	14		26	10		12	26		56	22		10	06		31	12		34	04		11
M	3	10	40	45	11		03	01	08		44	03		36	17		33	01	14		28	10		21	27		25	22		07	06		30	12		34	03		59
T	4	10	54	41	12		01	08	09		56	05		01	29		30	26	14		31	10		31	27		53	22		05	06		29	12		35	03		46
W	5	10	58	38	12		59	17	11		06	06		25	11	♈	33	04	14		33	10		40	28		23	22		03	06		28	12		35	03		34
Th	6	10	02	35	13		57	27	12		20	07		47	23		42	29	14		35	10		50	28		52	22		01	06		26	12		35	03		24
F	7	11	06	31	14		55	40	13		32	08		07	06	♉	00	40	14		37	10		59	29		22	21		59	06		25	12		36	03		15
Sa	8	11	10	28	15		53	54	14		45	10		27	18		30	08	14		40	11		08	09		53	21		57	06		24	12		36	03		10
Su	9	11	14	24	16		52	11	15		57	11		44	01	♊	13	55	14		41	11		17	00	♑	23	21		54	06		23	12		37	03		07
M	10	11	18	21	17		50	29	17		09	13		00	14		15	28	14		43	11		28	00		54	21		52	06		22	12		38	03		06
T	**11**	**11**	**22**	**17**	**18**		**48**	**50**	**18**		**22**	**14**		**15**	**27**		**38**	**03**	**14**		**45**	**11**		**35**	**01**		**26**	**21**		**50**	**06**		**21**	**12**		**38**	**03**	**D**	**06**
W	12	11	26	14	19		47	13	19		34	15		28	11	♋	24	36	14		47	11		44	01		57	21		48	06		20	12		39	03	R	06
Th	13	11	30	10	20		45	38	20		47	16		39	25		36	32	14		48	11		52	02		29	21		46	06		18	12		39	03		04
F	14	11	34	07	21		44	05	22		00	17		48	10	♌	12	57	14		50	12		01	03		01	21		44	06		17	12		40	03		01
Sa	15	11	38	04	22		42	35	23		12	18		55	25		09	56	14		51	12		09	03		34	21		42	06		16	12		41	02		54
Su	16	11	42	00	23		41	06	24		25	20		00	10	♑	20	13	14		52	12		17	04		07	21		40	06		15	12		42	02		45
M	17	11	46	57	24		39	38	25		38	21		02	25		33	55	14		53	12		25	04		40	21		39	06		14	12		42	02		34
T	18	11	50	53	25		38	14	26		51	22		03	10	O	40	01	14		54	12		33	05		14	21		37	06		14	12		43	02		23
W	19	11	53	50	26		36	51	28		04	23		00	25		28	25	14		55	12		41	05		48	21		35	06		13	12		44	02		13
Th	20	11	57	46	27		35	29	29		17	23		55	09	♏	51	40	14		56	12		49	06		22	21		33	06		12	12		45	02		04
F	21	12	01	43	28		34	09	00	♑	30	24		47	23		45	46	14		57	12		58	06		56	21		31	06		11	12		46	01		58
Sa	22	12	05	39	29		32	52	01		43	25		36	07	♐	10	14	14		57	13		03	07		31	21		30	06		10	12		47	01		56
Su	23	12	09	36	00	D	31	35	02		58	26		22	20		07	15	14		58	13		11	08		06	21		28	06		09	12		48	01		54
M	24	12	13	32	01		30	21	04		10	27		03	02	♑	40	52	14		58	13		18	08		41	21		26	06		09	12		49	01		54
T	25	12	17	29	02		29	08	05		23	27		41	14		56	03	14		58	13		25	09		16	21		25	06		08	12		50	01		54
W	26	12	21	28	03		27	57	06		38	28		14	26		58	04	14		58	13		31	09		52	21		23	06		07	12		51	01		52
Th	27	12	25	22	04		26	48	07		50	28		42	08	♒	51	56	14	R	58	13		38	16		28	21		21	06		06	12		52	01		48
F	28	12	29	19	05		25	40	09		03	29		06	20		42	10	14		58	13		44	11		04	21		20	06		06	12		53	01		42
Sa	29	12	33	15	06		24	34	10		17	29		24	02	♓	32	33	14		58	13		51	11		40	21		18	06		06	12		54	01		33
Su	30	12	37	12	07	♎	23	30	11	♑	30	29	♎	35	14	♓	28	02	14	♊R	58	13	♋	57	12	♑	17	21	♒R	17	06	♒R	06	12	♐	55	01	♋R	21

53

Present Transits in 2008-2009 through the USA Natal Chart

♃ transits through house 8. When afflicted herein it denotes death of a noble man connected with royalty, legal and religious groups or a person involved in banking and finances.

On and off between 2 – 10/2008 ♃ ☍ ☉ □ ♄. In 9-10/2008 it is at its strongest before leaving these aspects. Scandals, waste of resources, increasing taxation, an overloaded court system as well as health problems and increased crime are matters of great concern. The □ ♄ affects monetary affairs, decline in revenues, bank and business failure, increase in bankruptcy and stock market losses. The affairs are much disturbed, thus, affecting the governments action towards the people. A person of high standing and leadership may pass on.

♄ presently transits through House 4: This represents obstacles and difficulties to the Government. The affairs of the nation will not proceed smoothly. It denotes depreciating of land values and disturbs property affairs. It influences the weather and adversely affects agricultural matters. Extreme rain may be experienced in the regions mostly affected by ♄. Disasters through mining, earthquakes and floods will be experienced. The masses are unfortunate and unemployment will prevail.

♄ transit □ ♂ natal in Houses 1 and 4 around 10-12/2008 and thereafter on and off through 2009. Serious difficulties arise in national life. Discontent of the people, riots and crime increases. The Government will lose popularity and support, or may act autocratically. A very eminent person may die or be assassinated.

♅ transit □ ♂ natal in Houses 10 and 1 around 9-12/2008 and on and off during 2009. This is unfortunate for the ruling power of the nation. It denotes sudden trouble to the Government. It exposes false steps taken, bad faith or broken pledges. Defeat of Government may occur through a general election. Some statesman may fall ill or die. The country is in turbulence, is lawless and explosions may occur.

♇ in House 7: When afflicted, as here, it denotes international disputes, disagreements and danger of war. Foreign affairs produce awkward and unexpected complications of a serious nature.

♇ transit ☍ ♀ natal in House 7 and 1, which is beginning now but increasing in 2009. Dislike between the population and the countries involved in war. Dislike by other countries against the USA for being an aggressive war monger. Lawsuits may involve prominent people over war issues and foreign involvement. Associations maybe formed with undesirable elements for the prospect of gain. However, these relationships are not enduring but will result in a power struggle and dissolve as soon as benefits are not forthcoming to either party.

♅ transit through House 10 and at the same time being afflicted by ♂ now and throughout 2009 denotes sudden and unexpected developments in government circles, which will require careful management, or defeat and resignation will ensue. Possible attacks against the Government and its officials. A change in Government due to unpopularity and discontent of the people. It could foreshadow the attack on a statesman.

♆ ☌ **M**. This aspect is forthcoming and indicates scandal, disgrace to notable people, agitation against the Government and disrespect for the ruling class. The ruling Government will be defeated and the country will lose its national prestige. Scandal and disgrace among prominent people is likely to occur.

♅ □ **A** represents sudden strange, aggressive and peculiar action by the political party in power thereby disturbing affairs, hence bringing disappointment.

54

Pluto Rules Society and its Evolution

In Greek mythology, ♇ was already known, named and assigned to the god of the underworld. Society only heard of this most remote planet of our solar system through its official discovery in 1930. Its power is associated with death and destruction, including the discovery of atomic energy. Its most powerful influence is power itself. The use and abuse of it has turned the world, mostly in a destructive way. But out of the ashes of destruction something new has always formed. Its ability to totally annihilate as well as transform, renew and regenerate has helped accelerate evolution on our planet earth. Despite its long established influences, its compulsion with power, the need for control and persistent violence in society have barely changed since mankind arrived. Man has not yet learned to understand the function of control over the masses but abused its power solely for self aggregation. Eventually, we all have to face ♇ as our death will fall under its influence. Its transit through a single house takes an average of 20 years, thus providing an impact of long duration. When ♇ travels through a particular sign it affects society through the influences of that sign. It recently traveled through ♐ and has changed the way we travel and the merging of cultures to become one melting pot rather than stay individual units.

In 2008 ♇ enters the sign ♑ and already now, at the beginning of this transit, do we feel its powerful control. Society will be unhappy. Anarchy and uprising against political powers will emerge and lead to mass exodus of people, hence, changing existing boundaries and economic patterns in our world. This period will be enormously destructive as the old has to break down and go before a new system can be established. On page 454 is a chart of Manhattan Island on September 11, 2001. ♇ transit was 12 ♐. The 7th house represents war and the enemy involved. 12 ♐ herein falls exactly opposite the natal ♇ of 12 ♊ located close to the Ascendant when Manhattan was formed. ♇ ☍ itself represents utter distraction. Bad elements will surface. Destruction is certain and society will forever be changed thereby. ♇ ☍ **A** is indicating an abuse of power that needs correcting or ultimate destruction will result. ♇ influence over the USA is manifest by current destructive events that will escalate until a balance of power is achieved. America entered into war with Iraq when ♇ transit ☍ its natal ♂ (the lord of war) and ♂ transit ☍ ☉ natal (hasty acts out of ego confrontations)

♇ now transits into ♑, the sign of business and money. It will greatly affect financial institutions and the earning power of the people. The connection between the leader and the masses is broken and each carries on until the confrontation is inevitable. Natural and man made disasters will fall upon the people and change the concept of the United States of America, even to the point of recreating individual state powers independent of the federal government. The concept of being 'united' will dissolve.

By the year 2010 the mass migration from third world countries, together with bringing in religious structures, may topple governments and social control. Many corporations will go bankrupt. In short, the big power has to yield to the up and coming new wave. Global warming will seriously change the distribution of the food chain.

♇ is traveling into America's 8th house. Money received from others will be hard to come by and, at times, disappear altogether. Upcoming events include ♇ transit ☍ ♀, ♃, ☉ and □ ♄, which affects partnerships, involvement in war and losses sustained therefrom which will affect the country in devastating manners. Successful Kings and Queens of past centuries had astrological advisers to prepare and thus permit minimizing of disasters. Maybe today's ego has grown so out of proportion that destruction is needed to reign in what is out of control before man takes over and destroys nature. Any transit of ♇ affects not only a specific individual but also society per se.

55

Notes

It is interesting to notice that Russia, based on Lenin's declaration on November 7, 1917, has a ruling sign of 22 ♉ with a ☉ 14 ♏. It represents a power involved in secrecy and with the self. However, when compared to the chart of the USA, Russia's A □ ☉ is also □ and ☍ USA ☽ in the 9th house. This explains the prolonged power struggle between the two countries. As the USA progressed chart also contains ☉ ☍ ☽, which indicated a struggle within the self, a positive relationship between these two countries in the near future is very unlikely.

By 2008 Russia's ♇ will ☌ ♀ and ▲ ♂ establishing its might as a military ruler. In 2014 ♇ will reinforce Russia's 10th house of power. It will cumulate its power drive to gain ultimate authority and establish itself as a world power. The regime will act dictatorial to keep its subjects in line. When ♂ ✶ ♇ around 8/2008, which was positive in the natal chart, Russia successfully attacked Georgia but the fighting ended quickly. In its progressed chart there is ♂ □ ♇ but supported by ♂ ▲ ♃.

By 2021 ♇ ☍ ♇ reflects the desire for power that will be practiced behind the scene by secret and underhanded tactics.

THE FUTURE OF AMERICA

A brief look into the United States immediate future brings ♄ □ ♆ and ⛢ from the 5th and 7th house which will negatively influence the people and bring dispute, distress and discontent, loss of work and increase of poverty. Lawlessness and crime will increase. Any government will not gain the support of the masses and possible death or scandal in higher office may affect the trust of the people.

The transit by ♄ through the 5th house will begin by 10/2009. It afflicts theatres, amusements and general entertainment which will not do well during this transit. The birth rate will decline and trouble with children and schools could become prominent. Misfortune will affect the social side of town. High society has to take a step back and will come under scrutiny. Some great personality may pass away and becomes the subject of extensive mourning. Crime will increase. Much vice, distress and immorality will be felt.

♄ □ ♆ will bring confusion of the people who are unfortunate and discontented. Secrecy associated with crime may bring discredit or a downfall to police, municipal officials or state administrators. Stocks and investments may bring loss. Plots, schemes and secret actions may lead to crimes, scandals and legal actions.

♄ □ ♅ brings trouble to the ruling power through politicians who attempt great and sudden changes, however, they are either resisted or will be achieved only with difficulties. Changes within the government may take place. Strife surfaces within the parties. Foreign affairs produce unexpected complications.

The USA progression by 2008 indicates the following positive aspects.

☉ ▲ ♄ - houses 2 + 10 for another 4 years

☽ ∗ ♄ - houses 8 + 10 this aspect last only months and has already past

☽ ▲ A - house 8 " " "

☿ ▲ ♂ - houses 2 + 9 this aspect ends 2010

☿ ∗ A - house 2 " "

The most notable aspect here is formed by the ☉ and supports the craving of power by the Government. The ☽ moves ahead too quickly to form a longer lasting aspect and by traveling ahead forms positive and negative aspect for the duration of several months. ☿ positive aspects are separating and have no longer enough strength to affect and negate negative events.

The USA progression by 2008 indicates the following negative aspects.

☉ ☍ ☽ - houses 2 + 8 — this aspect has past now
☉ □ ♅ - houses 2 + 6 — its getting stronger, lasting for about 6 years
☽ □ ♅ - houses 8 + 6 — this aspect has past now
♀ ☍ ♂ - houses 3 + 9 — this is very strong, lasting 4-6 years
♀ □ ♃ – houses 3 + 7 — lasting another 4 years
♀ ☍ **M** - house 3 — this remains as both travel at about the same speed
♂ □ ♃ - houses 7 + 9 — both planets are retrograde. Due to ♂ faster movement this aspect increases in strength.
♂ ☌ **M** - house 9 — last another 4-6 years
♃ □ **M** - house 7 — last another 2 years
♄ □ ♇ - houses 1 +10 — due to ♄ retrograde this aspect is getting stronger
♆ □ **A** - house 9 — this is exact and last for about another 6 years.

By concentrating on the strongest affliction a pattern emerges that is a layout of existing and future events.

The government incurs mistrust and trouble. It engages in wrong acts, rash, hasty and ill-considered legislation that will lead to enormous difficulties in the near future. Friends are lost and more enemies are made. Reforms made will be unpopular and bring more harm than progress. Power is displayed in an autocratic way that leads to internal disagreements and power plays. Intended bills will either not come about or fail miserably and internal strife will bring many defeats to the government. After the election great changes will occur that could involve riots and unrest. The finances will be affected (house 2), the public health, the army, the navy and employees per se, will suffer (house 6) Many promises are made but only few will be fulfilled. The morality will suffer, scandals emerge also in connection with military affairs. Foreign relations are strained due to a forceful attitude. This affects all kinds of communications, accidents via car, train or plane (house 3). It afflicts long distance travel, foreign countries, the shipping industry, religion, courts of law and publications. (house 9).

Money is spent without forethought. Undue optimism is blinding to the fact that expenditures outstrip any income. Finances will turn sour, taxation becomes a problem. Fraud, extravagance and scandal become the norm. Luxury is embraced without the means to sustain it. Religious organizations are embroiled in scandal and suffer a similar fate as the government by living beyond their means. Communication is used to embellish rather than adhere to correct and truthful information. (house 3) Foreign affairs suffer from inconsistencies. Due to extreme over-confidence deals are made but turn sour soon after the ink is dry on any agreement. (house 9)

Social interactions are difficult. Financial extravagance will deplete resources that affect the reputation. Embellished communications are used to camouflage financial problems. (house 3)

Disagreements arise over religious, military, legal and public affairs. There is excessive optimism in regards to war that will lead to failure. Foreign affairs are stressed because of aggressive and military attitudes and attacks. Hostile actions are leading to loss (house 7). The law, foreign relations and religious enterprises are subject to bully and criminal behavior. Crime by and through foreigners will increase (house 9)

Of great concern is ♄ □ ♇ which will gain strength in the near future and bring disaster and disintegration of conditions in nature and government. A tough attitude, as well as an intense power struggle, combined with secret acts, will embroil the government resulting in disintegration of present conditions. Crime will increase, so will disagreement over money obtained from others. Tax revenues will fall and foreign investors may bail out for more secure heavens. Corruption and dishonesty will be the new norm. An internal power struggle by the government, engaged in to obtain the ultimate control over the masses, will bring annihilation and in the end a downfall will make room for a new system. This aspect will not pass without the destruction of the old. It affects the people of the country as well as the ruling government. The wealth will decline and a reversal of status will occur (house 1). The government will suffer through attacks on its reputation, credit and power. The power structure will eventually disintegrate. (house 10)

The mind is confused about the self-expression and relating to others, especially foreigners. (house 9) Unrealistic approaches are used for self-gratification. Desires emerge from a dreamy disposition that lacks reality. Self-deception is practiced that dissolves important relationships.

PROGRESSION IN ASPECT WITH NATAL PLANETS

While several aspects are formed when progressed planets affect natal positions in the USA chart, the major impact will be felt when a transit hereto aspects the natal and progressed planet. The strongest formations are:

☉ ☌ ♃. When afflicted it denotes a craving for self-importance and a desire for ultimate power.

☉ □ ♂. Quarrels and disagreements exist between the ruler and its desire for military actions and the people. This aspect increases in power and will lead to more military engagements. The ego is aroused to act rashly and hastily resulting in action that give reason to repent. The people will be up in arms against the ruling class and upper society. The military will incur trouble and death will increase.

♀ ▲ ♄. A positive aspect hereto during transit helps increase prosperity.

♄ ☌ ♂. The influences of these planets are increasing. The government will be unfortunate losing its ability to govern by facts and in a calm manner. The people will rise up against military engagements. Crime, riots and outrage against the ruthless rulers will increase. There is no support for the government which acts dictatorial, rashly and without much foresight. Errors are plenty and give reason for worry. When activated by transit (such as ♄ transit 2011) the full effect will be felt. It involves foreigners and investments as well as military engagements.

♄ □ ♃. Due to over-confidence and lack of foresight the financial affairs are in shambles. Business will suffer, revenues decline, taxation may be increased while investments turn sour. Bankruptcies will increase sharply. Religious enterprises will be troubled possible through hostile legislation affecting the financial well being. Foreign investments may generate a "divorce" process for relationships in which financial interest were at stake.

The upcoming election in the USA, even so it may trigger a change of party, may not serve as a miracle to halt the law of cause and effect. Let us hope that no assassination occurs, although a strong indication thereof appears in the chart. A more moderate old fashioned and conservative approach to life and its problems may be a tool that will help guide the ship through the storm.

A note on world events related to the USA

The Ephemeris discloses as of 2008 and well into 2010 an opposition of ♄ ☍ ⛢ which, in mundane astrology, is always interpreted as meaning the destruction of the economic life of much of the world. Throughout 2012 America's ♇ will be in □ with the transit ♄ increasing the change of war, disturbing the economy and most likely will create panic in the financial circles. This will increase around 2011-2012 when the transit ♄ ☌ ♂ (progress) □ ☉ (natal) ☍ ♀ (progressed). This will create aggressive and warlike conditions affecting the 2 & 8 house. It will act primarily on finances and ending of institutions that are involved in the market of finances. Also house 1, 3 & 9 express that the aggressor is the USA against a foreign country (represented by the 9th house). It begins with aggressive communications (3rd house)

Such acts will have far reaching consequences for the USA.

All charts are set up for the United States of America, based on a birth date of July 4, 1776 assuming, 3:01 AM as the birth time in Philadelphia. The exact birth time is somewhat uncertain and may vary.

The progression has been advanced to 2008

All calculations thereon were performed by Halloran Software, Los Angeles, California who has granted permission for this publication.

Index to all Planets

Index

N

R

S

V

W

Z